PRIVACY IN THE AGE OF NEUROSCIENCE

Neuroscience has begun to intrude deeply into what it means to be human, an intrusion that offers profound benefits but will demolish our present understanding of privacy. In *Privacy in the Age of Neuroscience*, David Grant argues that we need to reconceptualise privacy in a manner that will allow us to reap the rewards of neuroscience while still protecting our privacy and, ultimately, our humanity. Grant delves into our relationship with Technology, the latest in what he describes as a historical series of 'magnitudes', following Deity, the State and the Market, proposing the idea that, for this new magnitude (Technology), we must individually control rather than be subjected to it. In this provocative work, Grant unveils a radical account of privacy and an equally radical proposal to create the social infrastructure we need to support it.

David Grant is a senior fellow at the University of Melbourne Law School. After serving the administration of justice, Grant has authored four books, radically reconceiving the relationship of the citizen with Christianity, the State, the Market and Technology. His third book was co-authored with Professor Lyria Bennett Moses of the Law School, University of New South Wales.

Privacy in the Age of Neuroscience

REIMAGINING LAW, STATE AND MARKET

DAVID GRANT

University of Melbourne

CAMBRIDGE
UNIVERSITY PRESS

University Printing House, Cambridge CB2 8BS, United Kingdom

One Liberty Plaza, 20th Floor, New York, NY 10006, USA

477 Williamstown Road, Port Melbourne, VIC 3207, Australia

314–321, 3rd Floor, Plot 3, Splendor Forum, Jasola District Centre, New Delhi – 110025, India

79 Anson Road, #06–04/06, Singapore 079906

Cambridge University Press is part of the University of Cambridge.

It furthers the University's mission by disseminating knowledge in the pursuit of education, learning, and research at the highest international levels of excellence.

www.cambridge.org
Information on this title: www.cambridge.org/9781108835428
DOI: 10.1017/9781108883931

© David Grant 2021

This publication is in copyright. Subject to statutory exception and to the provisions of relevant collective licensing agreements, no reproduction of any part may take place without the written permission of Cambridge University Press.

First published 2021

A catalogue record for this publication is available from the British Library.

ISBN 978-1-108-83542-8 Hardback
ISBN 978-1-108-79336-0 Paperback

Cambridge University Press has no responsibility for the persistence or accuracy of URLs for external or third-party internet websites referred to in this publication and does not guarantee that any content on such websites is, or will remain, accurate or appropriate.

Contents

Acknowledgements		*page* vii
1	Introduction	1
	PART I PRIVACY	23
2	Privacy, Neuroscience and Algorithms	25
3	The Frailty of Privacy Theory	71
4	Privacy as the History of Normalisation	91
5	Privacy, Its Values and Technology	138
6	A New Sense of Privacy	175
	PART II REGULATION	197
7	Reimagining Regulation	199
8	Regulation and the Law	216
9	Regulation and the State	244
10	Regulation and the Market	272
Bibliography		303
Index		307

Acknowledgements

Since this work is the culmination of the development of some central ideas over fifteen years, there have inevitably been many people to whom I owe a debt of gratitude for their encouragement, forbearance, constructive criticism, good humour and wisdom far greater than mine. The first of them was Stephen Gaukroger at the University of Sydney, with whom I completed my master's degree in philosophy. Stephen not only opened my eyes but was generous and set intellectual standards that I have always tried to honour. I then moved to the University of New South Wales Law School, where I was extremely fortunate to be able to undertake my doctoral studies with Martin Krygier. It would be an understatement to say that Martin has been, right up to now, both patient and encouraging well beyond what was reasonable to ask and over a long time. And a more civilising person one could not meet. Dean David Dixon was resolute in his support during much of that time and remains so. It was David who introduced me to Dean Carolyn Evans of the University of Melbourne Law School, shortly after I had relocated. I was welcomed by Dean Evans, a welcome that has been extended by Dean Pip Nicholson. Standing behind that welcome has been Deputy Dean Matthew Harding, who not only has encouraged my efforts but has introduced me to Rosemary Langford and to a line of thought that has been most helpful in the present work. His encouragement has also been instrumental in its publication. I would also like to thank the anonymous reviewer for a number of helpful suggestions. I have also been greatly assisted by the practical good graces of the team at the Melbourne Law School Academic Research Service, Robin Gardner, Louise Ellis and Fiona MacDowall. I must thank those at Cambridge University Press who have brought this book to publication – Matt Gallaway and Cameron Daddis – and also Catherine Smith, Matt Rohit and Stephanie Sakson, all highly professional in ensuring the highest standards and hugely supportive. And of course my wife Dianne, who has ever been a loyal champion of my efforts. How fortunate can one person be?

1

Introduction

We have no proper understanding of privacy. Even if we did, we lack the social infrastructure to put it and keep it in place.

This work is concerned with identifying the problems inherent in contemporary accounts of privacy. It will do so by placing privacy in an entirely new context, that of a mythological social dynamic that has long constrained the West. This will reveal why privacy is vulnerable to the imminent impact of the latest form of that dynamic, emerging neuroscience. That is, while privacy is the product of early forms of this dynamic, neuroscience is now the most powerful form and will overwhelm current notions of privacy. Privacy therefore needs to be removed from this dynamic and be reconceived. It will then survive this challenge but will also be able to, counter-intuitively, embrace the range of neuroscientific benefits, including as they could promote a new sense of privacy but under the technological control of the citizen. How this could be realised will be argued by examining the nature of the dynamic, how it has produced present notions of privacy through a singular form of normal-isation, and how it is being re-formed by the mythological algorithms of neurosci-ence. To disengage privacy in this way, other elements are required, that is, a new ethical framework and the reimagining of the social infrastructure – law, the State and the Market – to provide necessary support, all these under the rubric of a reconceived notion of regulation. A new sense of regulation would be essential to sustain this new privacy.

Contemporary Privacy and Its Environment

None of this is to say that there is not a wide range of observations about what privacy is. Neither is it to say that there are not elaborated accounts of how we should go about protecting it. The problem is that these observations, these accounts and these protective plans are all 'of their time' and their weaknesses are shown as the social theories on which they rest change and move on. Such accounts reach out from the

Introduction

past – and some from the present – to cloud attempts to look at the field afresh. But as we shall see, we must do so. Emerging forces are such that, if we do not completely reconceive privacy and how to protect it, there is every prospect that fundamental changes will embed themselves in the social fabric in a way that will irreversibly change that fabric and the sense of ourselves on which it is built.

Unearthing a Foundational Dynamic

This work looks afresh – both close-up and from a historical distance – at the variations in social conditions and the dominant accounts of privacy those conditions have produced. This long perspective allows one to see what is typically obscured from only a proximate examination, that is, that there has been a social dynamic that has shadowed the history of the West, manifest in different forms, and which has created the varying conditions from which accounts of privacy have emerged.

Although we shall be looking at this dynamic extensively in what follows, we can say here briefly that it is a modern mythology. That is, the deep fears and desires generated by the awareness of our conditions of existence – the unsympathetic and recalcitrant absolutism of our existential reality – have led to the serial imagining of *mythological magnitudes*.[1] These were each initially absolute in their presence, by that presence distancing the absolutism of reality. We did not have to worry about it, only them. So, they have been entities that we have then sought to remake or engage as sympathetic by having them camouflage that existential reality with constructed but manageable fears and desires. They are mostly familiar but here they are seen in a new light: Deity, the State, the Market and now Technology on behalf of each individual as an Absolute Self.

These serial imaginings have been generated by their respective dominant interests. They were each created to overcome 'moments' of existential crisis. The Christian Deity, borrowing heavily from Judaism but amending those beliefs, was created by the attempt to establish a New Testament faith in the face of Roman persecution during the first four centuries. The State was created as the established notion of the Christian Deity was shattered in the face of the turmoil of the Reformation due to the thought of Ockham, Pomponazzi and Luther, between

---

[1] The notion of a mythological magnitude was originally conceived by German philosopher Hans Blumenberg in *Work on Myth* (1979). The present author has worked with this notion, initially to apply the implications of it to another major work by Blumenberg, *The Legitimacy of the Modern Age* (1966), arguing (in D. Grant, *The Mythological State and Its Empire* [Routledge, 2009]) that the modern age is not legitimate due to its mythological characteristics. Ongoing work by the author led to the characterisation of the phases of modernity, and its predecessor, Christianity, as comprising a series of myths each centred on a magnitude, thereby constituting a trajectory. That further work was elaborated by the author (in D. Grant and L. Bennett Moses, *Technology and the Trajectory of Myth* [Edward Elgar, 2017]). The notions of mythological magnitude and trajectory are signature reference points in the present work.

Introduction 3

the fourteenth and sixteenth centuries. The Market, as the credibility of the democratic State faded before the totalitarian catastrophe in the mid-twentieth century. Technology on behalf of the creation of an Absolute Self, still emerging into dominance out of the economic and health crises in this early part of the twenty-first century.[2]

However, there are two further important features of these magnitudes, features which also mark the dynamic that has driven them. The first is that, as each has been engaged or 'brought to earth' to be sympathetic, it not only lost its absolute status by that very concession but was shown to be insufficiently sympathetic, as these 'moments' of crisis and replacement demonstrated. So, although the vacuum was on each occasion filled by a new absolute magnitude, we have by that had a series of failed, absolute magnitudes: the 'trajectory' of Deity, then State, then Market and now, apparently, Technology. Second, for this dynamic to work, it requires the – typically complicit – subjection of individuals to the residual field of the ideas and practices of these failed but persisting magnitudes, a field in which we all exist. If we are subject, by that we empower those dominant interests, who can then claim that they are able to deal conclusively with these constructed fears and desires. They present as the solution to the problem they have created. This constitutes a continuing subjection to serially failed, apparently weakened but persisting magnitudes.

This dynamic is not the uncovering of an explanatory narrative which, by that understanding, enriches individual existence. Such narratives are rightly unfashionable. On the contrary, this is an uncovering which reveals the serial failures of the attempts to avoid confronting our existential reality. *This is best understood as a trajectory of failures away from existential reality and not towards some specific ideal condition.* These are failures which have left behind an accumulating field of institutional arrangements, of ideas and practices to which we have agreed – or have been made – to be subject, a subjection which is at the same time the distancing and camouflage of our existential reality. So this long dynamic has not enriched but has demeaned. The present work is a critical dismissal of that dynamic and suggests a different perspective which sets up some signposts for an embrace of the absolutism of reality but which is not intended to be in any way prescriptive. It is suggestive. This work is, beneath the examination of these magnitudes, unhistorical and existential. There is no 'progress', as we each time ended back where we started. This work is an attempt to understand where we have been and why we yet still need to confront the same existential reality by embrace not by diversion. It has two parts: Part I examines these serial, failed diversions; Part II proposes those signposts.

---

[2] The author has presented an account of this trajectory in ch.2 of Grant and Bennett Moses, *Technology and the Trajectory of Myth*, pp. 32–79, elaborating his account of the emergence of the State as myth in Grant, *The Mythological State and Its Empire*, pp. 19–40.

This dynamic is a matter of real significance. Recognising it, seeing those varying forms in which it has been elaborated and seeing its constituting impact on both social arrangements and individual belief and practice, will allow a very different view of both historical and contemporary arrangements. Dealing with its implications will require far more than changing legislation. It will mean going to the conceptual foundations and the practices of our institutions and how they have functioned as forces that act deeply on us as human beings.

We will begin this exploration with an account of the most recent of the historical forms of this dynamic, that is, emerging Technology in pursuit of an Absolute Self and, more specifically, the deep interventions of emerging neuroscience. This will point to a sense of immediacy in this dynamic and, in that, bring the issue of privacy into mid-picture as something requiring urgent attention. That is, emerging neuroscience will reveal our current thinking about privacy as tied to this mythological dynamic, distracting us from what needs to be an urgent rethinking about its nature and how we manage it. That urgency is needed due to the imminence and fast pace of the development of neuroscientific technologies.

NEUROSCIENCE AND THE NEW TECHNOLOGICAL TERRITORY

Something with a significance of the highest order is taking place within neuroscience and virtual reality, yet this development is not in full public sight. It is the progress being made in understanding and intervening in the human brain. The reason for this lack of visibility is that the purposes of these technologies are, on the one hand, the remediation of serious cognitive handicap and, on the other, the search for imaginative forms of education and entertainment. Uncontroversial, even welcome developments. However, along with these benefits – and as so often happens with new technology – an effect is emerging that is far less than desirable, even something of genuine concern.

These developments – brought to us by functional magnetic resonance imaging (fMRI), neural implants, optogenetics, brain–computer interface (BCI), nanoneuroscience and increasingly sophisticated virtual reality (VR) – are opening up our capacity to understand the most intimate human behaviours, which go to the heart of what it is to be human. That is, we are revealing the location and the functioning of our senses, our cognitive abilities, our beliefs, our thoughts, our dreams and even our very sense of ourselves as individuals. More importantly, with this knowledge comes the capacity to intervene to substantially control each of these features. The research is telling us not only how the brain functions but also how it might be brought to function, both in itself and by augmentation.

This has a further implication. That is, these interventions are not merely to deliver improved capacity but will increasingly constitute a digital embedding of the individual citizen. The consequence is that, if these interventions are made through a process of subjection to such regimes – even if they are chosen by the individual citizen as a result of claims made about personal enhancement – then they can constitute a serious loss of privacy, of identity and a denial of 'respectful self-responsibility'.

This *respectful self-responsibility* is a phrase we shall hear repeatedly throughout this work as it is at the centre of the proposals being put here, proposals regarding the need and means to reject the mythological denial of existential reality and the creation of a new sense of privacy. The frequency of its use – and those of its alternatives *non-mythological existence* and *living existentially* – should not lead to them acquiring the status of passive mantras. They are better understood as the active distillation of the broad argument of the present work.

Issues such as this embedding are explored here through a range of templates, especially that we cannot consider advances in neuroscience without looking at the evolution in the nature and impact of algorithmic technology. That template has important implications, including that the apparent success of interpreting data is leading some to argue that the way we think and how we will best live and even understand the world *in toto* should be algorithmic. This would be deep techno-logical embedding. However, seeing ourselves as algorithmic raises not only issues associated with the decodability and trustworthiness of algorithmic conclusions but, even more significantly, that what constitutes data is itself the result of conscious decisions and that the designs of algorithms to explore them are imbued with the perspectives and conclusions of the designer. This happens inevitably and does not merely apply to now-common concerns about race, gender and creed but impacts far more fundamentally on the ways in which we see and understand ourselves in the world.

This will become of the greatest significance as neuroscientific interventions go wider and deeper: we should look beyond issues related to decoding and see that the designs of algorithms are creators of reality. To put it more strongly, we need to consider whether we are entering a world of Kantian, idealist, digital metaphysics which is being overlain on and reconstructs the realities we know. So, dominant theories of digital information, such as those of Floridi and Domingos, comprise an increasingly influen-tial field to which these arguments about Kantian Idealism need to be applied.

Even more significantly, to the extent that neuroscientific interventions will be justified as means to deal with fear and satisfy desire – both of which, and much more, are now being shaped as means of enhancement – on condition of subjection to the algorithmic regime, then their algorithms are mythological artefacts. This algorithmic Technology may be promoting the first serious stage in the creation of the mythological Absolute Self, the claim that we are each able to fully control the conditions of our existence. This has real significance for how we should think about the nature of human capacity, human agency and privacy, among other fields.

The functioning of both virtual reality and augmented reality is also considered within this frame, especially as their use will become common and extensive through the long exposures of education, health and entertainment programming.

However, neuroscience need not follow this path, a path that would otherwise be highly attractive to the contemporary political and corporate worlds. It can be aware of the high plasticity of the self, the highly laden nature of data selection and algorithmic design but choose not to impose such alternative mythological realities. Instead, to open up not just a variety of worlds of interpretation, but worlds that are determined by individual citizens, each pursuing respectful responsibility to and for themself. Taking such an alternative path would have significance for thinking about privacy and would produce a very different sense of it than we now have.

PRIVACY THEORY, ITS CONCERNS AND ITS COMPLICATIONS

As soon as we start to think about the nature of privacy, a series of questions immediately arise. Some of these include whether privacy relates essentially to the individual. Is privacy only about knowledge of us and our close relationships that is sought by other citizens or agencies? Is it just wanting to be left alone or should it actually have content? Does it have layers, with some personal matters deserving heavier protection? Should its content be a matter for only the citizen themself or do the Church or State or Market or Technology agencies always have intervention rights regarding what we are thinking and doing? Should attitudes of dissent be included within it? So, should privacy have legal status, and then whose rights should have priority? Is privacy necessary to being able to act autonomously and responsibly? Does privacy vary with the cultural context or is it a universal idea? Does the media have special rights regarding certain people? What are the ethical principles to guide us in responding to these questions?

Or can privacy be seen apart from its place in the life of a citizen? Is it better understood by looking at the way information flows, how this is controlled by various groups and the norms established to manage that? Is it therefore properly considered within specific social contexts and within which principles of informational integrity can be applied? Are such contexts thereby comprised of common knowledge and is that knowledge 'relational' such that control over it – and the quality of the privacy – can be exercised by groups of various kinds? If so, what is the status of the individual within this social context and what are their reasonable privacy expectations?

Cutting across all these questions is the notional barrier between oneself and the world, one that is the boundary of the private within which we can explore our thoughts and feelings in confidence. Is that a viable notion in our present world of already widely interactive technologies? If technologies that intrude ever more deeply are actively sought out by citizens, what function should they be allowed to serve and how does that relate to privacy? Is there something inherent in being human that demands we be treated as individuals with dignity and respect or is that really an unsustainable presumption? Is privacy nothing like the answers to these questions at all but something very different?

In attempting to answer such questions, we need to keep in mind a number of themes. First, the interventions that come from neuroscience will increase in range and depth. Second, there is at least one fundamental element that current privacy theories, by their design, have distanced and camouflaged, that is, the *absolutism of existential reality* and its significance for individual citizens. Third, and related to that, no valid account of privacy can ignore the significant impact of the mythological dynamic on each citizen.

From this it will be argued that existential absolutism has been consistently distanced and camouflaged for mythological reasons. The consequence is that psychological space of individuals has become colonised and normalised by the application of the techniques developed by the dominant interests of Deity, State, Market and Technology on behalf of the Absolute Self, with the specific purpose of camouflaging this absolutism and over a very long period. This is at the same time the production of the content of what we see as private. That is, our primary private concerns are the issues to do with each of the magnitudes: morality, power, material ambitions and the embedding in technology. These are the concerns that displace our deepest, existential fears and desires. This particular – mythological – understanding of normalisation will be the means by which we can bring the answers to all the above questions within a single frame.

We shall see that these mythological strategies of normalisation that comprise current privacy theory break down into two groups. The first is what we have inherited from Deity, State and Market and constitutes the first of the two current theories, that is, the Constitutional account. The other is what we are now embracing through modern Technology in the form of digitised information, that is, the Selective Flow of Information account. Together they comprise the foundation of the impact of the mythological dynamic on our psychological space, and it is through these that we displace any experience of our most primal – existential – fears and desires.

To arrive at a valid account of privacy by accounting and correcting for these three themes – that is, neuroscience, existentialism and the mythological dynamic – will have us forgo these mythological accounts and develop one which embraces respectful self-responsibility. However, because it would be counterproductive to deny the benefits of neural enhancement, the way forward will require that we work substantially – but not of course completely – through technology. This will be an account in which this technology is under the control of the individual citizen. The outcome will be an entirely new understanding of the nature of privacy. We will then also refer to the political and economic conditions that will be required to sustain it. A new sense of privacy needs a new understanding and capacity of its social and political context.

NORMALISATION: THE REASON TO SEEK A NEW SENSE OF VALUES

Current privacy theories are the symptoms of the mythological displacement of existential concerns, whereby dominant interests have led the processes of constructing in their stead the circumstantial fears and desires that those interests claim will be conclusively dealt with on condition of individual subjection. However, before we seek to develop an alternative, non-mythological account of privacy, we need to understand the normalising which is that 'constructive' process. This is not the socialisation we see from Piaget or Freud, or even the normalising argued for by Foucault, but a particular form of normalising that serves modern mythology. Privacy – and the answers given to the questions we have just canvassed – is the product of this normalising.

This account will have strong historical features, as we examine the serial strategies of subjection established by the dominant interests of each of the magnitudes in their respective absolute phases but which persist as each has been engaged to be sympathetic, leaving behind an accumulating field of subjecting ideas and practices. That is, the impact of these respective magnitudes has been discrete but there is also continuity and accumulation across this long field.

Before doing so, we present – for contrast – an alternative account which also argues for a continuity across historical eras, that of Lyon. That account argues, as does the account presented here, that this historical perspective has been ignored. That said, the outcomes of these two broad arguments are radically different.

In the context of the notion of normalisation adopted here, we proceed to consider in turn selections from the means by which the mythologising of individual psychological space and material practice was and continues to be promoted by the dominant interests of Deity (through confessional pastoralism), State (through governmentalisation of the pastorate, subjectification of the individual through discipline for increased productivity and the emergence of the bourgeois economy) and Market (through its eventual dominance of the State by the arguments of liberal and neoliberal economists and the professionalisation of consumer debt).

The work of Foucault is thoroughly considered in these respective analyses, although this is prefaced by an argument that he had no theory of mythology. As a result, although his work was highly complementary to the analysis here, it cannot be considered an endorsement. The argument here ultimately stands on its own. The arguments of Elias regarding the creation of a personal bourgeois habitus that appeared along with the appearance of early forms of the State – and had significance for the emergence of a mythological notion of privacy – are also considered.

We then examine the impact of the latest of these serial magnitudes, that is, Technology on behalf of the Absolute Self. This is done by contrasting Heideggerean authenticity with the emergence of algorithmic technology, this as a means of normalisation. In the context of the latter, we explore the notion of technologies of the self and how this will increasingly lend itself to the promotion of the Absolute Self as the final mythological failure. This technological Self should be understood not as a rectification or correction of this serial mythologising but as a further example of the failure of the modern mythological project.

Normalisation: The Reason to Seek a New Sense of Values 9

In short, in our search to displace our existential concerns, we have attempted, first, a theological solution (an Absolute Deity), then a political solution (the Absolute State), then an economic solution (the Absolute Market) and now are moving towards a technological creation of the Absolute Self.[3]

Bringing all this back to the nature of privacy, the argument here is that this is not to be seen as a personal, confidential space within which we can exist largely uninterrupted – in the physical world or the infosphere – nor is it the reflection of the control of information flows, normative or not. Both of these are ultimately absorbed into the frame of the psychological space constructed long-term from the detritus of each of the magnitudes of the mythological trajectory. It is in this space that we have been led to struggle with our notions of right behaviour, where we mull over power and opportunity, or imagine the kind of material life we want and consider how technology could impact our lives. To the extent that these are based on a willingness to be subject to the ideas and practices of each or all of the magnitudes, these are mythological questions. It is therefore in this space that not only are we now exploring and planning what we seek within our lives but, equally importantly, where we thereby are creating the model of ourselves, our subjectivity.[4]

So, the implanting of ideas and practices based on the claims of agents – within, once or further removed – of Church, State, Market and Technology is intrusion into the very centre of our sense of self, establishing presumptions that dominate a wide range of personal considerations. These magnitudes largely drive the intentional content of our subjectivity[5] and, to the extent that we adopt these intrusions rather than other, non-aligned personal decision-making, they are mythological.[6] That is, our existential concerns are well covered over as dominant interests imagine the problems and opportunities to which they claim to have the resolution if we are subject. Privacy is now the product of a mythological history that brings us right up to the present.

By this normalisation, an individual variously arrives at a condition about which such terms as autonomy and responsibility are now typically used. With this status, one then can claim the right 'to be left alone' to enjoy the right to a self-fashioning of one's own choosing and also to have access to and control over currently available information selected by the citizen themselves in their social context. Such a status, however, is typically based on a lack of awareness of the distancing and camouflage of existential concerns and their displacement by constructed fears and desires. By this experience one has reached a condition far from the existential reality which humanity would otherwise both acknowledge and be concerned and inspired by. Instead, one exists in a mythological condition of bourgeois normality produced by

---

[3] For a full elaboration of this notion, see part 1 of Grant, *The Mythological State and Its Empire*, and ch.2 of Grant and Bennett-Moses, *Technology and the Trajectory of Myth*.

[4] T. Metzinger, *Being No One* (MIT Press, 2003), pp. 354, 452.

[5] Ibid. pp. 114, 177.

[6] Ibid. pp. 365, 593.

the mythological dynamic. So, one is thereby in no real sense autonomous or responsible, as one is too far beholden. In contrast, those two characteristics would be authentically available to those experiencing existential reality and engaging re-imagined, non-mythological agencies in the deeper and wider challenges and opportunities of living. It is in the non-mythological context that fundamental fears and desires, then shame, personal intimacy, respect, political authenticity and life plans take on very different meanings and where they would then re-emerge with an entirely different sense of privacy.

We conclude the examination of the history of this normalising by reflecting on the role and function of the bourgeoisie as dominant players in the broad process of mythological normalisation.

THE VALUES FOR A NEW PRIVACY

A fresh account of privacy needs, *first*, to acknowledge the mythological status of current theory and then focus on personal and reimagined social resources to realise an authentic, non-mythological condition. *Second*, it needs to embrace all citizens rather than simply stand as an apparent reward for one group or class. *Third*, it needs to be able – counterintuitively – to take advantage of and manage the valuable interventions and potentially malevolent intrusions of modern neuroscience and virtual reality and do so in a manner that allows us, far differently conditioned, to confront and manage deep fear and desire, to be ashamed, to plan our lives in self-reliance, to develop our own political views, to conserve what is singularly personal and to respect others who are also doing so.

Given the need to understand the history and very foundations of our social arrangements and psychological condition, especially as they provide the context for our relationship with Technology and our sense of privacy, what is required is a new sense of ethics to guide this fresh understanding. This preferred notion of the ethics for privacy therefore cannot be simply selected from what is presently available but needs to be developed from the ground up. This new ethical approach can be properly founded on the principle of respectful responsibility to and for oneself (*respectful self-responsibility*).[7] This new ethical frame would satisfy those three essential conditions. It would not be beholden to currently dominant ideologies, would be universally available and would use but manage emerging technology.

There are various reference points of which such an original ethics also needs to take note. These include Heidegger's principle of authenticity, Foucault's account of *parrhesia* or 'truth talk' and Capurro's critique of Floridi's informational ontology. Against that background, each of the ethical values commonly used to condition the

---

[7] As with the notion of the mythological trajectory, this is a further elaboration of the work done in *The Mythological State and Its Empire*, pp. 9–12, and *Technology and the Trajectory of Myth*, pp. 25–26, 32–34 and 209–210. It will be further explored in Chapter 6 herein.

field of Technology – human dignity, human rights, equality, identity, freedom as non-domination, the common good and responsibility[8] – needs to be examined. This will demonstrate instead the primary value of respectful responsibility to and for oneself. Doing so would not deny the secondary worth of those values. A full account of all these issues will produce a new ethical framework for a new sense of privacy.

THE FUNCTIONING OF THE NEW SENSE OF PRIVACY

This new ethical frame can readily fulfil a new notion of privacy, that is, one which forgoes mythological features. Such a notion would have existential reality at its core. It would be seen as embracing the full suite of the primal fears and desires, the risks and opportunities of existence, the development of meaning for oneself, the responsibility to develop the wherewithal to stand resiliently while being prepared to fail and the willingness to work with other like-minded individuals to address existential challenges. This is the essence of respectful self-responsibility, the refusal to be subject to the ideas and practices other than those freely chosen by the individual, while maintaining the wide sense of respect for others that constitutes a reformed, equitable quality of social existence.

Given the mythological forces of State and Market that are presently visited on individuals – including through the constantly extending technological means at their disposal – establishing the conditions for this will require, first, a conducive frame of regulation, law, State, Market. Only by this will both the free access to developmental information and related opportunities be available to each citizen, as well as the opportunity to assume ownership of all personal information and the value of working equitably in cooperation.

To ensure we can take advantage of all that emerging technologies will have to offer by way of correction and enhancement, any new sense of privacy needs to combine self-responsibility with the use of these technological possibilities. That is, the argument here is not only that Technology – including the advances in neuroscience – is of fundamental importance but that it, like State and Market, is not inherently mythological but is so whenever it assumes responsibility for the individual citizen.

---

[8] See *European Union Charter of Fundamental Rights* – Article 1 – Human Dignity; United Nations *Universal Declaration of Human Rights* inc. Article 7 – Right to Equality before the Law; Article 8 section II D of the *European Convention on Human Rights* regarding personal identity; I. Kant, *Critique of Pure Reason* at A533/B501 on freedom; P. Pettit, *Republicanism*, and D. Grant *The Mythological State and Its Empire*, ch.8, regarding freedom as non-domination; J. J. Rousseau, Book II of *The Social Contract*, and T. Hobbes, *Leviathan*, ch.22, regarding the common good; M. Heidegger, *The Essence of Human Freedom – Introduction to Philosophy*, in Complete Works, vol. 31, pp. 279ff., regarding personal responsibility; see also part II of *The Oxford Handbook of Law, Regulation and Technology*, R. Brownsword, E. Scotford and K. Yeung (eds.) (Oxford University Press, 2017).

What follows is that the aspirational aspects of this new sense of privacy will, first, need to be elaborated in a socio-technological frame. This will be represented in a *personal technology strategy* that provides access to all information and skills development that will allow the development of respectful self-responsibility but where it is the citizen who is at the centre – and in control – of such information sharing. This will require that various technical conditions be set on both the development of and access to data, including the means of its uploading and downloading. Uploading would include one's plans for development as well as recognising one's respect for others, the latter by contributing selected, valuable information – appropriately protected – to agencies of State. Downloading would include the full range of chosen enhancements and the means by which they are absorbed. This is the *progressive* element of the new privacy.

Second, given the importance of protecting one's sense of agency, including as the citizen explores all options without prejudice within the principles of self-responsibility, the opportunity will be needed to conserve one's evolving personal data, a data set that will be unique to the individual. This is not the sense of self-absorbed privilege than reflects bourgeois existence in the Constitutional account nor the simple demand for access to appropriate information that the Flow of Information account demands, since both those exist within the mythological frame. This is the assurance that each citizen can consider, develop and plan the implementation of their *personal technology strategy* without having to negotiate its conditions of availability with external agencies or others, while demonstrating respect for others' self-responsibility. This is the *conservation* element.

Such a strategy is distinct from those proposed, for example, by the algorithmic frame of Domingos and the Artificial General Intelligence networks of Goertzel. It is also distinct from that put by the IEEE regarding the management of personal information, although that body does place the individual at the centre of the data management process. All these remain prey to the incursion of mythology.

The robustness of this new approach would need to be tested against practical real-life circumstances where privacy is in contest. A beginning is made in that regard here by the presentation of a selection from case law, indicating what outcome this non-mythological approach to privacy would produce.

Bringing all this together, we say that this comprises a new sense and a new practice of non-mythological privacy.

ESTABLISHING THE NEW SENSE OF PRIVACY WILL
REQUIRE INSTITUTIONAL SUPPORT

But respectful self-responsibility – as the means to realise a reimagined sense of privacy in the neo-technological age – needs a conducive institutional environment to prosper, as no individual can engage its existential opportunities or fulfil its demands by themself. This will not be available from the mythological magnitudes with which the West has become fully accustomed over two millennia but from reimagined institutions and arrangements. So, the first question is what models of regulation, of the rule of law, of the State and of the Market, are required to provide that support, promoting the respectful self-responsibility of each individual, and what role would technology play therein to avoid the inducements of the Absolute Self?[9] More specifically, how would the law, the State and other agencies regulate the social-political-economic environment to do so? What is the sense of regulation in this arrangement?

REGULATION

It may be put that the elements of the institutional environment which need to be created to promote self-responsibility should be understood and elaborated before any regulatory framework to support them is presented. The position here is opposite to that. That is, not only do the law, the State and the Market – especially as they increasingly use technology in a particular way – represent a mythologised institutional framework but this framework is therefore subjecting and, in that sense, regulatory in the broad sense. It is therefore necessary to be clear about the nature of this regulation – which they all share – before we proceed to explore how we may 'deregulate' them. This is a sense of deregulation that is the opposite of that frequently proposed by neoliberal economists.

This is also a position against those who may say that we no longer live in a world in which the State and the Market are characterised by the exercise of 'sovereign' power, that is, that the Hobbesian/Kantian State has been or, in the case of the neoliberal Market, is perhaps being constrained – especially by the legislative regulation of their power – and so are no longer absolutist mythological magnitudes. That is, the mythological frame is outdated. Here it is argued that regulation has not constrained State and Market power – especially when seen in the context of their technological use of data – but is the form of their increasingly empowered dispersal across the social field: sovereign power may have been engaged but this is only by way of transformation. By this, regulation is mythological.

There are of course very different accounts of the nature of regulation, some which see it in its paralegal form as responsible for significant increases in the quality of life by constraining Market players large and small to operate in a manner that produces sympathetic outcomes for citizens. Some such as Schleifer argue that,

---

[9] No attention is given here to the question of Deity. The position here is that Deity is thoroughly mythological and any contribution that might be claimed for it on grounds of moral guidance or social cohesion can be provided alternatively by a rational moral framework of the kind that is being provided in this work. Regarding the relevance of Deity in governance, the position is that notions of Deity have no place in this field, again arguing that a rational political framework which also emphasises respect is sufficient: the influence of the Church on the political field is anathema.

Introduction

especially in advanced economies, better outcomes are obtained through deregulation. What is argued in the present work is that the mythological features of regulation are revealed by the way that both of these approaches strengthen the credentials of the State and the Market players to induce the subjection of the citizen through, for example, the satisfaction of created desire. We shall look closely at this issue.

The arguments of Schleifer peg out the ground that is variably occupied by the presently dominant form of regulation theory, that of Responsive Regulation as proposed by Braithwaite. Before exploring that theory, and to provide a perspective on it in a way that introduces how the position in the present work differs radically from it, it is helpful to refer to Foucault's notion of governmentalisation.[10] This notion describes the increasing disciplining of the social space, and the individual located within it, that emerged through the strategy of 'police' that took control of every aspect of human practice in the eighteenth century and which was a historical transformation of the Christian pastorate. However, governmentalisation has persisted and can be seen in three manifestations: biopower, urban planning and algorithmic regulation. These are means of subjection and will be explored as a context for the critique of Responsive Regulation on the grounds of its profoundly mythological character.

Looking closely at Braithwaite's account of Responsive Regulation reveals that character. That is, although promoted primarily as a means to engage citizens and agents of the Market cooperatively in compliance so that all may benefit, there is the constant shadow of more severe, and ultimately capital, measures to ensure subjection to the prescriptive regulatory regime. This complement of prescription, inducement, proscription and subjection is classically mythological.[11] The key to understanding Braithwaite's mythology is his heavy reliance, both early and still, on Pettit's form of 'non-dominating' republicanism, wherein agents of the State may interfere in my affairs if it is seen, in the context of what is generally accepted, that doing so will be in my interest.[12]

From this critique we shall see that there are ways of dealing with disrespectful behaviour – through fundamentally reimagined regulation which is embedded constitutionally and in a realigned legal framework – which do not fall into the trap of themselves being disrespectful in the way Responsive Regulation does. The point

---

[10] M. Foucault, *Security, Territory, Population*, pp. 108–110, 313. In considering the value of regulation, the primary intellectual reference points used here are the works in this area undertaken by Foucault but, before him, that by Bentham. See his *The Theory of Legislation*. The work on policing, broadly defined well beyond the criminal field, undertaken by Donzelot is also relevant here. These works are the lens through which regulation is seen here, often against the general themes presented especially in *Regulation Theory*, P. Drahos (ed.) (ANU Press, 2017).

[11] J. Braithwaite, 'Fasken Lecture – The essence of Responsive Regulation', *UBC L. Rev.* 44:475 (2011).

[12] For a full account of the mythology of Pettit's Republicanism, see Grant, *The Mythological State and Its Empire*, ch.8.

is that, for the values of respectful self-responsibility to work in response to the serious challenges of such new technologies as neuroscience, the State must itself have such a value fully embedded in it, rather than be compromised when it is faced with what it sees as robust deviance. The State needs to be non-mythological.

BEGINNING TO REIMAGINE THE LAW

Seen in the context of this regulatory frame, law demonstrates its mythological credentials, due to the impact on it of the dominant interests of Deity, State and Market. That is, the democratic institutions – and especially legislatures– are a field in which those interests have dominant influence.[13] This has happened variously over time. For example, Foucault points to the vast array of specific police regulations that were utilised to strengthen the State in its emergent phase, but also how, reflecting changing regimes of power, it subsequently represented liberal and then neoliberal forms of governmentality that have promoted productivity and market-based freedoms.

In this context, reimagining the law as non-mythological would need to begin with a revised Constitutional frame. The US Constitution contains no significant reference to any sense of self-responsibility, but it can be argued that elements of the First, Fourth and Fifth Amendments would provide an opportunity for a clarification of such a notion, as does Article 7 of the European Union Charter of Fundamental Rights. Doing so would aid an attempt to resist some of the fundamental challenges being presented to the US Constitution, now showing its age, especially due to recent developments in Technology.[14]

To fulfil the opportunity from such Constitutional reinterpretation, it would be necessary to re-examine current notions of the Rule of Law. Many of these fall into an 'anatomical' frame, whereby they provide lists of what their respective authors regard as essential characteristics of law. But none of those, perhaps bar one, can be seen to have 'teleological' features, that is, regarding the purpose of law in the first place. However, there is one rule of law theorist who confronts this fundamental issue head-on. That is Krygier. He seeks to open up the entire issue by looking at what social conditions drive the call for a rule of law and sees there what for him is its principal purpose, that is, the constraint of the arbitrary exercise of sovereign power.

However, in rightly focussing on this problem, the argument here is that Krygier does not look closely enough at the source of sovereign power with which he is concerned, so he misses the other forms of power into which the powerful, sovereign

---

[13] As one example of such influence, see Grant and Bennett Moses, *Technology and the Trajectory of Myth*, ch.4, where a detailed case study is presented revealing the influence of dominant interests on the legislative process for gene technology legislation in Australia.

[14] U. Kohl and D. Rowland, 'Censorship and Cyberborders through EU Data Protection Law', in U. Kohl (ed.), *The Net and the Nation State* (Cambridge University Press, 2017), ch.7.

16 *Introduction*

forms of State power have morphed and spread widely though subjecting regulation. These are mythological though in a different form than that which properly concerns Krygier.

The foundation of a re-imagined rule of law is then elaborated here through Langford's argument for the legislative establishment of purpose-based organisations that operate on fiduciary principles. While there are certain flaws in current thinking about such matters, this is an argument for non-mythological social arrangements that could promote existential, respectful self-responsibility and which would, at the same time, avert the possibility for any arbitrary use of sovereign power.

BEGINNING TO REIMAGINE THE STATE

The argument has been made that the State is a mythological magnitude, its Hobbesian and Kantian roots long 'engaged' by democratic institutional arrangements and now largely transformed into a regulatory form that extends across the socio-economic field.[15] In that form, and as we have just seen regarding Braithwaite and Pettit, it is still driven by the mythological dynamic of dominant interest, claims that constructed fears and desires which distance and camouflage existential reality will be conclusively dealt with, and consequent subjection. There is good evidence for this regulatory form of the State and this is explored here, principally through the work of those who have followed the Responsive Regulation framework of Braithwaite. This brings the analysis up to the present time as we look at the development of smart regulation and meta-regulation and their significance for public accountability.

This State form has significant impact on individual citizens, for example, in the fracturing of responsibility for crime control through privatisation and the consequent emergence of risk-based and predictive strategies which blur the boundaries of individual responsibility. The entry of neuroscience into criminal justice is a further disruption, including through the interpretation of neuroscientific research which lessens criminal culpability and shifts decision-making away from the judiciary.

Perhaps even more significantly now, the impact on the State made by the emergence of a range of technologies has left a deep imprint on its managerial role and how it interfaces with the Market and with its citizens. In short, the agencies of the State, those both close and distant, are digitally avaricious and are increasingly constituted by their use and misuse of their own data and that of the Market, the latter available through their symbiotic relationship. This use is typically justified on security and economic development grounds, but it is raising a wide range of issues, including a threat to democratic values and individual rights. The governance of

---

[15] The author has presented a full account of the development of the State as mythology in *The Mythological State and Its Empire*, see ch.1, Introduction, for the broad outline of the argument and ch.11; see also *Technology and the Trajectory of Myth*, ch.2.

cyberspace is in the centre of these difficulties, as is the issue of individual privacy, the present accounts of which are as a consequence appearing fragile or, in the argument here, unsustainable. That is, the regulatory nature of the modern State is operating in a manner that increasingly displaces a valid sense of rightful autonomy while it assures citizens of their security and economic well-being.

To contrast all this and as a way forward, an entirely different model of the State will be presented – one based on Langford's notion of purpose-based agencies operating upon fiduciary principles – that is, where the interests of the self-responsible citizen are brought to centre-stage. In this context, by way of example, the principles of an alternative criminal justice model which would promote respectful self-responsibility will be presented, including through the use of regulation in an entirely different manner than that which is shadowed by sovereign power. This is to say that regulation can be used as constraint, empowerment or a socially reconstituting device so long as it returns respectful self-responsibility to rather draws it from individuals. The importance of reconstructing the use of data and the implications for the use of other technologies by the State is also considered.

BEGINNING TO REIMAGINE THE MARKET

We begin by explaining the sense in which the Market is properly seen as a mythological magnitude, that is, that it has come to occupy a place in the social and economic landscape whereby claims are consistently made about its pre-eminent capacity to bring well-being within a sympathetic existence both generally and in relation to each citizen, so long as one is subjected to its regimes of lifestyle imagery, technological 'availability' and continuous indebtedness.[16] The significance of such landmark legal initiatives as *Salomon* v. *Salomon* and the Fourteenth Amendment to the US Constitution for this mythological status are explored to support this argument, in particular, how the ultimate effect of these was the personalising of the corporation in a manner that is argued to be patently mythological.

A particular model of corporate activity, linking it to the responsive regulatory frame, is then examined. That model is Regulatory Capitalism, wherein capitalism is seen as a regulatory arrangement. Its originating position includes that the processes of regulatory empowerment can lead to a range of outcomes within the field of *commodification*, as the transformation of social relations into or from commodity relations and involving every citizen.[17] This framework includes the now well-developed tendency to reconstitute employees as contractors. This Market

---

[16] An account of the Market as myth has been presented by the author in *The Mythological State and Its Empire*, ch.7, and *Technology and the Trajectory of Myth*, ch.2.

[17] D. Levi-Faur, 'Regulatory Capitalism', in P. Drahos (ed.), *Regulatory Theory – Foundations and Applications* (Australian National University Press, 2017), ch.17, pp. 289–299.

model is anathema to respectful self-responsibility. We explore the reasons why, critiquing the conditioning of the individual by their economic status rather than as a self-responsible citizen with economic interests among others. It is the latter that needs to be set as the frame for a reimagined Market and its elements include the need to reconstruct the notion of consumer protection,[18] the elimination of the disposition of the Market to construct desire through manipulation of personal and Big Data, along with other themes.

Calling on the work of Trentmann, we undertake an exploration of the motivation for a wide range of corporate activity, and with a particular focus on this creation of desire through data mining. This leads into and connects with the examination of the nature of algorithms that we looked at in Chapter 2. In this context, the works of Christl, Zuboff and Yeung are brought into the discussion.

Drawing together these features of the modern corporation into the mythological frame then provides the basis of a non-mythological way forward. This begins by briefly referencing the key elements in the history of the corporation. That is, the corporation was originally conceived as a public institution whose purpose was to serve national interests and advance the public good, radically different from the function it serves in the contemporary, neoliberal context where it is effectively programmed solely to advance the private interests of its owners.[19] As a sign of some of the re-thinking that is presently being expressed, we see that corporate responsibility is the subject of moves by the French National Assembly – by passing Article 61 of its Action Plan for Business Companies' Growth and Transformation – and certain English initiatives to make businesses more sustainable and in line with collective social and environmental interests. This is a revision of the very definition of corporate purpose.[20]

That commentary is followed by the reintroduction of the work of Langford, and her argument for the feasibility of the transformation of the corporation into an entity which not only is purpose-based but can operate on fiduciary principles, and by examining that of du Plessis, who argues that such purpose should be driven not by the interests of shareholders but more broadly by stakeholders.

These arguments are drawn on to then argue that corporations can, against the flow of the vast majority of current interests, be conceived and brought to operate non-mythologically. Further than that, they can be re-imagined, as can the agencies of the State, as promoters of individual respectful self-responsibility. There are roadblocks to this, of course, and many lie in current corporate legislation and

---

[18] Improvements in consumer protection can be seen as the result of bourgeois activism, in response to which the Market has raised its standards; see John T. D. Wood, 'Consumer Protection: A Case of Successful Regulation', in *Regulatory Theory*, p. 650.

[19] J. Bakan, *The Corporation – The Pathological Pursuit of Profit and Power* (Simon & Schuster, 2005), p. 153.

[20] B. Segrestin et al., 'French Law Revisits Corporate Purpose', *Stanford Social Innovation Review* (29 November 2018).

judicial interpretation. However, these are argued to be resolvable through the strategies outlined in Chapters 6–9. This move would also require the consequential reconception of competition law, of consumer protection provisions and those for the corporate use of personal data outlined in Chapter 6. We then examine the implications of this change of direction for the development of smart cities and for employee relations and, finally, revisit the importance of the creation, the ownership and control of personal data by the citizen, the latter being critical in any discussion of the corporation in the neoliberal era and the notion of the Absolute Self therein.

AIM OF THE BOOK

What is being presented here are new accounts of both privacy theory and regulatory theory, necessary to respond to the highly interventionist technologies of neuroscience and virtual reality, each of which is still in its embryonic stage but looming large. It does so by arguing that the standard accounts fail to see that privacy has been a field of modern mythological normalisation and thereby of subjection, believing instead that it is a confidential zone which should be left alone to allow one's self-fashioning within a field of rights or that it should be constituted by assured access to available data within a normative, contextual flow of information. The constructive process which leads to this subjection – in which we have always been complicit – has mythological roots in the ideas and practices of the trajectory of historical magnitudes in the West: Deity, State, Market and now Technology on behalf of the Absolute Self. The empowerment of these magnitudes – an empowerment ironically created by the transfer of self-responsibility which is at the heart of that subjection – is the source of the distancing and camouflaging of our existential concerns and of the claims that their dominant interests will deal with the daily concerns with which they have been replaced. This mythological engagement of the individual is thereby founded on intrusion into and construction of our psychological disposition by the ideas and practices promoted within those magnitudes. This is thereby the opposite of 'leaving alone' or 'ensuring access to all relevant information'. Even the normalised individual is continuously monitored or denied information to ensure ongoing compliance, a compliance not shared with the non-normalised – the mentally or physically incompetent or the criminal – who are thereby subject to deeper and wider and continuous intrusion.

The fragility – the unreality – of the standard accounts of privacy is fully revealed by the current suite of new technologies, especially neuroscience and virtual reality. Although developed for the purpose of delivering radically corrective data inside the human brain, applications of these technologies have the potential to be highly interventionist and thereby potentially highly reconstructive in their bidirectional management of neural data. The reconstructive nature of algorithms is fundamental to this consideration. None of the standard accounts of privacy can properly accommodate this intervention into privacy except by attempting the weak claim of selective adoption. The new account presented here deals with this circumstance by widely embracing – rather than being excessively cautious about – these new technologies. It does so by proposing the use of this new technology itself both to draw on the corrective opportunities and to provide the capacity to conserve what is prioritised by the respectful citizen without unjustified interference, by taking advantage of the many potential enhancements of the citizen's choice by engaging with reimagined State and Market, and by providing control over the creation of and access to a wide range of personal information, although some is rightfully shared. By this, this 'respectful responsibility to and for oneself', we have the new sense of *privacy*: the '*to and for oneself*' is what constitutes a different sense of privacy that also ensures respect and cooperation. This is far from the current dominant accounts.

However, given that respectful self-responsibility is weighty, its success would require that regulatory, legal, political and economic conditions of support and promotion exist. To that end, an outline for the reimagining of regulatory theory – and in that context, Constitutional principles, law, the State and the Market – is presented, all based on a reconception of the ethical foundations of the management of technologies. Doing so in no way plays down the challenges of realising this sense of privacy across these various fields. However, the position here is that the challenges from such emerging technologies as neuroscience and virtual reality, which will increasingly go to the heart of what it is to be human, are deeply significant, and the provision of a reimagined institutional framework will be necessary to allow the reimagined account of privacy to be established. Establishing the wide scope of these arguments is the aim of the book.

PLAN OF THE BOOK

The emergence and proliferation of interventionist technologies, in particular, through innovations in neuroscience, are argued to be initiatives of the greatest significance for the nature of human agency and therefore for both privacy and for the manner in which we regulate these and related fields. A detailed account of the emerging technologies within neuroscience and virtual reality, along with a full examination of the reconstructive nature and function of algorithms in this, is presented in Chapter 2.

The consequentially implicit shortcomings of current privacy theories, the essential elements of which include the claim to be left alone to pursue a project of self-fashioning or the development of one's personality within a rights framework and a claim for the reconstitution of the currently selective flow of information, is critiqued in Chapter 3.

A further key argument is then presented, that it is mythologically normalised individuals who claim to have the right to a private zone or to achieve privacy by correcting present distortions in the flow of information. This argument is supported by three fields of further evidence: the nature of the history of the magnitudes of the trajectory of Deity, State and Market and now Technology on behalf of an Absolute Self; the denial of privacy to the non-normalised; and that, even for the normalised, surveillance does not stop. Privacy now is not 'the right to be left alone to refashion oneself' or access to a wider range of normalising information but is the long-evolved mythological construction of our psychological and social dispositions, how we should think and act. This argument is presented in Chapter 4.

The notion of privacy thereby needs to be completely rethought so that these 'constructive', mythological interventions can be replaced by an arrangement by which the interests of the respectful, responsible citizen are promoted and protected. This first requires a reconsideration of the current ethical principles upon which privacy theory is presently based. In its place, but without denying the secondary value of those, respectful self-responsibility is argued to be that base, in the process providing a solution to the well-known dilemmas of current privacy theory: what is private is this respectful responsibility 'to and for oneself'. This is undertaken in Chapter 5.

The conversion of this new value system into a practical arrangement of privacy, based significantly on the embrace of a newly devised technology, and an outline of the nature of the support required of a new institutional framework, is presented in Chapter 6.

The need for this ethical-technological-privacy arrangement to be supported through an institutional frame begins with the reimagining of regulation. This functions as the subtext for a new law, a revised notion of the State, and reconceptions of the Market and Technology. The result is the presentation of a new regulatory theory, drawing on the lessons from the Foucauldian account of governmentality but relocating that into the context of the mythological trajectory. The new theory bypasses the currently dominant theory of Responsive Regulation due to its mythological nature. This is presented in Chapter 7.

The necessary consequential reimagining of the law, including the call for new Constitutional provisions and a new rule of law, to fulfil the undertaking of the new regulatory theory, is based on a substantive extension of the social context of rule of law. This is explored in Chapter 8.

The consequential reimagining of the State dispenses with the mythological account presented by the political theoretical tradition and focuses on a refounding of the State on purpose-based fiduciary principles. This account includes a reassessment of the responsibility of the State regarding the production, use and management of personal data and Big Data. A model for a non-mythological system of criminal justice is included. This reimagining is presented in Chapter 9.

Finally, the necessary reimagining of the Market covers parallel ground, dispensing with the neoliberal frame of the majority of modern corporations and exploring a frame which would also be founded on purpose-based fiduciary principles that favour the self-responsible citizen. This also explores the changes necessary in the gathering, use and management of personal data and Big Data. This is presented in Chapter 10.

The outcome of this broad argument is a new account of privacy, one protected by a new ethic and a new account of regulation, one facilitated by reimagined institutional arrangements of law, State and Market. By all this, it would be possible not only to resist the otherwise deeply disruptive, imminent interventions of neuroscience but to take full advantage of the corrections and enhancements that neuroscience will increasingly have to offer.

PART I

Privacy

Part I has been concerned with the significance of emerging neuroscience for the idea and practice of privacy and with a range of contextual factors through which that significance needs to be understood.

First, neuroscience is emerging as a tool for human clinical therapy and enhancement that is unlike anything seen before. Its force as a tool is due to its method being founded on the fast-evolving capacity of algorithmic technology.

Second, the speed of this evolution, and the fact that it is being championed by highly regarded theorists and practitioners, is delivering to this technology a pre-eminent, even fully dominant, status in human affairs. However, this dominance is obscuring the facts that, not only does algorithmic technology have technical limitations, but it is also leading to a progressive subjection of humanity to its regimes that have not been properly acknowledged among the claims made about it.

Third, a key effect of this subjection is that the connection of humans to algorithmic technology, which will increasingly occur through bi-directional data exchange, will demolish our current notions of privacy – a field already fraught with contradictions and shortcomings – even as it moves to repair and enhance human cognitive capacities.

Fourth, these shortcomings of current notions and practices of privacy are not only outdated – in that they are the product of former historical scenarios – but they are so riddled with shortcomings that they barely provide value to individuals, especially in the face of the tide of technology and now the deep intrusions of neuroscience therein. We need an entirely new conception of privacy.

Fifth, a pointer to the challenge of developing such a new conception is the revelation that this subjection by algorithms echoes the historical instances of wide human subjection that have preceded it. That is, this is the recurrence of a dynamic that points to the human disposition to subject oneself to absolute magnitudes so long as claims are made that existential concerns will be eliminated. The dominant interests who have adopted such strategies – serially through Deity,

State and Market – have all claimed that existential concerns can be banished, but do so by shifting the focus onto constructed fears and desires which they claim to conclusively deal with. This shifting focus is given effect by the processes of normalisation that have characterised their respective ideas and practices over historical time and which have thereby provided the content of how we presently understand privacy as an accumulation of historical ideas and practices. This recurring – mythological – dynamic is the foundation of the present elaboration of algorithmic technology, by which an Absolutism of the Self is promised but which will deliver only absolute subjection.

Sixth, a concept of privacy is required that is capable of resisting such deep algorithmic intrusion without losing the opportunity for clinical therapy or cognitive enhancement. Given that *responsibility to and for oneself* is the preferred antidote to any application of this mythological dynamic, it is presented here as the foundation of a new account of privacy. This preference is based not only on the manner in which it counters the materiality of this dynamic but also on its credentials as a new ethic.

Finally, this new conception therefore embraces algorithmic technology – to take advantage of these therapies and these enhancements – but is conceived in such a way that it is the individual citizen who must have control over every aspect of the interface with this technology. This is the meaning of responsibility to and for oneself, the 'to and for oneself' comprising the new understanding of privacy. This is not to say that this reconception is sufficient, as it will require to be supported by the institutions of the social infrastructure, the focus of Part II.

2

Privacy, Neuroscience and Algorithms

It is not possible to present an account of the spectacular developments in neuroscience without at the same time considering the evolution of algorithmic technology. Following some preliminary comments about artificial intelligence to set the scene, we shall proceed to examine in some detail a range of neuroscientific developments and then look at the role that algorithms perform therein and why they are significant. This will consist of four themes:

- The breadth and depth of neuroscientific research
- Algorithmic neuroscience as problematic
- Algorithmic constructivism
- Kantian informational Idealism as mythological.

We will complete this chapter with an exploration of the significance of virtual and augmented realities.

The Artificial Intelligence Context

The claimed advantages and risks of artificial intelligence as it relates to neuroscience have for some time been placed before us, with a wide range of material exploring its operation and monitoring its progress.[1] The Royal Society's *iHuman*

---

[1] For example, 'Intelligence explosion: Evidence and import', *Machine Intelligence Research Institute* (2012); S. Armstrong et al., 'Racing to the precipice: A model of artificial intelligence development', Technical Report 2013-1 Future of Humanity Institute; N. Bostrom et al., 'The Ethics of Artificial Intelligence', in *Cambridge Handbook of Artificial Intelligence* (2014); A. Browser et al., 'Artificial Intelligence: A Policy-Oriented Introduction', *Wilson Centre* (2017); T. Everitt et al., *AGI Safety Literature Review* (ANU, 2018); M. Buitten, 'Towards intelligent regulation of artificial intelligence', *European Regulation of Risk Regulation* 10:1 (2019); Fei-Fei Li and J. Etchemendy, 'We Need a National Vision for AI', Human Centred-Artificial Intelligence (HAI), Stanford University, October, 2019; P. Engelke, 'AI, society and governance: An introduction', for the Atlantic Council, March 2020.

report[2] examines the operation of the various kinds of neural interface – recording, stimulating, invasive and non-invasive – as well as such looming challenges as how they will increasingly merge with our intelligence, future likely developments in thought transfer, enhanced memory and learning, along with a consideration of important ethical questions. Further in that space, the paper 'Neurotechnologies for Human Cognitive Augmentation: Current State of the Art and Future Prospects'[3] – which understands augmentation as relevant to attention; the formation of knowledge, memory, judgment and evaluation; reasoning and computation; problem solving and decision making; comprehension and production of language – emphasises the same need for the development of an ethical framework which deals with challenges in the fields of mind reading, privacy, agency, responsibility, liability, safety and social impact. All this material argues for both the benefits of these technologies and the importance of dealing with any risk to the individual or society. Examining the related arguments will make up the substance of much of this chapter and this work more broadly.

It is, however, a particular issue which these reports do not specifically address but which lies at the centre of this field that is the concern here, that is, rather than what the impact that such technologies had and will increasingly have, how the algorithms – especially at the more complex end of the spectrum in machine and deep learning – actually function. Variously referred to as interpretability, explicability or the black box problem, this has sustained a cloud over the claimed value of these technologies, not the least element of which is the well-known inequity due to algorithmic bias.[4] It is relevant across fields, for example, in law regarding the threat to intent and causation;[5] in medicine regarding explicability rather than prediction[6] (where there is even Orwellian potential[7]); and in finance, especially regarding credit rating.[8]

In response, there has been a concerted effort to come to terms with and resolve these concerns. One prominent movement in this is Explainable AI (XAI), in which attention is being given to prediction accuracy (explaining how conclusions are reached and how future decision making can be improved), decision understanding (including improved trust from human users) and the inspection and

---

[2] 'iHuman: Blurring Lines between Mind and Machine', The Royal Society, September 2019.

[3] C. Cinel et al., 'Neurotechnologies for human cognitive augmentation: Current state of the art and future prospects', *Frontiers in Human Neuroscience* 13:13 (2019).

[4] T. Panch et al., 'Artificial intelligence and algorithmic bias: Implications for health systems', *Journal of Global Health* 9:2 (2019).

[5] Y. Bathaee, 'The artificial intelligence black box and the failure of intent and causation', *Harvard Journal of Law and Technology* 31:2 (2018).

[6] D. Watson, 'Clinical applications of machine learning algorithms: Beyond the black box', *BMJ Clinical Research* 364:1886 (2019).

[7] S. Eickhoff, 'Neuro-imaging based prediction of mental traits: Road to Utopia or Orwell?', *PLOS Biology* (November 2019).

[8] D. Fagella, 'AI transparency in finance – Understanding the black box', Emerj (October 2019).

traceability of actions undertaken by AI systems.[9] These efforts are supported by the independent conclusions by such leading theorists as Stuart Russell, who argues that artificial intelligence should be made to err on the side of obedience to humans but should be allowed to intelligently decide when to obey humans, due to our capacity to give orders which may well not be in our interests.[10] This is reinforced by his application of the principle of inverse reward design, which aims to overcome the difficulty that AI achieves 'sought' rewards in scenarios specified by us but misapplies those lessons in generalisation to other scenarios.[11] Further, he argues that we should change the definition of AI itself, from a field concerned with pure intelligence, independent of the objective, to a field concerned with systems that are provably beneficial for humans.[12] Within this approach, because algorithms applied to malleable humans can have drastically different and pernicious side effects on a global scale, he recommends that they undergo FDA-style digital clinical trials to ensure safety while protecting innovation.[13] While all this is an acknowledgement of the challenge posed by algorithms,[14] it is also recommending means by which that can be mitigated and they be made safe and beneficial to our stated purposes.

This seems reassuring, apparently pointing a way both to trust the algorithmic process and thereby to share the as yet untold benefits of artificial intelligence. However, not only are there grounds for caution in this, but, if one steps back and takes a broader perspective, these measures in fact point to a confirmation of a deeper concern than that produced by worries about the trustworthiness of algorithms. This concern is justified by the increasingly wide and deep exploration of our neurological capacity and the aspiration to control that capacity at all levels. That is, we need to look at the purpose of shoring up the investigative capacity of algorithms in the manner recommended by XAI and the work of Russell. We shall now examine how deep and how wide this exploration is becoming. In doing so we shall see that these improvements in algorithmic transparency and explicability will make them more – not less – troublesome.

---

[9] S. Mueller et al., 'Explanation in human-AI systems: A literature meta-review synopsis of key ideas and publications and bibliography for explainable AI', *DARPA XAI Literature Review* (February 2019), especially section 1, 'Purpose, Scope and Organisation', p.5.

[10] S. Milli, D. Hadfield-Menell, A, Dragan, and S. Russell, 'Should robots be obedient', *Proc. IJCAI-17* Melbourne (2017).

[11] D. Hadfield-Manell, S. Milli, P. Abbeel, S. Russell, and A. Dragan, 'Inverse Design Reward', in *Advances in Neural Information Processing Systems*, Papers of the NIPS Conference 2017 (MIT Press, 2018).

[12] S. Russell, 'Provably Beneficial Artificial Intelligence', in The Next Step: Exponential Life BBVA *OpenMind* (2017)

[13] O. Groth, M. Nitzberg and S. Russell, 'AI algorithms need FDA-style drug trials', *Wired* (August 2019).

[14] See M. Krishnan, 'Against interpretability: A critical examination of the interpretability problem in machine learning', *Philosophy and Technology* (August 2019).

THE BREADTH AND DEPTH OF NEUROSCIENTIFIC RESEARCH

There is proper concern about the intrusion into our personal circumstances by those who undertake widespread data gathering through various techniques that are one step removed from the person. There is properly even more concern when the distribution – the flow – of that data is then made selective by those who take hold of such data. However, those technologies – for example, that operate in the service of political security, social connection, corporate interests and online entertainment – have far less significance than those emerging out of neuroscience and related fields.

How should we react when we read that, by sending an electric current into certain neurons, we can restore a person's sense of touch or hearing? Or that we can send simple signals from one brain to another? Or that we will each be able to control robots through thought and from a distance? Or even that we will be able to zap nerves that connect our brain and spinal cord to our body and so learn skills faster or drive more safely? What if we are told that installing a neural chip will not only fix a range of such health issues as Parkinson's disease or dementia but will vastly improve short-term memory, allow us to pick up a new language quickly, even play chess better? How about discovering that such chips would enable us to upload, store externally and then reload our memories or those of others? What of brain implants that will boost such cognitive capacities as reasoning, willpower or judgement? Such powers raise questions not only about what it is to be human but also about who will control and use the data collection and the manipulation upon which such powers are based.

Technological intervention into the human brain is well established but is becoming more profound as technologies become more sophisticated. At present, these technologies are dominated by techniques and methods intended to address a wide range of human ailments and shortcomings. The value of these technologies for improving the quality of human lives cannot be underestimated. They are increasingly manna from heaven for the afflicted. However, as these beneficial interventions do increase in sophistication, as more is learned about the brain, as they draw increasing amounts of data from individual brains, as they download an increasing range of data into brains and as bidirectionality increasingly constitutes the framework for these processes, it is clear that the capacity to influence and restructure the brain and thereby to effect human thought and behaviour is beginning to undergo profound change. It is obvious that this has deep significance for what it means to be individually and socially human, for what we think, how we imagine, how we decide, what we sense and how we feel.[15] That is, there will be an increasingly soft line between what is intervention and what is intrusion. We could well be on a road that sees this line disappear altogether. In saying so, we should

---

[15] S. Fairhall, 'Cross-recruitment of domain-selective cortical representations enables flexible semantic knowledge', *Journal of Neuroscience* (2020), doi:10.1523/jneurosci.2224-19.20207.

The Breadth and Depth of Neuroscientific Research 29

remember that the notion of intrusion is not merely technological. As we saw in Chapter 1 and will see further below, the impact of technology should be seen in the context of the mythological trajectory, as its latest phase, so intrusion carries this far wider import than the functional capacity of the technology, although it includes that.

What Emerging Neurotechnologies Are Telling Us about the Brain

We need to begin by acknowledging that the range and pace of discovery in the field of neuroscience is so continuous that any selection here of research under development will be outdated with the passage of even a modest period of time. So, what follows are some of the new technologies that so far are most relevant for the broad argument being put here. That is, the important point is not that this is a rapidly changing field but that the meaning of the continuous evolution of these discoveries will not change. Since technology is argued here to be – typically but not necessarily – mythological, that meaning includes that understanding these technologies includes seeing them as attempts to influence and control human idea and practice by subjection through inducement. We shall see why.

Even a quick scan of recent developments in this field shows that these technologies are beginning to explore, to amend and to extend our knowledge of our cognitive features and experiences. The range of these discoveries is bordering on the astounding. They include methods that can map the brain at high levels of detail[16] and which can 'image' and read activity deep within the brain,[17] that have revealed a new form of neuronal communication within the brain,[18] clues to its evolution,[19] the basis of sensory experience,[20] as well as the possibility of neural repair and the means to one's self-control of waves in the deep brain (subthalamic

---

[16] E. Boyden, 'Mapping the brain at high resolution', *Science* (January 2019); P. Wang, 'Inversion of large-scale circuit model reveals a cortical hierarchy in the dynamic resting human brain', *Science Advances* (January 2019); A. Iraji et al., 'Space: A missing piece of the dynamic puzzle', *Trends in Cognitive Sciences* (2020), doi:10.1016/j.tics.2019.12.004; J. Stein et al., 'The genetic architecture of the human cerebral cortex', *Science* (2020), doi:10.1126/science.aay6690; A. Burton et al., 'Wireless, battery-free subdermally implantable photometry systems for chronic recording of neural dynamics', *PNAS* (2020), doi:10.1073/pnas.1920073117.

[17] 'How deep learning is transforming brain mapping', Singularity Hub (24 June 2019).

[18] Chia-Chu Chiang et al., 'Slow periodic activity in the longitudinal hippocampal slice can self-propagate non-synaptically by a mechanism consistent with ephaptic coupling', *The Journal of Physiology* (October 2018); M. Triplett et al., 'Probabilistic encoding models for multivariant neural data', *Frontiers in Neural Circuits* (online January 2019).

[19] M. Marchetto et al., 'Species-specific maturation profiles of human, chimpanzee and bonobo neural cells', *eLife* (February 2019).

[20] V. Axelrod et al., 'Neurons in the visual cortex that respond to faces identified', *Neurology* (January 2019); Y. Zhou et al., 'The current research of spatial cognitive evaluation and graining with brain-computer interface and virtual reality', *Frontiers in Neuroscience* 13:1439 (2019).

nucleus [STN]).[21] We can also now clone brain organoids (miniature organs resembling the brain grown in vitro).[22] We know more about the brain–body connection[23] and can see opportunities for the control of human behaviour.[24] Even more widely, we are gaining insight into the way we form representations of ourselves: not only do we not access all the available memories when creating our personal narrative, but we select and even persistently reconstruct the memories which comprise much of our preferred sense of self.[25]

However, if one looks more closely and behind what this quick scan reveals, one can see not only an emerging pattern that presents the brain as well situated within our phylogenetic past but right through to a future where it is being seen as linked to – and becoming part of – the elaborated infosphere of artificial general intelligence.

Primal Cognitive Experience

Research is revealing some of our basic cognitive experiences. At the most fundamental level, this includes not only evidence for the presence of magnetic receptors in the human brain[26] – and so adds to our knowledge of our earliest evolutionary past[27] – but also our experience of fear and pain[28] and

[21] P. Brundin et al., 'Repairing the brain: Cell replacement using stem cell-based technologies', *Journal of Parkinson's Disease* (December 2018); R. Fukuma, 'Real-time neurofeedback to modulate B-band power in the subthalamic nucleus in Parkinson's disease patients', *eNeuro* (February 2019).

[22] 'Scientists can now clone brain organoids. Here's why that matters', Singularity Hub (27 June 2019).

[23] P. Kells et al., 'Strong neuron-to-body coupling implies weak neuron-to-neuron coupling in motor cortex', *Nature Communications* 10: article 1575 (2019); J. Touryan et al., 'Automated EEG mega-analysis 1: Spectral and amplitude characteristics across studies', *PLOS One* (2020), doi:10.1016/j.neuroimage.2019.116361.

[24] B. Kim, 'Dopamine D2 receptor-mediated circuit from the central amygdala to the bed nucleus of the stria terminalis regulates impulsive behaviour', *PNAS* (November 2018); J. Zhou et al., 'Prefrontal cortex corticotropin-releasing factor neurons control behavioural style selection under challenging situations', *Frontiers in Behavioural Neuroscience* (2020), doi:10.1016/j.neuron.2020.01.033.

[25] W. Klemm, 'Neural representations of the sense of self', *Advances in Cognitive Psychology* 7 (2011); G. Mazzoni, 'The "real you" is a myth', *Neuroscience News* (19 September 2018); see also G. Mazzoni, 'Nonbelieved memories', *Psychological Science* 21:9 (September 2010).

[26] C. Wang, 'Transduction of the geomagnetic field as evidenced from alpha-band activity in the human brain', *Neuroscience News* (18 March 2019).

[27] M. Shreyas et al., 'The evolutionary evolution of visual and somatosensory representation in the vertebrate pallium', *Nature Ecology and Evolution* (2020), doi:10.1038/s41559-020-1137-2.

[28] A. Asok et al., 'The neurobiology of fear generalisation', *Frontiers of Behavioural Neuroscience* (15 January 2019); G. Corda et al., 'An amygdala neural ensemble that encodes the unpleasantness of pain', *Science* (January 2019); D. Nobbs et al., 'Brain has separate fear circuits for dealing with immediate and distant threats', *Neuroscience News* (6 March 2018); X. Li, 'The DNA modification N6-methyl-2'-deoxyadenosine (m6dA) drives activity-induced gene expression and is required for fear

desire.[29] These in turn are significant for our consideration of risk, a topic which will be significant in the broad argument here.[30] Research is also pointing to the expression of the 'dark triad' of personality disorders – narcissism, Machiavellianism and subclinical psychopathology – by which some individuals desire pleasure through the displeasure of others, including by the creation of fear through their own desire.[31] Research has also shown that it is possible to identify neural patterns of consciousness in unconscious individuals and that it is possible to use fMRI to predict streams of consciousness.[32] We are also now getting an indication of the neural basis of expectation[33] and where it is in the brain that both spiritual and value experiences are processed.[34] Regarding the latter, we have seen that it is central to the broad argument here that the notion of Deity has had both a deep and broad significance in the history of the West. It is undoubtedly true

extinction', *Nature Neuroscience* (18 February 2019); A. Besnard, 'Dorsolateral septum somatostatin interneurons gate mobility to calibrate context-specific behavioural fear responses', *Nature Neuroscience* (February 2019); A. Lacagnina et al., 'Distinct hippocampal engrams control extinction and relapse of fear memory', *Nature Neuroscience* (2019), doi:10.1038/s41593-019-0361-z; G. Lettieri et al., 'Emotionotopy in the human right temporo-parietal cortex', *Nature Communications* (2020), doi:10.1038/s41467-019-13599-z; T. Hua et al., 'General anaesthetics activate a potent central pain-suppression circuit in the amygdala', *Nature Neuroscience* (18 May 2020), doi:10.1038/s41593-020-0632-8

[29] K. Berridge, 'Affective valence in the brain', *Nature Reviews Neuroscience* (online 4 February 2019); H. Baumgartner et al., 'Desire or dread from nucleus accumbens inhibitions: Reversed by same-site optogenetic excitations', *Journal of Neuroscience* 40:13 (2020); R. Sanders, 'Dopamine's yin-yang personality: It's an upper and a downer', *Neuroscience News* (10 December 2018); J. Munuera, 'Shared neural coding for social hierarchy and reward value in primate amygdala', *Nature Neuroscience* 21:3 (February 2018); J. Kesby, 'How pleasure affects our brains', *Neuroscience News* (29 April 2018); F. Bartolomei et al., 'The role of the dorsal anterior insula in ecstatic sensation revealed by direct electrical brain stimulation', *Brain Stimulation*, doi:10/1016/j.brs.2019.06.005; E. Mitricheva et al., 'Neural substrates of sexual arousal are not sex dependent', *PNAS* 116:31 (July 2019).

[30] P. Sacre et al., 'Risk-taking bias in human decision-making is encoded via a right-left brain push-pull system', *PNAS* (January 2019).

[31] F. George et al., 'The cognitive neuroscience of narcissism', *Journal of Brain, Behaviour and Cognitive Sciences* (28 February 2018); Jing Jie et al., 'Self-interest induces counter-empathy at the late stage of empathic responses to others' economic payoffs', *Frontiers in Psychology – Psychopathology* (25 February 2019); M. Zajenkowski et al., 'Who complies with the restrictions to reduce the spread of covid-19?: Personality and perceptions of the covid-19 situation', *Personality and Individual Differences* (2020), doi: 10.1016/j.paid.2020.110199.

[32] A. Demertzi et al., 'Human consciousness is supported by dynamic complex patterns of brain signal coordination', *Science Advances* (February 2019); C. Fernyhough et al., 'Investigating multiple streams of consciousness: Using descriptive experience sampling to explore internally and externally directed streams of thought', *Frontiers of Human Neuroscience* 12:49 (2018); Z. Huang et al., 'Temporal of macroscale dynamic brain activity supports human consciousness', *Science Advances-Research Article* 6:11 (2020); C. Whyte and R. Smith, 'The predictive global neuronal workspace: A formal active inference model of visual consciousness', *bioRxiv* (2020), doi: https://doi.org/10.1101/2020.02.11.944611.

[33] L. Muzzacato et al., 'Expectation-induced modulation of metastable activity underlies faster coding of sensory stimuli', *Nature Neuroscience* 17:4 (2019).

[34] 'Where the brain processes spiritual experiences', *Neuroscience News* (2 June 2018); T. Komiyama, 'Scientists locate brain area where value decisions are made', *Neuroscience News* (9 May 2019).

32 *Privacy, Neuroscience and Algorithms*

that this belief system relates to a range of psychological and social – and, I argue, albeit in a contrary sense, existential – concerns.[35]

In short, we are coming to understand the brain – and therefore will have the capacity to intervene therein – at these most basic of levels.

How the Brain Functions

Less fundamental but equally important, research is unveiling various elements of the decision-making functionality of the brain. This includes how the interaction between the thalamus and the cerebral cortex leads to us consciously perceiving something.[36] It also reveals how different parts of the brain and the body work together to help us function in daily life, including not only breathing, sleeping, reading, walking, learning but also complex decision making;[37] also how we can identify hidden intentions and reconstruct speech through the use of algorithms in deep learning, including of covert speech.[38] This of course raises the entire question of free will versus determinism[39], a subject to which we shall return in Chapter 5.

Scientists have also identified a strategy that the brain uses to rapidly select and flexibly perform different mental operations.[40] This complements separate pieces of

[35] Why are people religious? A cognitive perspective', *Neuroscience News* (January 2019).

[36] A. Campo et al., 'Feed-forward information and zero-lag synchronisation in the sensory thalamocortical circuit are modulated during stimulus perception', *Proceedings of the National Academy of Sciences* (March 2019).

[37] H.-D. Park et al., 'Breathing is coupled with voluntary action and the cortical readiness potential', *Nature Communications* 11:289 (2020); M. Zust et al., 'Implicit vocabulary learning during sleep is bound to slow-wave peaks', *Current Biology* 29:4 (2019); F. Deniz, 'The representation of semantic information across human cerebral cortex during listening versus reading is invariant to stimulus modality', *Journal of Neuroscience* (2019); A. Selfslagh et al., 'Non-invasive, brain-controlled functional electrical stimulation for locomotion rehabilitation in individuals with paraplegia', *Scientific Reports* 9: article 6782 (2019); S. Sardi et al., 'Adaptive nodes enrich nonlinear cooperative learning beyond traditional adaptation by links', *Scientific Reports* (2018); M. Sarafyzad, 'How we make complex decisions', *Neuroscience News* (16 May 2019); L. Groschner et al., 'Dendritic integration of sensory evidence in perceptual decision-making', *Cell* (14 March 2018).

[38] V. Saigle et al., 'The impact of a landmark neuroscience study on free will: A qualitative analysis using Liber and colleagues' methods', *AJOB Neuroscience* 9:1 (2018); H. Akbari et al., 'Towards reconstructing intelligible speech from the human auditory cortex', *Scientific Reports* 9: article 874 (2019); G. Anumanchipalli et al., 'Speech synthesis from neural decoding of spoken sentences', *Nature* 568 (2019); S. Rainey et al., 'Brain recording, mind-reading and neurotechnology: Ethical issues from consumer devices to brain-based speech decoding', *Science and Engineering Ethics* 26 (2020): 2295–2311.

[39] A. Lavazza, 'Free will and neuroscience: From explaining freedom away to new ways of operationalising and measuring it', *Frontiers in Neuroscience* 10:262 (2016); L. Vervoort and T. Blusiewicz, 'Free will and (in)determinism in the brain: a case for naturalized philosophy', *PhilArchive* copy v1: https://philarchive.org/archive/VERFWAv1.

[40] 'How the brain performs flexible computations', *Neuroscience News* (6 June 2018); 'How the brain makes choices', *Neuroscience News* (11 January 2019); A. Banerjee et al., 'Value-guided remapping of sensory cortex by lateral orbitofrontal cortex', *Nature* 585 (2020): 245–250.

The Breadth and Depth of Neuroscientific Research

recent research concerning a proposal for a new model to explain how neural networks facilitate the flow of information[41] and how self-monitoring 'error' neurons fire immediately after a mistake is made.[42] We are thereby acquiring knowledge that could ultimately allow us to intervene deeply in brain function, that is, how it might be brought to function better.

How the Brain Can Be Brought to Function – Prostheses, Stimulation, Nanotechnology, Genetics

In the drive to develop methods by which cognitive and other disabilities can be addressed[43] – in the form of cochlear implants, artificial retinas, neural stimulation to treat Parkinson's, implants to help in stroke rehabilitation, neural interfaces to facilitate the use of artificial limbs – such research is also continuing to focus on means by which intervention allows the brain to be augmented per se. There are many examples. These include the use of prostheses to extend the capacity to solve complex, sequential decision-making problems by helping people overcome motivational obstacles for the achievement of personal long-term goals.[44] Optogenetic and such other techniques as electrical, ultrasonic and magnetic stimulation are being shown to be effective not merely in treating brain disorders but also in the augmentation of such brain functioning as communication, attention and situation awareness.[45] Further innovations have included the prospect of predicting human behaviour from its links to neural activity[46] and the counter-intuitive abilities to hear colours, see music and taste numbers as pre-eminent examples of brain

---

[41] G. Hahn, 'Portraits of communication in neuronal networks', *Nature Reviews Neuroscience* (December 2018).

[42] Z. Fu et al., 'Single-neuron correlates of error monitoring and post-error adjustments in human medial frontal cortex', *Neuron* (December 2018).

[43] J. Frank et al., 'Next-generation interfaces for studying neural function', *Nature Biotechnology* 37 (2019).

[44] F. Leider et al., 'Cognitive prostheses for goal achievement', *ResearchGate* (February 2019), doi: 10.13140/RG.2.2.16279.06564/1.

[45] C. Cinel et al., 'Neurotechnologies for human cognitive augmentation: current state of the art and future prospects', *Frontiers in Human Neuroscience* 13:13 (2019); S. Jarvis, 'Prospects for optogenetic augmentation of brain function', *Frontiers in Systems Neuroscience* 9: article 157 (2015), doi:10.3389/fnsys.2015.00157; see also; J. Garcia et al., 'Reconfigurations within resonating communities of brain regions following TMS reveal different scales of processing', *Network Neuroscience* (2020), doi:10.1162/netn_a_00139; 'Poking neurons and nerves precisely', editorial, *Nature Biomedical Engineering* 4 (2020): 133–134.

[46] K. Walsh et al., 'Evaluating the neurophysiological evidence for predictive processing as a model of perception', *Annals of the New York Academy of Sciences* 1464:1 (2020): 242–268; G. Etter, 'A probabilistic framework for decoding behaviour from in vivo calcium imaging data', *Frontiers in Neural Circuits* 14:19 (2020); A. Pak et al., 'Top-down feedback controls the cortical representation of illusory contours in mouse primary visual cortex', *Journal of Neuroscience* (2019), doi:10.1523/jneurosci.1998-19.2019.

plasticity,[47] not unlike the synaesthesic experience. These enhancements will continue to proliferate as the methods of intervention continue to develop.[48] Such developments will likely follow through the potential of nanotechnological methods into the mammalian visual cortex,[49] the use of robotic body surrogates by those with motor deficits[50] and improving the accuracy of long-term memory and thereby various aspects of intelligence, extending the human nervous system over the internet, allowing long distance robotic control and so on.[51] More recently, the prospect of genetic intervention to improve cognitive performance has become more real.[52]

How the Brain Can Be Brought to Function – Bidirectional Interfaces

It is clear that, as these more elaborate interactive interventions emerge,[53] they will increasingly raise a range of ethical issues. Examples of these interventions include the current hypothesis that spinal cord–spinal cord connection is a means of sharing information between brains and nervous systems[54] and the demonstration of brain-to-brain communication through BCI (brain–computer or brain–machine interfaces).[55] This has been complemented by other work which indicates that brain

[47] A. Alfaro et al., 'Hearing colours: An example of brain plasticity', *Frontiers in Systems Neuroscience* 9: article 56 (April 2015); '"Seeing" music or "tasting" numbers? What we can learn from those with synesthesia', *Neuroscience News* (23 May 2018).

[48] P. Gutruf, 'Fully implantable optoelectronic systems for battery-free, multimodal operation in neuroscience research', *Nature Electronics* (December 2018); 'Chinese scientists have put human brain genes in monkeys – And yes they may be smarter', *MIT Technology Review* (10 April 2019).

[49] Yuqian Ma et al., 'Mammalian near-infrared image vision through injectable and self-powered retinal nanoantennae', *Neuroscience News* (28 February 2019).

[50] A. Saniotis et al., 'Integration of nanobots into neural circuits as a feature therapy for treating neurodegenerative disorders', *Frontiers in Neuroscience* (March 2018); P. Grice et al., 'In-home and remote use of robotic body surrogates by people with profound motor deficits', *PLOS One* 14:3 (2019).

[51] R. Hampson et al., 'Developing a hippocampal neural prosthetic to facilitate human memory encoding and recall', *Journal of Neural Engineering* (March 2018); N. Martins et al., 'Human brain/cloud interface', *Frontiers in Neuroscience* 13:112 (2019); Z. Sun et al., 'The mechanisms behind learning and long-term memory in the brain', *Neuroscience News* (2 October 2019).

[52] A. Lavazza, 'Cognitive enhancement through genetic editing: A new frontier to explore (and to regulate)', *Journal of Cognitive Enhancement* (October 2018).

[53] E. Smalley, 'The business of brain–computer interfaces', *Nature Biotechnology* 37 (August 2019); R. Gaunt and J. Collinger, 'Brain–machine interfaces are getting better and better – And Neuralink's new brain implant pushes the pace', *The Conversation* (26 July 2019).

[54] A. Silva-dos-Santos et al., 'The hypothesis of connecting two spinal cords as a way of sharing information between two brains and nervous systems', *Frontiers in Psychology* 8:105 (2017); J. Weller, 'Spinal stretch reflexes support efficient hand control', *Nature Neuroscience* (February 2019).

[55] R. Saracco, 'Brain-to-brain interface. Where are we?', *IEEE Future Directions* (7 September 2018); see also A. Degenhart et al., 'Stabilization of a brain–computer interface via the alignment of low-dimensional spaces of neural activity', *Nature Biomedical Engineering* (2020), doi:10.1038/s41551-020-0542-9.

plasticity flows quickly from brain–computer interfacing.[56] Similar results were obtained in BCI-assisted collaborative control of a spacecraft simulator when compared with decisions by single users. Beyond any therapeutic benefits, these developments clearly raise deep questions about the extent and significance of their intervention, for example, regarding agency, responsibility, liability and current notions of privacy.[57]

Yet such questions go even deeper, in particular as they relate to the question of whether thoughts can be read, reconstructed or even brainjacked, the latter through implants which could determine cognitive or behavioural outcomes.[58] Barbara Sahakian has expressed views about these matters,[59] saying that fMRI techniques are increasingly able to uncover private thoughts[60] and unravel the brain processes related to self-control and morality. She refers to reconstruction of images from viewed video clips by applying machine learning algorithms to a subject's brain activity.[61] In this regard the work of Tomoyasu Horikawa is also significant. He uses brain decoding and computational models in computer vision to explore neural substrates of vision, including perception and dreaming.[62] Also relevant is that it has been shown to be possible to utilise neural plasticity to implant memories which persist after consciousness is regained in unconscious mammals with the use of optogenetic technology and to manipulate memories in various other ways.[63] A cautionary assessment of certain of these developments has been provided by Mecacci and Haselager.[64]

[56] T. Nierhaus et al., 'Immediate brain plasticity after one hour of brain–computer interface (BCI)', *The Journal of Physiology* (November 2019).

[57] E. Hildt, 'Multi-person brain-to-brain interfaces: Ethical issues', *Frontiers in Neuroscience* 13: 1177 (November 2019).

[58] J. Pugh, 'Brainjacking in deep brain stimulation and autonomy', *Ethics and Information Technology* 20:3 (September 2018).

[59] B. Sahakian 'Opinion: Brain scanners allow scientists to "read minds" – could they now enable a "big brother" future?', *University of Cambridge Research* (13 February 2017), www.cam.ac.uk/research.

[60] J. Makin et al., 'Machine translation of cortical activity to text with an encoder-decoder framework', *Nature Neuroscience* 23 (2020): p.575; T. Love, 'An MIT lab is building devices to hack your dreams', *OneZero* (April 2020).

[61] G. Shen et al., 'End-to-end deep image reconstruction from human brain activity', *Frontiers in Computational Neuroscience* (April 2019), https://doi.org/10.3389/fncom.2019.00021.

[62] G. Shen et al., 'Deep image reconstruction from human brain activity', *PLOS Comput. Biol.* 15 (2019): e1006622; see also B. Jarosiewicz, 'Evidence that human brains replay our waking experiences while we sleep', *Cell Reports* (May 2020); B. Lechat et al., 'Beyond K-complex binary scoring during sleep: Probabilistic classification using sleep learning', *Sleep* (2020), doi:10.1093/sleep/zsaa077.

[63] L. Carrillo-Reid et al., 'Imprinting and recalling cortical ensembles', *Science* 353:6300 (2017); see also G. Vetere et al., 'Memory formation in the absence of experience', *Nature Neuroscience* (April 2019).

[64] G. Mecacci and Pim Haselager, 'Identifying criteria for the evaluation of the implications of brain reading for mental privacy', *Science and Engineering Ethics* 25:2 (2019).

Privacy, Neuroscience and Algorithms

Beyond these developments, the emerging field of brain–computer interaction has opened up entirely new grounds and means of intervention.[65] These include speaking silently with a computer, correcting robot mistakes – some claim increasingly unlikely as robot intelligence improves[66] – through thought alone and both humans and computers both learning better through cooperation, including through game theory.[67] One notable spin-off is brain-to-brain communication, utilising a combination of elements: the reading of neural codes to identify intended speech, implanted devices and brain plasticity. This plasticity has been shown separately to enable the modification of neural connectivity through BCI learning.[68]

Expanding the Brain: Whole Brain Simulation, Substrate Extension, Neurohybrids

But the potential from BCI goes well beyond these significant developments. One example is the prediction that a full 'internet of thoughts' will arrive before long, that is, the development of a brain–cloud interface that connects neurons to cloud computing in real time.[69] This is predicted to occur through developments in

---

[65] J. Rosenfeld, 'Neurobionics and the brain–computer interface: Current applications and future horizons', *Medical Journal of Australia* 206:8 (2017); A. Vallejo, 'Propofol-induced deep sedation reduces emotional episodic memory consolidation in humans', *Science Advances* (20 March 2019); see also M. van Kesteren et al., 'How to optimize knowledge construction in the brain', *Nature Partner Journal Science of Learning* 5:5 (2020).

[66] R. Bauer et al., 'Patterns in the brain shed new light on how we function', *PLOS Computational Biology* (30 January 2020).

[67] A. Kapur et al., 'AlterEgo: A personalized wearable silent speech interface', IUI'18 23rd International Conference on Intelligent User Interfaces (March 2018); N. Jarasse et al., 'Phantom-mobility-based prosthesis control in transhumeral amputees without surgical reinnervation: A preliminary study', *Frontiers in Bioengineering and Biotechnology* 6 (2018); Y. Li et al., 'Differential game theory for versatile human-robot interaction', *Nature Machine Intelligence* (January 2019); A. Batula et al., 'Virtual and actual humanoid robot control with four-class motor-imagery-based optical brain–computer interface', *BioMed Research International* (2017), doi:10.1155/2017/1463512; S. Perdikis, 'The Cybathlon BCI race: Successful longitudinal mutual learning with two tetraplegic users', *PLOS Biology* (2018), doi:10.1371/journal.pbio.2003787; A. Schaefer et al., 'Massively parallel microwire arrays integrated with CMOS chips for neural recording', *Science Advances* (2020), doi:10.1126/sciadv .aay2789.

[68] K. Kornysheva et al., 'Neural competitive queuing of ordinal structure underlies skilled sequential action', *Neuron* (January 2019); A. Anderson et al., 'Predicting neural activity patterns associated with sentences using a neurobiologically motivated model of semantic representation', *Cerebral Cortex* 27:9 (2017); I. Monsalve et al., 'Theta oscillations mediate pre-activation of highly expected word initial phonemes', *Scientific Reports* (22 June 2018); E. Chang et al., 'Encoding of articulatory kinematic trajectories in human speech sensorimotor cortex', *Neuron* 98:5 (2018); K. Balasubramanian et al., 'Changes in cortical network connectivity with long-term brain–machine interface exposure after chronic amputation', *Nature Communications* 8: article 1796 (2017).

[69] A. Serb et al., 'Memristive synapses connect brain and silicon spiking neurons', *Scientific Reports* 10:2590 (2020).

nanotechnology, nanomedicine, artificial intelligence and computing and is claimed to be able to allow immediate access to wide accumulated knowledge and the experience of parts of the lives of other willing participants.[70]

This next phase is also being facilitated by further new techniques.[71] First, those which allow the scanning of a preserved brain's connectome, that is, the whole-brain nanoscale imaging and preservation of neural content. This data may subsequently be used to construct a whole-brain emulation for uploading into a computer or into a robotic, virtual or synthetic body. Second, the invention of new expansion microscopy which achieves super-resolution with standard confocal microscopes. This is not cryonics but the building of a bridge to future mind-uploading technology by preserving the informational content of the brain, encoded within the connectome.[72] This process has been encouraged by researchers who have taken a significant step towards enabling the simulation of brain-scale networks of the exascale class,[73] achieved through the development of a new algorithm which allows representation of larger parts of the human brain, using the same amount of computer memory. This algorithm also significantly speeds up brain simulations on existing supercomputers.[74]

Through these and other methods, researchers can see the prospect of not just reading but expanding the substrate – the underlying substance – of our mind by integrating brain and computer, thus overcoming our phylogenetic past.[75] This would allow the extension of our nervous system, allowing control of not one but swarms of robots by paying attention to multiple things simultaneously via a hierarchy of attentional spotlights or miniature conscious selves but subsumed within the primary conscious self.[76] This notion has been further extended by conjecture

---

[70] N. Martins, 'Human brain/cloud interface' *Frontiers in Neuroscience* (29 March 2019).

[71] C. McIntyre et al., 'Holographic reconstruction of axonal pathways in the human brain', *Neuron* (November 2019).

[72] A. Amico, 'Mapping hybrid functional-structural connectivity traits in the human connectome', posted online (24 August 2018), doi.org/10.1162/netn-a-00049; M. Canatelli-Mallat et al., 'Cryopreservation of a human brain and its experimental correlate in rats', *Rejuvenation Research* (June 2020 online), doi: 10.1089/rej.2019.2245.

[73] 'Exascale' refers to computing systems capable of at least one exaFLOPS or a billion billion calculations per second. This capacity is a thousandfold increase over the first petascale computer – allowing one quadrillion floating point operations per second – which became operational in 2008; S. van Albada et al., 'Performance comparison of the Digital Neuromorphic Hardware SpiNNaker and the Neural Network Simulation Software NEST for a full-scale cortical microcircuit model', *Frontiers in Neuroscience* (2018), doi: 10.3389/fnins.2018.00291; S. Marrink et al., 'Computational modelling of realistic cell membranes', *Chemical Reviews* 119:9 (May 2019).

[74] J. Jordan et al., 'Extremely scalable spiking neuronal network simulation code: From laptops to exascale computers', *Frontiers in Neuroinformatics* 12 (2018), doi: 10.3389/fninf.2018.00002.

[75] Y. Zhang et al., 'Synthetic polymers provide a robust substrate for functional neuron culture', *Advanced Healthcare Materials* (January 2020 online), https://doi.org/10.1002/adhm.201901347.

[76] Singularity Hub (5 June 2019) regarding the work of Dr. Jacob Robinson (Rice University) for DARPA in developing the MOANA Project (Magnetic, Optical and Acoustic Neural Access device).

about the possibility of connecting one's brain with an array of coordinated external emulations, including a 'whole brain' simulation which could compensate for any dysfunction in the original individual brain.[77]

Further, we have seen that algorithms that facilitate many of these developments are playing a part in the decoding process in certain forms of research, including as they relate to the development of forms of BCI.[78] But algorithms are also being applied to other, equally interventionist forms of research. In this vein, we have the development of neurohybrids. That is, through the increasing cross-connections between neurophysiology of brain microcircuits, neural interfaces and neuromimetics (the creation of physical elements and circuits emulating living neurons and circuits) together with the development of physical elements with synaptic-like neuroplasticity, we are approaching the stage in which natural and hardware-based neuronal circuits could be integrated into new entities, operating in vivo through brain implants and evolving together on the basis of shared plasticity and processing rules inspired by algorithms.[79] The transfer of information between the elements of such devices, which should be seen to include the current and future development of brain chip technology, employs continuous bidirectionality.[80]

Researchers have also shown that machine learning algorithms are able to demonstrate a link between personality and eye movement, the algorithm able to recognise four of the 'big five' personality traits: neuroticism, extroversion, agreeableness, conscientiousness but not openness.[81] The significance of this for privacy conservation is clear. Machine learning has also been used to demonstrate links between dimensions of mental illness to brain network abnormalities[82] and to use modelling to predict the neural representations of events and states, including the propositional content of sentences.[83]

---

[77] M. Serruya, 'Connecting the brain to itself through an emulation', *Frontiers in Neuroscience* 11:373 (2017) doi.org:10.3389/fnins.2017.00373; H. Yamaura et al., 'Simulation of a human-scale cerebellar network model on the K computer', *Frontiers in Neuroinformatics* (April 2020), https://doi.org/10.3389/fninf.2020.00016.

[78] M. Shomrock et al., 'A characterisation of brain–computer interface performance trade-offs using support vector machines and deep neural networks to decode movement intent', *Frontiers in Neuroscience* (24 October 2018).

[79] Y. Mosbacher et al., 'Toward neuroprosthetics real-time communication from *in silico* to biological neuronal network via patterned optogenetic stimulation', *Scientific Reports* 10:7512 (2020); V. de Feo et al., 'State-dependent decoding algorithms improve the performance of a bidirectional BMI in anaesthetised rats', *Frontiers in Neuroscience* 11:269 (2017).

[80] H. Yeon et al., 'Alloying conducting channels for reliable neuromorphic computing', *Nature Nanotechnology* 15 (2020): 574–579; S. Choi et al., 'SiGe epitaxial memory for neuromorphic computing with reproducible high performance based on engineered dislocations', *Nature Materials* (2018), doi: 10.1038/s41563-017-0001-5; see also S. Kriegman et al., 'A scalable pipeline for designing reconfigurable organisms', *PNAS* 117:4 (2020).

[81] 'Artificial intelligence can predict your personality by simply tracking your eyes', *Neuroscience News* (27 July 2018).

[82] 'Machine learning links dimensions of mental illness to brain network abnormalities', *Neuroscience News* (2 August 2018).

[83] F. Pulvermuller et al., 'Semantic prediction in brain and mind', *Trends in Cognitive Sciences* 24:19 (October 2020): 781–784.

We are hereby beginning to see the increasing sophistication of the use of algorithms as they are adapted to a wider and deeper function within artificial intelligence, machine learning and deep learning. Other examples of this include the use of deep learning to single out neurons exponentially faster than a human can;[84] as we have seen, the development of explainable machine learning (XAI) to generate unifying models of brain function and behaviour (e.g., sociability);[85] the testing of heuristic neural systems models of motivated human behaviour through applications of machine learning;[86] and the use of Bayesian decision theory – Bayes's theorem being the basis of a branch of machine learning – in determining the nature and implementation of human emotions.[87] The 'reverse' of all this is that neuroscience is being looked at to produce models by which we may not only improve artificial intelligence, thereby opening the possibility that physical and social skills may be developed more readily in computers,[88] but also better understand the brain–behaviour relationship in humans.[89]

A further pointer to the spread of algorithmic representation of the brain is that some research proposes that algorithms are the best means of integrating various levels of neural analysis, for example, implementation, computational and algorithmic. In this, algorithmic models can be used to interpret brain imaging data and that data can be used to select among competing models. That is, algorithms operate at both the functional and meta-functional levels.[90] Further research has been presented that some functions of the human brain involve carrying out and remembering non-symbolic algorithms, that is, sequences of steps to perform tasks or achieve ends: in effect, explaining some functions of cognition through the operation of inherent neural algorithmic activity.[91] Further again, evidence has been presented regarding theoretical modelling of brain function, for example, by resolving the ongoing debate in category learning between exemplar theory (knowledge is based on representation of individual instances of category members) and prototype theory

---

[84] S. Soltanian-Zadeh et al., 'Fast and robust active neuron segmentation in two-photon calcium imaging using spatio-temporal deep learning', *Proceedings of National Academy of Sciences* (12 April 2019).

[85] Mai-Anh Vu et al., 'A shared vision for machine learning in neuroscience', *Journal of Neuroscience* 14 (February 2018).

[86] M. Ernst et al., 'Sketching the power of machine learning to decrypt a neural systems model of behaviour', *Brain Sciences* 9:3 (2019).

[87] D. Bach et al., 'Algorithms for survival: A comparative perspective on emotions', *Nature Reviews Neuroscience* 18:5 (May 2017).

[88] B. Yirka, 'How learning more about neuroscience might influence development of improved AI systems', *Tech Xplore* (15 February 2019).

[89] A. Arac, 'Deep behaviour: A deep learning toolbox for automated analysis of animal and human behaviour imaging data', *Frontiers in Systems Neuroscience* (7 May 2019).

[90] S. Sardi et al., 'Brain experiments imply adaptation mechanisms which outperform common AI learning algorithms', *Scientific Reports* 10:6923 (2020).

[91] S. Yildirim et al., 'Does the human brain have algorithms?', in *Proceedings of the 2006 International Conference on Artificial Intelligence*, ICAI (2006), Las Vegas, Nevada, 26–29 June, vol.2.

(knowledge is an abstracted representation coding a category's prototypical features). This was achieved by decoding the brain's capacity for categorisation from its neural implementation to show that it is the representation of individual experiences, not the abstraction of experiences, which is critical for category decision making.[92]

Other research has been argued to show that the brain has a basic computational algorithm and that it is organised by power-of-two-based permutation logic and, further, that 'this simple mathematical logic can account for brain computation across the entire evolutionary spectrum, ranging from the simplest neural networks to the most complex'. This means that evolution has been forced by this mathematical cost-and-benefit analysis to use neuron resources 'efficiently and wisely, as evident from the evolutionarily conserved specific sensory pathways and cortical modalities'.[93] Further, it has been proposed that the brain differently changes its algorithms in parallel processing of visual information. That is, descending neural pathways change contrast for colour and luminance in the classical receptive field (CRF), and spatial grouping of similar attributes by interneurons and by horizontal connections within each area can be changed by still higher areas, 'which modulate interneurons and/or horizontal connections and directly change responsiveness of centre-to-centre cells'.[94]

A further application of the use of algorithms in neural research is their use in deep learning,[95] a biomimetic approach originally inspired by the brain. We shall have cause to come back to such applications, but one example of this is their use – it is the currently prevalent method of doing machine learning – in the reconstruction of perceived images from human brain activity as gathered by fMRI techniques. Improved reconstruction of such images has been obtained by utilising deep learning techniques in the form of a deep generative multiview model (DGMM) algorithm.[96] Further, researchers have developed an algorithm that claims to simulate how a deep-learning network could work in our brains, thereby representing a

---

[92] M. Mack et al., 'Brain mechanisms of concept learning', *Journal of Neuroscience* 39:42 (2019): 8259–8266; U. Topalovic et al., 'Wireless programmable recording and stimulation of deep brain activity in freely moving humans', *Neuron* (February 2020), doi: 10.1016/j.neuron.2020.08.021.

[93] Kun Xie et al., 'Brain computation is organised via power-of-two-based permutation logic', *Frontiers in Systems Neuroscience* 10:95 (2016); A. Oliva, 'Dissecting artificial intelligence to better understand the human brain', *Cognitive Neuroscience Society* (25 March 2018); P. Poirazi et al., 'Illuminating dendritic function with computational models', *Nature Reviews Neuroscience* 21 (2020): 303–321.

[94] A. Przybyszewski, 'Brain differently changes its algorithms in parallel processing of visual information' (2014) at www.researchgate.net/publication/221501506.

[95] Deep learning is a part of machine learning. It is the capability of learning in an 'unsupervised' manner from data that is unstructured. It is thereby different from the functioning of task-specific algorithms.

[96] Changying Du et al., 'Sharing deep generative representation for perceived image reconstruction from human brain activity' (2017), www.researchgate.net/publication/316471441.

biologically realistic way by which real brains could do deep learning.[97] In short, there would appear to be good evidence that algorithms can functionally 'mine' valuable data to support theories about brain function.

However, whether an algorithmic approach can be accepted to be the defining explicans regarding the ultimate nature and function of the brain is contested here.

ALGORITHMIC NEUROSCIENCE AS PROBLEMATIC

Before proceeding to consider further key developments in neurotechnology, we need now to return to some of the principal points we have just raised. That is, the technology itself, especially to the extent that it is beholden to algorithmic design and interpretation, is not unproblematic; and, although considerable attention is being given to these issues, the problems not only are not disappearing but are perhaps worsening and – counter-intuitively – due to such attention.

In the argument here, these problems are not persisting because the attention being given them is inadequate. Ironically, such attention is likely to improve their performance in their own terms. But it is those terms which are themselves problematic. To explain: both the XAI movement and the work of such theorists as Stuart Russell acknowledge, by their efforts to address concerns about the coherence and explicability of algorithms, that there are issues. These include that, even in the context of the moves to improve transparency and reliability, deep learning systems lack common sense regarding the meaning of their results, typically operate in an opaque manner, learn inefficiently, make mistakes and are undermined by 'missing data'.[98] A good example relates to the very nature of decoding, in particular, regarding the 'decoder's dictum', that is, that 'if information can be decoded from patterns of coded activity, then this provides strong evidence about what information those patterns represent'. There is an argument that this dictum is false, that decodability is a poor guide for revealing the content of neural representations and, further, that while connection to behaviour supplies valuable evidence, it is not enough to warrant inferences to representational content.[99] In short, the process

---

[97] J. Guerguiev, T. Lillicrap and B. Richards, 'Deep learning with segregated dendrites', Cognitive Computational Neuroscience Conference (2017), linclab.org; see also Z. Bi et al., 'Understanding the computation of time using neural network models', PNAS 117:19 (2020): 10530–10540; T. Lillicrap et al., 'Backpropagation and the brain', Nature Reviews Neuroscience (April 2020).

[98] M. Waldrop, 'News Feature: What are the limits of deep learning?', PNAS 116:4 (22 January 2019): at 1074; M. Milkowski et al., 'Replicability or reproducibility? On the replication crisis in computational neuroscience and sharing only relevant detail', Journal of Computational Neuroscience (October 2018); Will Knight, 'The dark secret at the heart of AI', MIT Technology Review (11 April 2017); D. Heavens, 'Deep trouble for deep learning', Nature 574 (2019).

[99] J. Ritchie et al., 'Decoding the brain: Neural representation and the limits of multivariate pattern analysis in cognitive neuroscience', British Journal for the Philosophy of Science 70:2 (2019).

of decoding is vulnerable to being over-read to satisfy the expectations or theories of the decoder: meaning can be imposed on the decoding process.

Further, not only can artificial intelligence not necessarily be trusted functionally but neither can it be trusted ethically. As Metzinger observes in response to the release by the European Union of its Ethics Guidelines for Trustworthy AI:

> The Trustworthy AI story is a marketing narrative invented by industry, a bedtime story for tomorrow's customers. The underlying guiding idea of a 'trustworthy AI' is, first and foremost, conceptual nonsense. Machines are not trustworthy; only humans can be trustworthy (or untrustworthy).[100]

Beyond these concerns, what is proposed in the present work is that there are more significant problems with the use of algorithms than either their functional or their ethical limitations and weaknesses. As the breadth and depth of neuroscientific research purposes and outcomes make clear, we have embarked on a project not only to eliminate disease and malfunction but also to understand – and thereby to provide the means to intervene in and reconfigure – our fears; desires; secondary emotions; sensory experience; intellectual, cognitive and physical capacities; spiritual beliefs; and, as we will see, our imagination. The more we improve the friendliness, the provability and the transparency of the performance of algorithms, as Strauss and others assure us, the more extensive and effective will this understanding and these expansive outcomes be. We shall return shortly to what is of concern in this.

The Widening Application of Algorithms

Extending from the individual research outcomes we have looked at, there are arguments that the relevance of algorithms for neural activity should be understood even more comprehensively. We look at two. The first comes from the work of Tom Griffiths at UC Berkley. He has undertaken research into the application of deep learning algorithms,[101] for example, how well they predict human 'similarity' judgements[102] and into the modelling of the human categorisation of natural images to

---

[100] T. Metzinger, 'Ethics washing made in Europe', *Der Tagesspiegel* (8 April 2019). Metzinger is director of the theoretical philosophy group and research group on neuroethics at Johannes Gutenberg University of Mainz. His research centres on the analytic philosophy of mind, applied ethics and philosophy of cognitive science.

[101] J. Peterson, T. Griffiths et al., 'Evaluating (and improving) the correspondence between deep neural networks and human representations', *Cognitive Science* (3 September 2018). Neural networks are a set of algorithms, modelled loosely after the human brain and designed to recognize patterns. They interpret sensory data through a form of machine perception, labelling or clustering raw input. The patterns they recognize are numerical, contained in vectors, into which all real-world data – images, sound, text or time series – must be translated.

[102] J. Peterson et al., 'Adapting deep network features to capture psychological representations: An abridged report', *Proceedings of the 26th International Joint Conference on A.I.* (2017) (IJCAI-17).

Algorithmic Neuroscience as Problematic

understand human minds and to advance artificial ones.[103] However, he also proposes that there are advantages in approaching life problems more broadly by being aware of and applying a range of algorithms, in fact, that we already do so unknowingly.[104] So algorithms are a means of determining when we should stop looking within various fields of activity to make a choice, thereby to begin taking advantage of or exploiting such knowledge; how we can optimally sort the elements of some chaotic field of elements; how we can apply Bayes's rule to predict the future usefully; how we can understand when it is better to leave things to chance; how we can use game theory to guide our understanding of the minds of others. For Griffiths, all this leads to the conclusion that 'as we go about managing such everyday tasks as using a motor vehicle, 'recognising the algorithmic underpinning of our daily lives ... would not only allow drivers to make the best decisions when they're in a particular scenario but also encourage planners to be more thoughtful about the problems they're forcing drivers into in the first place'.[105] This is a plea by him not that we adopt any idealistic computational attitude towards problem solving – that we mimic the view that computers make rational decisions by considering all available options and take the best one – but that we act algorithmically in doing what makes the most sense in the least amount of time in real world situations. One might quickly add that there is still the strong overtone remaining of the advisability of adopting algorithmic techniques in managing our lives.

But the shift towards algorithmic thinking has gone much further even that all these current strategies. In 2011 Pedro Domingos demonstrated his confidence in the application of algorithms for an enhanced understanding of the brain by proposing a new class of deep learning algorithm – sum-product networks (SPNs) – which not only represent functional partitions within the brain but which have 'intriguing potential connections to the architecture of the cortex'.[106] He developed this further through the application of discriminative learning principles to create a probabilistic modelling of the dependence of target variables on observed variables and applied this to demonstrate improved image classification.[107]

However, it was his expressed ambition for a master algorithm expressed in 2016[108] which invited even more attention. By this he claimed that the five dominant but

---

[103] R. Battleday et al., 'Modelling Human Categorisation of Natural Images Using Deep Feature Representations', arXiv:1711.04855v1 (cs.CV) (13 November 2017).

[104] These arguments are set out in detail in Brian Christian and Tom Griffiths, *Algorithms to Live By – The Computer Science of Human Decisions* (Henry Holt, 2016); see also TEDxSydney (16 June 2017).

[105] Christian and Griffiths, *Algorithms to Live By*, p.260.

[106] H. Poon and P. Domingos, 'Sum-product networks: A new deep architecture', arXiv: 1202.3732 (cs.LG) (2012).

[107] R. Gens and P. Domingos, 'Discriminative learning of sum-product networks', conference paper for Neural Information Systems (2012), https://homes.cs.washington.edu/-pedro/papers/nips12.pdf.

[108] P. Domingos, *The Master Algorithm – How the Quest for the Ultimate Learning Machine Will Remake Our World* (Allen Lane, 2015); see also interview with Domingos by Jim Pethokoukis,

competing classes of algorithms[109] would ultimately be integrated into such a single, master algorithm. Domingos was prepared to make both wide and deep claims about the outcomes of this integration. These include that, should an individual hand over all personal data to the control of such an algorithm, it could develop a model of that individual which could be carried in a thumb drive and then carry out the widest range of tasks for that person. These would include, in phase 1, searching cyberspace for personal preferences, keeping the refrigerator stocked, filtering emails and replying, checking credit card bills and disputing improper charges, doing tax returns, renewing subscriptions, consulting doctors about personal ailments, recommending job opportunities, screening partners and suggesting which political candidates one might support.

In phase 2, after further development, the model would stand in as an avatar for the individual and interview other models on one's behalf, say, for job opportunities, on an almost instantaneous basis; so also with dating. It would screen all marketing and service offers. In effect, 'Your digital half will be like power steering your life: it goes where you want to go but with less effort from you. This does not mean that you'll end up in a filter bubble ... the digital half knows better than that. Part of its brief is to leave some things open to chance, to expose you to new experiences and to look for serendipity.' But this model would be continuously learning about the world as it impacts on one, sharing information with you. In short, it would have a model of the world as it relates to you. As yours and the models created for others improve, 'their interactions become more like the ones you would have in the real world ... Tomorrow's cyberspace will be a vast parallel world that selects the most promising things to try out in the real one. It will be like a new, global subconsciousness, the collective id of the human race.'[110] Regarding the privacy implications of all this, he prefers the thin option of urging that individuals be made aware of the issue and encouraged to make individual choices about what to share or not.[111]

But Domingos's claims for a master algorithm did not stop at the digital modelling of one's world. He goes well beyond this to claim that the master algorithm would provide a unifying view of all of science and potentially lead to a new 'theory of everything'. Because of its foundation in data, Domingos makes the extraordinarily strong claim that, unlike other theories, including some of a scientific nature, it has power 'across all fields ... The Master Algorithm is the germ of every theory.'[112] It is not unreasonable to observe from this that current developments in AI, whereby

'What happens when AI scientists develop the "master algorithm"? A long-read Q&A with Pedro Domingos', *AEIdeas* (20 June 2018). Also H. Cai et al., 'Once-for-all: Train one network and specialise it for efficient deployment', conference paper (2020), ICLR 2020, arXiv:1908.09791.

[109] That is, Symbolist, Connectionist, Evolutionist, Bayesian and Analogistic.
[110] Domingos, *The Master Algorithm*, pp.269–270.
[111] Ibid. pp.275–276.
[112] Ibid. pp.46–47.

Algorithmic Neuroscience as Problematic

software applications can reconstruct reality[113] by rewriting themselves,[114] might be proposed as first steps on the pathway to this outcome.

Whether or not such an algorithm is created, what we should note is that the very strength of his claims for it encourage belief in its potential power. Very many individuals can and will see it as the single ultimate opportunity to deal with problems in biology, psychology, sociology or economics, so long as one is subject to the regimes of practice that would derive from it.[115] It will be seen as a significant means to deal conclusively with both existential and constructed fears and desires, despite the shadow of its post-Kantian Idealism. In the argument here, it has mythological implications.

Emerging Implications

One might properly respond to the work of Griffiths and Domingos, dominated by mathematics as it is, by observing that it is only one mode of decision making, of rationality, of perceiving – it is not one driven by aesthetic or intuitive principles, unless one wants to claim that the image of Botticelli's *Primavera* is ultimately founded in mathematics. It is not holistic but extrudes mathematical factors from the available range – social, psychological, spiritual, political, economic, mythological and so on – that far more typically are embedded in human decision making, even if not consciously so, and proposes that the result of that extrusion should be the dominant framework by which coping with life problems should be guided. One is tempted to say, as we shall see, that it would be more beneficial to examine those wider factors and their impact on such coping. This is particularly so when we note that, although algorithmic interventionism clearly points to a range of significant benefits, at the same time there lies a range of issues that reveal problems at the foundation of their use.

First among these is that the algorithmic 'reading' of neuronal activity can be technically erroneous, producing false positives. For about the last ten years, researchers have been using artificial intelligence machine learning techniques to decode human brain activity. Applied to neuroimaging data, these algorithms can reconstitute what we see, hear, and even what we think. For example, they show that words with similar meanings are grouped together in zones in different parts of our brain. However, by recording brain activity during a simple task – whether one hears 'BA' or 'DA' – neuroscientists from the University of Geneva, Switzerland, and the Ecole normale supérieure (ENS) in Paris now show that the brain does not necessarily use the regions of the brain identified by machine learning to perform a task. Above all, these regions reflect the mental associations related to this task.

---

[113] W. Knight, 'An AI that writes convincing prose risks mass-producing fake news', *MIT Technology Review* (14 February 2019).

[114] K. Varshney, 'Introducing AI Fairness 360', *IBM Research Blog* (19 September 2018).

[115] J. W. Krakauer, 'Neuroscience needs behaviour: Correcting a reductionist bias', *Neuron* 93:3 (2017).

While machine learning is thus effective for decoding mental activity, it is not necessarily effective for understanding the specific information-processing mechanisms in the brain.[116]

ALGORITHMIC CONSTRUCTIVISM

Apart from such technical problems, there are equally significant issues regarding not only algorithmic interpretive bias[117] but also the conceptual limitations of AI, for example, its inability to apply common sense.[118] But a larger problem seems to relate to the issue of constructivism. On the one hand, there is a recognition that AI programmers should be drawing on a wider range of theoretical frameworks in their design processes. One argument to that effect has been put that Piaget's theory about the manner in which babies process information in their learning experience may be a way forward. On the other, however, it seems that adopting particular theories or theoretical frameworks could result in a constructivism of the Kantian variety, in which facts about the world are forced into such theories or frameworks. This seems to be the way that we should view the biases inherent in AI.[119] The mathematization of which algorithm design is comprised is thereby both an advantage – in sorting selected data in a meaningful way – and a significant handicap – by either biasing the interpretation or 'short changing' the value of the data being interpreted.[120] It seems that a proper response might be to adopt an approach of the Kantian variety but, instead of embedding a single, dominant theoretical approach, to reinvent data and to have the data interpreted through competing theories, including by each subject. This would avoid reductionist approaches.[121] Artificially intelligent interventions might then avoid misinterpretation or inadequate interpretation, at least in their worst forms. In that latter regard, we should consider that the application of

[116] S. Bouton et al., 'Focal versus distributed temporal cortex activity for speech sound category assignment', PNAS (23 January 2018).

[117] A. Caliskan et al., 'Semantics derived automatically from language corpora contain human-like biases', Science (14 April 2017); also a wide range of such biases and their social implications have been detailed by Cathy O'Neil in Weapons of Math Destruction Crown/Archetype (2017); see also P. Lewis, 'Fiction is outperforming reality: How YouTube's algorithm distorts reality', The Guardian (3 February 2018).

[118] Tom Simonite, 'When it comes to gorillas Google photos remain blind', Wired (11 January 2018); see also Janelle Shane, 'The neural net hallucinates sheep', Nautilus (7 March 2018); Knight, 'The dark secret at the heart of AI'.

[119] M. de Graaf et al., 'Explainable Robotic Systems', in Companion of the 2018 ACM/IEEE International Conference on Human-Robot Interaction (2018), pp.387–388; L. Grabot et al., 'Alpha activity reflects the magnitude of an individual bias in human perception', Journal of Neuroscience (2020), doi:10.1523/jneurosci.2359-19.2020.

[120] Regarding the discovery of mathematical rules that are claimed as the foundation of brain growth, see M. Khariton et al., 'Chromatic neuronal jamming in a primitive brain', Nature Physics (2020), doi:10.1038/s41567-020-0809-9.

[121] J. Krakauer et al., 'Neuroscience needs behaviour: Correcting a reductionist bias', Neuron 93:3 (2017).

quantum mechanics to artificial intelligence or the automation of machine learning[122] could significantly compound the problem.[123]

We shall return to this but the point is that algorithms – especially those that are used for social analysis – are 'biased' in a much broader manner than is usually understood. That is, cultural beliefs – including those that relate to Deity, the State, the Market and Technology itself – not only are embedded neurologically but form the context in which algorithmic design is undertaken. This is a much broader point than the now-common criticism that algorithms are biased regarding race, gender and class. It is that these ideologies, embedded neurologically, must thereby be informing the selection of data and algorithmic design process. This is the risk of algocracy.[124]

These references to Kant and their implications for the nature of algorithms need to be elaborated. We can get a good sense of the Kant–algorithm connection by looking at the field of predictive processing (PP), a field that covers – among other elements – both philosophy and artificial intelligence. PP is a theory that sees the brain as essentially a device for anticipating the upcoming sensory states of the organism. The lessons here derive in an interesting way from the Kantian argument that we have inherent a priori dispositions of cognition that largely determine what we perceive. This is the opposite of much theorising about cognition, that we have primary sensory experiences from which we develop frameworks of understanding.

As Hohwy states:

> Much work has equated PP with *predictive coding*, leading to a quite basic version of PP. In predictive coding, a given system (such as the human brain) harbours an internal model of the causes of its sensory input. These are *hidden causes* in the sense that the system does not have direct access to them but must infer them on the basis of its sensory input and prior knowledge. The model specifies hypotheses about how hidden causes generate input, used to predict what the sensory input to the system will be. Predictions are messages that descend in the internal structure of the system, to be tested against the incoming, ascending sensory signal.[125]

And further: 'There is a wider, very rich intellectual history, and a vibrant contemporary context, to PP.... PP themes are evident early, in Alhazen, Kant and Helmholtz.'[126] Swanson elaborates, stating that it is inherent perceptual structure that itself causes perception:

---

[122] Will Knight, 'You could become an AI master before you know it', *MIT Tech Review* (17 October 2017).

[123] Will Knight, 'A start-up uses quantum computing to boost machine learning', *MIT Tech Review* (December 2017), referring to the work of Will Zheng of Rigetti Computing.

[124] See T. Kariotis et al., 'Fighting Back Algocracy: The Need for New Participatory Approaches to Technology Assessment', in *PDC'20: Proceedings of the 16th Participatory Design Conference 2* (2020), pp.148–153.

[125] J. Hohwy, 'New directions in predictive processing', *Mind and Language* (March 2020): p.2.

[126] Ibid. p.2. See also D. Zahavi, 'Brain, mind and world: Predictive coding, neo-Kantianism and transcendental idealism', *Husserl Studies* 34:2–4 (2017).

I argue that several core aspects of PP were anticipated by Kant in his works on perception and cognition. Themes from Kant active in PP include: (1) the emphasis on 'top-down' generation of percepts; (2) the role of 'hyperpriors'; (3) the general function of 'generative models'; (4) the process of analysis-by-synthesis; and (5) the crucial role of imagination in perception.... PP echoes Kant's general project in that it aims to explain how minds track causal structure in the world using only sensory data, and ... uses a reverse-engineer or 'top-down' method of analysis.[127]

Saying so is of course not enough to establish Kantianism as the nature of the functioning of algorithms and their design. For the argument here that social algorithms are more widely biased than regarding only race, gender and class, we need to identify other steps in the process by which the cultural framework – and thereby the beliefs and practices regarding Deity, State, Market and Technology itself – inform algorithmic design.

In fact, there are evidentiary-based arguments as to the neural embeddedness of culture and that this informs cognition. As Gintis states:

Because of the importance of culture and complex social organisation to the evolutionary success of *Homo sapiens*, individual fitness in humans depends on the structure of social life. Because culture is both constrained and promoted by the human genome, human cognitive, affective and moral capacities are the product of an evolutionary dynamic involving the interaction of genes and culture. We call this dynamic *gene-culture coevolution*.[128]

Further, for Kitayama:

Culturally shaped activation patterns of the brain foster culturally scripted behaviours when these behaviours are called for by the specific situation at issue. They therefore enable the person to enact the required behaviours both automatically and seamlessly. This in turn can help individuals achieve biological adaptation as assessed by their reproductive success. Culture then can serve as a context for biological selection.... Behaviour (and the brain), culture and genes are mutually related to one another. First, gene expressions are contingent on environments, including cultural environments. Second, genes themselves are contingent on relatively long-lasting environmental conditions, including cultural conditions. Third, cultural environments themselves are the creation of humans who show various culture-contingent behavioural tendencies.[129]

---

[127] L. Swanson, 'The predictive processing paradigm has roots in Kant', *Frontiers in Systems Neuroscience* (October 2016): p.1.

[128] H. Gintis, 'Gene–culture co-evolution and the nature of human sociality', *Philosophical Transactions* 366:1566 (2011): 878888.

[129] S. Kitayama and A. K. Uskul, 'Culture, mind, and the brain: Current evidence and future directions', *Annual Review of Psychology* 62 (2011):419–449, p.449; more generally, L. Kirmayer and S. Kitayama (eds.), *Culture, Mind and Brain* (Cambridge University Press, 2020), chapter 3, 'Mutual Constitution of Culture and the Mind'.

Algorithmic Constructivism

49

Bender adds the important further connection between culture and cognition, in the forms of language and writing, number representations and causal framework theories, in particular:

> Cultural evolution made us what we are today, by ratcheting up cultural innovations, promoting new cognitive skills, rewiring brain networks and even shifting gene distributions. Building on what (our evolutionary past) has endowed us with enables us to take another step further. Its pivotal role in human evolution renders culture a constitutive feature of the specifically human brand of cognition and prime source of its diversity. Crucially, this implies that even in the absence of cultural differences, cognition remains a product of human nature – profoundly shaped by the very fact that humans are a cultural species.[130]

The point in all this is that human cognition in the West – comprised significantly by the integrated capacities that include language, numerical ability and the inherent causal frameworks – is brought to bear in the development of technologies, including the selection of data and the design of algorithms. Williamson makes this clear in his assessment of the IBM Smart Cities project, which was conceived with the intention of developing algorithmic software – that reflected human neural capacity – to be embedded across a city to minimise the impact of disruptive events and to convert schools into neuro-pedagogical brain/code spaces for a new kind of Big Data–driven learning experience.

However, as Williamson point out, the algorithm comes *after* the generation of a model, that is, after the formalisation of the problem and of the goal in computational terms. Further, for the algorithm to function – especially with machine learning algorithms – it first has to be trained with existing data so that it may 'learn' and then it needs to be constantly retrained. But:

> *The models and the training data are always constructed and operationalised according to the values and assumptions of their designers.* Fundamentally, learning analytics such as those developed and deployed by IBM depend on the construction of models of learner actions, and learning processes, which can then be subjected to algorithmic processes that have themselves been designed to learn. *These models are the product of complex sociotechnical practices and are embedded in the methodological commitments, assumptions, values and styles of thinking of their designers,* such as those associated with Smarter Education at IBM.[131]

In the argument here, both data and their algorithms are the product of such assumptions, values and styles of thinking as are embedded in the culture of the

---

[130] A. Bender, 'The role of culture and evolution for human cognition', *Topics in Cognitive Science – Levels of Explanation in Cognitive Science: From Cultures to Molecules* (August 2019): pp.4 and 12–13; J. Breedlove et al., 'Generative feedback explains distinct brain activity codes for seen and mental images', *Current Biology* 30:12 (2020): 2211–2224.

[131] B. Williamson, 'Computing brains: Learning algorithms and neurocomputation in the smart city', *Information, Communication and Society* 20:1 (2016): p.86, emphasis added.

West, including especially by the dynamic of the mythological trajectory of Deity, State, Market and Technology on behalf of the Absolute Self. Algorithms are mythological artefacts that reflect, reproduce or generate the subjecting, cultural framework in both their corrective and enhancement of cognitive processes.

Therefore, the proper way to appreciate this range of widening and deepening interventions is to adopt a gestalt shift and to see them as the grounds to reproduce old perspectives (Deity, State and Market) and construct new but selected worlds (Technology) of capacity and imagination. In short, we construct and reconstruct particular senses of reality. That is, we are not trying to draw more 'imaginative' interventions into the frame of techniques we are using but are reinventing and extending the old into the new dominant senses of reality. Although not in the sense that is now usually intended, algorithms are therefore inherently – and are becoming more reliably – biased in this sense. That is, they will increasingly carry this role of reconstruction, in every sense of that notion. Even more significantly, unless these come to be applied at the behest and in the control of informed individuals, they carry the capacity for extensive mythological subjection.

In the context of neuroscientific intervention, this means that, to the extent that algorithms will increasingly be used to eliminate constructed fears and create and satisfy desires on behalf of citizens who will be induced to be subject to them, they can be directly mythological in the sense intended in this work. The 'mechanism' by which they can best be understood is post-Kantian Idealism. As in Kant, but well beyond his theological-political frame, such applications of these neurotechnologies can well become an attempt to deny the absolutism of existential reality, distancing and camouflaging its features into a cultural framework imposed upon it for the purpose of reimagining it.[132] This may be an argument ultimately that we should seek to identify the culturally laden, hard-wired *synthetic a priori* in the neurological manifold of command and control.[133] Whether or not that is feasible, this is an argument that humanity can and does select from the wide range of possible conceptual frameworks, the purpose being to order our understandings and perceptions and that individual citizens may be induced – or in some cases forced – to adopt these to satisfy the mythological purposes of dominant interests. Just as those interests within the magnitudes of Deity, the State and the Market in their respective

---

[132] For an account of the manner in which Kant saw nature as a source of existential contingency, chaos and thereby fear and thereby sought to reconstruct it as made by God, see *Technology and the Trajectory of Myth*, pp.89–92.

[133] Some, like S. Papert, argue this in relation to W. S. McCulloch – see the introduction to McCulloch, *Embodiments of Mind* (MIT Press, 1965); Warren S. McCulloch, 'What is a number, that man may know it, and a man, that he may know a number?', *Vordenker* (Winter edition 2008–2009). Others, like L. Weatherby, argue that McCulloch's position was that we have to find a way not to defer to a data-based understanding of a world that nevertheless includes data: the digital is real but not inevitable. See L. Weatherby, 'Digital metaphysics – The cybernetic idealism of Warren McCulloch', *The Hedgehog Review* (Spring 2018). This latter position is closer to what is put in the present work.

absolutist forms undertook to do so, so also will the dominant interests of Technology, including neurotechnology, do the same, the latter algorithmically. This might be called a digital metaphysics. Improvements in algorithmic design and operation – their transparency, their friendliness, their explicability – will, counter-intuitively, promote this. In following chapters, the means to avoid this trend of algorithmic subjection will be explored.

Digital Metaphysics

To explain further: within the frame of what has just been put forth, we may now see that there is a profound theme sitting behind both the unidirectional and bidirectional engagement of algorithms being used to reveal the neural code and thereby to develop neural applications. It is that there are those who regard the brain itself as deeply – if not fully – algorithmic[134] and that this is the reason why algorithms are useful in reading the neural code. There is a range of projects the results of which are used to point to this conclusion. What will now follow is not a denial of the usefulness of the application of algorithms to neuroscience. There are many examples – and not only in the field of health and medicine – of such technologies that are reaping the benefits of algorithmic technique and method. What is now to be argued is that algorithms, and the data created to serve them – especially as they will serve social objectives – have mythological potential, and we need to examine their design to ensure they are founded on conceptions that avoid the inducement of subjection, that is, that are non-mythological.

Some Deeper Themes in Kantian Idealism

As we have begun to see, this argument for explanatory values beyond but relying on the mathematical is at the same time a critique of the vulnerability that algorithmic representations have to the bias that inheres not just from personal preferences of the designers of algorithms but also due to the challenge of overcoming the ineffable and absolute qualities of reality itself. Without denying the value that can be extruded from the material world through mathematics, by placing such increasing trust in the application of mathematics, we have really entered and will be extending the tenuous frame of post-Kantian Idealism.[135] That is, the categories by which we

---

[134] A. Gidon et al., 'Dendridic action potentials and computation in human layer 2/3 cortical neurons', *Science* 367:6473 (2020): p.83; W. Dabney et al., 'A distributional code for value in dopamine-based reinforcement learning', *Nature* 577 (2020): p.671.

[135] J. Whittlestone et al., 'Ethical and social implications of algorithms, data and artificial intelligence: A roadmap for research', *Technical Report* 978-1-9160211-0-5 (2019).; J. Magelhaes, 'Do algorithms shape character? Considering algorithmic ethical subjectivation', *Social Media + Society* (2 May 2018); M. Ananny, 'Towards an ethics of algorithms: Convening, observation, probability and timeliness', *Science, Technology and Human Values* (24 September 2015).

52 *Privacy, Neuroscience and Algorithms*

understand the world are a priori products of our judgment,[136] and even if each of us then combines these with our sense data, the unified 'whole' is then imposed on Nature and without which Nature and Society as we know it would not exist.[137] This does not mean that Nature does not exist, only that we cannot know it, in itself. It is only what we judge it to be. So also for our psychological and social constitutions, as we shall see. The deep problem with this Idealism is twofold: first, the categories of the understanding[138] for Kant are an abstract logical framework that exclude a range of other, less abstract categories; second, these categories take the form they do in Kant because he wants to deny immediate experience of Nature, of which he was fearful,[139] and promote a theological-political agenda. The point is that, for existential reasons, Kant imposed an abstract rationality on the natural world which denied the sources of fear and desire that humanity can find there. Algorithms may be seen to be performing the same function for the range of natural, psychological, social and increasingly mythological circumstances.

Kantianism in the World of Information – Floridi

Perhaps the most prominent approach of this kind in the field of information theory is presented by Floridi. He acknowledges the influence of Kant's transcendental logic in his own work, for example, where he presents an argument that the digital re-ontologises our world by transforming the very nature of the concepts by which we understand it. What this in effect means is, following the first three revolutions due to the work of Copernicus (who moved humanity away from the centre of the physical universe), Darwin (who displaced us from the centre of the biological world) and Freud (who revealed that we are not exclusively rational beings), Turing has shown that we now live in an informational world, this constituting a fourth fundamental revolution.[140]

What is 'fundamental' here is that prevailing ontologies – materialism, biocentrism and androcentrism – should now be seen as replaced with information as the primary ontology. Any other sense of the real must be understood as information: '[Information ethics]) is ontologically committed to an informational modelling of *Being* as the whole infosphere.'[141] This is post-Kantian Idealism, the imposition of a

---

[136] I. Kant, *Critique of Pure Reason* (Palgrave, 2007), at A77/B102ff.; A81/B107.

[137] Ibid. A124–127/B125–129.

[138] Ibid. A80/B105, 106.

[139] See D. Grant, *Technology and the Trajectory of Myth*, pp.89–92, where this argument is elaborated.

[140] L. Floridi, 'The information society and its philosophy: Introduction to the Special Issue on "The Philosophy of Information, Its Nature and Future Developments"', *The Information Society* 25:3 (2009).

[141] L. Floridi, *The Ethics of Information* (Oxford University Press, 2015), p.133; regarding Floridi's position, see my analysis in Grant and Bennett-Moses, *Technology and the Trajectory of Myth*, pp.204–208. None of my analysis of Floridi's ontology is diluted by more recent observations by

Algorithmic Constructivism

philosophical construction on – one might say as with Kant – the fearsome absolutism of the nature of reality, subsuming all other claims about the nature of reality. Floridi is not unaware or unappreciative of the significance of this move for personal identity, stating that this produces a dephysicalisation and typification of the individual,[142] in turn leading to self-branding and online presence. This awareness has led to the development of an ethical framework which is intended to preserve the interests of individuals.

Several points need to be made in response. First, Floridi is not an innocent in the emergence of this informational transformation, a mere reporter on or analyst of it. He is a primary constructor and promoter of it. This begins with two claims, that is, that individual human beings are their information[143] and that the objects of the infosphere as *Being* are deserving respect because, as such objects, they have inherent value.[144] The result is that individuals must minimise the entropy – fight the decay and death – of the infosphere, in fact, to tend and grow it.[145]

There is a strong theological theme in his justification of the latter position, that *Being* as the whole infosphere 'makes much sense from many religious and spiritual traditions, including, but not only, the Judeo-Christian one, for the whole universe is God's creation, is permeated by the divine, and is a gift to humanity worthy of care'.[146] Apart from the highly dubious inference that we should care for the world as a gift from God, he offers no adequately elaborated justification for the theological reference. This failure opens him up to criticism, as we shall see.

Further, this all-inclusive informational-moral ontology – one which is a further echo of the Kantian claim for the inherent value of all Being – is, on closer examination, a tactic he uses to incorporate artificial agents as morally responsible entities. As I have argued,[147] Floridi has two senses of responsibility: first, the standard usage of being blameable, by which he initially excludes artificial agents, and, second, the usage by which moral agents must – *ecopoietically* – care for Being, thereby the infosphere. Although artificial agents are initially seen by him as moral but not responsible, they can become so as they will develop into 'human-like or indeed superhuman agents, such as a newly enhanced humanity, fully intelligent futuristic robots, extraterrestrial forms of life, angels, demons or gods'.[148] Artificial agents may then become co-responsible for sustaining and growing the infosphere, of which human 'informational' individuals are a part.

---

him that we should assess what AI is realistically and beneficially capable of; see L. Floridi, 'AI and its new winter: From myths to realities', *Philosophy and Technology* 33 (2020): 1–3.

[142] L. Floridi, *The Ethics of Information*, p.10.

[143] Ibid. p.309.

[144] Ibid. pp.127 and 318.

[145] Ibid. pp.130, 168, 315.

[146] Ibid. pp.133 and 315.

[147] See my commentary on Floridi's position in Grant and Bennett-Moses, *Technology and the Trajectory of Myth*, pp.204–208.

[148] L. Floridi, *The Ethics of Information*, p.161.

The significance of all this is that Floridi is properly seen as a mythologist. There are two issues here, one broad and one specific. Broadly, there is no problem in principle with constructing a particular view of what constitutes reality, although one can object to particular constructions should there be justification for doing so. What is unacceptable is the pretence that any particular construction deserves to be understood as a final ontology. Floridi, like Domingos, does just this. Doing so has totalitarian features. Specifically, Floridi combines elements of what is properly seen as a combined Deity–Technology myth. Its features include fear of death (of the infosphere of which we are all a part), totalised subjection to the moral infosphere, full adoption of informational practices, and the foregoing of any proper sense of self-responsibility (to and for oneself), instead having responsibility for the care and growth of the infosphere as all Being. It is this which should be seen as the context for the criticism of Floridi's arguments put by Capurro that this philosophy of information undermines the responsibility of human beings as key moral agents.[149]

It is relevant to observe further regarding the mythological credentials of Floridi that he remains in admiration of Augustine, whose primary intellectual endeavour was to unify Christian theology, thereby overcoming Gnostic dualism, by placing Christianity on a Neoplatonic foundation. Thereby was Christianity to become the final form of metaphysics, natural philosophy and ethics[150] and so as both fully integrated and fully explanatory. Even a casual eye can see a similar approach in Floridi's ontology. It is also worth noting in this context that it was the flaws – his discouragement of interest in natural philosophy[151] and his insistence on personal immortality[152] – in this attempt to force unity onto diversity that brought the Augustinian metaphysics down and saw it replaced by the Aristotelianism of Aquinas.

Floridi is also consistent in his post-Kantian constructivism or *poietic* approach to epistemology:

> *Poietic*, as opposed to *mimetic* science, relies on a conceptual logic of construction that does not start from the system to analyse it in terms of a model, but actually starts from the model (the blueprint) to realise the system. In this case understanding is constructing.... This information manufacturing, this poietic knowledge, is implicitly based on a logic of design. We find its roots in Kant and Hegel.[153]

As indicated, there is no inherent flaw in constructivism. However, not only may there be flaws in particular competing constructivist models, but this is especially so

---

[149] R. Capurro, 'On Floridi's metaphysical foundation of information ecology', *Ethics and Information Technology* 10:2–3 (2008).

[150] S. Gaukroger, *The Emergence of a Scientific Culture* (Oxford University Press, 2006), 53–55.

[151] H. Blumenberg, *The Legitimacy of the Modern Age* (MIT Press, 1985), pp.336, 341.

[152] S. Gaukroger, *The Emergence of a Scientific Culture*, p.84.

[153] L. Floridi, 'The logic of design as a conceptual logic of information', *Minds and Machines* 27:3 (2017): pp.459ff.

when – as several elements of the mythological trajectory and Floridian informational theory all do – a construction is preferred above all others to the point where it
is given the status of a fundamental ontology. This ontological flaw, by which
individuals are seen as totally subject to the infosphere, might be seen to be
corrected by Floridi's search for an informational ethics, whereby the flourishing
of individuals is to be promoted. We shall see in Chapter 5 that his ethics does not in
fact correct that flaw. This is not to say that his ontological-technological arguments
are not without value, however, since some lead to a sense of individual privacy that
coextends with that presented in the present work, although the argument to be
presented later in Chapter 6 comes from a position which, in reaching many of the
same conclusions about the nature of privacy, contradicts the arguments of Floridi.

One can see the limitations of Kantian-Floridian Idealism by considering the
work of Hoffman. He has shown that belief in object permanence starts very young
and stays with us for a lifetime and that an account of objects can be given without
an account of subjects. Applying evidence from evolutionary science, he argues that
selection does not favour veridical perception, and so the objects of our perceptual
experience are better understood as icons of a species-specific interface rather than
as an insight into the objective structure of reality. This means that we cannot
assume that physical objects have genuine causal powers nor that space-time is
fundamental, since objects and space-time are only species-specific perceptual
adaptions. So, he sees the prospect of object consciousness replacing object permanence.[154] Objects are the result of how evolution has caused us to perceive. They
are not things in themselves. What we can take from this is that how we see and what
we see are not an internal reflection of the external world but are in a real sense
constructed by our cognitive, perceptual disposition. However, very differently from
the abstract rationality of Kantian judgment, for Hoffman the reality we construct
derives from our evolutionary disposition. That is, what is real for us is what has
emerged from our evolutionary coping with natural reality, not the denial of it as in
Kant or as in Floridi.

KANTIAN INFORMATIONAL IDEALISM AS MYTHOLOGICAL

What is being put forward in the present work is that this human cognitive disposition to construct 'reality' is displayed not only regarding the physical world of
objects. It is also displayed in the manner in which we have constructed the social
and psychological worlds, and these are related. The heavy lifting for this has been
done in the history of the West within the framework of the mythological trajectory,
that is, by the serial, dominant myths of Deity, then the State (in which, as in the
myth of Deity, Kant plays a key role), then the Market and now technology as a way

---

[154] Donald D. Hoffman, 'Objects of consciousness', *Frontiers in Psychology – Perception Science*
(17 June 2014); see also Hoffman's *The Case against Reality* (Penguin Books, 2019).

to claim the creation of the Absolute Self. By this constructive and selective flow of information, existential reality is distanced and camouflaged and the cognition of the physical world of objects is saturated with the combined beliefs and practices of Christian theology, those of the political State and the Market economy. Technology is now beginning to function as the latest iteration of this, especially in neuroscience, which is now emerging as the claimed means to eliminate our existential shortcomings thrown up by evolution. We typically see and understand by these mythologies. This trajectory is much closer to Kant than to Hoffman, in that its premise is the attempted displacement of existential reality rather than an accommodation of it.[155] From this, we may see Floridi as but the latest in a long tradition of mythologists who have attempted to 'finally' determine reality, that is, to see it only as the information we can control.

In a direct sense, the mythological trajectory can properly be understood as an attempt to overlay on or be the claimed correction of the kind of evolutionary process that Hoffman describes. The dominant interests of the phases of the trajectory have 'constructed' and then serially 'reconstructed' both the physical and the socio-psychological world[156] by following through the claim that our existential concerns – most fundamentally our primal (or 'natural') fears and desires that persist in our evolutionary condition – can be dispensed with – eliminated in the case of fear and reimagined in the case of desire – on condition of our subjection to their respective regimes. We see it still regarding Deity,[157] the State,[158] the Market[159] and now technology as it begins to create the conditions for claims about the Absolute Self.[160] In this context, neuroscience is properly seen as the means both to eliminate

---

[155] For a more full account by the author of the place of Kant within the Trajectory, see D. Grant, *The Mythological State and Its Empire*, ch.5, 'The Reason of Protestant Politics'; D. Grant and L. Bennett Moses, *Technology and the Trajectory of Myth*, chs.2 and 3.

[156] It is worth noting in this regard that recent research suggests that culture shapes how we reason; see A. Carstesen et al., 'Context shapes early diversity in abstract thought', *Proceedings of the National Academy of Sciences* 116:28 (2020): 13891–13896.

[157] S. Dein et al., 'COVID-19, mental health and religion: An agenda for future research', *Mental Health, Religion and Culture* 23:1 (2020); H. Campbell, 'Contextualising current digital religion research on emerging technologies', *Human Behaviour and Emerging Technologies* 2:1 (2020): 5–17.

[158] P. Esaiasson et al., 'How the corona virus affects citizen trust in government institutions and in unknown others – Evidence from the "Swedish Experiment"', *European Journal of Political Research* (September 2020), https://doi.org/10.1111/1475-6765.12419; I. Freckelton, 'COVID-19: Fear, quackery, false pretences and the law', *International Journal of Law and Psychiatry* 72 (2020): 101611.

[159] S. Butler, 'The impact of advanced capitalism on well being: An evidence informed model', *Human Arenas* 2:2 (2019): at para 2 and ff.

[160] J. Firth et al., 'The online brain': How the internet may be changing our cognition', *World Psychiatry* (6 May 2019), regarding claimed benefits of the Internet and transactive memory; E. Broadbent, 'Interactions with robots: The truth we reveal about ourselves', *Annual Review of Psychology* 68 (2016); A. Bejjani, 'AI has the potential to enrich our lives in so many ways – If we use it properly', *World Economic Forum* (4 April 2019); C. Salge, 'Empowerment as replacement for the three laws of robotics', *Frontiers in Robotics and AI* (29 June 2017).

Kantian Informational Idealism as Mythological

deficiencies and to offer enhancements beyond the present state of our evolutionary development. To achieve this, the brain therefore not only needs to be understood but has to have its shortcomings eliminated and its claimed unlimited capacity widely fulfilled through enhancement, an Absolute Self.

The Trajectory Persists through the Finessing of Its Flaws

The problem with all this is that, as has been demonstrated over the history of the trajectory, it is a flawed model, which is why there have been serial failures of the absolutisms of Deity, State and Market, the darkly ironic outcome of which is the trajectory itself. There are two sources of this flaw. First, there is the irreconcilable contradiction that each of these three magnitudes must both be absolutely powerful – to materialise the absolutism of existential reality – and yet be brought under control so it benefits humankind. Second, the subjection required to empower these magnitudes cannot be reconciled with the benefits that flow to those who design and champion each magnitude far more than to the bulk who are subject. These flaws have typically been camouflaged – as existential fears and desires have been camouflaged by the artificial creation of 'manageable' fears and desires – by processes of normalisation, which has been the foundation of the historical reconstructions of the psychological space of each individual, as we shall see. One key outcome of these reconstructive, camouflaging normalisations is what is currently considered to be privacy.

We have already referred to – and will see in detail in Chapter 4 – various techniques applied to this 'normalised' construction of psychological space, each specific to its respective mythological magnitude. Now, in the age of neuroscience, we will see that the technique of normalisation turns to the brain and the means by which it can be 'reconstructed' to produce new realities: algorithms acting as artificial intelligence, machine learning and deep learning. This is a new, post-Kantian Idealism, but like its 'predecessor' normalisations, it reveals the mythology within it wherever it is based on the forgoing – induced or imposed – of individual self-responsibility.

Emerging Neuroscience Finds a Place in the Trajectory

This 'technological constructivism' has three strategies, the second of which refers to the exploration of the neuroscience with which we began this work. The first, simplest strategy is the operation of algorithms in the manipulation of personal and public data. Facebook and Twitter have received much attention in this regard[161] and there is evidence that YouTube has tolerated, even encouraged, the

---

[161] R. Kelly Garrett, 'Social media's contribution to political misperceptions in the US Presidential elections', *PLOS One* (27 March 2019).

distortion of truth enabled by its algorithms.[162] In that vein, other research argues that the algorithmic functioning of the internet is wider than these platforms, in particular, showing that, compared with the construction of reality by traditional mass media, algorithmic 'reality construction' tends to increase individualization and promote commercialization, inequalities and deterritorialization. It also tends to decrease transparency, controllability and predictability.[163]

The second strategy is both implicit and explicit in the account of the neuroscientific technologies outlined at the beginning of this chapter. There we saw developments in the understanding and control of the bases of vision,[164] learning, aging, neurodegenerative disease and so the repair of sensory, cognitive, motor and memory functions. We saw the identification of the process of an individual's spatial location and the ability to reconstruct one's mental images. Importantly, we saw the neural location of fear and desire, the prediction of subjective affective states more generally and the location of the capacity to distinguish between the emotional categories of words. The centres of self-control and the experience of morality have also been identified.

Beyond this we saw that there has been location of decision-making functionality and the reading of hidden intentions, including of both overt and covert (i.e., one's own inner voice) speech. Also, that it is possible to stimulate and predict one's stream of consciousness without sensory input, and the augmentation of such brain functions as predictive cognition and the acquisition of novel skills (e.g., the hearing of colours).

On another level, we saw the possibility of the use of remote neural devices through direct, bidirectional brain-to-brain communication, including of other mammals and the prospect of neural connection to and from external knowledge sources, including specific databases and the internet. In this vein we saw the possibility of expanding the neural substrate (e.g., for expanded mathematical capacities and multidimensional perception) and 'whole brain' simulation, as well as the prospect of integrated neural and hardware-based circuitry. Related to all this is the possibility of the implantation of memory and the uploading and preservation of neural content.

The point of this selective catalogue is to show that these are not random incidents of algorithmic development and application. In fact, there are two clear functions of all these developments. Even though laboratory or clinic-based

---

[162] Karen van Es, 'YouTube's operational logic: "The View" as pervasive category', *Television and New Media* (2 January 2019); P. Lewis, 'Fiction is outperforming reality: How YouTube's algorithm distorts truth', *The Guardian* (2 February 2018).

[163] N. Just and M. Latzer, 'Governance by algorithms: Reality construction by algorithmic selection on the internet', *Media, Culture and Society* 39:2 (2016); G. Smith, 'The politics of algorithmic governance in the black box city', *Big Data and Society* 7:2 (2020): 205395172093398 (2020).

[164] See K. Hao, 'A neural network can learn to organise the world it sees into concepts – Just like we do', *MIT Review* (10 January 2019).

researchers may well not have these functions in front of mind, the outcomes of these technologies – through their enabling data and algorithms – either are such that they correct a wide range of neural dysfunctions or are such that they offer enhancements of high-level depth and breadth, so long as the individual themself is brought to be subject to the technological regime.[165] These technologies overcome the conditions and limitations of our evolutionary past. Such subjection crucially involves the algorithmic method operating not only without the step-by-step concurrence of the individual but typically without concurrence at all beyond the initial acceptance of the neural technology involved. This is not of particular concern regarding technologies that are only correcting for sensory malfunction, stroke, Alzheimer's or Parkinson's, but it is of great concern regarding every technology involved in giving effect to all the other capacities just canvassed.[166] Subjection under those circumstances, the forgoing of self-responsibility in response to claims that our constructed – not existential – fears and desires will be conclusively dealt with, is mythological. Non-mythological engagement with technology would require that the interested individual be vitally involved in its design and application at each key step and that the experience promote, certainly not threaten, self-responsibility.

The third strategy is lateral; that is, it is a neural overlay, for example, as with virtual and augmented reality. This is a strategy, like most artificial intelligence applications, that brings with it both great benefits and significant risk. We shall explore this, and its essentially constructivist nature, in some detail below in this chapter.

All this is not to say that it is impossible to construct a correcting framework to the risks of bias inherent in AI, as elaborated in machine and deep learning. Attempts have already been made regarding Ethically Aligned Design of the Institute of Electrical and Electronics Engineers (IEEE), but there are shortcomings therein and they will be addressed in the context of a new proposal put forward in Chapter 6.

Some Summary Comments

Bringing the elements of this part of the argument together, we can say the following.

---

[165] See L. Cabrera and J. Carter-Johnson, 'It's not my fault, my brain implant made me do it', *Scientific American – The Conversation* (3 April 2018); L. Kangassalo et al., 'Neuroadaptive modelling for generating images matching perceptual categories', *Scientific Reports* 10 (2020): 14719.

[166] It is worth pointing out in this context that there are significant problems associated with the very notion of decoding, that is, regarding the 'decoder's dictum': that 'if information can be decoded from patterns of coded activity, then this provides strong evidence about what information those patterns represent'. There is a strong argument that this dictum is false, that is, that good decoding is not enough to accurately indicate neural representations of real-world objects and that 'working back' from behaviour is also not enough: J. Ritchie, 'Decoding the brain: Neural representation and the limits of multivariate pattern analysis in cognitive neuroscience', *British Journal for the Philosophy of Science* 70:2 (2019).

60 *Privacy, Neuroscience and Algorithms*

First, there is a strong connection between the use of algorithms in correcting and enhancing brain function through to the arguments of Griffiths, Domingos and Floridi by which the algorithmic framework is both an essential interpreter of cognitive function and the dominant means to create a wide understanding of the physical and social worlds, to see the world on a digital basis.

Second, such a process is akin to a post-Kantian Idealism which not only is intended to subject Nature to human digital reasoning but is best understood as part of a broader understanding of the dynamic that has deeply informed the culture of the West, that is, as part of a trajectory of modern mythology.

Third, algorithmic knowledge should therefore be understood as carrying important parts of this modern mythological revolution of technology, a technology which is intended to subject Nature and thereby humanity. This is a subjection at two levels, social and neurological, in that it claims the overcoming of the limits of the individual's phylogenetic past by inducing their subjection to an algorithmic regime per se; and which is to achieve that specifically by subjecting the brain to reconstructive, bidirectional capacity.

In short, algorithms applied to the brain should not merely be seen as an intended means of understanding cognitive function or even as a possible interpretive tool for understanding the world but also as the latest phase of a culture-long process of claims regarding the kind of overcoming of the limits of Nature promised by dominant interests and which depend on inducing the subjection of the individual to an intrusive, algorithmic regime by which the individual typically forgoes their respectful self-responsibility. Neuroscience is mythological whenever its enhancements are used to promise the Absolute Self rather than the respectfully existential.

BROADER IMPLICATIONS

These technologies raise a new set of problems regarding the boundaries of the self, the limits of sentience and the scope of what is private, whether focused on the individual or on its societal distribution.[167] As Jasmine Berry stated:

> [W]e propose that forthcoming brain augmentation studies should insistently include investigations of its potential effects on self-awareness and consciousness. As a first step, it's imperative for comprehensive augmentation to include interfacing with the biological brain in a manner that either distinguishes self (biological brain) from other (augmentation circuitry) or incorporates both biological and electronic aspects into an integrated understanding of the meaning of self. This distinction poses not only psychological and physiological issues regarding the discrepancy of self and other but also raises ethical and philosophical issues when

---

[167] S. Jensen et al., 'Sienna D3.4 Ethical Analysis of Human Enhancement Technologies', *European Commission Sienna Project D3.4 Ethical Analysis of Human Enhancement Technologies* Ref.2512574 (2020).

the brain augmentation is capable of introducing thoughts, emotions, memories and beliefs in such an integrated fashion that the wearer of such technology cannot distinguish his biological thoughts from thoughts introduced by the brain augmentation.[168]

For thoughts, one might substitute reasoning, desires, memory, perception, beliefs, emotion, intentions, behaviour and actions. One might also therefore add prejudice, positive and negative.[169]

Neurotechnology is not in itself mythological. But the very breadth and depth of current research – and the design of data and algorithms to pursue this – clearly extend well beyond the attempt to resolve medical problems, and this research ultimately seeks to create new cognitive realities and thereby to change the nature of what we understand to be the world and to be human. This trend will allow very wide claims to be made by dominant interests to citizens about the transformation of their cognitive experience, and when this is added to the quantum leap in the level of interconnectivity between citizens and non-human databases and intelligences of various kinds, then it would be wise to heed the lessons of history and foresee neurotechnology as the next phase in the trajectory of myth. Something mythological is going on.

VIRTUAL REALITY

Although it is emerging as among the most powerful forms of technology regarding the question of what it is to be human, neuroscience as we have considered it is not alone in this field. Virtual reality (VR)[170] will also have an increasingly profound impact on our fundamental notions of self, on our consciousness of the world, on our sense of what is real and on how as individuals we relate to others. It has ethical and metaphysical implications.[171] In this regard, its development may also be giving an indication of one direction which neuroscience more broadly might be taking. VR intervenes in a manner that allows its techniques to increasingly be used in neuroscientific research. Its capacity to create alternative senses of reality – and

---

[168] J. Berry et al., 'The elephant in the mirror: Bridging the brain's explanatory gap of consciousness', *Frontiers in Systems Neuroscience* 10 (2017): article 108.

[169] J. Shaw, 'Do false memories look real? Evidence that people struggle to identify rich false memories of committing crime and other emotional events', *Frontiers in Psychology* (April 2020), https://doi.org/10.3389/fpsyg.2020.00650; B. Calado et al., 'Implanting false autobiographical memories for repeated events', *PsyArXiv Preprints* (April 2020), doi:10.31234/osf.io/5yw6z.

[170] Virtual reality is taken here to be the computer-generated simulation of three-dimensional imagery, which is separate from the common experience of reality, and with which one can interact in a seemingly real or physical manner by wearing purpose-built electronic equipment. That is, the technology is a delivery system for a wide range of alternate reality content.

[171] M. Slater et al., 'The ethics of realism in virtual and augmented reality', *Frontiers in Virtual Reality* (March 2020), https://doi.org/10.3389/frvir.2020.00001.

62 Privacy, Neuroscience and Algorithms

thereby to reconstruct psychological space – will likely become so deep and broad that it is important not only to provide an acceptable operational and ethical framework for its development and its use but also to ensure that the broad – as well as the immediate – existential interests of the individual are placed to the heart of such a framework.

As a way to consider this technology, we shall look at examples of both beneficial and negative impacts of virtual reality. However, as with the technologies of neuroscience, we will move away from this binary approach in presenting the new ethical framework, placing this dualism into a broader perspective. That will be presented in Chapter 5.

Virtual Reality as Beneficial

It is clear that virtual reality is and will continue to grow as a tool which is positive for humanity. This is attested to by a range of experiments. For example, immersive virtuality allows subjects to acquire the virtual superpower of flight above an imagined city, which has led to altruistic behaviour.[172] Embedding subjects in an avatar with lighter or darker skin or with no body at all led to decreased racial bias.[173] An immersive environmental experience linking excessive paper consumption with deforestation led to a greater reduction in napkin use compared with those who merely read about such matters, while virtual embodiment promoted pain relief.[174] Further, the virtual experience may broadly improve empathy.[175]

Virtual reality has proved helpful in easing the tension of patients undergoing physical rehabilitation and in inducing calmness and so benefits the psychology of

---

[172] R. Rosenberg, S. Baughman and J. Bailenson, 'Virtual superheroes using superpowers in virtual reality to encourage prosocial behaviour', *PLoS ONE* (2013) 8:e55003, doi:10.1371/journal. pone.0055003; P. Breves, 'Bringing people closer: The prosocial effects of immersive media on users' attitudes and behaviour', *Nonprofit and Voluntary Sector Quarterly* (February 2020).

[173] N. Salmanowitz, 'The impact of virtual reality on implicit racial bias and mock legal decisions', *Journal of Law and the Biosciences* (2018): 174–203; see also S. Bielen et al., 'Racial bias and in-group bias in judicial decisions: Evidence from virtual reality courtrooms', National Bureau of Economic Research Working Paper 25355 (May 2019); A. de Borst, 'First person virtual embodiment modulates cortical network that encodes the bodily self and its surrounding space during the experience of domestic violence', *eneuro* (2020), doi: 10.1523/ENEURO.0263-19.2019.

[174] M. Matamala-Gomez et al., 'Immersive virtual reality and virtual embodiment for pain relief', *Frontiers in Human Neuroscience* (2019), https://doi.org/10.3389/fnhum.2019.00279.

[175] F. Herrera et al., 'Building long-term empathy: A large-scale comparison of traditional and virtual reality perspective-taking', *PLoS ONE* (17 October 2018), doi: 10.1371/journal. pone.0202294; A. van Loon et al., 'Virtual reality perspective-taking increases cognitive empathy for specific others', *PLOS One* (30 August 2018); but see also Josiah Nelson, 'Bicycles for the Mind', www.theculturecrush.com/bicycles.

disabled patients.[176] Research has also found that, even in non-immersive gaming where players choose their own avatars, acting as a hero causes people to perform coincident behaviours, and so creating games with more heroic – rather than villainous – avatars could encourage more prosocial behaviour.[177] More radically, it has been found that creating the perceptual illusion of body swapping could be a valuable tool for clinical research on body image disorders or regarding issues of self-identity.[178] There is also preliminary evidence that entering a virtual environment can help control burn pain during wound care[179] and that virtual reality exposure therapy (VRET) appears to be an effective psychotherapeutic tool in reducing general anxiety and specific phobia symptoms.[180] In this vein, there has also been success in using immersive virtual reality to treat subjects both in pre- and post-traumatic stress situations, such as is produced in battlefield conflict.[181] Virtual reality is also showing medical clinicians how to improve their haptic skills, for example, in needle insertion.[182] The technique is also shown to help in the management of unwanted thoughts, clearly an aid for those battling depression.[183] In short, virtual reality is likely to have increasing impact on healthcare.[184]

Beyond these, this technology is being shown to be a useful tool in experiential learning – although this can include processes in which virtual experiences are recognised as direct experiences – with lasting subsequent beneficial effect.[185] This

[176] Chih-Hung Chen et al., 'Psychological benefits of virtual reality for patients in rehabilitation therapy', *Journal of Sport Rehabilitation* 18 (2009); A. Araujo et al., 'Efficacy of virtual reality rehabilitation after spinal cord injury: A systematic review', *Biomed Research International* (2019): article 7106951.

[177] R. Ratan et al., 'Avatar characteristics induce users' behavioural conformity with small-to-medium effect sizes: A meta-analysis of the proteus effect', *Media Psychology* 23:5 (2020).

[178] B. Porras-Garcia et al., 'Virtual reality body exposure therapy for anorexia nervosa: A case report with follow-up results', *Frontiers in Psychology* (May 2020), https://doi.org/10.3389/fpsyg.2020 .00956.

[179] N. Amadpour et al., 'Design strategies for virtual reality interventions for managing pain and anxiety in children and adolescents: Scoping review', *Journal of Medical Internet Research Serious Games* 8:1 (2020): e14565.

[180] D. Boeldt et al., 'Using virtual reality exposure therapy to enhance treatment of anxiety disorders: Identifying areas of clinical adoption and potential obstacles', *Frontiers in Psychiatry* (October 2019), https://doi.org/10.3389/fpsyt.2019.00773.

[181] A. Rizzo et al., 'STRIVE: Stress Resilience in Virtual Environments: A pre-deployment VR system for training emotional coping skills and assessing chronic and acute stress responses', *Studies in Health Technology and Informatics* 173 (2012).

[182] R. Gourishetti, 'Improved force JND in immersive virtual reality needle insertion simulation', *Virtual Reality* (2018), doi.10.1007/s10055–018-0369-9.

[183] A. Prudenzi et al., 'Testing the effectiveness of virtual reality as a defusion technique for coping with unwanted thoughts', *Virtual Reality* (November 2018), doi: 10.1007/s10055-018-0372-1.

[184] T. Pareek et al., 'A survey: Virtual reality model for medical diagnosis', *Biomedical and Pharmacology Journal* 11:4 (2018).

[185] C. Kwon, 'Verification of the possibility and effectiveness of experiential learning using HMD-based immersive VR technologies', *Virtual Reality* (28 August 2018), doi.org/10.1007/ s10055–018-0364-1; D. Checa et al., 'A review of immersive virtual reality serious games to enhance learning and training', *Multimedia Tools and Applications* 79 (2020).

includes the provision of immersed multimodal environments enriched by multiple sensory experiences, through both virtual and augmented realities,[186] experiences that can also improve memory.[187]

More generally, the technology is now being shown to be an environment in which collaborative, rather than only individual, activity can be effective.[188] Although a contrary view is also presented below concerning the use of virtual reality in support of the commercial world, this has significance for a range of fields, including simulation models for manufacturing,[189] and thereby greater productivity through improved memory.[190] It is also evident that this technology enhances the impact of advertising,[191] although this is, of course, a two-edged sword.

Even such a brief scan of research outcomes makes it clear that virtual reality, including outside the gaming environment,[192] presents a valuable tool for a range of clinical and other conditions and dispositions and programmes. One can reasonably expect that, as its use is explored and expanded, such benefits would become socially broader and personally deeper.

Virtual Reality as Problematic

There is, however, also accumulating evidence that immersive virtual reality can have negative, even destructive, effects on human subjects, especially with the extended data gathering that VR makes available about the user.[193] Many of these effects derive from the inherent plasticity of the human mind, the result in turn of the 'context sensitive' nature of behaviour. This is obvious and usually accepted when it comes to the impact of the physical and cultural environments. However,

---

[186] G. Papanastasiou et al., 'Virtual and augmented reality effects on K–12, higher and tertiary education students' twenty-first century skills', *Virtual Reality* (August 2018), doi: 10.1007/s.10055-018-0363-2. See also Chien-wen Shen, 'Behavioural intentions of using virtual reality in learning: Perspectives of acceptance of information technology and learning style', *Virtual Reality* (May 2018), doi: 10.1107/s10055-018-0348-1.

[187] L. De Sousa et al., 'Virtual reality and its therapeutic uses in the elderly: A narrative clinical review', *Journal of Geriatric Mental Health* 7 (2020): 21–28.

[188] A. Erfanian et al., 'Verbal and vibrotactile cues on multiuser usability within collaborative virtual reality', *Virtual Reality* (November 2018), doi: 10.1007/s10055-018-0375-y.

[189] G. Lugaresi, 'Real-time simulation in manufacturing systems: Challenges and research directions', *Winter Simulation Conference*, Gothenburg Sweden (December 2018), doi: 10.1109/WSC.2018.8632542.

[190] E. Krokos, 'Virtual memory palaces: immersion aids recall', *Virtual Reality* (May 2018), doi: 10.1007/s10055-018-0346-3.

[191] L. de Gauquier et al., 'Levering advertising to a higher dimension: Experimental research on the impact of virtual reality on brand personality impressions', *Virtual Reality* (May 2018), doi: 10.1007/s10055-018-0344-5.

[192] There are increasing benefits to be seen by a cross-fertilising of gaming and virtual reality: see D. Checa et al., 'A review of virtual reality serious games to enhance learning and training', *Multimedia Tools and Applications* 79 (2020): 5501–5527.

[193] https://extendedmind.io/xr-privacy.

the totality of the immersive virtual reality experience and the potential for disturbingly alienating experiences can also make this a matter of concern, especially when stable character traits and phenomenological experience are put at risk.[194] For example, one's very senses of embodiment, of presence, of agency, of social interaction and thereby of reality can be made illusory in nature. Research has shown that immersive virtual reality can lead to an increase in dissociative experience – for example, through depersonalisation and derealisation – including a lessened sense of presence in objective reality.[195] Of equal concern is the potential for these forms of experience to make the subject vulnerable to deep manipulation, since the effects of long-term immersion can constitute a real threat not only to the user's sense of agency but also, more deeply, to an individual's 'unit of identification' (UI), one's integrated sense of embodiment and phenomenality.[196]

This is properly understood as a consequence of the argument that, for about two-thirds of our conscious lifetime, we are in fact not mentally autonomous subjects: epistemic agency is an exception, not the rule. Then cognitive processing – unlike allowing one's mind to wander – becomes a personal-level process only by being functionally integrated into an actively controlled context with the help of a specific form of transparent conscious self-representation. Beyond the range of normatively induced activity, virtual reality would be one environment in which this could be made to occur and thereby a sudden shift in one's unit of identification could be manufactured.[197] This would be made an easier achievement because one's constructed view of oneself in the world is itself a 'virtual reality'.[198] The significance of this for the adoption of mythological ideas and practices promoted by the dominant interests of Deity, State, Market and Technology on behalf of an Absolute Self is clear: the all-encompassing potential of these mythologies can be described as different virtual realities that could be implanted or reinforced by the use of this technology.

Of equal concern is that the impact of the virtual reality experience can last beyond the experimental phase and extend into real life. Such is the Proteus effect,

---

[194] See Kent Bye VoicesOfVR at https://twitter.com/kentbye/status/1134602685645111297?s=20.

[195] E. Bezzubova, 'Virtual reality as a mirror of depersonalisation', *Psychology Today* 23 (April 2017); R. Lavoie et al., 'Virtual experience, real consequences: The potential negative emotional consequences of virtual reality gameplay', *Virtual Reality* 470 (2020).

[196] M. Madary M. and T. Metzinger, 'Real virtuality: A code of ethical conduct. Recommendations for the good scientific practice and the consumers of VR-technology', *Frontiers in Robotics and AI* (2016), doi: 10.3389/frobt.2016.00003.

[197] Thomas Metzinger, 'The myth of cognitive agency: Subpersonal thinking as a cyclically recurring loss of mental autonomy', *Frontiers in Psychology* (2013), doi:10.3389/fpsyg.2013.00931; J. Vance, 'Commentary: The myth of cognitive agency: Subpersonal thinking as a cyclically recurring loss of mental autonomy', *Frontiers in Psychology* (20 August 2018).

[198] T. Metzinger, *Being No One – The Self-Model Theory of Subjectivity* (MIT Press, 2003), pp.312, 365, 416; also U. Pompe-Alama, 'Being Strange While Being No One', *Frontiers in Psychology – Theoretical and Philosophical Psychology* (9 April 2018), an article which analyses and extends Metzinger's theory of personality

experienced when subjects retain characteristics of their avatar after the experiment is over, for example, by behaving more aggressively.[199] That is, there is a lasting psychological impact. This is shown further by research that reveals the significance for mental health of virtual reality and social media use on perceptions of one's self and one's body.[200] Another relevant extension of this kind of application is the inducement of visual hallucinations through the use of virtual reality in combination with deep convolutional neural networks (DCNNs), the long-term impacts of which are not known.[201]

Taking this scenario further and wider, other researchers show that using immersive virtual reality is a particularly powerful way of eliciting false memories in children. As a consequence, they conclude that third parties may be able to elicit false memories without the consent or even any mental effort by an individual.[202] Related to this, the use of avatars to engage children in virtual reality allows the gathering of large amounts of data on the subjects to infer psychological characteristics and thereby a range of social dispositions, without their knowledge.[203]

Beyond these particular risks lies the increasing connection between virtual reality and social networks. This connection will increasingly threaten not only our privacy – both physical and associational – but also our autonomy, the latter in the form of freedom, knowledge and authenticity.[204] Perhaps ironically, this greater embedding in social networks can have the effect of subjects neglecting their bodies, their physical environments and those others with whom they are not directly connected: there is a loss of true intercorporeality.[205] This effect could be ameliorated – although unnaturally – by such an emerging suite of methods for generating well-being as predictive algorithms, psychopharmacology, non-invasive brain stimulation and virtual reality.[206]

---

[199] N. Yee and J. Bailenson, 'The proteus effect. The effect of transformed self-representation on behaviour', *Human Communication Research* 33 (2007), doi: 10.1111/j.1468-2958.2007.00299.x; R. Reinhard et al., 'Acing your avatar's age: Effects of virtual reality avatar embodiment on real life walking speed', *Media Psychology* 23:2 (2020).

[200] K. Kruzan, 'Embodied well-being through two media technologies: Virtual reality and social media', *New Media and Society* (February 2019), doi: 10.1177/1461444819829873.

[201] K. Suzuki et al., 'Hallucination machine: Simulating altered perceptual phenomenology with a deep-dream virtual reality platform', in *ALIFE 2018, Artificial Life Conference Proceedings* (MIT Press, July 2018), https://doi.org/10.1162/isal_a_00029.

[202] Kathryn Y. Segovia and Jeremy Bailenson, 'Virtually true: Children's acquisition of false memories in virtual reality', *Media Psychology* 12:4 (2009), doi: 10.1080/15213260903287267.

[203] M. Peters et al., 'Video ethics in educational research involving children: Literature review and critical discussion', *Educational Philosophy and Theory* (January 2020), doi: 10.1080/00131857.2020.1717920.

[204] 'Facebook's VR isn't about gaming, it's about data – Surprise, surprise', *The Conversation* (27 September 2020).

[205] Madary and Metzinger, 'Real Virtuality', p.16.

[206] D. Yaden et al., 'The future of technology in positive psychology: Methodological advances in the science of well-being', *Frontiers in Psychology – Human-Media Interaction* (18 June 2018).

But there is an even darker side to immersion and connectivity regarding virtual content. That is, virtual reality allows the exploration of extreme attitudes and behaviour, for example, the 'dark triad' of personality features of narcissism, Machiavellianism and subclinical psychopathy. In this, narcissism includes grandiosity, entitlement, dominance and superiority; Machiavellianism refers to the manipulative personality; and psychopathy includes high impulsivity, low empathy and anxiety.[207] Most of these are properly seen as exploring the fear experience of others.

But in addition to satisfying one of the two deep human experiences, that of fear, VR appears to be also satisfying the other: desire. In saying so, we may remember that these are typically experiences constructed by dominant interests to camouflage their existential sources rather than experiences that explore those sources themselves. Regarding desire, this is already in evidence regarding both sexual experience – or digisexuality[208] – and in the field of market consumerism.[209]

One might add that there is an increasing possibility that, beyond this technology being taken up by individual citizens for their (sometimes nefarious) pleasure and by State agencies for the purpose of mainstream education, clinical therapy and security monitoring, the option will loom increasingly that it will be engaged to correct socially unacceptable behaviour. Those before the courts or in punitive or rehabilitative custody may well be induced to undergo highly intrusive programmes of 'rehabilitation' through virtual reality. This immediately raises a range of serious civil rights issues, given the circumstances of the subject and the highly intrusive nature of the virtual experience.[210]

AUGMENTED REALITY

Before concluding, it is worth making a comment about the emergence of the allied field of augmented reality. This means of adding both information and interpretation to one's sensory and cognitive fields could have benefits in such fields as education and entertainment. However, the interpretive element of this is prey to the kind of post-Kantian constructivism or overlay which can bias or misrepresent the value of those fields. This misrepresentation would be exaggerated by the extension of this technology into a 'whole world' or 'mirror world' frame in which

---

[207] M. Slater et al., 'The ethics of realism in virtual and augmented reality', *Frontiers in Virtual Reality* (2020), doi 10.3389/frvir2020.00001; T. Yen et al., 'The interplay of gaming disorder, gaming motivations and the dark triad', *Journal of Behavioural Addictions* 9:2 (2020): 1–6.

[208] N. Doring et al., 'Design, use and effects of sex dolls and sex robots: Scoping review', *Journal of Medical Internet Research* 22:7 (2020).

[209] S. Loureiro et al., 'Understanding the use of virtual reality in marketing: A text mining-based review', *Journal of Business Research* 100 (July 2019).

[210] See XRSI (Extended Reality Safety Initiative); S. Seinfeld et al., 'Offenders become the victim in virtual reality: Impact of changing perspective in domestic violence', *Scientific Reports* 8:2692 (2018).

68   *Privacy, Neuroscience and Algorithms*

every aspect of the sensory – and thereby the cognitive – field has such an augmented or virtual overlay, by which every meaningful aspect was re-interpreted for the individual.[211]

THE PLASTICITY OF THE SELF

With the outcomes of the wide neuroscientific research that we have explored in this chapter in mind, together with a disposition by individuals to respond to the claims of empowerment by the advocates of these outcomes, we can see a potentially deep impact on the individual self. We shall explore this more extensively below, especially in Chapter 4, but it is appropriate to make some broad comments about this impact before we proceed to examine current privacy theories in the following chapter.

The first point to make is that the notion of the self – one's self-representation – is, in the argument here, significantly impacted by the processes of normalisation that apply now but have been inherited from the dominant mythological ideologies of magnitudes past and present. This is, of course, not to say that these weighty intrusions constitute all we think and do. But it is a claim that these mythologies provide a frame which projects into our lives the matters that are foundational to our ideas and practices, concerns about right and wrong, how we manage relationships, how we relate to political and bureaucratic power, how we should pursue the material existence we want and how we engage with the technologies that proliferate in our lives. We have seen earlier in this chapter that these cultural artefacts end up in our neural structures. These become central to our self-representation, our sense of self and how we navigate the world as agents.

The second point is that this normalising self is thereby inherently plastic. While we are continually subjected to iterations of these mythologies, we continue to adjust our sense of self. We may become less active in one area, for example, to do with Deity or the State; we may become more active within the mythology of the Market or Technology. We may stop attending church or stop voting but we may become more active consumers or be more active online. Further, ceasing mythological activity does not of itself eradicate the imprint of the ideas and practices within our psychological space.

Advances in the field of social cognitive neuroscience are beginning to provide an increasingly sophisticated account of self-referential processing and person perception and are thereby beginning to reveal how the brain represents knowledge about the self and others. That is, we are obtaining a clearer understanding about how knowledge of self and others is neurally located and retrieved by each of us. This understanding will increasingly lead to an appreciation through multivariant pattern

---

[211] www.artefactgroup.com/ideas/the-mirrorworld-bill-of-rights/; D. Gelernter, *Mirror Worlds* (Oxford University Press, 1993).

The Plasticity of the Self 69

analysis (MVPA) of the manner in which representations in various brain regions are transformed, communicated to other regions and ultimately associated with behaviour, that is, a comprehensive model of the neural basis of social perception and the cultural themes therein.[212]

We can take this notion of plasticity further by considering the argument that there is no thing as the 'self', only a neuroscientific process which produces a phenomenal self in consciousness as a transparent self-model.[213] Metzinger adds: 'Of course, sensory body and motor maps are highly plastic and subject to the influence of experience, even in the adult organism. And, of course, one has to see on theoretical grounds that there is probably no such thing as *absolute* invariance or functional rigidity in highly complex, dynamical systems like the human brain.'[214] In the terms of the argument of the present work, the self would then be an evolving construction embedded in an evolving global meta-representation or world view. Not only would the ideational elements of the self then be mythological – to the extent that they are accepted from the ideologies of the respective dominant interests of the mythologies of the trajectory – but the self is thereby a substantially mythological construct. As Metzinger states regarding the Western philosophy of mind:

> Christian philosophy ... finally *denaturalised* and *personalised* the concept of mind. In the way the Western history of the concept of mind can be read as a history of a continuous differentiation of a traditionalistic, mythical, sensory proto-theory of mind, which gradually led to mind being a more and more abstract principle, which finally, culminating in Hegel, is devoid of *all* spatial and temporal properties.[215]

We can draw some preliminary conclusions from these points. First, cultural artefacts related to the dominant mythologies are embedded neurologically, not only influencing algorithmic design but existing more generally within the self-representation of individuals in the West. Second, the plasticity of our inherent neural infrastructure and content means that, if we are living mythologically, then we can live non-mythologically. That would require a non-mythological normalisation, which would be very different from that to which we have been subject. That is the subject of Chapter 4. The frame for such a non-mythological normalisation – in

---

[212] D. Wagner et al., 'Decoding the neural representation of self and person knowledge with multivariant pattern analysis and data-driven approaches', *WIREs Cognitive Science* 10:1 (2019): p.14; see also O. Vilarroya, 'Neural representation. A survey-based analysis of the notion', *Frontiers in Psychology* (29 August 2017), https://doi.org/10.3389/fpsyg.2017.01458; see also N. Herz et al., 'Overarching states of mind', *Trends in Cognitive Sciences* (2020), doi:10.1016/j.tics.2019.12.015.

[213] T. Metzinger, *Being No One – The Self-Model Theory of Subjectivity* (MIT Press, 2003), pp. 14, 311, 434, 564, 578.

[214] Ibid. p.356.

[215] Ibid. p.505.

regulation, law, governance and corporate purpose – is the subject of Chapters 7 to 10, and by which a new account of privacy can be promoted.

CONCLUSION

We may conclude by affirming that, well beyond the already clear medical benefits being delivered by neuroscientific developments, we can easily imagine data-gathering and data-manipulating technologies sponsored by the State and the Market through the latest neuroscience and through virtual reality. These are capable of introducing what can properly be considered quantum changes in such gathering and use.

This gathering and use needs to be seen as potentially unbounded. Such interventions are founded on an algorithmic strategy which, despite its success in neurological repair to date, is vulnerable to a post-Kantian constructivism – the establishment or re-establishment of new or old realities through a further reconstruction of personal neural and psychological space – that could deeply constrain or even deny any sense of self-responsibility. This would be a mythological process.

In this context, the notion of privacy takes on an entirely new and vital significance. The need for a full reconsideration of the ethics of the interface between citizens and their technologies seems clear – the production of a new moral code for their operation – but an entirely new operational framework for that interface is also needed, one which does not settle into a binary relationship but which fully embraces these new technologies while counterintuitively conserving and progressing our individual humanity at the very same time. It is the challenge which the balance of this work attempts to address.

3

The Frailty of Privacy Theory

The Absence

Before we look at what privacy theory is now, we need to recognise what it does not take into account. In fact, the key element that is absent is the most important issue. It is the silent factor that underpins not only our accommodation to the State, the Market and now Technology but also thereby our accounts of the nature of privacy. It is the lacuna at the very heart of how we think about how we live.

That 'absence' is the awareness of the absolutism of existential reality. This is absent because, although always in fact present, it is typically distanced and camouflaged in the lives of most people. For a wide range of thinkers from Kierkegaard[1] to Heidegger[2] to Klein[3] to Blumenberg[4] to those of modern psychology,[5] existential fear and desire (to eliminate this fear) are nevertheless within the core of how we come to view the world.

In this regard we might notice the attempts to bring a new focus on existential risk by the Future of Life Institute in Boston – with the attention it is giving to the impact of climate change, biotechnology, nuclear weapons and artificial intelligence – and by the Centre for the Study of Existential Risk at Cambridge University, with its focus on risks from technology, biology, climate change and artificial intelligence. Both centres are leading research in all these respective areas, which are rising too slowly in both global and individual consciousness. These institutes are attempting

---

[1] S. Kierkegaard, *Fear and Trembling* (Cambridge University Press, 2006), pp.65–66.
[2] M. Heidegger, *Being and Time* (Blackwell, 1997), 189 at p.233.
[3] R. Blass, 'On the fear of death as the primary anxiety: How and why Klein differs from Freud', *International Journal of Psychoanalysis* 95:4 (2014): pp. 613, 616.
[4] H. Blumenberg, *Work on Myth* (MIT Press, 1985), pp.6, 13–14.
[5] R. Menzies et al., 'Death anxiety: The worm at the core of mental health', *Ipsych* 40:6 (2018).

to remind us of what we have suppressed, to bring existential concerns back to the centre of both our collective and private concerns.

This distancing is the first stage in the dynamic that has generated the mythological magnitudes that guide our theological, political, commercial and technological aspirations. But what is achieved at the macro level is also realised with the individual. This occurs in two ways. First, through the processes of the normalisation which have been sponsored by the dominant interests of the magnitudes. Thereby, as we shall see in Chapter 4, the normal is significantly framed by the mythological. Second, thereby through the construction of one's private world, wherein this mythologically 'normal' frames our private thoughts, emotions, instincts and ambitions. That is, those thoughts, emotions, instincts and ambitions come up against and are heavily impacted by the spiritual-ethical-social, the political, the consumer-commercial and the technological aspirations that have displaced the 'existential'. So, the private mirrors the mythology of the normal, which distances and overlays our existential concerns and comprises the range of our subjections. Current notions of privacy are therefore what we are left with when we do replace existential fears and desires with those derivative, constructed, mythological substitutes, the fears and desires of the workaday world. We are left a privacy that is the residue of our mythologising.

The Evidence That Points to Existential Concerns

Neuroscientific research provides evidence for the centrality of these existential concerns. For example, in research at Johns Hopkins, 'the clinical use of psilocybin produced rapid and sustained anxiolytic and anti-depressant effects, decreased cancer-related existential distress, increased spiritual well-being and quality of life, and was associated with improved attitudes towards death'.[6] This phenomenon is not only evident in those experiencing serious illness. It has been found that 'Existential anxiety concerns were highly prevalent in this sample of adolescents and thus it may be reasonable to consider them a normative phenomenon.'[7] Further, 'In middle age, finality becomes an intimate personal issue and, as a result, there is a renewed search for the meaning of life which confronts the individual with questions of freedom and responsibility, along with a painful sense of isolation. It is the conjunction of these elements that I have sought to stress, thereby demonstrating the

---

[6] S. Ross et al., 'Rapid and sustained symptom reduction for anxiety and depression in patients with life-threatening cancer: A randomised controlled trial', *Journal of Psychopharmacology* 30:12 (2016): p.1177. See also L. Berra, 'Existential depression: A non-pathological and philosophical-existential approach', *Journal of Humanistic Psychology* (2019), https://doi.org/10.1177/0022167819834747.

[7] S. Berman, 'Existential anxiety in adolescents: Prevalence, structure, association with psychological symptoms and identity development', *Journal of Youth and Adolescents* 35:3 (2006): p.290.

importance of existential emphases in psychotherapy for the middle-aged.'[8] Further again, it is clear that citizens in old age but not facing serious illness are also fully aware of existential issues: 'Death anxiety is a common phenomenon when older adults acknowledge their own mortality. [This study's] findings indicated that self-esteem has a mediating effect in the connection between meaning in life and death anxiety in the Chinese elderly.'[9] Finally, irrespective of age, we can see that mortality awareness has neurological correlates at the most significant level.[10] We also see that 'the results suggest that, although we believe human extinction is a bad thing, it's not until we're forced to think beyond the immediate, short-term consequences that we tend to agree that extinction is a far worse outcome than any other.'[11]

None of this is featured in the present dominant accounts of privacy. A defender of those accounts might say that these existential experiences are part of the content of what is psychologically internal, whereas the theories are about how to set up means and devices – legal or technological – to allow the individual to fully experience those 'internals'. Not only is that incorrect given the disposition to 'distance' such experiences, but it is this conceptual separation which is the foundation of the problem. As we shall see below and in Chapter 4, the form of this internal/external divide – which was emphasised in early Christian confessional practices and was later taken up by the bourgeois merchants with the emergence of the early forms of the State – has been the mechanism by which existential fears and desires have been – and remain – camouflaged by secondary fears and desires created by the State and the emerging Market. Deity was the first magnitude, used to quash existential fear and replace it with the fear of an absolute, fearsome but eternally loving entity and so was the initiation of the mythological trajectory, reimagined in subsequent magnitudes. The hard God of the Jews needed the creation of the loving Christ.

We will now elaborate this point, as we examine currently dominant theories of privacy as products of those magnitudes and note the absence – in the argument here, the attempted elimination – of existential concerns.

PRESENT UNDERSTANDINGS OF PRIVACY

Even without the complication of its effective denial of the centrality of existential concerns to privacy, privacy theory is fraught. There remain apparently unresolvable

---

[8] D. Becker, 'Therapy for the middle-aged: The relevance of existential issues', *American Journal of Psychotherapy* 60:1 (2006): p.98.

[9] J. Zhang et al., 'Relationship between meaning in life and death anxiety in the elderly: Self-esteem as a mediator', *BMC Geriatrics* 19:308 (2019): p.6.

[10] M. Quirin et al., 'Existential neuroscience: A functional magnetic resonance imaging investigation of neural responses to reminders of one's mortality', *Social Cognitive and Affective Neuroscience* 7:2 (2012): p.193.

[11] M. Warren, 'We're not great at thinking about the long-term consequences of catastrophes that threaten our existence', *The British Psychological Society – Research Digest* (October 2019), published online.

contests between the responsibilities and opportunities of a range of agencies and entities and what are presently seen as the conditions of privacy. Although we will examine these further in Chapter 6, we can say that these contests exist across a range of fields, including political governance generally; security, law enforcement, health and education specifically; media; the Market; religion; and close personal associations.

One could fairly say that, within this world of contradiction and confusion, there are two major intellectual locales or frames of thought, although that is not to indicate that there is coherence between those two frames. Further, what is proposed here is that neither of those two frames should be considered as adequate. A new approach to its understanding will be outlined, to be further developed in Chapter 6. The trigger for such a new account, revealing both the 'external' (existential) problem and the deep fissures within the present understandings of privacy, is the impact of the extensive interventions of emerging neuroscience on such understandings.

The two currently dominant privacy frames will be presented here as the 'constitutional', focused on individuals and their qualified rights, and the technological 'informational', in which its normative and 'controlled flow' elements have prominence.

Context and Themes

Before that presentation, it is necessary to make some observations about two contextual factors regarding these two dominant frames of privacy theory and to some themes featured therein. The first factor relates to certain constituting elements present at the emergence of the notion of privacy in the early modern period. The arguments here will be informed by the nature of these early elements, which we will see developed later as perceptible themes in the emergence of modernity. At the centre of these elements was the appearance of the bourgeoisie. This class became a key factor within the initial consolidation of State power and was central in the mercantilist movement, which in turn was a key informing factor in the emergence of the modern economy and ultimately the appearance of the Market State. Along with that, whereby it both collaborated with the centralising sovereign power and promoted the proper place of etiquette within that collaboration, was the establishment of a bourgeois sensibility and the modern creation of a personal private world. These elements which will be elaborated in Chapter 4, may be noted as relevant within the history of what was to become the 'constitutional' notion of privacy.

The second contextual factor relates to the nature and role of information in privacy theory. Here three themes are relevant. The first of these themes is the status of information. A central issue there is the control and ownership of information and whether this ownership is significantly constitutive of, if not equivalent to, notions of privacy. That is, whether my personal information – say, facts of various kinds about me – is mine to deal with irrespective of any social implications – theological, political, economic or technological – that it might carry. This issue of ownership appears to set up a possible distinction between personal and social implications and raises many issues about who can claim rights to such information. It seems fair to say, given the very wide range of contests over the rightful use and distribution of information, that current privacy theory struggles in the face of these issues, although attempts have been made to address them. These matters have been further complicated by the emergence of Big Data. Irrespective of any assurances that personal information is depersonalised in that Big Data context, it is still true that the agglomeration of individual data is transferring very significant influence over individuals to those who gather, analyse and materialise such data.

The second theme – related to the first – is whether privacy should be regarded as having some objective nature or whether it is always context dependent, that is, whether for example the privacy provisions that apply in public are the same as apply in one's home, whether different provisions should apply between cultural groups within one society, whether the notion of privacy changes in response to such external factors as the emergence of new technologies, and, if so, whether the notion of privacy is so stretched and varied that it begins to lose validity or at least sufficiently widespread applicability to keep it as a commonly understood idea. This raises the question of whether privacy can be seen in the context of rights.

The third of these themes is whether privacy can be extended – beyond protection – to include notions of anonymity or, even further, of being forgotten. That is, should personal information be able to be depersonalised, if it all can be, or even expunged so that a person can be forgotten in that sense?

It will be argued that these questions about context and theme are either wrong or at least derivative questions. The idea of context will be argued to be relevant but in an entirely different sense than this; that is, the notion of context needs to be seen much more broadly than the matters we have just referred to.

The Constitution, Case Law and Privacy

Constitutional and case law are at the centre of one of the two currently dominant accounts of privacy. This constitutional consideration emerged through several instances of case law in the nineteenth century but drew on earlier cases. We shall now refer to a selection of these to see the roots of this account of privacy. Various themes will be identified within this selection and these will be drawn together to highlight their significance.

Entick v. *Carrington* (1765) was concerned with preventing improper search and seizure by the English King's Men in the home without warrant, thereby clarifying the powers of the State in this regard and affirming the views of John Locke regarding private property rights. This also became an informing argument for the Fourth Amendment to the US Constitution. Further to this question of ownership,

76   *The Frailty of Privacy Theory*

Southey v. *Sherwood* (1817) was a case in which the poet argued that his early poem 'Wat Tyler' was not seditious, as claimed, and the injunction against its later publication should not have been denied, since this was a matter of property right over an unpublished work. One reason proffered was that the judge ignored the property right to warn the public, through a trial over sedition, that insurrection in a period of widespread fears of popular uprising would not be tolerated.

In *Gee* v. *Pritchard* (1818) an injunction was granted to prevent publication of personal letters which related to personal conduct and morals of a member of the clergy. The legal argument pleaded that publication without the writer's consent would be against the 'welfare of society' as it unjustifiably raised questions about the author's honour in the minds of his parishioners. It was a case of property rights over the letters but also about wounded feelings and thereby of an interior, private life. *Wyatt* v. *Wilson* (1820) was a successful attempt by the radical publisher Wilson to prevent the publication of prints of the ill and secluded King George III, thereby shoring up the privacy of the head of State. In *Prince Albert* v. *Strange* (1849), the crux of the case was the protection of the 'thoughts, sentiments and emotions' of the 'Royal Family' as expressed through the arts, due to the leaking of etchings that were intended to be enjoyed privately and by limited circulation. The case was framed in terms of an author's property right – and so in terms of the early modern Market – and a matter of breach of confidence, though a reference was also made to the principle of privacy. In that context we may properly see that this case brought the issues of legitimate self-fashioning and 'intrusion of celebrity' into prominence. But the view of the Romantics, for example, of Wordsworth, was that a greater knowledge of human nature and a more comprehensive notion of the soul was also emerging at this time, a view shared by the utilitarian Bentham and his circle. This was a fuller sense of interiority.

Richardson points out that all this connects with the plea for privacy by Bentham's acolyte, lawyer Romilly in *Gee* v. *Pritchard* and was a drift towards liberal-utilitarian ways of thinking throughout the nineteenth century, a high point of which was Mill's liberal-utilitarian defence of private life *On Liberty* (1859).[12] Thereby were issues of personal freedom joined with property rights. Of course, notions of freedom were not straightforward. It is worth pointing out that, for all his talk about the rightful freedom of the individual, Mill was an elitist. As Friedman shows regarding Mill's concept of rational democracy, rulers should have wide discretion because 'the many will not only defer to their authority but cheerfully acknowledge them as their superiors in wisdom and the fittest to rule'.[13] Neither did he believe that 'backward societies' should enjoy these liberal rights. That is, liberal utilitarianism was not conceived as so radically free for the ordinary citizen as might be thought,

---

[12] M. Richardson, *The Right to Privacy* (Cambridge University Press, 2017), p.6 .
[13] R. Friedman, 'An Introduction to Mill's Theory of Authority', p. 405, in *Mill – A Collection of Critical Essays*, J. B. Schneewind (ed.) (Macmillan, 1968).

Present Understandings of Privacy

even if the agreement of the few implied they had forgone prejudice,[14] as it would be open for such an elite to prescribe the meaning of privacy. One could fairly characterise this elitist freedom as a bourgeois view of freedom and privacy.

In France, there were somewhat different justifications for privacy. Due to concern about 'intimate sentiments and respectable aspects of human nature', celebrity issues led to a dignitarian right to privacy that emerged from *Felix c. O'Connell* (1858), where a deathbed portrait of France's charismatic *tragedienne* was made available for sale.[15] In *Dumas v. Liebert* (1867), the specific issue of intrusion through photography into private life became the focus. In this, the court referred to 'upsetting the most intimate and respectable sentiments of nature and of domestic piety'. In *Bonnet c. Societe Olibet* (1882), the Tribunal held against Olibet for depicting Bonnet, a performer in the Palais Royale, in a photo on a biscuit tin. This was a case about the commercial control of an image by the subject, that is, within the Market. The court said there was no tangible prejudice to someone who had presented herself publicly but that a portrait should not be circulated without the subject's permission: this was an absolute principle.[16]

In Germany, dignitarian arguments, especially in their Kantian mode, became more widely influential. This was to become particularly so regarding early American thought about privacy through the expressed opinion of the legal personalities Warren and Brandeis. For example, they read von Jhering,[17] whose view was that German law should reflect the 'idealism' of the man who looks on himself as his own end and esteems all else lightly when he is attacked in his 'personality'. From the use of a Kantian-Hegelian dignitarian rhetoric, we can see a parallel claim by Warren and Brandeis that tort law should respond to spiritual needs by supporting the right to privacy as a right to have one's 'personality'. It is proper to see this development of 'personality' as a notion significantly comprised of processes or programmes of self-fashioning or self-cultivation and undertaken in private from one's self-formed opinion. Such is dignity.

Warren and Brandeis did not merely derive from but added to von Jhering, as he added to the English utilitarians. That is, they located the right to privacy in snapshot photography and the rising tabloid feeding off (or one might say generating) a public need for gossip. In their 1890 article Warren and Brandeis pointed to all this as the need for an affirmation of the 'right to privacy' characterised as the 'right to be let alone'[18] subsumed within a broader right of 'inviolate personality'.[19] For example, in *Manola v. Stephens* (1890), photographing an artist on stage in tights but who was dressed with appropriate modesty was seen as a matter of public

---

[14] Ibid. p.406.
[15] M. Richardson, *Right to Privacy*, pp.64ff.
[16] Ibid. p.73.
[17] See R. von Jhering, *Law as a Means to an End* (Boston Book Company, 1913).
[18] S. Warren and L. Brandeis, 'The right to privacy', *Harvard Law Review* 4:5 (1890): p.193.
[19] Ibid. p.206.

embarrassment: in this, everyone was seen as vulnerable to such intrusion by the use of photography by the press. This also raised the issue of ownership of the imagery. Their argument was influential in some legal circles. In *Pavesich* v. *New England Life Insurance Co.* (1905), the court decided that the unauthorised use of an artist's portrait in advertising was a violation of his 'right to privacy', including the publication of one's picture without consent to increase profits. It cited the Warren and Brandeis article. Brandeis went on to argue in dissent in *Olmstead* v. *United States* (1928) that the prohibition of unreasonable search and seizure in the Fourth Amendment should be construed as a constitutional 'right to be let alone' against the government, including regarding wire-tapping.

For Richardson, Warren and Brandeis's article took on a life of its own, emerging as a leading modern scholarly statement of the problem of privacy and its solution, and influencing American cases where the right to privacy took shape as a species of tort, especially a tort of public disclosure of private facts, even if this was ultimately overshadowed by a broadly interpreted Constitutional right to freedom of speech. We can see the work of Prosser (1960) in this vein. He argued that the law recognised not one but four torts: intruding upon the seclusion or solitude of the plaintiff or into her private affairs, the public disclosure of embarrassing private facts about the plaintiff, publicity that places the plaintiff in a false light in the public eye, and the appropriation of the plaintiff's name or likeness for the advantage of the defendant.[20] It would be a fair point that, even though they were seen as unfortunately neglecting the principles of inviolate personality and human dignity, these four torts formed the basis of the Constitutional protection of privacy, both generally and through the Fourth Amendment.

It helped that the Warren and Brandeis argument for a right to be let alone was expressed in terms that were broad and mainstream, providing the basis for a right that could be invoked by multiple individuals responding to a range of modern circumstances of intrusion on privacy, some already identified (photos, newspapers, gossip) and others to come. And if a second major irony of American law is the way that the right to privacy they talked about – as a way of dealing with an intrusive press – ended up being subsumed under a more expansive right of freedom of speech (the First Amendment), they offered a model of law reform that would be taken up in other parts of the common law world where freedom of speech was less overwhelming.[21] We see developments of this kind especially in the European and other jurisdictions, for example, in the European Convention of Human Rights (1953) and in the Human Rights Act (UK 1998).

It is worth noting again that, apart from having an influence on the Anglo-American account of privacy, thinking about privacy has a continuing strong

---

[20] P. Schwartz and K. Peifer, 'Prosser's privacy and the German right of personality: Are four privacy torts better than one unitary concept?', *California Law Review* 98:6 (2010).
[21] M. Richardson, *Right to Privacy*, p.104.

Present Understandings of Privacy

tradition of its own in Europe. Much of this does go back at least to Kant and the notion of the right to develop one's autonomous personality and the dignitarian theme behind that. It manifests itself in the three spheres of personality, that is, intimate, private and individual with differing levels of protection under the Basic Law and the Civil Code. It is fair to characterise this tradition as focused at its heart on the rights of the morally autonomous individual. As Kant stated:

> If we look back upon all previous efforts that have ever been made to discover the principle of morality, we need not wonder now why all of them had to fail. It was seen that the human being is bound to laws by his duty, but it never occurred to them that he is subject only to laws given by himself but still universal and that he is bound to act in conformity with his own will, which, however, in accordance with nature's end is a will giving universal law.[22]

And

> Now, morality is the condition under which alone a rational being can be an end in itself, since only through this is it possible to be a lawgiving member in the kingdom of ends. Hence morality, and humanity insofar as it is capable of morality, is that which alone has dignity.[23]

Strong views about privacy also apply in France and Italy. In fact, one can fairly say that the Europeans have had a stronger sense of the importance of privacy than do the Americans, who also treasure the value of revelation as a demonstration of free speech and of a free press, as expressed in the First Amendment.

Overall, privacy might thereby be argued by some to have extended from the seclusionary rights of the self-fashioning, dignified *bourgeois* individual to a constitutional and universal right due to widespread attention given Warren and Brandeis. Even though the focus in the United States remained on intrusion by the State and Markets rather than by the press – which in the 1960s established its rights in the First Amendment – this focus reflected the right of every individual to be let alone to develop their personality. This made the universal right to privacy possible in the twentieth century, allowing a response to what sociologist Georg Simmel saw as the deepest problems of modern life flowing from the intrusions of society on the individual, and establishing itself as one of an agreed list of international rights in the post-war Universal Declaration of Human Rights (1948). In this vein, privacy had, for Richardson, transcended its restricted beginnings to become a general right to protection from others, which denied accountability to 'them' and which valued the intimacy of family and friends.[24] Looking forward, for her the question is how to continue to develop this notion in the face of such emerging technology as surveillance, profiling, archiving and image proliferation. Yet there are modern parallels

---

[22] I. Kant, *Practical Philosophy* (Cambridge University Press, 1996), 4:432 at p.82.
[23] Ibid. p.84.
[24] M. Richardson, *Right to Privacy*, pp.9–10.

with older cases, even if there is more blurring of public and private. The result will be that right to privacy will contribute to modern case law, concerned with the basic human interest in 'personality'.

A summary of all this might emphasise, with Richardson, that an important source of the right to privacy can be located in these shifts taking place in cases, statutes and arguments from the nineteenth century but that the now-traditional idea of the right to privacy as one with an external and an internal face (both a right 'to be let alone' – or not to be accountable to 'them' – and a right to interiority, intimacy and self-fashioning)[25] has developed unevenly over a long period of social and cultural transformation. Further again, one might well understand that this notion is challenged presently by a range of factors the origin of which lies well beyond this constitutional-legal frame in the field of emerging technologies. But it was an account of privacy based on a certain notion of the individual, to be left alone in dignity to develop their unique personality. It was bourgeois.

To emphasise the bourgeois nature of this sense of privacy, one can properly observe that the notion of being left alone to develop one's unique personality does not apply either to lower socio-economic classes[26] or to other categories of individuals across the social spectrum, including those located within prisons or psychiatric facilities, about whom Foucault has written in his consideration of Bentham's Panopticon.

Lessons from Constitutional Privacy Theory

This conception of privacy, rooted in such case law from the late eighteenth century, has problems that are technological, sociopolitical, legal and mythological in nature.

Technologically, a notion that is based on such a dual right to be let alone and to a self-fashioning interiority is inadequate to deal with the kind of profound cognitive embeddedness and connectivity that has emerged from the mainstream information and communication technologies, let alone from those neurotechnologies which we have examined. We cannot describe this embeddedness in any sense as 'being let alone', as intended by Warren and Brandeis and their later interpreters, or as is intended by the European notion of autonomy. Nor can the sense of self-fashioning interiority that forms the other side of current Constitutional privacy theory be accommodated within that embeddedness. We cannot – nor should we – deny some form of technological embeddedness, but we need to think through a sense of privacy that can accommodate – and take advantage of – the technologies of both

---

[25] Ibid. p.118.
[26] M. Shamir, *Inexpressible Privacy – The Interior Life of Antebellum American Literature* (University of Pennsylvania Press, 2008), pp.150–155.

Present Understandings of Privacy

the mainstream information and communications technology (ICT) and neurological varieties.

Sociopolitically, the practices that concerned Warren and Brandeis – the intrusion into, the gathering and publication of private aspects of personal life – did not stray even minimally into the conditions under which the working class, including children, existed at that time.[27] Throughout much of the nineteenth century and right up to the time that Warren and Brandeis wrote their paper for the Harvard Law Review (1890), those people suffered seriously unhealthy living conditions and paltry wages, conditions which saw widespread protest and which resulted in harsh responses from what have been described as the industrial barons and their supporters in the State police and State legislatures and courts. A good example of the distance Warren and Brandeis kept from both the practical and legal implications of this was *Spies* v. *Illinois*, which we shall examine below. The question of defending the private aspects of personal life – one's letters, poetry, etchings, image, thoughts, sentiments, emotions and so on – were so remote from the reality of the mass of working class lives as to be irrelevant. Those concerns were bourgeois and covered a range that ironically spread upward to include the middle-class lifestyle of the English sovereign Victoria. Beyond this, the practices common in factories and prisons[28] – in all of which the notion of privacy was anathema – were of no apparent interest to Warren and Brandeis. We shall see that this sociopolitical problem is also indicative of deeper and wider mythological implications.

Legally, it is worth noting that just because certain human behaviours are constitutionally regarded as private does not point to such privacy as having any solid objective status. For example, even though various pieces of legislation to ban contraceptives, abortion and homosexual acts were serially deemed to be unconstitutional (in *Griswold* v. *Connecticut*, *Roe* v. *Wade* and *Lawrence* v. *Texas*, respectively), this has not prevented interest groups, especially Christians, attempting to have the Supreme Court reinterpret the US Constitution to disallow such behaviours. We shall look more closely at the role of vested interests shortly, and in that context at the mythological elements within the Constitutional approach to privacy, that is, the Constitution as a field within which notions of normality are contested and imposed.

Finally, it takes little effort to see these sociopolitical and legal problems as mythological. That is, the case law upon which the emergence of the Constitutional notion of privacy was based reflects a mythological influence: case law as an inducement or requirement to be subject to the magnitudes of Deity, State, Market and Technology in return for protection of a singular notion of

---

[27] M. Schuman, 'History of Child Labor in the United States – Part 1 Little Children Working', *United States Department of Labor – Bureau of Labor Statistics* (January 2017).

[28] C. Matthew, *Short Oxford History of the British Isles – The Nineteenth Century* (Oxford University Press, 2000), pp.70–74; W. Barney, A *Companion to 19th-Century America* (Blackwell, 2006), pp.164–176.

82 *The Frailty of Privacy Theory*

privacy. Cases such as *Entick* v. *Carrington* (1765) and *Prince Albert* v. *Strange* (1849) effectively established the conditions under which the State could properly intrude into private lives and created a sympathetic and familiar view about the heads of State and their inviolable property rights. *Southey* v. *Sherwood* (1817) revealed how privacy could be denied for the purpose of warning against insurrection against the State. In *Gee* v. *Pritchard* (1818), we see the private interiority of feelings linked to the protection of private property. *Wyatt* v. *Wilson* (1820) revealed how the principle of privacy could be used to deny any perception of the head of State as weak and vulnerable. *Pollard* v. *Photographic Company* (1888) established the illegality of capturing one's personal image with the then-new technology of photography. *Manola* v. *Stevens* (1890) was used by Warren and Brandeis to argue that the unauthorised photographic image was in fact a violation of inviolate personality. Further, to the extent that Warren and Brandeis were informed by Kantian dignitarianism and autonomy, they were thereby informed by a strictly Christian ethic to which the individual must subject themself to attain the status of citizen of the State.

Beyond this they were clearly defending the personal and social affairs of the middle classes – as the social class that encapsulated Deity, State, Market and cultural self-development and whereby the relations of private life are sacred. In the fin-de-siècle Oscar Wilde trials, the case was turned away from Wilde's prosecution of Lord Queensbury into an exploration of Wilde's own homosexuality, this seen as an attempt to expose and root out social English decadence. We have also just referred to the continuing attempt by Christian interests to have the Supreme Court reinterpret the Constitution to outlaw certain behaviours now regarded as private. Special mention is also due to *Spies* v. *Illinois* (1887). There, the spectre of rising socialism and the fear associated with it led Warren and Brandeis to refuse to refer to it in their famous paper despite real constitutional privacy issues resting in that case, that is, that Spies had been subjected to highly questionable search and seizure.[29]

It is worth noting at this point – especially regarding the broad absence of any concern for the tenuous and decidedly unprivate existence of the working class or regarding the refusal to recognise that those conditions of existence could justify social insurrection – that Warren and Brandeis steered clear of any recognition of existential issues as they might apply to either class.

The point about all this is that one can see signs throughout the emergence of this account of privacy not only of the key role played by the interests of Deity, State, Market and early modern Technology but also that the purpose of their efforts was also directed to the protection of the privacy of the middle classes. That is, privacy was a matter inextricably bound up with the interests of Deity and State and of the normalised, propertied, bourgeois middle classes in which those interests were embedded. We shall see in the following chapter how these signs were in fact

---

[29] H. Zinn, *A People's History of the United States* (Harper Perennial, 2003), pp.270–271.

Privacy as the Selected Flow of Information

indicative of a more thoroughgoing embeddedness which stretched back long before the modern era yet is alive at present.

In short, what we have with the Constitutional notion of privacy is the argument to protect a particular form of bourgeois individualism spread large, and which is long embedded in and so representative of the mythologies of Deity, State, the early modern Market and early modern Technology. Further, as we shall now see, this form has been challenged by one form of late modern information and communication technologies. We shall also see that this alternative has flaws of its own.

PRIVACY AS THE SELECTED FLOW OF INFORMATION

There is an alternative set of accounts of privacy which shift the primary focus away from the rightful individual and their personal property, including information, to the status and movement of information. Part of the reason for the emergence of an alternative has been the claim that the Constitutional arguments against intrusion into one's private life are themselves flawed. For example, Stern challenges the constitutional claim regarding the inviolability of the home, as a locale of personhood, a claim that dominates the Fourth Amendment. In fact, she sees little evidence to support the broad territorial conception of privacy inherent in the sanctity of the home or even any robust privacy expectations in varying residential contexts.[30]

The more expansive account of this new frame can be seen in the work of a range of theorists, the views of some having become well established. For Nissenbaum, protecting privacy is not a matter of strictly limiting access to personal information or assuring people's right to control information about themselves. Instead, what people really care about is ensuring that information flows appropriately. Her account of such an appropriate flow is housed in a notion of contextual integrity, by which she means that social activity occurs in contexts and is governed by context-related norms. Such norms include informational norms which govern the flow of information about a subject between parties and which take account of roles, types of information and the principles of its transmission. That is, norms circumscribe the nature of information about individuals which, within a particular context, is allowed, expected or required to be revealed.[31] Integrity in that circumstance is preserved when these norms are respected and damaged when they are contravened. These elements then allow her to consider the vast array of accumulating data, the impact of socio-technical systems on this, the public/private dichotomy – including the apparently low concern by many people about the public

---

[30] Stephanie M. Stern, 'The inviolate home: Housing exceptionalism in the Fourth Amendment', *Cornell Law Review* 95:905 (2010).

[31] H. Nissenbaum, 'Privacy as contextual integrity', *Washington Law Review* 79:119 (2004): 137–138.

sharing of personal information – and how privacy plays a foundational role for other moral and political rights and values.[32]

Others adopt a similar approach, seeing privacy as a matter of rules that govern the flow of personal information, reflecting changes to – rather than the demise of – privacy. For example, the analysis by Richards and King emphasises that shared information can remain 'confidential', since privacy is not a binary or 'on/off' condition, and that all data – including Big Data – must be transparent, thereby helping to prevent abuses of institutional power, but acknowledging that Big Data can compromise identity, given privacy is the ability of individuals to define who they are. In essence, for them, privacy is a shorthand we have come to use to identify information rules. So privacy should not be thought of as what is secret but is about what rules are in place (legal, social and so on) to govern the use and disclosure of information. There can be confidentiality, but this needs to be understood in a social context. These rules should continue to be driven by a legal-ethical frame-work and, more particularly, by principles of privacy (including Fair Information Principles [FIPs] through a continually revised notion of self-management of privacy that still honours 'notice and choice') and of self-definition as the means of shaping one's identity. The increased role and management of metadata can be seen as a fulcrum in all this, a means to share information while protecting the personal.[33]

In a further analysis that could be seen to bring the two alternative, dominant frames together, Irwin sees that privacy is, on the one hand, inherently comprised of a boundary between self and others, and that desired levels of privacy can be sought and achieved, and are reflected in personal space and territorial behaviour. On the other hand, this boundary is permeable, negotiable and interpersonal: a combin-ation of social stimulation and outgoing interaction of the self, resulting in either intrusion or isolation. So this is a dynamic process with continual readjustments in desired and achieved levels of privacy. Systems of regulation of privacy – personal and social – can therefore be applied. Self-identity is a central element in these processes, which in turn points to the histories of one's ability to regulate interactions.[34]

It might be argued that such an artificially bifurcated – secluded or integrated – but ultimately unifiable sense of individuality can be seen in the earlier work of Simmel, through his notion of the stranger, whereby each individual is both insider and outsider.[35] He gets to this understanding by seeing the large systems and super-individual organisations that customarily come to mind when we think of society as nothing but intermediate interactions that occur among people constantly, every

---

[32] H. Nissenbaum, *Privacy in Context: Technology, Policy and the Integrity of Social Life* (Stanford University Press, 2010), pp.4–17.

[33] N. Richards and J. King, 'Big Data ethics', *Wake Forest Law Review* (April 2014).

[34] I. Altman, 'Privacy: A conceptual analysis', *Environment and Behaviour* 8:1 (1976).

[35] See D. Levine (ed.), *Georg Simmel on Individuality and Social Forms* (University of Chicago Press, 1971), pp.143–149.

Privacy as the Selected Flow of Information 85

minute, but that have become crystallised as permanent fields, as autonomous phenomena. As they crystallise, they attain their own existence and their own laws, and may even confront spontaneous interaction.[36] But he emphasises the status of the individual within the social:

> Man's interactions would be quite different if he appeared to others only as what he is in his relevant social category, as the mere exponent of a social role momentarily ascribed to him.... A society is, therefore, a structure which consists of beings who stand inside and outside of it at the same time.... The individual is not incorporated into any order without confronting it.[37]

A further approach, by Coll, which attempts to bring together these three themes – privacy as a collective fact, contextual integrity and privacy as an individual fact – also refers to Simmel and his notion of privacy as secrecy. Here, such privacy is 'the feeling that ... an ideal sphere lies around every human being ... This sphere cannot be penetrated, unless the personality value of the individual is thereby destroyed.'[38] From this ideal, private sphere, it is secrecy, so understood, that guarantees social cohesion since any social relation requires a negotiated balance between concealment and disclosure, and it is information which is the subject of this negotiation within particular contexts.[39]

These various claims for 'integrated singularity' invite a view in the contemporary context that participation in the digital world – say, within social media, whereby one is both within and outside the group – should be seen in this way.[40] Information from and about an individual, through which myriad shapes of power and discourses of knowledge can be built, has these characteristics of the stranger: information is both personal and collective and its flow can be situated with such structures, within which important information about an individual and events may be shared or censored.[41]

Another perspective on this theme of privacy as the selected flow of information is that proposed by Warner and Sloan, who emphasise the relational nature of privacy. That is, people voluntarily limit the knowledge of each other and themselves as they interact socially and commercially. This amounts to a group coordination which ensures group control over what is thereby the selective flow of information. This coordination depends on common knowledge – everyone knows what everyone

---

[36] K. Wolff (ed.), *The Sociology of Georg Simmel* (Free Press, 1950), p.10.

[37] K. Wolff (ed.), *Georg Simmel: 1858–1918* (Ohio State University Press, 1959), pp.345–348.

[38] See G. Simmel, 'The secret and the secret society', in D. Levine (ed.), *Georg Simmel on Individuality and Social Forms*, pp.143–149, n.276.

[39] See Sami Coll, 'The social dynamics of secrecy: Rethinking information and privacy through Georg Simmel', *International Review of Informational Ethics* 17 (2012).

[40] Z. Feldman, 'Simmel in cyberspace', *Information, Communication and Society* 15:2 (2012): pp.297–319.

[41] Ibid. p.315. Feldman refers to the 'Arab Spring' in this context, where social media was used both to connect people and to inform authorities whom to arrest.

86 *The Frailty of Privacy Theory*

knows – that is, where everyone knows that everyone conforms to such informational norms.[42] This arrangement becomes undermined by some parties not abiding by the rules, so that what they know is not understood by others. An example is certain kinds of surveillance wherein there is a lack of knowledge of another's lack of conformity to the rules.

We can see similar themes in an approach which emphasises privacy as trust – especially as it is particularised – that is, as the sharing of personal information. This approach rejects the traditional separation of public and private – and therefore the basis of privacy in rights – and says instead that disclosures in a context of trust are private. Here, trust is seen as a social phenomenon: embedded in overlapping networks, identity sharing, interpersonal relationships and so on, as elements within a total experience. This includes an appreciation that information about one flows through networks irrespective of any influence we as individuals may have. In all this, breaches of trust are breaches of privacy. Therefore, privacy law should be protecting this social notion of privacy rather than one which is about protecting individual rights.[43]

Other approaches call back to Westin by critically assessing his individualist approach within a digital context, pointing out that personal data gleaned from online activity is typically not known to the individual and who thereby has no control over its content or dissemination. Further, due to one's personal biases, individuals are themselves handicapped in any attempt to decide what is in their best long-term interests. In this approach, it is therefore an examination of the context of information movement that offers the best chance of coming to terms with what is going on. This requires an appreciation of the actors and how they will impinge on system integrity. Doing so allows several key issues to be addressed: how to maintain contextual integrity across systems that are constantly changing and with varying players, many of whom are unknown to the individual; how we can protect marginalised groups; and how we can come to terms with the global nature of information flow.[44]

One emerging method by which this framework might be broadly addressed begins by avoiding naïve notions about how information flows within a context in the sense intended by Nissenbaum. This method takes contextual information flow and applies the statistical frameworks of Bayesian probability networks to clarify both how data flows across social systems and how those systems acquire their evolving meanings through data mining and machine learning. The claim is that, through this changed understanding – disciplining data in this way – the role of law, social

---

[42] R. Warner and R. Sloan, 'Relational privacy: Surveillance, common knowledge and coordination', *University of St. Thomas Journal of Law and Public Policy* 11:1 (2017): pp.5–6.

[43] A. Waldman, 'Privacy as trust: Sharing personal information in a networked world', *University of Miami Law Review* 69 (2015):559.

[44] P. Wu, J. Vital and M. Zimmer, 'A contextual approach to information privacy research', *Journal of the Association for Information Science and Technology* 67:1 (2019).

Privacy as the Selected Flow of Information 87

theory, statistics and computer science can be better aligned in information management to promote privacy.[45]

We may add here that many of these themes are brought together in a directly informational account of privacy, one which sees privacy breaches as nothing more than interference in the information of which the individual is (only) comprised. Here, instead of trying to stop moral agents treating human beings as informational entities, Floridi says we should ask them to realise that, when they deal with personal and private information, they are actually dealing with human beings themselves and so should show the same ethical respect they would show when dealing with other people, living bodies and environmental elements; a person, a free and responsible agent, is after all a packet of elastic information. 'Me-hood' is a bundle of information and the moral rights of me-hood include privacy. Intrusion in this me-hood is therefore a personal alienation.[46] Floridi continues:

> Privacy is nothing less than the defence of the personal integrity of a packet of information, the individual and the invasion of an individual's informational privacy ... is an infringement of her me-hood and a disruption of the information environment that it constitutes. The violation is not a violation of ownership, of personal rights, of instrumental values or of consequentialist rules but a violation of the nature of the informational self, an offence against the integrity of the me-hood and the efforts made by the individual to construct it as a whole, accurate, autonomous entity independent from and yet present within the world.... [I]nformational privacy requires an equally radical re-ontologisation of the infosphere and its inhabitants.... Such a re-interpretation is achieved by considering each individual as constituted by his or her information and hence by understanding a breach of one's informational privacy as a form of aggression against one's personal identity.[47]

In more recent work,[48] Floridi places privacy within his assessment of the five high-profile initiatives set up to promote socially beneficial AI. Within the principles (beneficence, non-maleficence, autonomy, justice and explicability) which he extrudes and elaborates from those initiatives, he places privacy as a key element within non-maleficence, but links it to autonomy as well.

Lessons from the Flow of Information Account

What should be said about this broad informational approach to privacy is that there are elements that can fit within a non-mythological account. The emphasis on an

---

[45] S. Benthall, 'Situated information flow theory', in *Proceedings of the 6th Annual Symposium on Hot Topics in the Science of Security* (2019), pp.1–10.
[46] L. Floridi, *The Ethics of Information* (Oxford University Press, 2015), pp.259–260.
[47] Ibid. p.260.
[48] L. Floridi and J. Cowls, 'A unified framework of five principles for AI in society', *Harvard Data Science Review*, no. 1 (2019).

appropriate flow of information has resonance, including where it connects information with its political and ethical context. Further, several of the elements of this broad 'flow' account rightly argue that the rules that govern information flow, the transparency of data to avoid tyrannous behaviour and the importance of individual control for the purposes of self-definition are all important. Further again, the notion of the individual as insider and outsider, interacting with 'autonomous' super-individual organisations but confronting the external order while being incorporated into it, is a fair account. That theme is complemented by the said sense of negotiated concealment and disclosure. Also, the notion of privacy as trust argued by Waldman is relevant, although care needs to be taken in prescribing its place. All these elements would fit within a non-mythological, reimagined notion of privacy, as we will see in Chapter 6.

However, these elements form no integrated sense of privacy. Is there an identifiable dynamic amid these differing approaches and, if so, what are its characteristics? What is the nature of this information? What is the template on which it flows? Where is the place for our existential condition and so the need for personal existential data to be generated by the citizen?

It might be argued that trust, and its reinforcement, is the common element to all these questions. All of the accounts that focus on the relationship between individuals and their social environments, especially as that argues for rules and ethical principles to manage information flow, in the end place varying degrees of reliance on trust. Trust brings together Nissenbaum's norms of integrity, the rules of the confidential sharing of transparent data (Richards and King), the incorporated secrecy of the stranger (Simmel and perhaps Irwin), the viability of group coordination of data (Warner and Sloan), Waldman's trust, the importance of online systemic integrity (Nissenbaum and Wu) and perhaps even Floridi's ethical ontology. Nonetheless, we will see in Chapter 8 that trust is best seen as a secondary ethical principle. That is, this reliance on the trust that comprises notions of systematic integrity, even if reinforced by rules, is an inadequate foundation for privacy. This is because trust does not trace back to the common, existential factors and so is not related to the framework of the dynamic of 'distancing, magnitude, camouflage and subjection' which determines the content and flow of dominant forms of information. Here trust camouflages the mythological dynamic which should inform their respective arguments.

To provide a valid sense of coherence, these theorists might have taken a different emphasis. They might have focused on who dominates the production of information, why and how it is produced, for what impact. This is not to say that information does not come from a range of sources, even every individual, only that the information that heavily biases social dialogue is not only untypically neutral, in that it serves the interests of some far more than others, but does so in a manner which has anti-existential subjection as its goal. Protecting privacy as the social integrity of information exchange, even looking at issues of exploitation of

Privacy as the Selected Flow of Information

information by major players or as informational rules and political rights, will not address this wider – mythological – context: applying principles of social integrity cannot be effective unless it is set in that particular context. This question will be explored in Chapter 4, where it will be put that privacy has been dominated by the production of information – including now algorithmically – created by the magnitudes through the dynamic of which we have spoken, to subject individuals for a variety of mythological purposes. Privacy is that subjection. Issues such as that of the individual as insider/outsider, the matter of negotiated secrecy, trust, self-definition, exploitation and rules and rights all need to be looked at principally in that light. Information, the focus of the technological age, and the question of its flow and integrity, are only the symptoms of this larger question and need to be informed by it.

Concluding Comments

There is a range of elements within both the Constitutional and selective flow of information frameworks within current privacy theory that deserve comment. First, we have already seen that the legal cases that contributed to the emergence of the Constitutional frame of privacy were heavily indebted to the influence of the dominant interests of Deity, State, the early modern Market and early modern Technology. Not only that, this influence carried the patent credentials of promoting the interests of the bourgeoisie. The connection of the bourgeoisie to modern mythology is clear from the case law.

Second, although the arguments for an alternative approach, focusing on the selective flow of information, have merit, they lack an adequate common and explanatory foundation and framework. The move to re-ontologising reality in favour of information (Floridi), thereby leaving praxis as at best a secondary presence, is troublesome. Further, the separate attempts to lay down the principles and rules of social integrity for a 'selective flow' account of privacy (following Nissenbaum) move too easily through the varying forms of trust and on to an algorithmic framework, a framework which we also questioned in Chapter 2. Neither would they survive the intrusions and subjections of individuals in the neuroscientific age of continuous bidirectional neural uploading and downloading of data. In fact, the group coordination elements of such accounts would worsen that subjection. A stronger notion of privacy is required.

So, we have moved from an account of privacy intended to protect the confidentiality and self-fashioning of bourgeois individualism to one which has as its principal focus a single aspect of individual activity: the production and flow of information that may be seen as based unreliably on trust. The former is the product of the early modern era of the mythological subjection – dominated by ideas of the State, the Market and early Technology – and the latter is equally a product of its time, the late modern age of information Technology. Each denies the reality of the existential condition that is at the centre of our private concerns and neither would survive – but could worsen – the impact of advances in neuroscience. Each in its own way is thereby illegitimate. We need to stand further back and see a bigger picture, which puts all these accounts in perspective, corrects the flaws and conceives privacy in response to that.

Replacing all these imaginative but insufficient accounts is the challenge. The argument here is that a non-mythological model – which recognises the centrality of the existential, which eschews the normalising ideas and practices of the dominant interests of the magnitudes, which promotes self-responsibility within an ethics of respect while acknowledging a significant contribution from technology – is a properly coherent way forward. This also needs to be one which can cope with and take advantage of neuroscience. To attempt this, we shall move first to an examination of that normalising that has generated each of the present accounts (Chapter 4), then propose a non-mythological ethical model as a basis for enhancing and protecting privacy in the neuroscientific age (Chapter 5) and then present an outline of a new account of privacy drawn from those considerations (Chapter 6).

4

Privacy as the History of Normalisation

The argument of the previous chapter is that current privacy theories are illegitimate, one displaying its mythological characteristics and the other simply unaware of the mythological dynamic in which it is embedded and which would change the shape and meaning of its various component theories, that is, that the social integrity of information flow has to be reworked existentially.

We therefore need to construct a framework for a new theory of privacy. This framework needs two preliminary elements. First, an appreciation of the ideas and practices – promoted by the dominant interests of the magnitudes – that camouflage existential factors, that create the secondary fears and desires which they claim to conclusively address, and of which current notions of privacy are comprised. This will be looked at through the frame of normalisation and is the subject of the present chapter. Second, a new ethical framework, upon which a new account of privacy can be imagined, is needed. That will be the subject matter of Chapter 5.

This chapter will be concerned with elaborating a central idea. That is, what we have just seen as those accounts of privacy is not the essence of privacy but need to be understood only as symptoms of a much deeper and broader dynamic. That dynamic began with early Christianity; proceeded through the formation of the State, as the Reformation undermined the still-problematic notion of the Christian Deity; then through the dominance of the Market, following the shattering of faith in the democratic State by the totalitarianism of the mid-twentieth century; and can be seen now being put in place with the emergence of Technology on behalf of an Absolute Self, following the crisis visited on Western societies by the failure of the Market and its Market State in the early twenty-first century.

Each of the first three of these magnitudes, as they passed through phases of absolutism and then were engaged, has left embedded in the social and psychological fabric a residue of concerns with which we continue to be constantly and personally engaged. Technology has not yet achieved absolute status but is beginning to seek to do so through this notion of the Absolute Self. These concerns are, respectively, the dominant matters of right and wrong, including the conditioning of our personal relationships; how we relate to power; what our material aspirations are; and how to respond to the transformative forces of technology. In short, how we manage ourselves in life. None of this is to deny that within our own increasingly rare quietude we do not think of many other things but the argument here is that it is to these dominant themes that we return – or that can be found at the heart of these many other things – as we seek to deal quietly with our most pressing personal matters.

These are the foundations of the concerns that we call private. Seeking to be left alone to pursue our self-enhancement or seeking to better control the flow of information as it impacts us are thereby secondary or derivative matters. To understand the nature of privacy, it is to these foundational matters that we should turn, how we have been impacted by the residue of ideas and practices of each of the magnitudes that have generated them. That is, privacy is the extent and the manner of how we have been normalised to this archaeology of influences, of how we have internalised these and how these have gone to forming or individualising us.

If we look at the sequence of the magnitudes and the manner in which their practices have functioned in the service of the mythological dynamic, we can see that each regime worked to construct a respectively preferred individuality and that each has done so through a particular management of ideas, practices and information about these. Thereby we see the two aspects of privacy theory that we have just examined. The result is that we can begin to understand how the content of the framework of psychological space has been put together – even up to now – from the nature of its founding dynamic.

AN ALTERNATIVE FRAME

For the purpose of clarity in the analysis of mythological normalisation that follows, an alternative frame will first be presented. This will allow a comparison with the mythological analysis that will follow it, especially since that analysis will include commentary of various attributes of this alternative frame. This frame comprises key themes from the work of sociologist David Lyon.

Perhaps the obvious element of Lyon's work is his continuing commitment to Christian theology. That theological reference point is the first element that is in common with the present work. But there are others. Lyon's primary focus on the techniques and impacts of surveillance also takes him through the work of such key Enlightenment figures as Bentham, into the nature of modern science in Kuhn and into the critical work of Foucault. From this, Lyon identifies the dehumanising features of modern technology and so the position of privacy theory. In the end, he retains a commitment to Christian values as a means to overcome the resulting misguided developments within modernity. These elements of his work clearly have

An Alternative Frame

93

a co-extensive focus with the matters under consideration here, albeit with vastly different outcomes.

One way in which Lyon approaches the surveillance that has proliferated across social space is through the notion of the Eye of God, wherein he sees the proper reading of Psalm 139 as describing the ever-watching God as deserving 'gratitude, wonder, reassurance'. Further, the understanding by the psalmist of this all-knowing vision resembles an 'epistemology of love' as 'Love is the deepest mode of knowing, because it is love that, while completely engaging with reality other than itself, affirms and celebrates that other-than-self reality.'[1] For Lyon, this positive sense of knowing is in stark contrast to that produced by Bentham's Panopticon and, thereafter, by modern technological surveillance. Bentham's late eighteenth-century design for a prison arranged people around a single point from which a lone guard could see everything due to the inherent one-way lines of sight. This arrangement was intended as a means to instil self-control by prisoners who could never be sure if that guard was watching.

The difference between these for Lyon was that the former, unlike the latter, was founded on relational connectedness, care rather than control and trust rather than suspicion.[2] Moving from this to an ethics of surveillance, Lyon draws on the 'goodness' of the Eye of God, which is contrasted with crucial elements of what He sees as unethical behaviour, for example, mistreatment of others. This combination of the *critical* and the *caring* would allow for a 'good looking' that is available to both individuals and institutions. This is not the social sorting of which post-Enlightenment biopower of surveillance is now generally comprised.[3] Significantly, this 'ethics of care' whereby one has *regard* for the Other goes beyond claims for privacy, data protection and civil liberties.[4]

All this needs to be seen within a broader context for Lyon. That is, not only is he unconvinced by almost all the arguments that we now live in a post-theological, secularised world, but this also leads him back to theological solutions to a wide range of social problems. In that, he has cast a wary eye on modern science, for example, through the work of Kuhn, and refers to the sociology of Elias. Out of all this he sees 'myths of secularisation' which demand a new way to understand and utilise this idea.[5] He gives a number of interesting reasons why we need to rethink secularisation. The first is the inadequacy of the standard secularisation hypothesis, that religion dies with the onset of modernity, especially with the rise of modern science. To this, he replies, from Kuhn – who argued that normal science was interrupted by a series of revolutions when the flaws in normal science were

---

[1] D. Lyon. 'Surveillance and the Eye of God', *Studies in Christian Ethics* 27:1 (2014): p.29.
[2] Ibid. p.29.
[3] Ibid. p.30.
[4] Ibid. p.31.
[5] D. Lyon, 'Rethinking secularisation: Retrospect and prospect', *Review of Religious Research* (1985): pp.240–241.

94   *Privacy as the History of Normalisation*

revealed – that science was no edifice in itself. Second, that there is no identifiable religion-in-decline theorem in the face of the waxing and wanings in the enthusiasms for religious beliefs, and that the State–Church tensions pre-dated modernity. The third is that there is no sociological agreement even about what religion is, so its secularisation is far from straightforward.

Fourth, secularisation arguments are often based on a naïve, nineteenth-century view of history that derives from arguments in favour of the pre-industrial/post-industrial divide, the latter being of what modernity is comprised. That is, the defining Church–State collusion in the medieval period may well be seen as an aberration, and modern science preceded, for Comte, later emanations of theology and metaphysics. In short, the sacred/secular divide may be seen as a relationship in which the lines were blurred. Fifth, secularisation proceeded differently in different cultures. Sixth, secularisation studies ignore the role of individual and group action in favour of social patterns: formal sociological discussions about the relationship between the individual and society are sterile and need to be replaced by individual biography and the development of structure in a historical context. An example of this is the work of Elias on civilising from the thirteenth century. The seventh reason is that proliferating questions about legitimacy in contemporary society – and associated questions about sources of identity – have rekindled interest in what secularisation means and how this might open the door to rethinking the significance of religion.[6]

From all this, Lyon comes to the view that secularisation has wrongly been used as a global explanatory concept when a historical sociology that is sensitive to context and detail is needed. Yet he remains of the view that the term should not be dispensed with, given its identification of a valuable field of study. We need a new conception of it that is more modest but within a broader historical sociology and cultural analysis that does not have the constricting blinkers of this overworked concept.[7]

There is value in many of these observations by Lyon, in fact, either allowing or affirming certain themes that are proposed in the present work. For example, secularisation is used here but elaborated in an entirely different manner that is not vulnerable to his criticisms of that notion. It not only contributes to a broader historical sociology but also can in no sense be seen as global in that. Further, although it contributes to a dynamic that is argued to repeat across history, it derives all its meaning from the manner in which it points to the heart of individual psychological space. This is the existential question. It is how each citizen is drawn into a mythological response to that through a series of dominant mythological experiences under the sponsorship of the members of dominant interests.

---

[6] Ibid. pp.233–240 passim.
[7] Ibid. p.241.

On the other hand, issue is taken here with Lyon's abiding commitment to the Christian frame, and his tendency to draw on the notion of Deity as a guiding entity. In the present work, despite how that notion might have elements that seem attractive, that notion is conceptually flawed and presents no elements that cannot be sourced from individual rational capacity. For example, that we should accept that the notion of care for others, where appropriate, should be drawn from God's love and His continuing, loving, omniscient surveillance is anathema.[8] Such is not a base for anything but a mythological normalisation and so a denial of the application of ethical reasoning. The balance of this chapter will focus on how this normalisation has worked across historical periods as a dynamic of mythological subjection.

Principles of Normalisation

The account of normalisation to be explored here has three particular emphases. First, normalisation is not to be understood as an abstracted process of socialisation that points to any universal process. Normalisation is always situated in historical context and reflects the ideas and practices of all participants in the process. In particular, these historical moments reflect the serial elements of the trajectory of absolute magnitudes but also the field of accumulating practices that are produced by the engagement of each as it persists in being made 'sympathetic' to those subject to its regimes. Second, normalisation reflects the situated but recurring mythological dynamic. That is, normalisation is never merely imposed on a citizen but requires the citizen's willing – to a greater or lesser degree – participation in their own subjection. Even for those normalised when very young, this dynamic applies due to the persistent, lifelong assurances by the respective dominant interests and their agents that the non-existential, constructed concerns of those subject will be conclusively dealt with. The influence of some may wax and wane – as with Deity – and some will vary in form – as with the increasing regulatory transformation of the sovereign State – and others may emerge – as with modern neurotechnology, but they each rely on the continuing subjection of the individual. Third, normalisation is not only concerned to attune an individual to the strictures and opportunities of subjection to a mythological regime but is, before that, concerned to ensure that existential concerns are put at a distance and camouflaged by such claims made by respective dominant interests that those secondary fears and desires will be dealt with.

We shall now proceed to explore the historical pattern of mythological normalising. We shall do so in the following way. Regarding Deity and the Market, we will examine, respectively, a central manifestation of their normalising methods, that is, the Sacrament of Confession and Consumerism. Regarding the State, which rests

---

[8] See Z. Bauman and D. Lyon, *Liquid Surveillance – A Conversation* (Polity Press, 2013), pp. 84, 123.

96 *Privacy as the History of Normalisation*

between these two magnitudes, there will be a wider examination of features. This is because the State transitioned out of the 'governmental' practices of the Christian pastorate and then itself became a sponsor of the early forms of the modern Market before becoming significantly embedded in it.

NORMALISING DEITY

Christian theology, and the place of the Christian Deity within that, can be seen as the quintessential example of a mythological magnitude. It fully distances existential reality and camouflages it in a regime of idea and practice that replaces that reality with the chimera of eternal, blissful existence so long as one is fully subject to its theological regime. This contract is incentivised by the threat that failure to be subject will deliver one to horrifying, eternal punishment. Further than this, the Christian theology – and the all-powerful but also all-loving Deity at its centre – includes rituals that remind everyone of the faithful of this dual promissory. Such rituals include the repeating reminder in Mass of the sacrifice of the Son of the Deity for each individual but also the sacrament of confession, which adds temporal peace to eternal bliss. We shall focus on confession as emblematic of the regime of subjection to Christian idea and practice.

Confession as a Ritual of Mythological Subjection

Among the range of normalising methods and techniques adopted and practiced by the dominant interests of the Christian Deity – which included the development and refinement of dogma, the practices of inculcation, the wide-ranging scope of pastoral care and Inquisitorial violence – is the sacrament of confession. In fact, it can be properly argued that the principles of confessionalism have been at or near the heart of each of those other methods. The benefits of this practice are several in that it satisfies theological, social and psychological needs. It is a key to achieving peace in this world and for the salvation that will bring the believer eternal peace in the next. It is also a means by which existential concerns are continuously kept at a distance and covered with controllable fears and desires.

Confession has a long history dating back to the Old Testament,[9] the purpose of which was to acknowledge sin and reconcile with God. In the New Testament, especially in the First Epistle of John, in Acts and in the Gospels of Matthew and John, the Christ emphasises its importance.[10] Drawn up into a Catholic Sacrament, this practice was founded on a combination of expressed repentance as

---

[9] *The New Oxford Annotated Bible*, New Standard Version with The Apocrypha (Oxford University Press, 1950), pp.148, 167, 929.

[10] Ibid. pp.1770, 1915, 125, 1953, 2139.

self-humiliation, absolution by a member of the priestly caste who requires subjection, and potentially public penance, the ultimate effect of which is the reconciliation with both the Church and God: peace by subjection to the Deity through its dominant interests on Earth. This last point is theologically important as it is a key point of difference between Catholic and certain Protestant dogma, the latter position being that what is important is faith, which leads to the possibility of salvation without the sacrament of confession.[11] In modern mythological terms, that is a forgoing of the dominant interests of the Church and the Church itself but not of the myth of the Deity.

Before we start to explore the essential elements of the sacrament, we need to place it in the present time and note its current standing. Here we see that participation in the sacrament of confession has suffered a severe decline.[12] Stotts's explanation for this is that the decline occurred within the context of the broad changes in social values in the 1960s, as notions of respect for established Church authority – and the focus on morbid and legalistic guilt – declined. The Church responded, attempting to replace the traditional language about venial and mortal sin with a more complex and multivalent notion. But there has been no resurgence of interest in confession. Instead, Stotts suggests, there needs to be a turn to psychoanalytic insights into the structure of guilt so that there can be a fresh ritualising of complex theological-psychological experiences like guilt, sin and forgiveness, if the Church rituals of penance are to be a source of healing: 'these rituals must provide a cathartic and self-reconciling context in which mercy and tolerance cooperate with law and restitution. Fault and the transgression of law ... are insufficient.'[13] This appraisal might be seen as a demythologising of morality but it is not. Certainly, this recommended approach is less straightforwardly mythological in its degradation of priestly authority and its turning away from traditional ritual forms, but the sought methods and outcomes have the same end. There is a sophisticating of subjection through psychoanalytic-theological means. Salvation remains the ultimate goal yet it still recommends the means to arrive at inner peace in the meantime. The eradication of existential concerns through the perpetual reconstruction of individuality remains at its core. In fact, given the intention to gather information at more deeply psychoanalytic levels, these reforms go far deeper into psychological space – and so face privacy more profoundly – than the traditional ritualistic forms.

---

[11] Martin Luther, *The Babylonian Captivity of the Church*, in *Luther's Works*, H. Lehmann (ed.), vol.36 (Muhlenberg, 1970), pp.82–83, 87. The Catholic Council of Trent (1545–1563) responded with reforms that reaffirmed the role of the priest in their sacramental dogma; see D. Coffey, *The Sacrament of Reconciliation* (Liturgical Press, 2001), pp.101–107.

[12] See J. Stotts, 'Obedience as belonging: Catholic guilt and frequent confession in America', *Religions* 10:6 (2019): 370 at nn.30 and 32, where it is stated that only a quarter of Catholics attend confession once per year.

[13] Ibid. pp. 17–18.

Privacy as the History of Normalisation

Although such reforms are under constant review, it should not be thought that traditional approaches to repentance have faded. This begins with a wide range of references in the New Testament wherein each of the matters canvassed in the Ten Commandments is given as the subject of exhortation by the Christ.[14] The First Commandment ('I am the Lord thy God. Thou shall not have strange gods before Me') is stated in Matthew 4:10; the Second ('Thou shalt not take the name of the Lord thy God in vain') in Matthew 12:31; the Third ('Remember to keep holy the Sabbath day') in Matthew 12:11–12; the Fourth ('Honour thy father and thy mother') in Mark 7:10; the Fifth ('Thou shalt not kill') in Mark 10:19; the Sixth ('Thou shalt not commit adultery') in Luke 18:20; the Seventh ('Thou shalt not steal') in Mark 7:22–23; the Eighth ('Thou shalt not bear false witness against thy neighbour') in Matthew 5:33–34; the Ninth ('Thou shalt not covet thy neighbour's wife') in Mark 7:22–23; and the Tenth ('Thou shalt not covet thy neighbour's goods') in Mark 7:22–23.

These ancient prescriptions persist to now. As prominent contemporary theologian and scholar Scott Hahn makes clear, they lead to a process of deep self-examination of one's thought and behaviour that needs to be undertaken to prepare for entering the confessional, a process that is highly refined and remains a priority. He presents an exhaustive list of questions for the believer, of which the following are excerpts:[15]

First Commandment

- Have I performed my duties toward God reluctantly?
- Did I neglect my prayer life? Did I recite my usual prayers?
- Did I fail to mention some grave sin in my previous confession?
- Did I put my faith in danger – without a good reason – by reading a book, pamphlet or magazine that contains material contrary to Catholic faith or morals?

Second Commandment

- Did I take the name of God in vain? Did I make use of God's name mockingly, jokingly, angrily or in any other irreverent manner?
- Have I been a sponsor in baptism or participated actively in other ceremonies outside the Catholic Church?

---

[14] Generally, see *The Holy Bible – The New Testament* (Kennedy and Sons, 1950), pp.1–148 passim.

[15] S. Hahn, *Lord, Have Mercy – The Healing Power of Confession* (Darton Longman Todd, 2017), pp.186–193.

Normalising Deity

Third Commandment

- Did I miss Mass on a Sunday or a holy day of obligation?
- Did I fail to dress appropriately for Mass?
- Did I allow myself to be distracted during Mass, by not paying attention, by looking around out of curiosity?
- Have I performed any work or business activity that would inhibit the worship due to God ... on a Sunday or a holy day of obligation?
- Did I fail to generously help the Church in her necessities to the extent that I am able?
- Did I fail to fast or abstain on a day prescribed by the Church?

Fourth Commandment

For Parents

- Have I neglected to teach my children their prayers, send them to church or give them a Christian education?
- Have I neglected to watch over my children; to monitor their companions, the books they read, the movies and TV shows they watch?
- Have I failed to see to it that my child made his first confession and first Communion?

For Children

- Was I disobedient towards my parents?
- Did I react proudly when corrected by my parents?
- Did I have a disordered desire for independence?

Fifth Commandment

- Did I easily get angry or lose my temper?
- Was I envious or jealous of others?
- How many persons did I lead to sin? What sins were involved?
- Did I neglect my health? Did I attempt to take my life?
- Did I eat or drink more than a sufficient amount, allowing myself to get carried away by gluttony?
- Did I consent to or actively take part in direct sterilisation (tubal ligation, vasectomy)? Do I realise that this will have a permanent effect on my married life and that I will have to answer to God for its consequences?

- Did I consent to, advise someone about or actively take part in an abortion? Was I aware that the Church punishes with automatic excommunication those who procure and achieve abortion? Do I realise that this is a very grave crime?
- Did I desire revenge or enmity, hatred or harbour ill feelings when someone offended me?
- Did I quarrel with one of my brothers or sisters?

Sixth and Ninth Commandments

- Did I wilfully entertain impure thoughts?
- Did I engage in impure conversations?
- Did I look for fun in forms of entertainment that placed me in proximate occasions of sin, such as certain dances, movies, shows or books with immoral content?
- Did I fail, before going to a show or reading a book, to find out its moral implications, so as not to put myself in immediate danger of sinning and in order to avoid distorting my conscience?
- Did I wilfully look at an indecent picture or cast an immodest look upon myself or another?
- Did I commit an impure act? By myself, through masturbation (which is objectively a mortal sin)?... With someone of the same or opposite sex?... Did this illicit relationship result in pregnancy? Did I do anything to prevent or end that pregnancy?
- In courtship ... [do] I degrade human love by confusing it with selfishness or mere pleasure?
- Did I engage in acts such as 'petting', 'necking', passionate kisses or prolonged embraces?

For Married People

- Did I, without serious reason, deprive my spouse of the marital right? Did I claim my own rights in a way that showed no concern for my spouse's state of mind or health?
- Did I take 'the pill' or use any artificial birth control device before or after new life had already been conceived?
- Did I, without grave reason, with the intention of avoiding conception, make use of marriage on only those days when offspring would not likely be engendered?
- Did I suggest to another person the use of birth-control pills or another artificial method of preventing pregnancy (like condoms)?
- Did I have a hand in contributing to the contraceptive mentality by my advice, jokes or attitudes?

Normalising Deity

Seventh and Tenth Commandments

- Did I steal? How much money?... Did I give it back or at least have the intention of doing so?
- Did I harm anyone by deception, fraud or coercion in business contracts or transactions?
- Did I unnecessarily spend beyond my means? Do I spend too much money because of my vanity or caprice?
- Do I give alms according to my capacity?
- Was I envious of my neighbour's goods?
- Do I neglect to pay my debts?
- Did I desire to steal?
- Did I give in to laziness or love of comfort rather than diligently work or study?
- Was I greedy? Do I have an excessively materialistic view of life?

Eighth Commandment

- Did I tell lies? Did I repair any damage that may have resulted as a consequence of this?
- Have I unjustly or rashly accused others?
- Did I sin by detraction, that is, by telling the faults of another person without necessity?
- Did I engage in gossip, backbiting or tale-telling?
- Did I reveal a secret without due cause?

While it would be difficult to deny that there are precepts among this list which are sensible and which contribute to both an equanimous social condition and to personal well-being – although none of which could not have been equally well drawn up within a thoroughly rational moral code – there are elements here which none bar the fervent would, or would need to, tolerate. There is clearly herein a consolidated strategy to intervene deeply into psychological and material space and to normalise human ideas and practices in Christian terms.

That strategy is clearly mythological in that none of the questions relates to the existential condition, all are based on fear of the absolute magnitude to which one must be subject, and all carry the reward of sacred blessing – passed on by the dominant interests of the magnitude, the priests – and, if continuously honoured, eternal bliss so long as one wholeheartedly subjects oneself to the process and sees it as valid. There is therefore a forgoing of self-responsibility by which one can respectfully relate to others but determine one's own moral compass.

Finally, a point here regarding privacy. That is, there is a right of access to the personal thoughts and actions of the faithful (in Catholicism rather than

Protestantism) – and the accompanying duty to reveal all breaches of canon and derivative laws – by those dominant interests that is complete. This domination is reinforced by the assurance of confidentiality on the part of the priest. Denial of such access by the confessing individual itself constitutes a breach of faith.

Clearly, the impact on the personal thought and behaviour of the faithful wrought by this ritual is intended to be extensive and repeated. Foucault has looked closely at its social and psychological significance.

A Word on Foucault

In what follows, there is a substantial reference to Foucault. However, Foucault is not accepted here on his own terms. We shall see below a range of criticisms of his work, but, even before we begin such a reference, one point needs to be made clear. That is, Foucault has no account of myth – or anything that approaches that – even though he does describe the State, for example, as a 'mythicised abstraction'.[16] This is a significant shortcoming since it leaves his forensic explorations as highly descriptive and compellingly analytic but short of a rationale beyond the immediate materiality of his work. He might say that is the very point, that meta-narratives are misleading. However, the kind of narrative argued in the present work is deconstructive of the major ideologies of the West, an explanation but the opposite of a construction of a progressive Idealism that one would find, for example, in Kant or Hegel. The explanation here reveals the serial failings of those major ideologies and the search for a way of living that eschews a meta-narrative.

Foucault himself – as Lyon did – pursued and established continuities across historical eras, as we do in the present work. His examination of the long impact of the pastorate is an example. Nonetheless, even though his work complements and illustrates the materiality of the mythological analysis presented here, he does not himself perceive such a wide context, a context which would have strengthened his forensic archaeology. So, he is not presented here on his own terms, only to the extent that his work is of illustrative value for the present argument. We rely on Foucault for evidence but not for the argument.

Foucault on Normalisation

There are arguments put by Foucault that are in sympathy with what we have just considered regarding confessionalism and which extend that in a manner that is useful with what follows in this chapter. In doing so, they will strengthen the argument about normalisation that is the theme of this chapter generally. That is, the embedded practices of the magnitudes go to the heart of what we see as our dominant private concerns.

[16] M. Foucault, *Security, Territory, Population* (Palgrave Macmillan, 2007), p.109.

Normalising Deity 103

The first is that confession – which itself had long existed as a practice – received strong institutional support and direction from its codification through the Lateran Council in 1215. The production of truth which it fostered became strongly connected to processes of individuation. The medieval experience of confession was, when required, shadowed by torture[17] and always, *post factum*, by punishment in some form as penance. This means not only that fear was ingrained in it but also that it must be understood within a relation of power. It was a mechanism for men's individuated subjection: 'their constitution as subjects in both senses of the word'. That is, it is a ritual discourse in which one does not confess without the presence of an interlocutor who is also the authority who requires the confession, prescribes and appreciates it and then intervenes to judge, punish, forgive, console and reconcile. The very expressing of the truths produces intrinsic modifications in the person who articulates it, as it exonerates, redeems and purifies, unburdens them of wrongs, liberates and promises salvation.[18]

Particularly relevant for the broad argument here, Foucault goes on to say that this is an obligatory speech which breaks the bonds of discretion. What secrecy it presupposes is owed not to the high price of what it has to say and the small number worthy of its benefits but to its obscure familiarity and its general baseness. Its truth is guaranteed only by the bond and intimacy of the discourse, and the agency of domination resides not in the constrained speaker but in the one who listens and who knows, in the one who questions.[19] The key elements here are secrecy – the privileged expression of one's most private thoughts and feelings – and its relation to the domination that subjects through fear, acceptance of contrition, the discourse of prescribed normality, imposition of penance and the promise of salvation. It is a method, as he points out, that has proliferated into the modern era across pedagogy, security and health and on television talk shows, all inheritors of the Christian pastoral[20] and all taking up the goals of private normalisation.

Second, Foucault widens this story of confessional repression and individualised normalisation by relating it to sex and the bourgeoisie. Here he claims the most rigorous application of the 'technologies' – or techniques – of sex, for example, through Freudian psychiatry, stretched back into the history of the Christian West and was especially productive in the sixteenth century. However, these technologies were not mostly applied to young men but – contrary to the well-told account of the Reformation connection to asceticism, the work ethic and the rise of capitalism[21] – by the bourgeoisie to themselves. Narrowing the range of accepted sexual practice, they emphasised the importance of vitality, longevity, blood, heredity and so the

---

[17] M. Foucault, *The History of Sexuality – An Introduction*, vol. 1 (Vintage, 1990), p.59.
[18] Ibid. pp.60–61.
[19] Ibid. p.62.
[20] Ibid. pp.18, 21, 63.
[21] Ibid. p.122.

establishment and growth of bourgeois hegemony.[22] This was therefore a focus on the bourgeois family and its private sexual practices, whereby it subordinated its soul to sex by conceiving of it as constituting the soul's most secret and determinant part to create a 'class' body.[23] This came to promote economic imperatives and social homogeneity, principles that sustained the progressive exploitation of the proletariat.[24]

We can draw a number of elements from this analysis of confession by Foucault. On the one hand, his analysis could seem to endorse the views of those who see privacy either as issues of the rights of the individual to manage their perceived wrongdoings without interference – until they present to either God or priest for reconciliation – or as a selected flow of discursive information between the believer and the informed and authoritative representative of the Deity. Further, he makes the point that, at least as far as the sexuality of the bourgeoisie is concerned, this is to be seen not as the subject matter of a repression but as at least one of the bases for their effective strength and the vitality of their heredity. However, when one takes into account Foucault's emphasis on fear, the self-humiliation within a power relation, a secrecy (or privacy) that is the basis of thorough individualised exploration, critique, admonishment and forgiveness by the empowered agent of the Deity – all as elements of wide pastoral 'care' of all members of the community – then such notions of privacy invite an entirely different account than those of which we are currently familiar. As for the apparently contrary response of the bourgeoisie, we shall see shortly that this is, like a different account of the private, well placed within the context of the dynamic of the modern mythological framework.

What is actually at play in confessionalism is the distancing of existential fear and its replacement with the prospect of eternal bliss on condition of complete subjection to the regime prescribed by the dominant interests of the Deity. In short, it is the internalised Christian normalisation of the individual that requires the forgoing of responsibility to and for oneself. It is the extensive catalogue of confessional matters present in the Bible and presented again by Hahn that is imposed upon and constitutes the foundations of the private for the Catholic Christian and informs the derivative forms of self and public examination. Ultimately, there is no Christian privacy, either in the sense of a right to be left alone or in the social management of the flow of information. Christians are not 'left alone' and information exchange is free flowing in an individual's interests but within a relationship of domination. We are beginning to see that the common notions of privacy need to be put aside.

THE NORMALISING STATE

We shall see now that this dynamic, and the place of the Christian pastorate within it, needs to be considered as having informed the emergence of the State, that a

---

[22] Ibid. pp.123, 124, 125.
[23] Ibid. p.124.
[24] Ibid. pp.126, 127.

theological normalisation was followed by a political normalisation that drew its central tenets from it.

The genesis of the modern Western State needs to be traced back at least to the practices of the Christian pastorate.[25] For Foucault, the Christian religious community constituted itself as a Church

> that claims to govern men in their daily lives on the grounds of leading them to an eternal life in the other world and to do this not only on the scale of a definite group, of a city or a state, but of the whole of humanity ... With this ... an apparatus was formed of a kind of power not found anywhere else and which was constantly developed and refined over fifteen centuries, from the second and third centuries after Jesus Christ up to the eighteenth century. This pastoral power ... was no doubt shifted, broken up, transformed ... but basically has never been truly abolished ... [and] is something from which we have still not freed ourselves.[26]

He proceeds to argue that, although this overall pastoral power remained distinct from political power, it is concerned with individual souls insofar as this direction of souls also involves a permanent intervention in everyday conduct, in the management of lives, as well as in goods, wealth and things. In this it concerns not only the individual but also the community.[27]

That is, the pastorate has been a form of governing men that gave rise to 'an art of conducting, directing, leading, guiding, taking in hand and manipulating men, an art of monitoring them and urging them on step by step, an art with the function of taking charge of men collectively and individually throughout their lives and at every moment of their existence'.[28] This is where he sees the origin, the point of formation or the embryonic point of the governmentality whose entry into politics, at the end of the sixteenth and in the seventeenth and eighteenth centuries, is the threshold of the modern state. That is, the modern state is born when governmentality became a calculated and reflected practice. Foucault's point is that pastoralism – although not exactly characterised by salvation, the law and truth – does feature each of these. That is, it establishes a context within which the merits and faults of every action, including of the pastor, are recognised and addressed as means to eventual salvation; it promotes the submission of one individual to another at a personal level, a humility rather than to a singular will, and this is without end; and third, that there is an examination of conscience in an effort to grapple with a sense of what has truth. This is a new form of power and produces modes of individualisation through analysis, universal servitude and internal or hidden truth.

---

[25] For a wider context of what is being put here regarding the Foucauldian view of the State, see D. Grant, *The Mythological State and Its Empire*, pp. 229–241, and D. Grant and L. Bennett Moses, *Technology and the Trajectory of Myth*, pp.51–53.

[26] M. Foucault, *Security, Territory, Population*, p.148.

[27] Ibid. p.154.

[28] Ibid. p.163.

106   *Privacy as the History of Normalisation*

He sees in all this the prelude to the governmentality that began in the sixteenth century.[29]

The pastorate thereby makes an entry into governmentality in various ways. Especially due to the impact of the Reformation and Counter-Reformation, the pastorate intervenes further into not only matters of material life, property and the education of children but also how to conduct oneself, one's children, one's family. It is here also that the distinction between private and public begins to be problematised.[30] These broad themes of directing conduct become the concerns for government. This invokes the question of the responsibilities of the political sovereign. Specifically, to follow the model of God's government on earth and to procure the common good of the multitude, as does the pastor of his flock, but through a system of obedience that functioned by a system of threats of chastisement and promises of salvation.[31] This is a process of transition and evolution from the Christian pastorate, not a transfer.

Beyond the pastorate and sovereignty, from the early seventeenth century, this is becoming the art of government and its rationale is not Machiavelli's godless whims of the Prince but raison d'état, by which the State is to be preserved while it satisfies its responsibility within a frame comprising salvation, obedience and truth. Salvation was the sustenance of the State even when special circumstances required coup d'état, a notion therefore still consistent with raison d'état. Obedience – for example, regarding the spread of rumours as 'opinion' and the forms of sedition triggered by the unsatisfied material needs of the people – was addressed, respectively, by manipulating such opinion (by the *publicistes*) and facilitating mercantilist economic policy (by the *economistes*). Truth required the sovereign to be wise and prudent by knowing the range of types of laws and the elements that constitute the State in strength, its statistics (regarding the population, wealth, trade), how to keep these statistics confidential and how to manage public opinion.[32] This was the emergence of the State as a set of practices, especially through the notion of 'police'.

Against this background and extending arrangements from the Middle Ages, the art of government transitions into a field of relations of forces, through manipulations and distributions whereby 'police' represents the exercise of public authority over a community: from the early seventeenth century, 'police' is the set of forces by which the State's forces are increased but while maintaining order, optimising the State's absolutist 'splendor'. The increase in State force is promoted by intrusions: to ensure the better education of children, forcing the poor to work, regulating both the operation of the mercantilist Market[33] and the sale of property. Within a whole of government approach, special powers came to bureaus of justice, the army and

[29] Ibid. pp.167ff.
[30] Ibid. p.230.
[31] Ibid. p.235.
[32] Ibid. pp.261ff.
[33] Ibid. pp.335, 337.

finance. 'Police' had to promote the loyalty of citizens, wealth and household management. The desired outcome was the true subject for the perfection of the State, that is, increasing the population, the provision of such necessities as food and health, as well as infrastructure. Not just living but living better, that is, with happiness, through regulatory discipline and the arts.[34]

What we are beginning to see here in the early development of what was to become the modern State is, drawn from the Christian pastorate, a particular sense of care for the subjects of the sovereign. This is a sense of care by the sovereign to manage the population in a way that begins to balance their security and standard of living with the aim of, at the same time, strengthening the capacities and resources of the mercantilist Market and thereby the State. The constant attention of 'police', overlain on the Christian way of life, gave no room for thought about existential matters as individuals became embedded in this normalising pastoral-'police' State.

The Eighteenth Century

During the eighteenth century, there was a reaction against many of these Statist themes, especially by the *economistes* and their views supporting the fundamental interests of individuals: the 'natural' working of the economy was primary for this movement and this emerged as reforms of modern governmentality. All this was the move from Renaissance government willed by God to the raison d'état of the *politiques* and 'police' then to the governmentality of the *economistes*, a correlate to civil society and which thought scientifically about and facilitated – to ensure the security of – the natural features of population, thereby providing forms of freedom that marginalised 'police' into a police force.[35] For Foucault these were contrary to the State as it had emerged. The *economistes* did not oppose the absolutist sovereignty of raison d'état but sought to reorganise thinking around it to promote a new domain, the economy. The State remained responsible for the regulation and promotion of the economy so that the State was stronger.[36] This is not yet the Market State.

The argument in the present work is that what we see at this point – well before the emergence of the modern, engaged, institutional State – is the emergence of what may be called the 'atmosphere' for that emergence, that is, the raw environmental conditions of government which would sustain the mythological, institutional State: the judging of actions; how to conduct oneself; the education of all children; the necessary material conditions; the inducement to obedience through the manipulation of public discourse and to avoid sedition; the artificial distinction between public and private life; a concern for demographics, including as that

[34] Ibid. pp.312ff.
[35] Ibid. pp.337ff.
[36] Ibid. pp.346, 348.

108   *Privacy as the History of Normalisation*

related to population, wealth and trade; the requirement to work; and the emergence of civil society, all this presaging the ultimate move away from absolutist State control to the natural laws of economy and the development of a police 'force'.

In short, we have serial transitions during the sixteenth to the eighteenth centuries. First, the State emerges out of the adoption of the methods of pastoral care; second, we see a phase of sovereign power strengthened by mercantilist and 'police' policies; and third, there is the continuing strengthening of the sovereign State but by replacing 'police' and allowing – and maintaining the conditions for – the appearance of the economy and civil society. Along with that we have the imagining and then the control over the population. Out of this would come the liberalism of the late eighteenth and nineteenth centuries[37] and, ultimately, the economic reversal in the twentieth century – through neoliberalism – by which the State has come to exist substantially to support the economy.[38]

Given the emergence of the public-private dimension, this programme not only was carried out at the level of policy but also operated on individual souls.[39] This form of governmentalisation was an extension or persistence of the aim of its progenitor, the Christian pastorate, to make subject through individualising and normalising. It pursued this end, first, by identifying and dissecting every merit and fault at each moment; second, through a network of servitude of everyone to everyone and the exclusion of 'the self as ego' as the central form of the individual; and, third, not by the production of recognised truth but by the production and revelation of secret, hidden truths. This is subjectivation as identification and subjection,[40] as a normalised and normalising strategy.

Such a strategy is also reinforced by techniques of discipline. Those techniques were a focus for Foucault at least as early as *Discipline and Punish*. He saw the operation of this micro-power as the proper focus, rather than the institutions of macro-power. Discipline operates by dividing everything according to a code of what is forbidden, what is permitted and then what is obligatory. The law prescribes what is forbidden so that what remains is order. Within that, discipline makes clear what must be done and how this is to be regulated, at every moment: the law prohibits and discipline prescribes.[41] The result is that discipline normalises: it analyses and breaks down individuals, places, time, movements, actions and operations. Thereby it produces components that can be seen and modified. It then classifies via particular objectives – what are the best actions for particular results – and how all these can be linked and coordinated so that permanent control can be established through regimes of training. This is a process that identifies the suitable and thereby divides the normal from the abnormal. Disciplinary normalisation first

[37] Ibid. p.61.
[38] Ibid. p.121.
[39] Ibid. p.231.
[40] Ibid. p.184.
[41] Ibid. pp.46–47.

The Normalising State

posits a model to achieve a particular result and seeks to adapt people, movements and actions to conform to this norm.[42] This conformity, this normalising, in turn produces docility. Referring to Le Mettrie's *L'Homme-machine* (published in 1747), Foucault sees this as joining the analysable body to the manipulable body: a body is docile that may be subjected, used, transformed and improved, and the techniques for doing so were new, treating the body not en masse but at the level of movements, gestures, attitudes and rapidity; the object of control was its economy, the efficiency of movements, their internal organisation; and the implication of an uninterrupted, constant coercion according to a codification of time, space and movement. All this makes possible meticulous control.[43]

Elias

Although he devotes much of his attention to the upper levels of French and other societies, the work of Elias complements some of the central themes of Foucault's thought. Elias presents a particular focus on the art of civilising and the development of a personal habitus; the relation of that to the emergence of court society, mercantilism and the rise of the bourgeoisie; and, in turn, the function of those within the centralisation of power and the emergence of the State. For him, thereby, psychogenesis is inseparable from sociogenesis.[44] Drawing on this background, one focus here is on the creation of an internal bourgeois psychological space, how civilising was fundamental to that, how such emotions as fear and shame were related to individual socio-economic status and how respective behaviours became habitualised. In short, how one dominant notion of privacy – being left alone for self-realisation – is related to processes of normalised bourgeois subjectification in the emergence and nature of the State.

The context for this focus is that, as competition between social groups – especially including court society and the rising mercantilist bourgeoisie – led to the centralisation and then monopolisation of power and taxation, the groundwork was thereby laid for the emergence of the State[45] and the eventual pre-eminence of the bourgeoisie.[46] The economic policy of mercantilism – as we saw in Foucault – was a key strategy in this as was the detailed shaping of the conditions of individual practice by the techniques of pastoralism, governmentality and discipline that Foucault laid out. At the same time, the tone of society was also changing through

---

[42] Ibid. pp.55–57, 63.

[43] M. Foucault, *Discipline and Punish* Vintage (1979), pp.135–169, especially pp.136–137.

[44] For a wider context of these arguments concerning Elias, see D. Grant, *The Mythological State and Its Empire*, pp.210–220, and D. Grant and L. Bennett Moses, *Technology and the Trajectory of Myth*, p.49.

[45] N. Elias, *The Civilising Process* (Blackwell, 2003), p.344; H. Kuzmics, 'Civilisation, state and bourgeois society: The theoretical contribution of Norbert Elias', *Theory, Culture & Society* 4:2–3 (1987: pp.515, 527, 531.

[46] N. Elias, *The Civilising Process*, p.275.

the influence of the humanists and their promotion of a more civilised manner of living. But increasing *civilitas* belied a widespread field of fears and anxieties as the growing atmosphere of competition which produced this early form of the State became a deep factor for social classes and individuals.

Civilitas

Promoted by, among others, the Christian humanist Desiderius Erasmus (for example, in *De civilitate morum puerilium*, 1530), the notion of *civilitas*, as expressed particularly in bodily carriage, gestures, dress and facial expressions, presented what it meant for a person to be civilised.[47] The content of this notion was a reform of a range of such behaviours as one's 'natural functions', behaviour in the bedroom, aggressiveness and so on. All these – and others – came to be internalised by the processes of training from childhood and throughout one's life:

> Since the pressure or coercion of individual adults is allied to the pressure and example of the whole surrounding world, most children, as they grow up, forget or repress relatively early the fact that their feelings of shame and embarrassment, of pleasure and displeasure, were moulded into conformity with a certain standard by external pressure and compulsion. All this appears to them as highly personal, something 'inside', implanted in them by nature ... adults, too, were at first dissuaded from eating with their fingers, to spare others a distasteful spectacle and themselves the shame of being seen with soiled hands, later it became more and more an inner automatism, the imprint of society on the inner self, the superego, that forbade the individual to eat in any other way than with a fork. The social standard to which the individual was first made to conform from outside by external restraint is finally reproduced more or less smoothly within him or her, through a self-restraint which operates to a certain degree even against his or her conscious wishes.... If one wished to express recurrent processes of this kind in the form of laws, one could speak ... of a fundamental law of sociogenesis and psychogenesis.'[48]

But such a process of internalisation was not confined to the field of personal behaviours. Due to the range of fears and anxieties that occur in social situations, even when fear of violence from others has been brought under control, civilised interdependence remains fragile. In fact, such fears are necessary whenever people live together: 'No society can survive without a channelling of individual drives and affects, without a very specific control of individual behaviour. No such control is possible unless people exert constraints on one another, and all constraint is converted in the person on whom it is imposed into fear of one kind or another.'[49]

---

[47] Ibid. p.49.
[48] Ibid. p.109.
[49] Ibid. p.443.

The Normalising State

This process constrains adults as well as children. It is made of '[s]hame, fear of war and fear of God, guilt, fear of punishment or of loss of social prestige, man's fear of himself, of being overcome by his own affective impulses'.[50] These are all constructed fears, even though there is an existential element in the fear of war.

A particular range of fears applied to membership of social classes. The competition between those on the same level and the tensions between those in different strata produce both anxieties and prohibitions. For those on lower levels, it comes from fear of dismissal, exposure to those in power, falling below a subsistence level; while for the middle and upper strata it is the fear of social degradation, of the reduction of possessions or independence or of the loss of prestige and status.

> Precisely these fears ... are particularly disposed to internalisation; they, far more than the fear of poverty, hunger or direct physical danger, become rooted in the individual members of such strata, through their upbringing, as inner anxieties which bind them to a learned code almost automatically, under the pressure of a strong super-ego.[51]

These bind the individual, from childhood, to a certain internalised norm of shame, embarrassment and guilt. In the argument of the present work, it is these emotions, the incidents that trigger them, the manner in which each individual quietly considers all the information around that impact, along with her planned response, that all need to be understood as informing the current 'internalised' notions of privacy. The most significant of those types of incidents have a religious-moral, a political, a commercial-financial or, lately, a technological flavour and the individual has to be 'left alone' to deal with them.

All this was particularly relevant to the bourgeoisie. Their aspirations were driven by a desire for both high social status – an ambition to compete with and ultimately replace court society[52] – and economic pre-eminence. However, the success they realised in this through their commercial and professional activity and by adopting the practices of *civilitas*[53] brought as much fear as it brought satisfied desire. Fear and desire – the circumstantial experiences that camouflaged the existential – were both strongly present. Their means of coping with these strong emotions was through a self-control which not only internalised the attitudes and practices necessary for this success but also normalised them to the features of the emerging State, just as the pastorate had normalised believers to the features of the Deity. They were forced to hide these constructed fears – in public at least – under a veil of *civilitas*.

Although this internalisation and normalisation became significantly embedded in them – to the extent that many of these attitudes and behaviours became

[50] Ibid. p.443.
[51] Ibid. p.444.
[52] Ibid. p.423.
[53] Ibid. pp.86, 88.

notionally automatic[54] – these processes also saw the emergence of an entirely new social and psychological structure. That is, they saw the separation of the public world from the private world and thereby the inception of a new, modern notion of privacy that is still present. For the bourgeoisie the public world was focused on their commercial or professional activity, and the private world had two elements: the world of the family[55] and the private psychological space[56] where a range of information was taken in, where emotional and rational experiences found their place, were explored and either became repressed or became the subject of aspirations to be progressed in the public world: fears of exclusion,[57] shame and embarrassment at vulgarity,[58] moral questions, attitudes towards the powerful, preliminary commercial planning and so on.

It is in this early phase that we also see the seeds of what is to develop into a bourgeois mentality and lifestyle, which was to burgeon throughout the long period up to the present consumer society. From the mid-eighteenth century we see the signs of self-fashioning in dress, the taking of pleasure in private. Taking the luxury of coffee, the collection of antiques and attending the theatre were such pleasures. These trends in consumption went along with such personal qualities as self-discipline and self-improvement, and an increased focused on the bourgeois home and its increasingly fashionable accoutrements.[59]

This was the creation of the origin of the field of current privacy theory, where we begin to want either the space to be left alone to deal with such psycho-social and consumption issues or to plan our self-enhancement or where the selective flow of information which inform these issues begins to find a place. The argument in this work takes a different perspective, whereby what we see there is nothing more than the creation of a psychological space and derivative practices in which the influence of the mythological dynamic becomes intensely personal: circumstantial fears and desires concerning notions of and attitudes towards theological right and wrong, how we manage relationships, embryonic State power and the material existence offered by the emerging mercantilist Market. That is, the promises of dominant interests and subjection – willing, induced or imposed – as the forgoing of respectful self-responsibility. In effect, this is the appearance of the internalisation of what comes to be understood as a second 'normal' – beyond but overlapping the Christian – as the means of individual subjection to the mythological dynamic and therefrom a modern, bourgeois notion of privacy.

---

[54] Ibid. p.118.
[55] Ibid. p.117.
[56] Ibid. pp.148, 153, 154; see R. van Krieken, *Norbert Elias* (Routledge 1998), pp.89, 92.
[57] Ibid. pp.423–424.
[58] Ibid. pp.127, 431.
[59] F. Trentmann, *Empire of Things* (Penguin, 2017), pp.86–87, 94, 117, 215, 227, 250, 311, 345, 374.

Foucault and Elias

None of this is to say that the differences between the approaches of Foucault and Elias have not been long known.[60] But the complementary nature of their work has also been acknowledged, for example, by van Krieken:

> The concepts and categories used in the debate (about the modern self) have in recent years displayed a heavy reliance on the work of Foucault and Elias.... Foucault argued that one of the definitive characteristics of European State formation ... was the transition from a sovereign State power which operated negatively by setting limits and constraints, to a decentred disciplinary power which penetrates our souls, bodies and minds, actively transforming them and producing positive effects which turn us all into self-managing citizens. By discipline, Foucault is referring to the techniques within such institutional setting as schools, workhouses, hospitals factories, monasteries and the confessional.

He continues:

> Elias also insists that we should see European social history in terms of a gradual transformation of personality structure, an intensifying 'constraint towards self-constraint', in which regulation of the human body, as well as our impulses, passions and desires, undergoes a 'civilising process', which he explains in terms of the increasing monopolisation of violence which accompanies the process of State formation, the effects of the intensified competition between and within social groups characteristic of a market economy, as well as an accompanying historical tendency towards increasing social interdependency.[61]

> The civilising process can thus be regarded more accurately as a project, as a 'conscious proselytizing crusade waged by men of knowledge and aimed at extirpating the vestiges of wild culture.... The differences between medieval and early modern disciplinary power were those of a transition from power relations rooted in communal village relations, exercised 'matter-of-factly', without conscious deliberation and direction, to an apparatus of power in which discipline was consciously planned, designed, implemented and imposed on a reluctant population.

> If we jettison the Boschian view of the Middle Ages and grant an effectivity to medieval social constraint, European social history can nonetheless continue to be perceived in terms of a particular transformation of social order from one based on external constraints to one located more within individual souls, in the sense that State formation itself contributed to the breaking down of old, communal forms of social order and a particular socialization process, one based on the State-individual (citizen) relationship, rather than, say, commune-Church, or village-Lord.[62]

---

[60] R. van Krieken, 'The organisation of the soul: Elias and Foucault on discipline and the self', *European Journal of Sociology* 31:2 (1990): pp.353–371.

[61] Ibid. pp.354–355.

[62] Ibid. p.364.

114   *Privacy as the History of Normalisation*

The differences that van Krieken sees between them are not profound. They include that Elias emphasises increased competition and social interdependency, whereas for Foucault (and indeed Weber) there is an intermediate step, the translation of those requirements into Protestant ascetism, rational bureaucracy and disciplinary techniques. The latter two agree with Elias that self-discipline emerged as a strategy of self-advancement for ruling social groups, the court aristocracy, the administrative and legal elite and the bourgeoisie, but they have different views about the emergence of the proletariat. They have a wider social profile in mind as the target of their respective strategies.[63]

Criticisms of Foucault and Elias

There have been various critiques of both Foucault and Elias which need comment in the context of the argument being put here. One such is that Foucault gives insufficient recognition to the significance of agency, irrespective of the acknowledged power of the techniques of governmentality to constitute subjectivities. Foucault's subjects are too passive. Further, he is accused of delineating the process of subjectification as linear and one-way. Responses to these criticisms would include that, in his late writings, Foucault emphasised a route to self-formation, even within historically constituted conditions, through the capacity of critique and creativity, and that the presence of a range of agents who sit between governmental strategies and citizens helps to reform strategies by taking account of the values of citizens. Thereby the lessons of pastoral power can be enlisted to subvert such criticisms.[64] Foucault has also been criticised for being too sympathetic towards neoliberalism. In response, Zamora has said that, apart from any influence on Foucault of the intellectual environment in which he found himself, this should be seen as an attempt to – mistakenly – perceive Hayek's notion of the Market as providing opportunities to invent one's life: micro-resistances rather than revolution.[65] A further common response to Foucault is that he has no substantial account of the State as a set of institutions, focusing as he does on the different account of power that we have looked at. There are accounts that disavow this claim, emphasising that, if one looks at the notion of the State through the field of functioning governmentality, one would accept that the State was never an entity that was planted and grew but can be seen as an 'object' that appears as the connection of different and diverse technologies, partnerships and interactions:[66] 'The State is superstructural in relation to a whole series of power networks that invest the body,

---

[63] Ibid. pp.361–362.

[64] G. Martin and J. Waring, 'Realising governmentality: Pastoral power, governmental discourse and the (re)constitution of subjectivities', *The Sociological Review* 66:6 (2018): pp.1294, 1297.

[65] 'How Michel Foucault Got Neoliberalism So Wrong – an interview with Daniel Zamora' (by Kevin Boucard-Victoire), *Jacobin*, 6 September 2019.

[66] S. Sawyer, 'Foucault and the state', *The Tocqueville Review* 36:1 (2015): p.158.

The Normalising State | 115

sexuality, the family, kinship, knowledge, technology and so forth.'[67] Regarding Elias, there also well-established criticisms.[68] The first echoes a criticism of Foucault, that his notion of social development is in some way blind, that the place of agency is not sufficiently prominent. A response to this is that of Haferkamp, that there is collective agency – a Church or a State or a corporation. Second, Elias's focus on long-term trends sees him undervalue discontinuities, to which Elias said he was increasingly aware of this issue as featuring counter trends. Finally, Elias's focus on demythologising has been seen as a political rather than sociological exercise and he has therefore been criticised for not being clear about the validity of scientific knowledge. Questions have also been raised about his central concern about civilising, regarding the degree to which civilising has transformed human conduct, how he accounts for 'civilised' barbarism and whether civilising has really been a single process or the subject of serial offensives.[69] Questions have also been raised about the level of his understanding of psychiatric theory and the validity of the links between, on the one hand, the social processes of State formation and civilising processes with, on the other, the theological or commercial contexts. More recently, there has been a repeat of the established criticism that his notion of civilising is Eurocentric.[70]

However, perhaps a more significant criticism of both Foucault and Elias is the early but well-made point by van Krieken, that the mere existence of disciplinary – and, one can add, civilising – strategies does not establish their causal effects 'and the *apparent* correspondence between these strategies and interventions and eventual changes in psychic make-up might therefore be misleading'.[71] Interestingly, in saying so, van Krieken refers to how the thought of Catholic clergy was often 'magicalised' by popular beliefs in the process of attempting to Christianise the rural populace.

Comment

These various criticisms of Foucault and Elias may seem to be telling, but, in the wider context of the present work, they are not. That is, if one takes the view that there is a valid notion of the State – a mythological notion by which we are all brought, variously but mostly, to a condition of subjection due to the claims of its historical and contemporary dominant interests that our existential fears and desires

---

[67] Quoted in ibid. at p.160; M. Foucault, *Power Knowledge, Selected Interviews and Other Writings* (Pantheon, 1980), p.122.

[68] The criticisms are outlined in R. van Krieken, *Norbert Elias* (Routledge, 1998), pp.78–83.

[69] See also R. Powell, 'The theoretical concept of the 'civilising offensive' (Beschavingsoffensief): Notes on its origins and uses', *Human Figurations* 2:2 (2013): especially section 2.

[70] N. Pepperell, 'The unease with civilisation: Norbert Elias and the violence of the civilising process', *Thesis Eleven* (2016).

[71] R. van Krieken, 'The organisation of the soul', p.365.

116   *Privacy as the History of Normalisation*

will be despatched and camouflaged – that is, seen in the context of the mythological dynamic – then these criticisms begin to fade. Regarding Foucault, it is inappropriate to criticise him for ignoring the notion of the State as his focus is on the power relations of governing rather than its institutional arrangements.[72] Regarding their respective notions of agency, these merely reflect their respective focus on the processes of governmentality and civilising, each of which comprises the processes of subjection in which citizens typically willingly submit to a transformation of individual human conduct. Further to this, the claimed 'gap' between the existence of disciplinary or civilising strategies and their causal effects should be seen in the context of the common willingness of individuals to comply, especially in the context of inducement from early childhood. That is, heavy doses of discipline and civilising practices are not at all necessarily required. Regarding Elias, there is no contradiction in the barbarity of civilised individuals, since civilising is nothing more than subjection to a mythological regime, which can introduce barbaric elements. Further to that, civilising can properly be seen as the consequence of serial offensives – rather than a single long-term process – as civilising always operates in the context of one of the series of elements of the mythological trajectory: Deity, State, Market (and more recently, Technology as agent of the Absolute Self). Finally, elaborated psychiatric theory is not a necessary foundation for an analysis of the mythological dynamic, since all that is required is an appreciation of existential fear and desire and the elaboration of the disposition to mythologise as the strategic response.

Analysis

Putting these matters therefore respectfully to one side, what is argued here is that, as was displayed by the strategy of the pastorate regarding the myth of Deity, these processes of governmentality (with its totalising yet attentive force of 'police'), discipline and civilising were intended to accommodate the individual to the internalising, subjectifying – but adequately comforting – and normalising required to sustain the mythological magnitude of the State. That magnitude came to replace Deity due to the conceptual flaws of the latter as pointed out by Ockham, Pomponazzi and Luther,[73] its replacement to ultimately emerge as the magnitude Leviathan conceived by Hobbes in 1651.

---

[72] Neither can the present author criticise Foucault for not reading the broad developments he explores as mythological. He had no theory of myth, although he does describe the State as a 'mythicised abstraction'. See *Security, Territory, Population*, p.109.

[73] For a full account by the author of the role of Ockham and Luther in effectively destroying the myth of Deity – whereby mankind was shown to be categorically incapable of negotiating with God, or to be the initiator of Him being 'brought to earth', see D. Grant and L. Bennett Moses, *Technology and the Trajectory of Myth*, pp.36–46.

Those strategies were established as widespread and engaging for dual purposes, that is, for precluding any concern for existential reality and thereby replacing them with a range of more immediate concerns that, by claim, would be addressed by a combination of pastoral practice, assured security and an economy that would provide for material needs and aspirations, so long as one were subject. So while there is difference between the magnitudes of Deity and State, there is similarity through the accumulated layering that constitutes what is normal and in the recurring application of the mythological dynamic. This dynamic – with the 'magicalising' to which van Krieken refers – is the true heart of the emerging notion of bourgeois privacy, as that class defined itself and manufactured its rise to social and economic pre-eminence with its aspiration to be left alone for self-enhancement and as it personalised the flow of information it assembled or which was made available to it.

It will be noticed that there has been no presentation here regarding the evolution of the institutional State, especially from the dominance of the Absolute State up to the late seventeenth century – at which point the process of its engagement began until it faded as an absolute following the catastrophes of the mid-twentieth century – as that has been elaborated by the author elsewhere.[74] What will be presented in Chapter 7 is what is argued to be the modernisation of the notion of the governmental State as regulation, as that applies up to the present.

We shall now examine the next phase of the trajectory and the efforts made to internalise and so normalise market strategies in return for claims for the satisfaction of created fears and desires.

THE NORMALISING MARKET

Hayek

There is a long-standing argument that market forces, allowed to work in a manner consistent with their inherent capacities, can deliver not only a widely comfortable but also a fairer existence for the vast majority of people. That argument readily acknowledges that these forces can be uncomfortable, but that in itself is not considered to be an intrinsically negative effect as it prompts positive changes to individual behaviour.

More profoundly, for many who – like the leading neoliberal thinker Hayek – champion such arguments, the current state of the Market is the result of a long evolution which is positively traditional and should not be tampered with. It has

---

[74] This elaboration was the subject of D. Grant *The Mythological State and Its Empire*, where the arguments for the evolution of the State form – from absolutism through the various phases that realised what is known as the democratic State form – was presented through an examination of the political tradition from Hobbes through Locke, Montesquieu, Rousseau, Kant, Rawls, Hayek, Pettit, Foucault and Elias.

served society well and is to be highly valued. These arrangements are best seen as *rules of just conduct* which bring order to society, which properly determine our ethical code, which are practiced by a few and imitated by many and are guided not by reason but by success. In fact, all progress must be sought on the basis of such tradition, which must not be tampered with through reason or by government.[75] These rules of just conduct, conceived by Hayek in response to the Fascism that overran Europe in the 1930s and 1940s – which in effect revealed the flaws in the myth of the State and led to the emergence of the absolute Market as a replacement myth[76] – are also the rules of the 'spontaneous' Market, which optimises knowledge and choice.[77] This eschews any imposition of social or distributive justice responsibilities on Market forces, as that limits the freedoms of an Open Society, in fact, contains the seeds of totalitarianism.[78] The hardness of this freedom can be ameliorated by a minimal level of provision of resources by government.[79]

Regarding the operation of the market system, Hayek is clear:

> The best way to understand how the operation of the market system leads not only to the creation of an order, but also to a great increase of the return which men receive from their efforts, is to think of it ... as a game which we may now call a game of catallaxy. It is a wealth-creating game (and not what game theory calls a zero-sum game), that is, one that leads to an increase in the stream of goods and of the prospects of all participants to satisfy their needs, but which retains the character of a game in the sense in which the term is defined by the *Oxford English Dictionary*: 'a contest played according to rules and decided by superior skill, strength or good fortune ... the outcome of this game for each will, because of its very character, necessarily be determined by a mix of skill and chance.[80]

And regarding the most important matter of prices and wages:

> [T]he importance of the functioning of the market order on particular prices or wages, and therefore of the incomes of the different groups and individuals, is not due chiefly to the effects of the prices on all of those who receive them, but to the effects of the prices on those for whom they act as signals to change the direction of their efforts. Their function is not so much to reward people for what they *have* done as to tell them what in their own as well as in general interest they *ought* to do ... it will often be necessary that the return of people's efforts do [sic] *not* correspond to recognizable merit.[81]

---

[75] F. A. von Hayek *Law, Legislation and Liberty* (Routledge, 1982), s. III pp.166–167.

[76] For an account by the author of this transition from State to Market, see D. Grant, *The Mythological State and Its Empire*, pp.158–163, and D. Grant and L. Bennett Moses, *Technology and the Trajectory of Myth*, pp.53–58.

[77] F. A. von Hayek, *Law, Legislation and Liberty*,s. II pp.8–11.

[78] Ibid. s. II pp.67–70.

[79] Ibid. s. II pp.87–88.

[80] Ibid. s. II p.115.

[81] Ibid. s. II pp.71–72.

The Normalising Market

He continues in a manner which elaborates the meaning of *'just'* by which these 'rules of *just* conduct'[82] are comprised:

> Men can be allowed to act on their own knowledge and for their own purposes only if the reward they obtain is dependent in part on circumstances which they can neither control nor foresee. And if they are allowed to be guided in their actions by their own moral beliefs, it cannot also be morally required that the aggregate effects of their respective actions on different people should correspond to some ideal of distributive justice. In this sense freedom is inseparable from rewards which often have no connection with merit and are therefore felt to be unjust.[83]

For him, benefit is derived from the individualism of strictly personal interest as shown by Adam Smith's 'invisible hand', which is akin to the outcome of evolution 'whose results nobody foresaw or designed'[84] and '[the successful entrepreneur] is led to benefit more people by aiming at the largest gain than he could if he concentrated on the satisfaction of the needs of known persons. He is led by the invisible hand.'[85]

However, there are other perspectives of these same themes.[86] Understanding that the market moved away from the eighteenth-century principles of liberalism to those of neoliberalism in the 1930s as championed by various economists including Hayek, Foucault saw this as a complete reversal:

> In other words, instead of accepting a free market defined by the state and kept as it were under State supervision – which was, in a way, the initial formula of liberalism: let us establish a space of economic freedom and let us circumscribe it by a state that will supervise it – the ordoliberals say we should completely turn the formula around and adopt the free market as organising and regulating principle of the State, from the start of its existence up to the last form of its interventions. In other words: a state under supervision of the market rather than a market supervised by the state.[87]

On the topics relating to principles of justice, he sees different consequences:

> Invisibility is absolutely indispensable. It is an invisibility which means that no economic agent should or can pursue the collective good.... This is what Adam Smith says when he writes: the common interest requires that each knows how to

---

[82] Ibid. s. II p.21.

[83] Ibid. s. II p.120.

[84] Ibid. s. I p.37.

[85] Ibid. s. II p.145. One needs to remember, however – as Picketty observed – that '[Smith] never really considered the possibility that the distribution of wealth might grow more uneven over the long run'; see T. Picketty, *Capital* (Belknap, 2014), p.579 at n.2.

[86] The author has given accounts of the nature and significance of Hayek's thought in *The Mythological State and Its Empire*, pp.146–166, and in D. Grant and L. Bennett Moses, *Technology and the Trajectory of Myth*, pp.53–57.

[87] M. Foucault, *The Birth of Biopolitics* (Palgrave, 2008), p.116.

interpret his own interest and is able to pursue it without obstruction. In other words, power, government, must not obstruct the interplay of individual interests.[88]

And seeing in this an unbridgeable gap between the economy and governing:

I think it is an important moment when political economy is able to present itself as a critique of governmental reason.[89]
... Juridical theory is unable to take on and resolve the question of how to govern in a space of sovereignty inhabited by economic subjects, since precisely ... the juridical theory of the subject of right, of natural rights, and of the granting and delegation of rights does not fit together and cannot be fitted together with the mechanical idea, the very designation and characterization of *homo oeconomicus*. Consequently, neither the market in itself ... nor the juridical notion of the contract can define and delimit in what respects and how the economic men inhabiting the field of sovereignty are governable.[90]

The Market, the Consumer and Marketing

What these differing perspectives on the nature of the Market raise is not only its place within the institutional environment but what this question indicates about the relationship between the individual subject, say, as consumer, Market forces and the methods by which these are brought together, for example, through marketing for consumption. We will take the notion of consumption forward in this part of the broad argument as a touchstone for the nature of the Market.

Referring to the work of Gary Becker, Foucault proposes that neoliberal thinkers have redefined what is to be *homo oeconomicus*, that is, a person who is no longer a partner of exchange for the purpose of consumption but an entrepreneur, a producer (not consumer) of their own satisfaction who utilises whatever capital is at their disposal for that purpose.[91] This is a complete revision by the neoliberals of the notions of consumption and the consumer, who is now claimed to be a creator as much as a standard consumer of products offered to them. In these terms, government must in no way obstruct but must facilitate such 'creative' consumption and must promote the idea of this new status for *Homo oeconomicus*.

Further, the marketing process is no longer merely in the hands of the producer and/or marketer of what is understood to be desired but is to be restructured to deliver what it is that the citizen with this new status desires. In fact, beyond this, the individual – with their property, capital, family, insurance and retirement – is now claimed to be an enterprise[92] in itself, thereby fully embedded in the neoliberal

---

[88] Ibid. p.280.
[89] Ibid. p.283.
[90] Ibid. p.294.
[91] Ibid. p.226.
[92] Ibid. p.241.

economy. An important implication of this is that *homo oeconomicus* has the authority to function as analyst and critic of non-economic domains.[93] This is thereby the basis upon which the economic grid can challenge governmental action on any economic ground: it has become a permanent political criticism of government.[94]

Freedom Is Claimed by Neoliberalism

This neoliberal view of the Market and the citizen as *homo oeconomicus* is clearly attempting to claim that, given the establishment of the Market with neoliberal features, the desires that such citizens want fulfilled – within agreed limits of law – will be satisfied. This is a claim for a particularly strong framework of liberal freedom. The question is whether this claim is valid.

There are arguments to the contrary. At the softer end of these criticisms are those – like John and Nicholas O' Shaughnessy – who argue that, although the hedonistic lifestyle has increased – irrespective of the persistence of guilt – and this reflects a value system that has become somewhat more self-centred, marketing has been more the facilitator than the creator of more widespread desires. That is, wants are not necessarily easy to create and many emerge from pre-existing dispositions. In short, consumer marketing should be seen more as value-neutral in itself than it has been seen and also as available to a wide cross-section of market interests, for example, regarding both sides of the debate regarding tobacco usage.[95]

However, others have taken a stronger line regarding the nature of the consumer– market nexus in that they attempt to address questions about the deeper causal factors of that nexus. For Csikszentmihalyi, the preferred approach to understanding consumerism is to see it in existential terms. Referring first back to Maslow's hierarchy of human needs, he reminds us that survival needs are usually attended to before the need for loving and belonging and then esteem and self-actualisation. However, he then argues that measuring the value of consumer behaviour in terms of how various choices may satisfy basic existential needs may not be satisfied by applying Maslow's model.[96] Instead, he prefers a slight shift of focus towards what he calls 'experiential' needs, whereby one may distinguish between such meaningful activities as, on the one hand, teaching, craft, cooking, athletics, music, dance, gardening and art and, on the other, shopping and surrounding oneself with possessions. The latter, which are relatively easy ways to forestall the dread of non-

---

[93] Ibid. p.243.
[94] Ibid. p.246.
[95] J. O'Shaughnessy and N. O'Shaughnessy, 'Marketing, the consumer society and hedonism', *European Journal of Marketing* 36:5–6 (2002): pp.544–545.
[96] M Csikszentmihalyi, 'The costs and benefits of consuming', *Journal of Consumer Research* 27:2 (2000): p.269.

being, contribute little to a positive experience. Research already shows that excessive concern with financial success is associated with lower levels of life satisfaction and self-esteem: this is the contingent worth of *having* not *being*.[97]

Csikszentmihalyi is, in the argument of the present work, close to a valid analysis of consumerism. That is, we might well say that, if placed within a mythological context – if consumerism were understood as the willing subjection of the consumer to the Market magnitude to 'distance' existential concerns, induced by the 'claims' of the dominant Market interests – then, due to the inherent failure of the mythological model to ultimately satisfy in any of the serial guises of the trajectory, the 'pointlessness' to which he refers is fully comprehensible. That is, what is lacking in his account is the coherence of an overall intellectual framework that provides a rationale for his various insightful points of argument, especially as they relate to the existential question.

A similar problem – although its themes give even more emphasis to the existential question – comes in Mary Wrenn's analysis of fear and neoliberalism.[98] Wrenn has existential anxiety as a principal reference point in her argument that, when citizens experience the fear that comes from disorder, most consider it best to stick to 'the devil one knows', even if that is a neoliberal market order that breeds anxiety due to its socially fragmenting impact. She also perceptively attributes that response to an individual's set of personal ideologies – as mental models – explained as system justification theory, and observes that we should not attempt to eliminate fear as it inspires and humanises us. But what she does not do is connect quite enough of the dots, so to speak. The relationship between fear, existential anxiety and ontological insecurity is unclear, in that fear and ontological insecurity are both referred to existential anxiety but not to each other. Further, religion and science-technology are referred to but they do not appear to be afforded similar status to the State or the Market (neoliberal or not). Nor is there any systematic relationship between them presented, other than as 'institutions' or 'social constructs'.

Further, there is no mention in Wrenn that the Market, now in its neoliberal form, is a mental model or an ideology of the kind to which she refers nor what other mental models might be in 'system justification theory', although included among these ideologies are the Protestant work ethic, meritocratic ideology, fair market ideology and economic system justification. Also, alienation is argued to having increased unusually in the industrial and post-industrial worlds, especially in the 'dislocating' neoliberal environment, but there is no serious consideration of the waves of seriously dislocating alienation which accompanied the breakdown of the unitary Christian Church in the early sixteenth century or the deep and

---

[97] Ibid. pp.270–271.
[98] M. Wrenn, 'The social ontology of fear and neoliberalism', *Review of Social Economy* 72:3 (2014).

widespread psychological responses to the totalitarian political forces the twentieth century, apart from a passing reference to Nazis. Her claim that the average individual interprets efficiency as fairness and thus is convinced of the ultimate fairness of the market economy seems highly questionable. In addition, little is made of the place that consumerism – which is central to the notion of neoliberalism that is the main focus of her argument – occupies within neoliberalism. Finally, and most importantly, there is almost no consideration of desire, the inextricable other side of fear, as a motivator of subjection to market forces.

The point is that the many perceptive points made by Wrenn bring the elements of her arguments close to a coherent and valuable whole. What is lacking is the identification of a dynamic which drives the relationships between them all and which would eliminate some of the inconsistencies therein. Such a dynamic not only would place the Market more strongly in a broader context – and so clarify its nature even more clearly – but would allow a proper exploration of the relationship between the neoliberal Market and the citizen as consumer, especially as that is revealed by desire as much as by fear.

A Different Understanding of the Consumer

These shortcomings could be addressed, without in any way denying the value of these existential issues, if we extended the field of understanding of the impact of the market on the citizen-consumer through a disciplinary analysis within the modern mythological model. That reveals an account of the market–consumer relationship which emphasises not neoliberal self-determination but the manufacture of desire, as well as the normalisation and internalisation of market attitudes and behaviour. Thereby, this internalisation – the space of self-monitoring and self-creation – is anathema to prevailing theories of privacy as being left alone for self-enhancement. Also, the flow of information on which this internalisation is based is selective in the sense of it being externally generated for surveillance and management by market forces. Information is again freely available but for purposes of subjection. This would see the private world of the consumer operating as a field for the dominant interests of the Market magnitude, a magnitude to which we subject ourselves due to the promises of self-fulfilment and self-control but which, because of that subjection, is incapable of delivering self-determination.

The micro-physics of disciplinary power thus shows that neoliberalism, far from delivering self-determination, elaborately constructs the citizen as consumer – through monitoring, using the assembling information to categorise the citizen and to pursue a strategy of correction against the preferred norms – in a manner that seeks to prescribe individual attitudes and behaviour and in detail. In this, market research is not neutral or value-free or liberating but is intended to gather information to profile individuals so that prescribed, normative messages can be promoted and adopted, thereby 'correcting' their behaviour in a manner that leads

124   *Privacy as the History of Normalisation*

to a self-control – through techniques of internalisation – to meet these prescribed ends.[99]

This is not a disciplinary system that operates only out of institutions but also works across the social field. It characterises the relations between individuals, groups and institutions and the discourses that connect them, thereby constituting 'truth' as it circulates. Its replacement of sovereign power – which emanated from the institutions of Church and State – with the developments of the Industrial Revolution[100] was ironic. This irony is due to the willingness of individuals to become subject to disciplinary power which still operates as regulation under the camouflage of the mythological remnants of those magnitudes, along with those of the Market itself and now Technology on behalf of the idea of the Absolute Self, an idea that features so strongly in neoliberalism via the individual as entrepreneur. Market research does not simply reflect the facts of individual behaviour but constitutes, conditions, affects, alters, influences, implicates, distorts and redirects what it claims to represent.[101] Unlike the remnants of sovereign power that camouflage it, this power is ingrained and so largely invisible. It is 'regulatory' power and it is subjecting.

The outcome is that the frame of reality of the individual is 'normalised' and she is re-formed as consumer-citizen. Market research – by accessing social media, online purchasing, GPS, Wi-Fi, loan applications, banking and credit details, email, medical and taxation records and so on – identifies people in stereotypical categories, so they may be measured and corrected against the governmental and marketing norms, in relation to which they are constantly monitored via this continuous information collection. The aim is to make these processes internalised in the citizen so that external control is replaced by self-control. None of this is to say there can be – and is not – resistance but the processes of internalised, normalised attitudes, beliefs and practices are the dominant forms against which resistances can be developed.

The actual process by which disciplinary power creates the consumer-citizen derives from this broad strategy. Contrary to the neoliberal discourse of empowerment through the exercise of free will as almost infinite choice – based on self-made preferences – power within the frame of governmentality is not a possession of consumers but formative of them through the discourses and practices they are urged to adopt.[102] The themes of normative individualisation – as subjectification – and internalisation are as much features of the disciplined consumer – through branding, targeted advertising, feedback and promotion – as in other applications of

---

[99] D. Marsden, 'Disciplinary power and consumer research: An introduction', *European Advances in Consumer Research* 5 (2001): pp.54–55.

[100] Ibid. p.55.

[101] Ibid. p.58.

[102] A. Shankar et al., 'Consumer empowerment: A Foucauldian interpretation', *European Journal of Marketing* 40:9–10 (2006): pp.1013–1030.

The Normalising Market

governmentality. Here the adoption of consumer self-control through choice – but which fulfil dominant discourses of self-creation or technology of the self – is the aim. For the Market, the discourse sees disciplined individuals as 'consumers', while the other magnitudes see them as 'faithful' or 'democratic' or 'digitised'.

One advantage of this account of the individual as micro-disciplined is that it does not only allow the point that neoliberal arguments have turned out to be failures, as many studies have shown that increased consumption has not led to the increased happiness as promised by dominant interests. It also offers an explanation. That is, that the mythological dynamic – which is flawed in itself as we have seen in the contradiction of absolutism and sympathy – is bound to repeat that sense of failure exhibited by the predecessor magnitudes of Deity and State and will be repeated with Technology in the form of the Absolute Self.

Consumerism as Debt to the Market

One of the key elements in the modern transformation of the consumer has been changes to the nature of debt in the form of credit. As Trentmann observes, debt and credit have a long history, but after 1900 they evolved into something qualitatively and quantitatively new. Consumer credit underwent a revolution as dramatic as the revolution on the industrialisation that made cheap, mass-produced articles available. Growth in consumption went hand in hand with growth in production. New forms of credit arrived in waves, starting with instalment plans and mortgages, then store cards and personal loans and, most recently, adding credit cards and equity withdrawal. By 2007, total household debt as a share of gross disposable income stood at 180 per cent in the United Kingdom, 140 per cent in the United States, 130 per cent in Japan and 96 per cent in France and Germany.[103]

This new regime gave people a chance to accumulate goods and 'move up in the world'. Instead of it being a character defect – lack of prudence regarding planning for the future – this became a sign of virtue, a wise investment in wealth and future happiness. At the forefront was the bourgeoisie: they traditionally saw the poor as feckless and the rich as wasteful, while they presented as productive. But now – at least in the United States – they regarded credit as a sign of both personal comfort and the national interest.'[104] For champions like the economist Seligman, freedom of credit and freedom of choice were two sides of the same coin. The United Kingdom parliament in the 1970s expressed the view that 'It remains a basic tenet of a free society that people themselves must be the judge of what contributes to their material welfare.'[105]

---

[103] F. Trentmann, *Empire of Things*, p.409.
[104] Ibid. p.412.
[105] Ibid. p.420.

126   *Privacy as the History of Normalisation*

In this context of reducing savings, the bourgeoisie invested more heavily in the stock market, the mortgage took the place of the savings account and credit cards reached the poor: consumer credit grew fast. In fact, due to rising incomes and market deregulation, there was a strong incentive to enlist increasing numbers of customers. In the United Kingdom, the number of people with credit facilities tripled between the mid-1970s and the mid-1990s, the icon of this evolutionary burst being the credit card.[106] This commitment to debt increased further into the 2000s through the introduction of second mortgages and home-equity withdrawal, especially for education and basic living expenses, with bankruptcies rising due to fragile living arrangements (unemployment, low income, ill-health and divorce) exacerbated by growing class inequality.[107]

What is particularly interesting in Trentmann's account is how successfully most have mastered the rising debt. Although commentators in 1900, and still many recently, have predicted moral corruption, social decay and bankruptcy from rising debt due to the spread of credit availability,

> By and large, people have proved their moral critics wrong.... Credit has oriented consumers towards the prospect of ownership. Paying the monthly mortgage or an instalment on a product focused the mind. The number at the mercy of loan sharks ... is much smaller today than it was a century ago. Yet the few who ... have been pushed off the escalator of credit, being excluded from regular credit is much harder now, because so many features of life today depend on a decent credit rating. Here is one of the first signs of polarization characteristic of contemporary consumer culture.[108]

This reveals several points. First, people have generally embedded themselves well into the market as consumers, beyond the individual acts of buying, and take pride in satisfying the expectations of them. Second, people feel better off in this arrangement than before. Third, a new polarisation has emerged from the manner in which debt as credit has both internalised and normalised itself as a fully acceptable discourse of ideas and practice for citizen-consumers. We shall return to the manner in which the flow of information in this regime has occupied the psychological space of the consumer and how those two elements do not adequately account for what is expected of the notion of privacy.

This theme of embedding has been pursued further, revealing the features of the normalisation of credit/debt as fully credentialled cultural phenomena, especially for the bourgeoisie. Among such studies is that by Penanzola and Barnhart.[109] The premise of this research is that, at least for the bourgeoisie, credit/debt is typically

---

[106] Ibid. p.423.
[107] Ibid. pp.431, 438.
[108] Ibid. pp.439, 440.
[109] L. Penalzola and M. Barnhart, 'Living U.S. capitalism: The normalization of credit/debt', *Journal of Consumer Research* 38 (2011): pp.743–762.

The Normalising Market 127

and necessarily a fact of life: the themes that the research uncovered point to its normalisation within US culture.[110] Reinforcing this, they also observed that market agents, realising that the achievement of viable credit scores is fundamentally important to socio-economic position and especially for the aspirational bourgeoisie, actively incentivise this normalisation.

However, when it comes to an explanatory framework for this – especially bourgeois – behaviour, the result is somewhat thin. For Penanzola and Barnhart, due to a tradition of 'abundance' in the United States, there is 'a relatively high level of consumption diffused across the middle classes as a matter of national policy through the latter part of the twentieth century, becoming a matter of national pride'.[111] Looking back further, they trace the results of their research to Weber's claim for the Protestant work ethic. More immediately, what they see is that 'Against a social backdrop of friends, family and neighbours with larger houses and cars and sons and daughters attending prestigious universities, it becomes more difficult, indeed old-fashioned and out of sync, not to leverage credit/debt as a normative activity to consume at higher levels now, and to generate future wealth, even as doing so has constrained some informants and left others with upside down mortgages.'[112]

As is clear by now, there is a more interesting – and more explanatory and predictive – account available in the operation of the mythological dynamic, even if there is reference in their work to such of its elements as willing subjection to the market due to the claims of its dominant interests, as well as in the notions of normalisation and subjectification. In the context of the argument of the present work, neoliberalism is little more than a mythological strategy. That is, there is in this world of consumerism, inextricably connected to the field of debt, no room for the consumer considering – let alone dealing with – a frame of existential concerns. There is only the distancing of it and its camouflage behind a veil of normalising, constructed, secondary desires to avoid another field of such secondary, constructed fears as poverty or loss of prestige. Both Csikszentmihalyi and Wrenn come close to understanding these forces but fall short through the lack of an appreciation of the kind of dynamic that a modern mythological analysis provides. Regarding privacy, it is clear that this analysis strongly foreshortens any claim that the two current, dominant theories can make to being valid. A claim for constitutional rights based on being left alone for the purposes of self-enhancement or on a management of the flow of information that will more fairly and more comprehensively represent the interests of the citizen is indefensible against the claims of agents of the Market to despatch existential concerns and deal conclusively with constructed fears and desires, so long as the individual is subject to the inducements and micro-discipline of the Market regime. We see that strongly in the case of the modern bourgeoisie.

---

[110] Ibid. p.757.
[111] Ibid. p.758.
[112] Ibid. p.759.

128 *Privacy as the History of Normalisation*

NORMALISING TECHNOLOGY

There are three reference points to put the argument that, as with its predecessor magnitudes, Technology – as the means by which dominant interests increasingly promote the idea of the Absolute Self – is in fact a field of subjectification and normalisation, not of liberation or self-enhancement. The first is the Heideggerean notion of authentic existence. The second is the further exploration of the account of algorithms given in Chapter 2 and relates to the associated notion of normalisation. The third, which further extends the latter point, is founded on the notion of technologies of the self, a notion allied to internalisation and subjectification.

Heideggerean Authenticity

For Heidegger, technology is anathema to personal authenticity. This derives in the first instance from his argument that what we know of technology is distinct from its essence, which is 'enframing'. Mankind has been drawn into perceiving nature as exclusively to be unlocked, transformed, stored and distributed.[113] As a 'standing reserve', we can always 'set upon it' as it is always at our disposal. Enframing blocks the kind of revealing which allows us to understand the truth of nature[114] and engage with it authentically: through enframing, objects lose their character as objects[115] and we see them only as opportunities for our use.

Techne, which was the original Greek revealing of truth and belonged to *poiesis* as the bringing of something into presence as 'unconcealment', was lost with the emergence of modern technology and modern science.[116] This inception – which he attributes to Descartes – was conceived at its very beginning as the means to 'order' nature to be at our disposal.[117] Importantly for Heidegger, it was by this transformation of how we perceive nature that we became at risk of ourselves becoming a standing reserve and so subject to Technology. This is because our way of revealing creates a veil that covers what comes to presence in truth[118] and through this we are continually approaching the possibility that our way of revealing is this ordering of nature, including ourselves. So nowhere do we encounter our own essence.[119] Technology tends towards such a totalising effect. This is the loss of authenticity – the loss of access to *Dasein* as full Being or existence of each

---

[113] M. Heidegger, *The Question Concerning Technology* (Harper, 1977), p.4. For a wider account by the author of the thought of Heidegger on technology in the mythological context, see D. Grant and L. Bennett Moses, *Technology and the Trajectory of Myth*, pp.117–122.

[114] M. Heidegger, *The Question Concerning Technology*, p.127.

[115] Ibid. p.17.

[116] Ibid. p.14.

[117] R. Descartes, *Discourse on Method* (1637; Penguin, 2003), p.144.

[118] Heidegger, *Question Concerning Technology*, p.25.

[119] Ibid. p.27.

Normalising Technology

individual in the world[120] – and technology is the means. Being oneself authentically is the capacity to exhibit 'care'.[121] Care includes – as *sorge* – the anxiety to provide for oneself. This 'self' is not the egotistical Cartesian 'I' but an integrated self as body, soul and spirit and by which we pull ourselves together into self-constancy[122] and avoid dispersal into the THEY-self where we are induced to do the homogenising bidding of others.[123] So every Dasein has an inner voice calling to authenticity and self-fulfilment.[124]

For the broad argument in this work, such authenticity may be read as 'respectful responsibility to and for oneself'. It is also founded by Heidegger on existential conditions of *angst*, whereby – through stripping the world of its significance – the absolutism of being-in-the-world of Dasein is revealed. Here there is no specific harm but there is the sense that we are not at home in the world, and it is this which causes us to flee and fall into a familiar, intraworldly condition. In such a fallen state, we experience – derivative – fear about things in this now-familiar world:[125] the tranquilised self-assurance of the – one can say mythologised – They-world.[126]

Heidegger does of course suffer properly from how he saw the politics of his time but he saw it as providing a means of disrupting this – mythological – condition so that Dasein may thereby be revealed and made accessible. In this dismantling of inauthenticity he returns to Descartes, urging not separation but embedding ourselves in the world: we should not focus on the *cogito* in the Cartesian *cogito ergo sum* but more on the *sum*. The *cogito* has led mankind to go beyond that condition, no longer constrained by any gulf between it and the world of objects, which are thereby all at an individual's disposal. This includes other people, who disappear as subjects in a comprehensible usability, and humanity itself is simply a resource.[127] More significantly, existence in a world in which we do not feel embedded and in which we decide the nature of objects in a totalised environment provides what is argued in the present work to be an Absolute Self, that is, separate from the world but claimed to be in control of it. This as the ultimate purpose of mythological Technology, irrespective of the inauthenticity. We can see its potential in the technologies canvassed in Chapter 2 and those to which we will refer as the fourth reference point below.

Algorithmic Normalisation

The argument was put in Chapter 2 that algorithms should not be seen as value-free data collectors and analysers but should be understood as technological means by

---

[120] M. Heidegger, 'Introduction to Philosophy', in *Complete Works* (Vittorio Klostermann, 1989), vol.27, p.136.

[121] M. Heidegger, *Being and Time* (Blackwell, 1962), p.322.

[122] Ibid. p.369.

[123] Ibid. pp.223, 299.

[124] Ibid. pp.26–28, 32.

[125] Ibid. pp.179–182, 233.

[126] Ibid. pp.233, 321–322, 333.

[127] M. Heidegger, *Nietzsche* (Harper and Row, 1991), vol. 3, p.180, and vol. 4, p.244.

which data are first 'created', following which perceptions of reality are coded and charged with creating then assembling data relevant to such perceptions. This is effectively the imposition of a world view in each case. It is not so much a problem with the search for data to relieve medical conditions – where there is a greater level of agreement as to what the problem and so the data is – but the difference between rehabilitation and enhancement is still blurred, and this is especially a problem when the design of both data and algorithm exercises a much freer range.

We shall now examine three further features of predictive algorithms that point to this problem. This will include reference to predicting the behaviour of subjects, controlling such behaviour and promoting personal enhancement. In this, to show the continuity that can rest within shifting frameworks, we shall maintain a focus on the Market (consumerism as it is effected by digitisation) and the State (algorithmic prediction of behaviour).

There is a strong argument that predictive algorithms have the capacity to discipline individual behaviour through its processes of surveillance and subjection to specific regimes of – at one end of the spectrum – training and – at the other end – promotion and suggestion. This can be seen as an extension of Foucault's account of this process, although such an extension needs to recognise that the processes of modern machine learning (ML) have incorporated more varied techniques, so that its outcomes are more general than those that Foucault saw in the disciplinary institutions which he examined.[128] Such differences include that causation (for example, of crime) was the key to the imposition of a regime of training that normalised – it worked *backwards* from the alleged crime to causation – but in ML the data gathered is not triggered by an event of misconduct, merely the possibility of one: the data looks *forward*. The misconduct has to be corrected before it occurs or the circumstances (in another example, providing a loan that data indicate may not be repaid) must be avoided (the loan is not approved, though there is no misconduct). Governance is now of risk: it causes the individual to imagine (since, continuing the example, typically no reason for the denial of loan decisions is given) what might have been the reasons and to adjust their behaviour accordingly (say, cancelling their credit cards). In predictive disciplining, centred on the mind, one only knows that one has failed, not why or even what data has been collected to reach the decision to deny. This is both individuation and internalisation.

But prediction has gone well beyond facilitating such enforced compliance. There is a substantial corporate and research capacity set up – drawing on the nexus of connected devices and data – to predict and shape the interests and wants, especially of the bourgeoisie. This relies on well-established data that social class is a predictor of consumption and identifiable through information management and

---

[128] P. de Laat, 'The disciplinary power of predictive algorithms: A Foucauldian perspective', *Ethics and Information Technology* 4 (2019): pp.325–326.

Normalising Technology 131

the persuasive advertising messages that can flow from that.[129] The *Harvard Business Review* reported as early as 2016:[130]

> Responsive retail has peaked, and we're about to enter an era of predictive commerce. It's time for retailers to help people find products in their precise moment of need – and perhaps before they even perceive that need – whether or not they're logged in or ready to click a 'buy' button on a screen. This shift will require designing experiences that merge an understanding of human behaviour with large-scale automation and data integration.
>
> ... Predictive retail involves inspiring consumers in different contexts – before, during and after a purchase. Commerce is already becoming less of a deliberative activity than an organic part of how we experience daily life.

Regarding privacy,

> There's almost always some trade-off between privacy and personalisation.... Many of us are inclined to share personal information for experiences that are magical and valuable ... Retailers will need to create experiences that make this magic and value happen.

This not only emphasises the creation of wants as desires and the threat to the privacy of personal information but also recognises that magic – one may properly say 'mythology' – is a key part of accepting that threat, that is, the subjection to the commercial regime and the associated forgoing of control over personal information in return for claims by dominant Market interests about a magical experience.

The point of this emphasis on the revolution in marketing for consumption, and that it is focused on the bourgeoisie, is that it has long been they who are the engine of consumption. One can see this most starkly in the massive class shifts occurring in emerging economies. In fact, already by 2016: 'The rapidly growing middle class of consumers in emerging nations, including Argentina, Brazil, Chile, China, Columbia, Egypt, India, Indonesia, Russia and Mexico numbers almost two billion people spending a total of $6.9 trillion annually. About 70% of consumption is contributed by the middle class category (15% upper middle, 32% middle and 23% lower middle).'[131]

Insurance is a further indicator of the trend in predictive AI and its relation to the bourgeoisie. The American Medical Association has reported on the link between lower socio-economic status and the increased risk of premature death.[132] Access to

---

[129] S. Shavitt, 'Stratification and segmentation: Social class in consumer behaviour', *Journal of Consumer Psychology* 26:4 (2016): pp.583–588.

[130] A. Sharma, 'How predictive AI will change shopping', *Harvard Business Review* (18 November 2016).

[131] M. Ahmed et al., 'Income, social class and consumer behaviour', *International Journal of Applied Business and Economic Research* (October 2016): p.6683.

[132] K. Fox, 'Social epidemiology: How socio-economic risk factors become health realities', *AMA Journal of Ethics* (November 2006).

quality health care varies by socio-economic status: more than 60 per cent of the uninsured are low-income families and those who lack insurance receive less medical care.[133] This is significant because the insurance industry has moved to the use of predictive AI analytics[134] as a means of assessing and minimising risk. This will clearly benefit the bourgeoisie, especially as they become aware of the evolving information that determines insurance decisions.

All this amounts to both normalisation and subjectification of preferred behaviour by the colonising of one's psychological space, a colonisation that contradicts modern notions of privacy of being let alone for self-enhancement or information flow that benefits the citizen: information is now largely for the purpose of subjection. This is thereby not a value-free gathering of data but the selection of data and the application of the values of the designer of the algorithm – without any prior discussion or post-factum sharing of information with the subject, so the information flow is so selective as to be virtually non-existent – and the consequential imposition of these values on individual behaviour. Making this information flow more transparent and comprehensive may allow other questions to be raised but it would not materially change the strategy of inequitable risk minimisation by the insurance corporates.

This effect of the application of predictive algorithms is not limited to the operation of the Market but is an increasingly common feature of the State as well. It can – or will be able to – deploy such algorithms across its functions, from anti-terrorist strategies to tax fraud to traffic control to political protest to health and education demands – all based on individual data that will be available to governments. Resistance will in part determine the extent of this, but governments will retain the high hand in this interplay, given their responsibility to protect and provide services. But it is in regard to marginal groups that the impact of the application of predictive algorithms is clearest, thereby in effect favouring the bourgeoisie over the poor, the disabled and racial minorities.[135] Valentine makes several points which themselves have wider significance. She argues that predictive algorithms introduce biases against subjects in both the criminal justice and social welfare systems and that this is intentional on the part of governments, despite the human rights implications. Such intentions are based not only on the claimed increased efficiencies of such processes – decision-making becomes more straightforward – but also on the claim that the application of the knowledge that results is a tool in itself for pre-emptive intervention into and control of the lives of such subjects.

---

[133] N. Adler and K. Newman, 'Socioeconomic disparities in health: Pathways and policies', *Health Affairs* (March–April 2002).

[134] N. Boodhun, 'Risk prediction in life insurance industry using supervised learning algorithms', *Complex and Intelligent Systems* 4:2 (2018) : see at 'Description of Data Set'.

[135] S. Valentine, 'Impoverished algorithms: Misguided governments, flawed technologies and social control', *Fordham Urban Law Journal* 46:2 (2019): article 4.

An argument which extends the negative reaction to such intentions is that such a process de-personalises and de-subjectifies[136] due to the loss of personal narratives that results. One might make the different point that all that is happening here is that one narrative – a personal one – is being replaced by another, which is the application of that constructed opaquely on the basis of the algorithmic formula. Like all narratives, over time and with constant force of the interaction with governmentalising practices, such alternative narratives tend to become embedded within the psychological space of the individual subject. This goes beyond management of risk to the manner in which there is normalisation and internalisation, this time through the imposition of the value system of control and self-redefinition housed within the predictive algorithmic framework.

Finally, questions need to be asked in relation to another emerging use of algorithms, that is, whether there is a clear distinction between rehabilitative and enhancement therapies, whether there is a blurred line between these or whether they exist on a continuum. If there is a clear distinction between them, further questions then follow regarding the distinction between apparently transparent rehabilitative therapies and those which are for enhancement, where the impact may not be transparent. We have seen that, for Heidegger, technology is inherently contrary to authenticity and so not transparent. We have also seen that, in examining Foucault, the practices of governmentality – whether by the State or the Market, including through the application of technology – are intended to expose individuals to regimes of subjection. All these questions are directly relevant to whether the algorithmic design of such therapies is set up to impose an alternative sense of reality and thereby to normalise and subjectivise in those terms. These questions point, in the end, to the function of these alternative data and algorithmic designs regarding current notions of privacy: How can there be privacy with the imposition of non-transparent algorithmic enhancements?

Consideration has been given to the relevance of Heidegger and Foucault in respect of this question of enhancement.[137] Pariseau-Legault sees enhancement, broadly, as augmenting an individual's psychological, physical or cognitive abilities through drugs, implantable electronic devices or genetic therapies. He recommends that the proper approach is to be guided by Heidegger's understanding of technology and by Foucauldian notions of power and subjectivation as a way of understanding the conditions of this new discourse of human enhancement. 'The enhanced subject is a new form of subjectivity (re)constructed through new power relations whose neoliberal orientation cannot be denied.'[138] Human enhancement is thereby a new discursive formation intimately tied to contemporary constructions of

---

[136] A. Zavrsnik, 'Algorithmic justice: Algorithms and big data in criminal justice settings', *European Journal of Criminology* (September 2019).

[137] P. Pariseau-Legault, 'Understanding human enhancement technologies through critical phenomenology', *Wiley Online* (5 October 2018), doi: 10.1111/nup.12229.

[138] Ibid. p.8.

134   *Privacy as the History of Normalisation*

selfhood. This is consistent with the broad position being put in the present work, especially regarding the impact of neuroscience, although we have begun to see that there is a way through these dilemmas which answers the questions raised by both Heidegger and Foucault. The development and application by a citizen of personalised data and algorithms, co-designed by the citizen, canvassed in Chapter 6, as a means of pursuing self-responsibility will be one part of such a strategy.

Technologies of the Self

We have referred above to the notion of self-creation – of technology of the self – as a key outcome of the Foucauldian processes of governmentality, including as it is applied to the construction of the consumer as subject to the Market. That is, repression is an inadequate explanation for such subjection. The argument of the present work is that it is better understood as a process of self-scrutinising and self-forming of the subject, usually complicitly entered into by them due to the desire to have their existential concerns set aside and the secondary, constructed desires conclusively dealt with. This is a reconception of Heideggerean loss of authenticity and in addition to the inducements of algorithmic technology.

The notion of self-creation as conceived by Foucault has continued to attract attention.[139] Drawing lessons from the Benthamite-Foucauldian notion of the Panopticon for wider and contemporary application, Manokha elaborates the notion of such a 'technology' – or techniques – as comprised of self-restraint and self-censorship, especially using that as a metaphor for the nature of modern information technology.[140] Thereby he emphasises that individuals are not only constantly surveilled but are aware of this, for example, by the digital platforms with which they constantly interact (Facebook, Google and so on). He also makes the point, significant for the argument here, that Bentham conceived the Panopticon in the context of emerging capitalism and that 'Foucault repeatedly emphasised the link between the development of Panoptic institutions and the rise of the capitalist society and the interests of the *bourgeoisie*. In this respect, the Panopticon may also be helpful in the analysis of the "technologies of the self" in the modern workplace.'[141] There are several responses to be made to this updated account of the significance of the Panopticon. First, the example of the optimal presence of surveillance in the contemporary era to which Manokha refers, that is, the Snowden revelations, was one in fact where subjects were unaware of the surveillance so were not complicit. Further, his subsequent point that becoming aware of such extensive surveillance can trigger a search for greater privacy rights may be

---

[139] I. Manokha, 'Surveillance, panopticism and self-discipline in the digital age', *Surveillance and Society* 16:2 (2018): pp.219–237.
[140] Ibid. p.221.
[141] Ibid. p.233.

correct, but it needs to be remembered that the inducements to remain 'open' are far stronger than to 'shut down' access to one's exposure. His point that the entire enterprise of surveillance was generated to promote the emergence of capitalism – and therefore of the Market – and that this was promoted especially by the bourgeoisie, is apt.

In fact, in the broad, what Manokha is doing affirms the overall point of the present chapter, that privacy is not best seen as the protection – or 'letting alone for self-enhancement' – of a personal zone or the consequence of some sense of the non-strategic selection of the flow of information. 'Privacy' is better seen as its opposite, the occupation of the psychological space of all citizens – especially including the bourgeoisie, given their pivotal role in the construction of the sense of personal space across the fields of State and Market formation.

What Manokha does not see is that the technology of the self is not only a matter of self-restraint and self-censorship. It is also – as even Foucault did not fully see – a matter of willing subjection by most individuals to these regimes. That is, it is not repression – as Foucault saw – and it is not merely Foucauldian constructivism because it is more than these. Foucault had no sense of mythology so did not see the psychological dynamic of imagining, claim, subjection and forgoing. Understanding this opens the opportunity to then see why there is the self-construction, subjectivation, internalisation and normalisation that is a reference point of the reimagined notion of privacy proposed here. Privacy is closely linked to the intrusions that would create the Absolute Self and not to any idea of being left alone for self-actualisation or controlling the flow of what passes for information in the current climate.

A Note on the Bourgeoisie

As a post-script to these observations about the nature of the self, it is worthwhile to reflect on how the bourgeoisie have featured repeatedly in both the previous and the present chapters. The reason for that is that the emergence and activities of this class have been significant at a number of levels. Their appearance as a merchant class was not only an essential element in the early stages of the formation of the State and what would become the economy, but they also took the lead in adopting and developing the notions of personal *civilitas* promoted by Erasmus and thereby the early forms of sensibility and self-fashioning as 'personality'. This may properly be described as a bourgeois form of individualism. It is unsurprising then, as Foucault points out, that this class became a particular target of Nazism, as that movement sought to destroy essential social and economic structures and create a new State form, supported by a new *Gemeinschaft*.[142]

The impact of the bourgeoisie has not only persisted in the form of political and economic activism and consumerism, in which it has been a primary target for the

---

[142] M. Foucault, *The Birth of Biopolitics*, pp.112–114.

normalising strategies of the Market in the modern era. It has also been central, by the construction of the private-public differential, to one of the two current dominant models of privacy. In fact, the bourgeoisie has been – following the beginning of the end of the myth of Deity with Scotus, Ockham and later Luther (from late fourteenth to the early sixteenth centuries) and the emergence of the early mercantilist State – not only a co-designer of that State and the Market and of its own place within them, but also a class that fully and widely experienced that environment and continues to do both. It is due to its dual functioning as creator and subject that it has over this time constructed what we still understand as privacy. This understanding remains substantially a bourgeois notion, even where it extends into claims about the importance of controlling the flow of information that welds one into the social fabric. This is the context in which we need to understand the inauthenticity[143] of the bourgeois 'heritage' sexuality, class-inspired political activism, capitalist entrepreneurship, psychological fragility, protective domesticity, cultural pleasure, exaggerated consumerism, defensive self-discipline, self-determination and as 'beneficiaries' of algorithmic technology that we have just looked at. In short, the bourgeoisie has been a co-creator and subject of mythological magnitudes of State, Market and now Technology. It is this panoply of characteristics – products of the trajectory of mythological magnitudes – that constitute current notions of privacy and that need to be disassembled for the new, viable notion to have the space to sustain itself.

Concluding Remarks

This chapter began by stating that it would be concerned with elaborating a central idea. We have attempted to do so by arguing that, rather than seeing privacy in its current formulations of being let alone to pursue our self-enhancement or by attempting to manage better the information of interest to ourselves – as outlined in Chapter 3 – there is another, wider and deeper framework within which privacy needs to be understood. That frame is the mythological trajectory, the serial elements of which have constituted the foundation of what is better understood as the concerns of privacy. Such concerns have been either willingly accepted or forced into our psychological space in a manner that is best understood as normalisation, internalisation and subjectification.

The first thing to be seen from the fields covered in this chapter is that, blatantly with the Christian Deity and through avoidance with subsequent magnitudes, existential concerns are distanced and camouflaged by secondary concerns constructed and promoted by the dominant interests of these magnitudes. Through

---

[143] For an exploration of bourgeois inauthenticity, see J. Aroosi, 'The causes of bourgeois culture: Kierkegaard's relation to Marx considered', *Philosophy and Social Criticism* 42:1 (2016); see also E. Labrousse, 'The bourgeois(ie) as concept and reality', *Semantic Scholar* (2004).

Deity we have developed a wide range of prescriptions concerning our ethical principles and our relationships of various kinds, personal and socio-economic; regarding the State, we have developed practices not only that relate us to sovereign and regulatory power that requires the prescribed disciplining and management of our lives but that have formed into an evolving habitus which created the public-private separation and also incorporate such personal practices as etiquette; regarding the Market, we are urged to see this as the place where our economic well-being and self-fulfilment can be satisfied rather than the site of micro-discipline; and regarding Technology, we are being subjected to a wide range of embedding practices which are increasingly being claimed will deliver to us unbounded capacity to resolve the widest range of fears and desires. A substantial inheritance. And one that is the framework within which we consider a range of other concerns, such as job security, financial stress and who is the major player there (typically the Market); international tensions (the relation between States); environmental degradation and who is the source of the problem (both States and Market corporations) and the solution (both, again); and the problems associated with social media (Technology) and so on.

As those constructed ideas and practices are willingly adopted or imposed on individuals, there is an accumulation of characteristics within the psychological and social space of the individual and this occupation is normalised. This is not a claim that such characteristics are the full range of what our private thoughts are comprised of – we spend much time thinking about a wide range of lesser matters, of course – but that these dominate what pre-eminently engages us. This is the methodology of distance and of camouflage. If we are to develop a new account of privacy which eschews the mythological dynamic which generated these processes, we need to start from a non-mythological position and develop an ethic which allows, promotes and defends respectful responsibility to and for oneself. That will mean a refusal to deny existential reality.

5

Privacy, Its Values and Technology

Given the impact that the predecessor mythological regimes of idea and practice have had on the foundations of our psychological and social spaces, any attempt to prevent the Technological regime from achieving the same impact would need to start by re-examining the ethical foundations upon which our relationship with technology is being built. The argument here is that a new, non-mythological frame is needed. Before doing so, it will be useful to revisit one current dominant ethical frame being applied to technology, and a response to that, by way of introducing a new frame.

The Recent Form of Floridi's Ethics

We have seen in Chapter 2 that Floridi has a strong – if distinct – ethical sense, one founded on the idea of his informational ontology and the sense that human individuals – as important elements in his infosphere – are fully comprised as their information.[1]

To appreciate what Floridi appears to be intending, it is useful to look briefly at what he considers to the future of artificial intelligence.[2] He sees this future as relying not on historical data – from the rules derived by observing behaviour – but on synthetic and hybrid data. This is data generated either by AI completely (synthetically) or with some historical data included (hybrid). He has a preference for the former. Synthesised data is achieved by abstracting rules that eliminate, mask or obfuscate some degrees of resolution from historical data. Hybrid and truly

---

[1] Floridi outlined his approach to privacy in L. Floridi, 'Four for a theory of informational privacy', *Ethics and Information Technology* 8:3 (2006): 109–119, where he rejected Western notions of individualism.

[2] L. Floridi, 'What the near future of artificial intelligence could be', *Philosophy and Technology* 32 (2019): 1–15.

Privacy, Its Values and Technology

synthetic data can be generated by either constraining or constitutive rules, these typified in gaming.[3] This will occur best by translating currently complex tasks into more easily analysable tasks by transforming the environment within which AI operates into an AI-friendly environment, for example, by a process of enveloping the environment around them[4] and by ludifying (or gaming) a problem into a 'constitutive-rule game'. The latter are design challenges. So, the future of AI will, for Floridi, depend on our ability to redesign reality and, he adds, on our ability to negotiate the resulting (and serious) ethical, legal and social issues (ELSI), from new forms of privacy to nudging and self-determination.[5]

We have already seen in Chapter 2 not only that Floridi's ontologising seeks to create an artificial ontology which will optimise the reconstruction and increasing manipulability of reality but that its Kantian overtones repeat in particular Kant's fear of the natural world that needs to be fully controlled through this abstraction and reconstruction. It is well to remember that Kant undertook this project for theological-political purposes, that is, to promote the myth of Deity by the reconstruction of the myth of the State and which subverted science for this purpose.[6] These problems are equally evident in Floridi's account of the algorithm. That is, not only does an algorithm have no purpose separate from data,[7] but, as we have just argued, the preferred data is itself fully designed and then manipulated by the designed algorithms of AI. He attributes to AI the status of interactive, autonomous and often self-learning *agency* (his emphasis).[8]

Regarding this 'algorithmic' problem, Floridi acknowledged in 2016 that a mature 'ethics of algorithms' does not yet exist.[9] It is at least arguable that this remains the case. There he expressed the view that there are six identifiable (epistemic and normative) ethical concerns raised by algorithms: inconclusive evidence leading to unjustified actions, inscrutable evidence leading to opacity, misguided evidence leading to bias, unfair outcomes leading to discrimination, transformative effects leading to challenges for autonomy, and traceability effects leading to challenges for informational privacy and lower moral responsibility. In the coverage of these issues he acknowledged inter alia that 'algorithms inevitably make biased decisions'[10] by the very process of their design and interpretation, although his view is that this is a remediable factor.

---

[3] Ibid. pp.5–7

[4] Ibid. p.11.

[5] Ibid. p.13.

[6] See my account of the Kantian State in *The Mythological State and Its Empire* (pp.100–119) and the account of the Kantian enterprise in D. Grant and L. Bennett Moses, *Technology and the Trajectory of Myth*, pp.88–98.

[7] L. Floridi, 'What the near future of artificial intelligence could be', p.3.

[8] Ibid. p.2.

[9] L. Floridi, 'The ethics of algorithms: Mapping the debate', *Big Data and Society* (July–December 2016): pp.1–21.

[10] Ibid. p.7.

140   *Privacy, Its Values and Technology*

For him, progress can be made in addressing these problems through improvements in design, for example, by 'fairness aware' data mining, personalised algorithms and smart transparency.[11] Within this context he considers the prospects and challenges of attributing moral responsibility to learning algorithms – attributing moral agency to them – due to the accountability problem and thereby considers the emerging suggestion of designing ethical principles into the operation of algorithms.[12] It might be added that in a more recent consideration of this field, especially as that relates to machine learning, the problems are no more tractable. There the author repeats the need to embed ethical consideration into the design of computational, specifically algorithmic artefacts.[13] That is, there still needs to be greater explicability, a greater focus on the individual over the collective, in addition to the need for greater usability. He concludes by stating that, unless such changes are initiated in the short term, the potential risks include that the costs of ethical mistakes outweighing the benefits of ethical successes; the undermining of public acceptance of algorithmic systems, even to the point of a backlash; and the reduction in the adoption of algorithmic systems. These are hardly trivial concerns.

Regarding the ethical, legal and social issues that he raises as being 'serious', Floridi has worked on and presented a wide-ranging strategy that he argues will cope with those problems.[14] He sees the issues as including the enabling of self-realisation, enhancing human agency, protecting human responsibility, increasing social capabilities, protecting human control, cultivating social cohesion, protecting human self-determination and so on. In doing so, he refers to a range of similar work undertaken by respected international agencies. Included in this is his reference to the Ethically Aligned Design project by the Institute of Electrical and Electronics Engineers (IEEE). We shall return to the work of that organisation, but there are problems within that account. In doing so, he promotes such principles as beneficence, non-maleficence, autonomy, justice and explicability. He then makes a series of recommendations about the kind of legal, organisational, investment, corporate and other elements of a preferred action plan – all admirable.

However, it appears that Floridi has missed the principal problem, one to which he is also a prime contributor. That is, the very move to artificially recreate and re-ontologise reality, to artificially create the basic data in a manner that enables AI to understand, interpret and manipulate it, to indicate that human individuals are only their data and so on – these are the sources of errors, biases, misinterpretations, distortions which his strategy is then intended to address. He is largely the creator of

---

[11] Ibid. pp.8–10.

[12] Ibid. p.11.

[13] J. Morley, 'From what to how: An initial review of publicly available AI tools, methods and research to translate principles into practice', *Science and Engineering Ethics* (2019), https://doi.org/10.007/s.11948-019-00165-5.

[14] L. Floridi et al., 'An ethical framework for a good AI society: Opportunities, risks, principles and recommendations', *ResearchGate* (November 2018).

Privacy, Its Values and Technology 141

the problems he is trying to solve, a characteristic displayed by the dominant interests of other magnitudes. Further, the principles that he catalogues suffer from a serious challenge, in that – although they have secondary value, as we shall now see – they do not stand on foundations solid enough to sustain them in the face of the deep and wide challenges of AI. This is especially so given what we have seen as the developments in neuroscience. His approach may make sense when we are dealing with easily agreeable data that has scientific credibility in such fields as medical therapy, but it loses value when the data is created from the social field for the purposes of explaining, predicting and manipulating human behaviour, such as is done with credit-worthiness, predictive justice, universal educational software, facial recognition, election outcomes, the value of corporations as reflected in share value, construction of consumer desires and so on. There, the construction of data for these purposes is not only untrustworthy but often destructive, both personally and socially. Social data and their interpretive algorithms have agendas.

Before moving on to give an account of the ethical frame for a new model of privacy, it is useful to place Floridi in a wider context of commentary on his thought and arguments. This will be done by briefly considering the work of Capurro, who not only has a view of AI that is at wide variance with that of Floridi but whose account, as it turns out, is well aligned with the arguments in the present work.

Capurro

There are a range of fundamental points on which Capurro disagrees with Floridi. Importantly for the argument in the present work, Capurro questions the metaphysical foundation of Floridi's entire information ecology, the status of the objects in the 'infosphere', the moral status of the so-called artificial agents and the foundation of information ethics as information ecology. Consistently, he challenges the ontological value of information as a first-order category. Positively, he proposes that we not forget the limitations of human actors and of their digital agent surrogates.[15]

He reached the conclusion that:

> What we need is then to 'de-ontologise' the 'infosphere' in order to weaken the demiurgic ambitions of Western metaphysics, including the somewhat exotic idea of creating artificial agents to whom we should be morally responsible.... We have some six billion moral agents on earth. Why should we create millions of artificial ones.

In a recent paper which undertook a retrospective view of the emergence of AI, Capurro has made a number of significant points of argument. He specifies what he sees as the important ethical issues in this field: human dignity, autonomy and

---

[15] R. Capurro, 'On Floridi's metaphysical foundation of information ecology', *Ethics and Information Technology* 10:2–3 (2008, updated 2017): pp.167–173.

responsibility, privacy, cultural diversity, inclusion, access to the labour market, the use of the precautionary principle, and the principle of transparency. We shall see that many of these are the subject of comment in the range of ethical issues to be considered shortly in this chapter.[16] In this paper, Capurro observes that 'the present casting of ourselves as *homo digitalis* opens the possibility of reifying ourselves algorithmically. The main ethical challenge for the inrolling digital age consists in unveiling the ethical difference, particularly when addressing the nature of algorithms and their ethical and legal regulation.'[17]

He also distinguishes between artificial intelligences and human beings, stating that the former might mimic a self, yet they are not a 'who' but a 'what'. Thereby regarding privacy, he states:

> The concept of privacy cannot be adequately determined without its counterpart, publicness. Privacy and publicness are not properties of things, data or persons, but rather ascriptions dependent upon the specific social and cultural context. These ascriptions relate to what a person or a self ... divulges about him- or herself. A self in turn is not a wordless, isolated subject but a human being who is and understands herself always already connected with others in a shared world. The possibility of hiding, of displaying or showing oneself off as who one is, no matter in what context and to what purpose, is in this sense as far as we know, peculiar to human beings, but precisely not as the property of a subject, but rather as a form of the interplay of a human being's life as shared with others.[18]

In summary, Capurro argues that the so-called digital enlightenment of the modern era needs itself to be enlightened. 'This enlightenment needs to be inspired by the resolution of the ambivalence of the project(s) of enlightenment coming from the social revolutions of the nineteenth century but going back to the dialectics between mythology and science that characterise European Enlightenment, particularly in the eighteenth century. Enlightenment must take care of this ambivalence that might revert digital enlightenment into digital mythology.'[19] The resonance with some key elements of the wide argument being put forward in the present work is interesting.

It might be noted in this regard that typical of the kind of organisation which should be given the role of taking care of the enlightenment of the digital era is the Institute of Electrical and Electronics Engineers (IEEE). We shall examine the approach to the ethics of the digital environment of that organisation in Chapter 6.

---

[16] R. Capurro, 'The Age of Artificial Intelligences' (S.II 'Distributed Intelligences'), his contribution to the AI, Ethics and Society Conference, University of Alberta, May 2019, reproduced in the *International Review of Information Ethics* (2020).

[17] Ibid. S.III 'Natural and Artificial Intelligences'.

[18] Ibid. S.II 'Distributed Intelligences'.

[19] Ibid. S.IV 'Conclusion: Enlightening the Digital Enlightenment'.

AN ALTERNATIVE ETHICAL PROPOSAL

Background

In light of this debate between Floridi and Capurro but before outlining an alternative ethical proposal as a foundation for a relationship between human individuals and technology, a few comments are made.

The first deals with resistance per se. That is, it is one thing to propose an alternative ethical frame as a foundation to a reimagined sense of privacy, one which has a denial of mythology at its core, but there needs to be a context in praxis to deliver force to that reimagining. We need to 'act against' what dissatisfies us as well as to 'act for' something new. Given that he devoted so much thought to the means of the regimes of constructed subjection that is argued here to ultimately be mythological in nature, it is unsurprising that Foucault also seriously considered the notion of resistance. How he undertook this has been well explored by Legg.[20]

Legg encourages us to consider Foucault's consideration of *parrhesia* not as any simple form of resistance but as the kind of 'truth talk' that was used in ancient Greece. What we find there are parrhesiastic subjects that use 'truth talk': 'to found Athens; to be brave enough to govern well through the Athenian Assembly; to fearlessly advise tyrants on how better to sustain their empires; to refuse political service in favour of personal tuition; and, finally, to see the Cynic who chooses militant and radical resistance to the satisfied norms of the people of the polis, but only so that he might save them'. Each of these reflected the importance of discourse located and performed physically, that is, in a sense of place:[21] *parrhesia* emerged as an ethical and political mode of thought that would enable ways of thinking about struggle and politics.[22] Legg proceeds: 'At the level of individual de-subjugation, critique allows virtuous self-transformation which might expose the limit of the present, mining out ways of "not being governed" and questioning doctrinal truths which owe their origins to the anti-pastoral (Reformation and counter-Reformation) movements of the sixteenth century.'[23] Foucault in fact ranges across various historical examples of *parrhesia* but does emphasise its presence in Ancient Greece. For him both Cynic and Socratic *parrhesia* emerged from their linking of one's way of life with 'truth telling'. For them, life should be studied in its reality and then one should live accordingly. The Cynics went further by adding the principle that one should courageously challenge what had constituted true life in its embodiment and in terms of a way of life. These were later adopted within the context of the Reformation and beyond.

---

[20] S. Legg, 'Subjects of truth: Resisting governmentality in Foucault's 1980s', *Society and Space* 37:1 (2019): pp.27–45.

[21] Ibid. p.29.

[22] Ibid. p.32.

[23] Ibid. p.32.

144 *Privacy, Its Values and Technology*

While the argument of the present work rejects the advantage that accrued to the Reformation – given its wide mythological purpose – it endorses the capacity of *parrhesia* to promote 'de-subjugation' and 'virtuous self-transformation' by adopting a 'Cynical' way of life that might help to realise a respectful way of being responsible to and for oneself.

Legg has a reasonable sense of the value of Foucault's notion of *parrhesia* – although his support for Foucault's sense of that as governmentality is not endorsed here – when he says:

> While insisting we pursue public liberation from domination, [Foucault's] lesson was that freedom must also be sought within the individual, so as to complement systemic challenges to ingrained injustice. To study these resistant acts as power, as *parrhesia*, is to acknowledge their fragile vulnerability to internalisation and neutralisation and their potential as future and insolent governmentalities.[24]

The second comment is that the notion of Heideggerean authenticity that is examined in this work is a strong, even if not fully determinative, presence in the consideration of a preferred ethical system. The notion of realising a presence within the available but veiled condition of *Dasein*, of reuniting body, soul (as the life principle) and spirit (as the intellectual principle) – so unpacking the habitual, governmental conditions revealed by Elias and Foucault – allows Heidegger to be understood an attractive alternative to the mythologising regimes of the trajectory.

What is therefore being proposed is that the foundations for a new ethical frame for a new sense of privacy need to start with a rejection of the metaphysical, mythological approach, for example, of Floridi. That would subsume the individual into the infosphere – defined fully within a fundamental informational ontology. This would follow how the predecessor magnitudes of the trajectory in their absolutist form had, through their respective regimes, sought relentlessly to produce 'the faithful', 'the apparatchik' and 'the ideal consumer'. It would instead seek an ethics which preserves and promotes what is left of individual autonomy.

Digital Ethics and Respectful Self-Responsibility

It was argued in Chapter 1 that the optimal strategy for dealing with the increasingly profound impact of neuroscience on our sense of privacy will be the idea and practice of *respectful responsibility to and for oneself*. It was also argued that adopting this framework required the reimagining of privacy itself so that it could be conserved and progressed by the moral and technological combination of elements of which this strategy is comprised. *Privacy would be seen thereby as the 'to and for oneself' of this respectful self-responsibility and not as a zone of confidential life experience or of fairer management of information within a social context.*

---

[24] Ibid. p.43.

An Alternative Ethical Proposal

145

We shall now look more closely at this notion. In part this is because it is a newcomer to the wide field of values by which we are currently being guided in coming to terms with these technologies and so its credentials need to be justified. But it is also because it is proposed to replace these other values as the primary reference point as we come to terms with them.

Doing so will also allow us to begin to understand how this ethical principle of a respectfully self-responsible regime should relate to the functions of the State – through law and regulation and through the allocation of resources – and the Market. In fact, this will point the way to the manner in which that institutional framework can be reimagined to promote that principle, a task to be followed through in subsequent chapters. The strong implication is that the functioning of State and Market should generally – that is, not only in relation to the management of new technologies – be founded on fervent adherence to that principle. But the frame through which we shall do this here remains that of technology since its relation to privacy is the opening focus of this work. That is, by looking at their relation to technology and privacy, we shall see how law and regulation should be conceived so that State and Market – as reimagined – ensure that their primary function is to reflect and promote that principle. This of course is somewhat different from any approach that would urge the primacy of State and Market, even within a democratic framework, and the responsibility of individuals as citizens to comply with State and Market regimes that claim responsibility to deal with the needs of such citizens. So we are reversing the usual manner in which priorities are established in the currently dominant mythological framework.

To undertake this task we shall begin by examining the broad ethical framework of human rights and then the particular suite of values which are commonly argued as the primary reference points for what should be allowed regarding the functioning of new technologies.[25] These values include dignity, liberty, the common good, equality, identity, responsibility, rights, justice and those claimed for liberal democracies. We shall look at each of these, but before doing so it will be helpful to make a point about the theme that is often seen as constitutive of the broad impact of new technologies, that is, disruption.

In what follows, the argument will be that new technologies, while clearly disruptive across a range of fields, are best not seen first as disruptive. A more fundamental feature of these technologies is typically that of subjection: the purpose of disruption – especially by such advanced algorithms as are used in machine and deep learning – is subjection, in that the adoption of technology requires the adoption of the interpretations imposed by the technology itself. That is, this adoption at the very same time leads to the necessary subversion of the decision-

---

[25] Part II of 'Legitimacy and Technological Regulations: Values and Ideals', in *The Oxford Handbook of Law, Regulation and Technology*, R. Brownsword, E. Scotford and K. Yeung (eds.), is used as an introductory reference here.

making capacity of the individual. This is a claim not that citizens or communities are necessarily involuntarily subjected to technology – though they often are – but that the adoption of technology requires the embedding of technological ideas and practices that constitute a regime. These are usually adopted in relation to a particular technology, but, of course, as these have proliferated, we should properly think of this as a more generalised technological regime to which citizens are becoming subject, largely if not universally but increasingly so. This issue of the voluntary/involuntary nature of such adoption will be fully explored in much of what follows, but the point here is that, before we consider new technologies as disruptive across such fields as communication, law, data collection and manipulation, industry, finance, transport, medicine, security, the environment and so on, we should understand technologies as a regime of interpretation that subjects. This is contrary to the claims of the dominant interests of the technology industry. This issue of subjection is to be kept in mind as we now explore the range of values currently presented as guides to the manner in which we should manage technologies. Doing so will make it clear how self-responsibility takes a place at the base of this framework and what is at stake in making a place for it. This will show that, although these specific ethical characteristics are noble, both they and the ethical framework itself that they represent ultimately fail to satisfy the ethical standards that will be required to deal with the continuing emergence of developments within neuroscience.

THE BROAD ETHICAL FRAMEWORK

We have long looked to a range of ethical declarations, covenants and conventions produced thoughtfully by such organisations as the United Nations, the European Union and – to a lesser extent – the United States, especially through its Constitutional amendments, to guide us in establishing ethical reference points for a wide range of social, political and, more recently, technological fields of activity.

We shall first concentrate on those declarations, covenants and conventions. One reason for doing so, apart from their proliferating effect, is that they are a significant reference point for the IEEE, which has done significant work on the impact of technology through its *Ethically Aligned Design (First Edition)*. That work includes a suite of provisions by which the ethical principles it recommends can guide the development and application of emerging technologies. I make substantial reference to the practical value of these principles in Chapter 6, but here I will begin the consideration of necessary ethical principles by referring to those declarations and conventions, as does the IEEE.[26] It might be noted that the IEEE associates these

---

[26] *Ethically Aligned Design (First Edition): A Vision for Prioritising Human Well-being with Autonomous and Intelligent Systems* (Institute of Electrical and Electronics Engineers, 2019), pp.18ff.

declarations and conventions with two other principles, that is, well-being and data agency, by which the benefit of technology should also be judged. I will avoid the former here, as that takes us beyond the field of ethics into the field of economic benefit, and I will leave comments about data agency to Chapter 6.

Regarding the Universal Declaration of Human Rights, it is fairly said that for over seventy years it has had a truly significant status in the field of human rights, placing a recommended range of rights in the public domain and doing so through the authority of the United Nations. These rights centre on such themes as human dignity and justice, personal development, the environment, the centrality of culture, gender equality and participation in community life.

However, its status has not prevented the Declaration from being the subject of criticism. Probably foremost among these are its claimed 'Western' bias, the related concern that certain nation-states have been an impediment to its universal acceptance and the 'siloing' that sees certain rights, for example, civil and political rights, given priority over such others as social and economic rights, thereby also interfering with the principle of universality.[27]

However, this Declaration – written in 1948 – is clearly deficient in a further particular, fundamental way. This is the absence of any sense of self-responsibility by which such rights would genuinely accrue to the individual. As a result, one must say that the value of such rights is seriously devalued. For example, Article 23 states the right to work rather than the responsibility to do so and thereby to demonstrate self-reliance; Article 26 states the right to an education rather than the responsibility to acquire skills that would optimise self-reliance; and in Article 29, the duty of each to the community is the only means to ensure the development of one's personality, rather than the reverse. Article 18 claims the right rather than the responsibility to freedom of thought and conscience, and in Article 11 there is a claim for proper principles of legal justice and punishment without reference to any requirement of the individual either to accept responsibility for an offence or to pursue means by which they can become respectful and self-reliant. Article 21 claims the right to political participation and that the will of the people should be the basis of political authority through elections but makes no reference to the need for the political process to promote wide individual political participation rather than a single electoral vote every several years. Important for the focus of this work, Article 12 states that no one shall be subjected to arbitrary interference with their privacy, family, home or correspondence, nor to attacks upon their honour and reputation and that the law should provide such protection. We have seen – and will see in detail in

---

[27] M. Ignatieff, 'The attack on human rights', *Foreign Affairs* (November–December 2001); J. Mende, 'Are human rights Western – And why does it matter?', *Journal of International Political Theory* (1 March 2019); S. Ozler, 'The Universal Declaration of Human Rights at 70', *Ethics and International Affairs* 32:4 (Winter 2018): pp.395ff.

148   *Privacy, Its Values and Technology*

Chapter 6 – the argument here that this is an outdated notion of privacy which will not deal with the intrusions or opportunities of neural and associated technologies.

In the absence of any requirement that individuals or social processes demonstrate or promote such self-responsibility, it seems particularly unconvincing that Article 22 claims the right for each individual that there be national and international effort to ensure the economic, social and cultural drive to ensure their dignity, thereby that – as with Article 25 – they have the inherent right to a standard of living adequate to health and well-being. In fact, one might go further and question the claim of Article 1 that each citizen has inherent – as opposed to having to realise – dignity, reason and conscience. We shall see why this is a fair criticism.

In short, the Universal Declaration makes presumptions about individual and social processes that are straightforwardly lopsided and thereby challengeable. The establishment of such a declaration induces rather than requires the engagement of the individual. The consequence is, typically, that this allows a space of activity that is instead constructed by other – typically dominant – interests. So the Church defines what constitutes a marriage or a family; the State effectively determines political participation; and the Market determines what is employment (and so full-time work has been largely replaced by casual part-time activity that tends to enslave rather than sustain). Access to the law – in the form of effective legal representation – is determined by claimed public financial priorities; there is long-demonstrated bias against lower income groups in police practice; the nature and extent of 'privacy' is ultimately determined by interests within State and Market; the right to own property is far out of the reach of many citizens; the right to education is largely determined by income; and so on.

One can make similar observations about other declaratory statements in the broad ethical framework. For example, the United Nations International Covenant on Civil and Political Rights, which was clearly influenced by the Universal Declaration of Human Rights, covers much the same ground, except for the provisions regarding the establishment of the Human Rights Committee and the Conciliation Commission. One particular emphasis within the Covenant worth noting is that individual States are to establish laws to progress the local installation of the suite of rights detailed within it. However, this does not contradict the point already made that, without any specification of an active role for individual citizens in the realisation of such rights, how they are delivered will be assumed and specified by dominant interests in a manner that suits those interests.

It is no argument in response to say that all these elements are negotiable, but they are not, in effect. Unless there is a requirement for active engagement of individuals – the opportunity and expectation of respectful responsibility to and for oneself – such declarations must be seen as indicative and therefore of only partial practical value.

Perhaps ironically, it is within the United Nations Convention of the Rights of the Child where we see a glimmer of the kind of approach that does attempt to embed respectful self-reliance in the individual. For example, Article 12 states that children have the right to say what they think when adults are making decisions that affect them and have their opinions taken into account; Article 13 states that children have the right to get and share non-damaging information; Article 14 specifies that children have the right to think and believe what they want so long as they are not stopping people from enjoying their rights; and Article 29 states that education should develop each child's personality and talents to the full and encourage respect for parents and their culture. This is not to say that these provisions fulfil the notion of the ethical principle preferred herein, but there is a hint here of what such a notion would comprise. As for the Convention on the Elimination of All Forms of Discrimination against Women and the Convention on the Rights of Persons with Disabilities, one might fairly say that in general these are intended to remove additional structural and incidental factors that interfere with the enjoyment of the rights, as expressed in, for example, the Universal Declaration of Human Rights for others, by women and the disabled. So, as with those other conventions, they lack provisions that require respectful self-responsibility, notwithstanding the additional constraints they experience in being either women or disabled.

Within this broad context, there have been calls for a Digital Geneva Convention, the purpose of which is to protect civilians from State-sponsored cyber attacks through the weaponizing of advances in technology. This involves the development of protocols for responsible development and deployment of cyber capacities and to establish norms to prevent the targeting of important infrastructure, which is increasingly in the hands of Market interests. It also calls for the non-proliferation of cyber weapons and international processes for dealing with cyber attacks. As with these other declarations, this is a top-down framework and provides no opportunity – let alone requirement – for individual engagement.

Against this background, it is not difficult to see some of the shortcomings present within the various elements of this human rights spectrum.

COMMON ETHICAL PRINCIPLES

Human Dignity

A good starting point in considering the values which should guide the introduction and operation of technologies is human dignity. That is, human dignity is one of a number of potential foundations which is often elevated to frame the regulation of new technologies. It recommends itself due to a number of credentials. First, it has the capacity to act as a barrier to human degradation, as well as its promotion of a sense of cooperative individualism, thereby of autonomy, which does not descend into atomism. It also invites the development of institutions to protect the individual rights that it would generate. These include the right to privacy, to security, to life

150   *Privacy, Its Values and Technology*

and to non-discriminate equality.[28] More importantly, human dignity might be seen as the source of the human capacity for moral reasoning – and thereby the foundation of rights and duties – that is the ultimate justification for it being elevated to a primary reference point in the assessment, regulation and management of technology.

However, there are at least two significant problems with such an elevation. First, the notion is ideologically vacuous in that it lends itself not only to a world view that honours respect for universal individual rights and autonomy but also to the hostile denial of a world view other than one's own, even including the elimination of what one would see as ideological threats. Each of the credentials just listed can be accommodated within a world view that would attempt to do so, including those persons with a religious or a political belief who would terrorise non-believers but who are regarded within that frame of reference as dignified, even heroic. Second, the Kantianism that lies behind the admiration for the human capacity to 'reason' universal moral standards is far from straightforward. As Hunter points out,[29] Kantian moral thought was inextricably linked to his aspiration to construct a form of State which would subject individuals to a metaphysical *paideia*, or broad cultural education – the sacralisation of politics. That is, for all of his presumption of the capacity of each individual to imagine categorical imperatives and to act autonomously, there was implicit in his account that there is an ontological gap between the empirical human and the pure rational being. The typical individual must remain subject to incentives and sanctions that can regulate their desires and prepare them for the rule of the rational self. This is inculcation.[30] We would do well to remain cautious about any claims that reason rather than inculcation is the primary source of present moral codes and that human dignity is a precondition of such reason.

What this latter point raises is the serious doubt that there should be any presumption about the practical rationality of human beings, let alone for the imagination of categorically imperative, universal moral principles. Qualifying the attribution of respect for individual potential for such reasoning, which would begin as provisional and which would progress towards full respect when there was a demonstration of an effort to realise this potential, would be a preferred, if challenging, position. Further, Kantianism has left us with the view that all moral principles must be universal, when there is a justifiable alternative view that moral principles should be individualised – I should decide such principles as should apply to me –

---

[28] 'Human Rights and Technology Issues Paper', July 2018, *Australian Human Rights Commission*, pp. 15–17.

[29] I. Hunter, *Rival Enlightenments* (Cambridge University Press, 2001), pp.315, 353–355.

[30] For a wider account of this point, see D. Grant and L. Bennett-Moses *Technology and the Trajectory of Myth*, pp.88–98. For a broader analysis of the nature of the Kantian State, see D. Grant, *The Mythological State and Its Empire*, pp.100–119.

so long as that was located within a moral-political-legal field that insisted on mutual respect.

On these grounds we should not accept presumptive human dignity as the foundation for a frame by which technology would be regulated. Neither should it be the template against which other normative systems such as rights and duties and the features of autonomy are developed. Another principal reference point is needed.

Liberty

The protection of liberty is a necessary focus when we consider the impact of new technologies, given these can both constrain or enhance our interaction with the world. But an effective framework is needed within which to see this relationship between the two. As a still-leading thinker in this field, Mill seems to provide one, although, as we have seen, referring to him needs to be checked against his own elitist views on liberty. Being a straightforward Millian is fraught.

Nonetheless, for him, 'the sole end for which mankind are warranted, individually or collectively, in interfering with the liberty of action of any of their number is self-protection', and 'the only purpose for which power can be rightfully exercised over any member of a civilised community, against his will, is to prevent harm to others'.[31]

The range of sources of the notion of liberty, which Mill is here tapping into, appears to justify a strong sense of liberty. For example, he draws on a religious frame, albeit one that stands in a radically different position than traditional dogma,[32] and on the value of law[33] in this. He even adopts the view that imperialism with a strong economic agenda – as with the British East India Company – can promote the protection of legal rights, respect for competing viewpoints and a commercial society that can cope with natural threats.[34] These sources are the origin of the familiar questions in this field: Do we prefer our liberties to be framed in legal or moral terms, or both? What weight, if any, do we place on religious views about this? Do we want these to be embedded in the resilient field of State law or are we served best by allowing greater flexibility so that we can respond more quickly to changing circumstances? What is the function of the Market in defending our liberties, and can State legislation ensure that? and How much do we want to rely on technology itself to determine where our liberties lie and what they are? The very multitude of its sources and forms seems to attest to the importance of liberty as a guiding principle.

---

[31] J. S. Mill, *On Liberty* (Pelican, 1974), p.68.
[32] J. S. Mill, *Theism*, www.earlymoderntexts.com/assets/pdfs/mill1873.pdf (2017), pp.36–41.
[33] B. Saunders, 'Reformulating Mill's harm principle', *Mind* 125:500 (October 2016).
[34] M. Tunick, 'Tolerant imperialism: John Stuart Mill's defence of British rule in India', *The Review of Politics* (2006).

However, the very fact of these different sources points to problems in dealing with the issue of liberty, especially in a rapidly changing technological world. Are these frameworks compatible? For example, are the laws and practices of the State the means of primary protection of our liberties or the principal means of intrusions into them? Are there suitable laws to ensure we can trust the Market to deal properly with the choices that should reflect our personal privacy, or do laws allow and even encourage such intrusion? What role does the relationship between the priest and the believer have on the latter's privacy and so their capacity to act freely? Should the State be encouraged to intervene in the confidentiality of the confessional in serious matters of misconduct?

Current debate about such conundrums is still mostly dominated by the question of whether these traditional institutions should remain the frame within which such questions are to be addressed, although these are increasingly accommodating the impact of emerging technologies. Within this debate there is a particular focus on the relationship between a right and a responsive claim against such right, as a means of determining rightful positions between individuals or between individuals and agencies. We might call this the traditional framework of liberty. Should our liberties remain determined by what we enshrine in the contested laws of the State, in the notions and practices prescribed by the dogmas of religion, in the assurances and interests of the Market and by whatever local arrangements we can establish in the shadows of these magnitudes?

What has now emerged as a key question is whether technology can take a place among these institutional determining elements of liberty. Should we allow the prescriptions of technology to be increasingly embedded in or even be brought to dominate this complex field? For example, should 'ethics by design', 'privacy by design' or 'crime control by design' be increasingly embedded in this contested field, pre-emptively determining what we can do or what others can know about us? This is a paradigm shift between fields, although it is currently presented as an evolution from the traditional field to selectively include elements of new technology.

Many might argue that classical notions of pre-technological liberty, such as those that concerned Mill, cannot and should not accommodate this evolution. To them it seems anathema. However, Mill himself is not so easily blocked off. There is a credible argument that he should be thought of as one who had uncertainty at the centre of his moral and political thought. From this he not only emphasised the plasticity of human nature, but offered accounts of custom, harm and progress based on this quality.[35] Liberty was no absolute. In fact, what he says about custom is telling:

> The despotism of custom is everywhere the standing hindrance to human advancement ... which is called ... the spirit of liberty or that of progress or

---

[35] M. Phillips, 'Troubling associations: JS Mill, liberalism and the virtues of uncertainty', *European Journal of Political Theory* (24 February 2016).

Common Ethical Principles 153

improvement. The spirit of improvement is not always a spirit of liberty, for it may aim at forcing improvements on an unwilling people ... but the only unfailing and permanent source of improvement is liberty ... the greater part of the world has, properly speaking, no history, because the despotism of custom is complete.[36]

In the present context, this would be no carte blanche for technology, but it is an opportunity for those who prefer a move away from standard frames of reference and towards technological initiatives to design privacy on grounds that this would be in favour of liberty.

However, there is a different, more fundamental question than that concerning the relationship between these two fields – the traditional and the technological – that we should be asking, that is, regarding the status of the individual citizen within both these paradigms. Should we be shifting the focus away from looking first at the dynamics within and between these paradigms and focus first on reimagining and re-establishing the status of the individual citizen, who is claimed to be the main beneficiary of these discussions about liberty? That is, the question is whether in our search for the answer to questions about individual liberty we have been moved to a position where it is the features of these institutional magnitudes (Deity, State, Market and Technology) that have come to determine how we may be free rather than ensuring that the magnitudes focus entirely on the individual citizen in this. Who is benefitting when the State claims to be the protector of privacy but is active across a wide range of its laws and activities to gather and even share personal data as part of a profiling policy? Who benefits when the Church claims the confidentiality of the confessional but in doing so protects some individuals from the investigation of crimes against other individuals? Who is the principal beneficiary when, under the guise of providing services to customers, Market corporations use the near-indecipherability of privacy agreements to gather wide-ranging information through technological means about individuals and then convert that into means to 'target market' back to the individual and to distil such information from Big Data to mount campaigns across a marketing field or to deprive individuals of reasonable access to credit and insurance?

One might well add at this point that Mill, for all his concern about liberty, was not wholehearted about his apparently wide sense of liberty. Not only has his perspective on the role of the East India Company been seriously challenged in recent scholarship,[37] but his views that for 'unimproved' nations 'their almost only hope of making any steps in advance depends on the chances of a good despot' also have been given more emphasis. That is, liberal rule is completely consistent with the authoritarian rule of colonial societies.[38] This points to the mythological theme

---

[36] J. S. Mill, *On Liberty*, p.136.

[37] C. Anderson, 'Convicts, commodities and connections in British Asia and the Indian Ocean 1789–1866', *International Review of Social History* (2019).

[38] M. Dean, *Governmentality – Power and Rule in Modern Society* (Sage, 2006), p.133.

154 *Privacy, Its Values and Technology*

in Mill, a theme that is present in the political theories of his predecessors Rousseau and Kant, who are also purported to be strong defenders of liberty as autonomy and whose views have come to the contemporary world through such thinkers as Rawls.[39] Mill is not the author of ethical principles that we seek to develop.

Therefore, there seems to be a clear need for a new paradigm, recommended here as one in which the respectful and self-responsible citizen is shifted to the centre of activity regarding the question of the nature of liberty. There are several immediate implications of such a shift. The first would be that technological solutions to questions that affect liberty would rarely, if ever, be the first step. That is, rather than extending the traditional framework to include – and possibly progressively be replaced by – technological solutions, this is a move in the other direction. That is, the field of technology – and more broadly the traditional framework for the answers to questions of liberty – would see the respectfully responsible citizen, rather than the dominant interests of the magnitudes, as the centre of attention. We shall explore this option in the final section of this chapter, but we can say here that this is not the complete supplanting of technology, let alone of law, dogma or the Market, only that the purpose of these forces would be to support and cooperatively enhance the development of respectful self-responsible behaviour by the citizen. Neither is it to dismiss the wide range of conundrums we have just looked at, only to state that these need to be looked at in a completely different light – in a new paradigm – and so with fully different outcomes.

Identity

It might be argued that the most significant element of a preferred value system as it relates to the management of new technology is one's identity, seen as the evolving features that define us each as an individual.[40] We have seen the central importance of this in Chapter 2. Identity points to what we fear, what are our imaginings, what goals we have for ourselves and others, what we are passionate about, what concerns us, what we value and so on. It reflects our world view – our unity of life – showing what we acknowledge, what we deny, what has helped form us and the direction we have decided we want our life to take. Identity reflects the extent to which we have come to understand ourselves in honesty and how we mean to take responsibility for and enhance our lives. Within this context, we might be aware of the extent to which we live – and want to live – technologically. This is a dynamic account of

---

[39] For an account of the mythological bias in Rousseau, Kant and Rawls, see D. Grant, *The Mythological State and Its Empire*, chs.4–6.

[40] P. Wu, 'The privacy paradox in the context of online social networking: A self-identity perspective', *Journal of the Association for Information Science and Technology* (19 November 2018); H. Nach et al., 'The impact of information technology on identity: Framing the research agenda', *ResearchGate* (June 2009).

identity but also points to the extent to which we might live authentically. It is also the field into which neuroscience is moving.

But what is missing from such an account of identity are the strategic implications of it. There are a number of elements we need to be aware of to explore these implications, but they are not transparently present. First, it should be noted, regarding how we each decide the boundaries between the categories that comprise our persisting and shifting characteristic features, that these features are typically significantly determined by forces outside us. Second, we need to consider the sources and nature of these determining forces and the relationship between them and the individual citizen. This is the extent and manner in which the individual may be imposed upon but also seeks to impose categories on themself – in trying to imagine their own identity in line with or against these external forces – and the extent to which these may be shared with others and imposed on the world. The latter question is strongly influenced by Kantian constructivism. Third, we should question the nature of such determinations, specifically whether they comprise both idea and practice and whether they fit within one's preferred identity. This is relevant in considering the personal impact of the magnitudes, now beginning to include the new technologies in their strategic aims. In questioning these external influences, this would mean not forgoing the wide range of sensible arrangements that help us navigate the world in relative safety and with some comfort but asking about the broader elements of how we think about and how we behave in the context of powerful, competing world views.

Taken together, these points suggest that we should be asking if there might be background strategic elements that include such determining forces, and even whether these are ideological and promoted on behalf of dominant interests. We would also ask what it would mean for one's identity not just to take responsibility in the usual sense but here in a broader strategic sense; whether this means that we should reimagine the notion of authentic living to address the sources of our fears and desires and, in a positive Kantian sense, come to impose our own constructed perspective on the social and natural world but with such a new sense of responsibility.

The outcome would be the realisation of a different sense of identity, one that combines our human, personal and self-identities and which is determined by the individual themself against the interests of external dominant elements. Employing the term 'technology' in a wider sense than it is presently used, Foucault positively explores much of this terrain.[41] Such a reimagined sense of identity fairly raises the question of the extent to which the individual might be substantially different, especially if the reimagining is deep and wide. We shall explore these questions

---

[41] M. G. E. Kelly, 'Foucault, subjectivity and technologies of the self', in *A Companion to Foucault* (2013), ch.26.

156   *Privacy, Its Values and Technology*

further in the final section of this chapter. But the constant negotiability of identity makes it at least an uncertain buffer against technology.

Responsibility

We have seen in Chapter 2 that the knowledge being gathered by neuroscientists not only increasingly and extensively indicates how the structure and operation of the brain links to self-awareness[42] and behaviour[43] but also will increasingly invite a level of intervention the effect of which will be to change that structure and that behaviour. Nonetheless, it remains true that individual human beings do make decisions, including those between what they consider right and wrong and between what they know to be lawful and unlawful. Further, in making these decisions they are typically conscious of such differences.

These two broad positions meet in the principle of determinism, where, at one end, individuals are fully briefed – and their decisions determined – by their neurological arrangements and, at the other, where a compatibilist account allows autonomous decision-making in a determinist world, allowing a claim of incomplete but substantial individual responsibility. Clearly, the latter position is crucial to the functioning of our ethical principles and legal system and therefore our political, commercial and social arrangements. In determining an outcome between these, it might seem fair to leave the burden of proof with the neuroscientists – as only the results of continuing research will determine whether the centre of gravity will be located with either neurology or autonomy – although even this may not provide a clear outcome.[44] In the meantime, it may be argued that we should continue to recommend autonomy and responsibility as foundational principles.

However, even if one does adopt this position, there are important unanswered questions. If one accepts that autonomy and responsibility must be qualified, that is, an individual never makes decisions fully autonomously and even makes some unconsciously,[45] what is the nature of the broader biological, psychological and social fields that 'qualify' full responsibility? It seems inadequate to say – beyond acknowledging that neural structure and content predispose us in various ways –

---

[42] See also H. C. Lou et al., 'Toward a cognitive neuroscience of self-awareness', *Neuroscience and Behavioural Reviews* 83 (December 2017): pp.765–773.

[43] See also J. W. Krakauer et al., 'Neuroscience needs behaviour: Correcting a reductionist bias', *Neuron* 93:3 (2017): pp.480–490, in which the authors explain that behavioural work provides understanding, whereas neural interventions test causality

[44] A. Lavazza, 'Why cognitive sciences do not prove that free will is an epiphenomenon', *Frontiers in Psychology – Theoretical and Philosophical Psychology* (26 February 2019); see also B. Gholipour, 'Philosophers and neuroscientists join forces to see whether science can solve the mystery of free will', *Brain and Behaviour – People and Events – Social Sciences* (March 2019) doi: 10.1126/science.aax4190; V. Saigle et al., 'The impact of a landmark neuroscience study on free will: A qualitative analysis of articles using Libet and colleagues' methods', *American Journal of Bioethics – Neuroscience* 9:1 (March 2018).

[45] See www.sciencedaily.com/releases/2008/04/080414145705.htm.

Common Ethical Principles

157

merely that rational decision-making is founded on the mental states comprised of our reasoning, desires, beliefs, intentions, plans and suchlike[46] or by a range of social customs, norms or moral systems. This all seems quite uncertain given the multitude of meanings that attach to each of these notions.

Further, and related to that, we need to be clear about the sense we give to responsibility, as it can properly refer to at least two notions: the condition in which a citizen makes autonomous decisions ('I am responsible for the action I took') and another sense in which one takes on a commonly agreed set of principles and practices ('I accept that I'm responsible for upholding the laws of the land' or 'I am responsible for promoting the interests of this or that agency') and which may involve being responsible to other individuals or agencies for such practices or behaviours. That is, in the range between the effects of neurological predisposition and the making of autonomous decisions is a wide, identifiable field which accommodates that rationality, those beliefs, attitudes and aspirations – along with their respective preferred behaviours – that are, on one hand, embedded in this neurology and which, on the other, impact on behaviour. In fact, beyond accommodating these, this field promotes the realisation of mythological strategies which impact deeply on individual decision-making and so on responsibility.

Although this may seem to constrain autonomy too severely, one should take the opposite view, that is, that radical determinism is undermined by this focus on this strategic field: our decisions are thereby not the result of deterministic predisposition since those predispositions are impacted by the elements of this strategic field and the ideologies it contains. This does not eliminate the problems since the argument might still be that our rational decisions – our autonomy – are determined by elements of that field. Yet these can be seen as social constructs that can be amended or eliminated: they are not hard-wired into our genes even though they become embedded into our neural structure. Being aware of – and being able to amend or eliminate – these elements is thereby asserting acts of rationality and autonomy. This implies that there will not be a paradigm shift in neuroscientific research that allows behaviour to be determined and eliminates autonomous decision-making. The paradigm shift will be in the understanding of the elements of the strategic field which impacts on both neurology and behaviour and our preparedness to take control of those strategies in a manner that ensures such rational autonomy and responsibility.

So it seems that, in an effort to unpick the respective significances of neurology and autonomy, our primary focus should be on this field. Because neuroscience cannot be credited with a dominant determinism at this point, relying on arguments about the validity of mental states – and the plethora of psychological and social elements which impact those states – seems to be an avoidance of this field.

---

[46] See S. Morse, 'Law, Responsibility and the Sciences of Brain/Mind', in *The Oxford Handbook of Law, Regulation and Technology*, p.157.

158   *Privacy, Its Values and Technology*

A systematic attempt to describe this strategic or mythological field will be presented in the final section of this chapter.

Democratic Principles

Clearly, the regulation of technologies, given their highly intrusive nature, is a principal function of Western constitutional democracies, and how this task is undertaken reveals much about the nature of abiding democratic values. The core of these values – a constitutional framework, representation, rule of law, equality, human rights and so on[47] – is often expressed, in the spirit of the influential republicanism of Pettit, as a non-domination distinct from the non-interference of which liberalism is claimed to comprise. In that republicanism, interference is justified so long as it is considered – on some basis of wide agreement – to be in the interests of the individual.

Against such a background, for example, the efforts of the State to fight crime and terrorism allows a range of State activities which, given the absence of individual consent, at first sight seem to seriously breach such individual rights as the right to privacy. Privacy is considered important in the formation of an individual's intimate attachments, their thinking through of new ideas which might lead to legitimate associations for dissent, and thereby the capacity for autonomous behaviour. But these State activities include mass surveillance in the form of the bulk collection of data, which not only might well transgress the exercise of these liberal democratic rights but, in doing so, might well suffer the mistakes that are not untypical of the application of algorithms to data, such as false positives. Such mistakes thereby threaten the conditional trust that is necessary between a citizen and the liberal democratic State. All this is made worse if official secrecy provisions apply.

Yet without such activities the State is said to be unable to effectively carry out its appointed role of fighting crime and terrorism and so protecting its citizens. This argument is usually accompanied by the assurances that if certain conditions are applied, then State domination is constrained within a limit that still protects citizens' freedoms. Such assurances typically include a primary reliance on meta-data rather than personal data but which can be pursued down to the personal level if there is sufficient evidence to convince, say, a judicial authority of the justification for that and that there is sufficient *post factum* publicity about such processes.

Corporations are a different matter and, although some changes in favour of the citizen are being considered,[48] they commonly have limited statutory responsibility to protect individual liberty, so that their justification for the levels of data

---

[47] M. Plattner, 'Illiberal democracy and the struggle on the right', *Journal of Democracy* 30:1 (2019); C. Skach, 'Constitutional democracy: Creating and maintaining a just political order', *International Journal of Constitutional Law* 7:1 (2008).

[48] N. Tusikov et al., 'It's time for a new way to regulate social media platforms', *Phys Org* (17 January 2019).

manipulation not only can be highly intrusive but is typically without supervision and so morally dangerous. In this context there is the need to acknowledge the subconscious level at which marketing works but also that little attention is given to the capacity of the State, even in its liberal democratic form, to operate in a similar way.

This latter point should be taken far more seriously, and doing so opens out into a range of issues with which the foregoing account of the State–citizen relationship should be reconsidered. That is, the psychological manipulation that is made possible by the gathering of large amounts of data, on which many corporations rely, can properly be seen as trading on the satisfaction of desire in return for varying degrees of subjection to the corporate strategy. If there is an argument that a similar strategy in is play regarding the State–citizen relationship, then the account of that relationship outlined above is erroneous. That is, Pettit's account of republican non-domination is unjustifiably intrusive. A reimagination of that relationship is necessary, including how the State undertakes the constraint of technologies for the purpose of protecting individual liberties. The outline of such a reimagined account is provided in the final section of this chapter and in Chapter 9.

Equality

The core democratic value of equality seems undeniably attractive as a guide to assessing the social and individual value of new technologies, especially when it is typically aligned with such other liberal values as dignity and individual rights and capabilities, all founded on the idea of the unconditional worth of each individual.[49] In fact, equality is a lens with particular advantages regarding new technologies, since some of these have been shown to have biases that deny the validity of some lives. Further, by applying the principle of equality, the entire issue of access – along with the relevance of that to distributive justice – is brought to the fore, raising important questions, for example, about the digital divide and genetic enhancement priorities.

Given the nature of liberal democratic government, the principle and practice of equality could then be properly seen in the broader context of legitimacy, with the quality and extent of the delivery of that principle to citizens being a key test for any government: from as long ago as the time of Locke, the test of the legitimacy of a government is its assurance of the equal rights of all citizens and the extent to which it pursues the common good.[50]

---

[49] J. Locke, *Two Treatises of Government*, Book II ss.54, 123, 135, 168; A. van Deursen, 'The first-level digital divide shifts from inequalities in physical access to inequalities in material access', *New Media and Society* (7 September 2018); M. Warschauer et al., 'Technology and equity in schooling: Deconstructing the digital divide', *Educational Policy* (September 2004).

[50] J. Locke, *Two Treatises of Government*, Book II s.149.

In short, equality carries with it both the seeds and the test of a government in its political, legal, social and economic functioning, not only in the extent to which it delivers on the quality of life of each citizen in terms of those functions but also in the extent to which it is constrained in that relationship to that delivery and no more. There is continuing debate about the extent and manner of the redistribution and equalisation required to fulfil the responsibilities of the State in this regard, including whether it is inextricably related to individual and group rights, and the extent to which it impacts on legitimacy, especially in the context of limited resources available for allocation. Rawls,[51] Sen,[52] Dworkin[53] and Nussbaum[54], among others, have significantly informed this debate, as – we have seen – has Hayek.

All this has an impact on how – to what extent and purpose – new technologies should be regulated. Key issues here include accessibility across the socio-economic spectrum, the respective advantages and disadvantages of corrective and enhancement interventions and their downstream effects on later generations. The liberal democratic principles regarding liberty, justice, dignity and protection from harm feature prominently in debates around these issues. Equality seems to a key reference point here.

However, there are problems that appear in these considerations of equality, both generally and in regard to the regulation of new technologies. There are all the obvious ones, for example, what equality actually is, does it relate to rights, to distribution of resources, to life opportunities? Then, how are disputes that arise from these various notions to be resolved, that is, what takes priority and on what criteria?

But perhaps the most significant problem is that there is strong and unresolved tension between, on one hand, the roles of the State (and its regulators) and the Market (and its strategists) and, on the other, the status of the respectful citizen regarding the responsibility to both define and to give effect to practices of equality. That is, although there is repeated reference to the rights, capabilities, experiences, conditions of existence, and aspirations of citizens, the centre of gravity in addressing these matters ultimately and continuously defaults to the State and Market, to whom authority is ceded. There is at least a Lockean sense in all this, even if one incorporates the limited input that rests in the democratic process, since the notion of authority depends very largely on wide tacit consent. The argument here is that, for equality to be an irresistibly pre-eminent value in the sociopolitical process, there

---

[51] J. Rawls, *A Theory of Justice*, ch.8, s.77; see also D. Grant, 'Reason and the Myth of Justice', in *The Mythological State and Its Empire*.

[52] A. Sen, 'Equality of what?', *The Tanner Lecture on Human Values*, Stanford (22 May 1979).

[53] R. Dworkin, 'What is equality? Part 1: Equality of welfare', *Philosophy and Public Affairs* 10:3 (1981); 'What is equality? Part 2: Equality of resources', *Philosophy and Public Affairs* 10:4 (1981); T. Finegan, 'Dworkin on equality, autonomy and authenticity', *American Journal of Jurisprudence* 60:2 (2015).

[54] M. Nussbaum, 'Women's capabilities and social justice', *Journal of Human Development* (August 2010).

Common Ethical Principles   161

is no reason why primary responsibility for defining and implementing equality must not ultimately lie with the respectful individual citizen. This in no way denies that both State and Market play important facilitating roles in that.

The source of this problem is twofold. The first is the traditional notion of the State–citizen relationship in which the legitimacy of the State derives from the forgoing of responsibilities by citizens in return for its protection and for the common good. In the modern era, this goes back at least to Hobbes. This is the wide empowering of the State and its derivative powers. The second is the persistent notion that each individual is unconditionally worthy due to the creation of each by Deity and to whom complete subjection is due according to His law, a notion that has emerged in the secular era as based on the value – or inherent dignity – of each life to the person themself and therefore by which they are due unconditional respect. The latter is clearly an erroneous notion, given the range of seriously unacceptable behaviour displayed by many individuals and would be better replaced by notions of provisional value and respect. Together, these references to Deity and the State have placed equality in a context which has continued to construct what equality may comprise. This context persists, irrespective of the presence of reinterpretation and revision.

One such revision is that by Dworkin. His associative account of political obligation – that we have obligations to obey the law due to our membership of the political community, separate from the authority of the State – and his account of the legitimacy of the State as deriving from equal concern for all citizens go some way to disengaging the citizen from the primacy of the State. However, by locating responsibility across a range of bonded social fields – friendships, families and nation-states – and without any notion of choice or consent, they do not move the responsibility for equality to the individual citizen. Further, Dworkin still sees government as *endeavouring* to respect human worth and as *allowing* citizens to realise their conception of the life they wish to lead. The primacy of the State persists.

These foundational, 'centre of gravity' issues regarding equality are what lie behind – and raise questions about – such issues as the location of decision-making regarding knowledge about and access to new technologies and on what grounds; how the notion of rights plays out in the political field and beyond; and, more broadly, the nature of government authority and legitimacy, the range of its policies and the relation of these to the nature and quality of individual capacity and opportunity; the meaning of both dignity and consent; and the justifications for distributing resources – that is, what equality is and how it works in a political community. These all look very different in a State- or Market-centred arrangement than they would where the respectful individual is the centre of gravity with the State and Market as a facilitator to that.

Human Rights and the Technologies of the Body

We have already looked at human rights in the context of the broad ethical framework. However, looking more closely at human rights in operation is revealing. For example, consideration of the impact of the new technologies – and of which frame of guidance should be preferred in response – acquires a particular relevance when looking at the human body and the technology of reproduction or transplant, for example. It is increasingly common to look for such guidance regarding technology and the body in the field of human rights, whereby questions of the ownership of the body and its parts came to be seen through the lens of property rights. Here we have seen the ground shift from a circumstance in which ownership of one's body was denied to one in which the law has outlined a range of conditions under which ownership of the body and its parts is prescribed: property rights have been established.

But this has brought to the fore a range of questions and challenged positions, the outcomes of which are far from determined. The main 'reference' position is that it is the stated intentions of the person whose body and body parts are under consideration that counts. However, this has been varied in the absence of a deceased owner's express intention and where there is no competing interest, and also varied if the owner had donated the body part to a public body bank, in which case it becomes property owned by whoever obtained it legally.

The purpose of seeking ownership has also become part of the mix where profit is set against the common good. With this we have seen the courts shift from the intent of the original owner to include other parties who may have an interest in body parts that become available down the track. Along with this has come the notion of limited property rights, where ownership of body parts is allowed but is limited to certain uses. This can include ownership for profit.

There has been a negative reaction to such profit seeking, as the excesses of the market have become increasingly obvious in this field. The reactions against this include an attempt to combine property rights with communality to resist such market incursion, whereby the originator of a body part continues to have a say about its use under the guise of a reinterpretation of the notion of gifting.[55] But legal pragmatism has not been the only response, as moral positions have also been put forward. Rather than relying on notions of fairness or consent and suchlike, these look to some intrinsic value in the body and its parts. But it is fair comment that, wherever property rights are introduced, even when used to protect a person's physicality, they still degrade and corrupt.

This argument about intrinsic value seems to appear most frequently regarding sperm, but the existential implications of that are more broadly applicable to organ donation. As a consequence, this line of argument can easily be drawn into commentary on the special and intrinsic nature of what it means to be human and consequential warnings about the commodification of the body and its parts encouraged by the application of property rights through the market. This is the

---

[55] I. Goold et al., 'Why does it matter how we regulate the use of human body parts?', *Journal of Medical Ethics* 40:1 (2014).

Common Ethical Principles 163

reduction of the body and its parts to a thing to enable possession for use or transfer, its alienation in the Cartesian manner: I am a thinking thing, therefore separate from my body. This argument is also extended to criticise an implied drive for control, preferring to accept that we cannot and should not aspire to or desire anything we can imagine, for example, regarding the state of our physicality: we should treasure what we are and not see our body or its parts as separable elements to be enhanced. In this our physicality is a gift,[56] and any provision of its parts to another who is in need should be seen in the same way. By this there is a presumption against a donor setting conditions regarding the characteristics of a donee, as this is argued as equivalent to monetising the body part. One outcome of this critique of property rights as human rights is a tendency to look to such other frames of value as human dignity, the limitations of which we have discussed.

There are a number of problems with these attempts to co-opt property rights as human rights. While it is patently so that such co-opting is a sign of the dominance of the Market – that is, commodification, alienation and monetarisation are pointers to its exploitative strategies regarding the body and its parts – property rights do not automatically lead to those outcomes. I could provide my body parts for a preferred recipient without any of these features coming into play. The proposal to reimagine the transfer of body parts as gifts under a property law regime seems to provide the necessary protection in my doing so. However, even in this frame, there are elements which go beyond the legal implications and beyond any moral reading that some might attempt to apply for the justification of such law. The political and commercial interests in such gifted property will remain robust and will keep these interests as strong contestants, including in a regime which highlights communal governance. A rationale is required which avoids this while protecting the interests of the parties.

Two other matters require comment. First, the notion of intrinsic value, be it of the body or its parts, is fraught with difficulty given the wide range of cultural contexts within which value, intrinsic or not, has to be considered. Second, the concern over the desire for control and the wish to accept circumstances as they are, for example, one's genetic features, not only appears to minimise the importance of bringing genetic diseases and defects under control but also ignores the political importance of bringing the Market – so widely recognised as predatory – under control. We will see that there is a frame for such rights that eliminates these concerns.

Common Good

The notion of the common good is another attractive value by which we might be guided in our management of the new technologies, especially given the disposition

---

[56] C. Stewart, et al., 'The Problems of Biobanking and the Law of Gifts', in *Persons, Parts and Property: How Should We Regulate Human Tissue in the 21st Century*, I. Goold et al. (eds.) (Hart Publishing, 2014), pp.25–38.

of sections of the Market to exploit a wide range of resources for commercial advantage and given the now-dominant tendency of the State to encourage commercial interests, including for its own bragging rights, but also in the enthusiastic pursuit of increased security. In response, Dickenson takes the reasonable view that the proper management of such new technologies as has emerged, for example, in the reproductive sciences, is best guided by communality rather than by the increasingly unrestrained liberal individualism we see. She cautions, however, that this communalism should not take the risky form of elaborate prescriptions of what is the common good, but should just rely on transparent, democratic institutional processes to provide its content.[57]

The search for foundations regarding the preference for communalism can understandably resolve into a critique of such liberal thinkers as Hobbes, Smith, Locke and Mill and a degree of sympathy for the thought of such as Aristotle,[58] Aquinas,[59] Rousseau[60] or even Kant,[61] although such sympathy would require caution. So while it remains so that there is a valid notion of common good – for example, the ending of global warming or the principle of education or value of the human genome or the banning of nuclear arms – what should be included in such a list and by whom is less clear, especially given the dominant influence of sectional interests in each area. That is, even with climate, education, genetics and nuclear arms, there are vast differences between positions on their status. What is certain is that scientific progress or democracy as such or corporate profitability or religious conviction should not be relied upon to establish such a status, all being fraught in this regard.

In this context it is perhaps unwise therefore to seriously downplay the importance of individual interest, so long as one approaches that from a position which is inclusive rather than one based simply on individual rights and desire. What is problematic about the argument that radical individualism should be seen as anathema to a common good, with the consequential move to provide for this through communal arrangements, is that it fails to see the dynamic which ties the State, the Market, scientific progress and rampant but normalised individualism together. So it is unable to see that a critique of that dynamic will make available a strong but different sense of individuality upon which a viable notion of common good can be constructed. Such a critique would be not only of Hobbes, Smith,

---

[57] D. Dickenson and A. Cattapan, 'On bio-ethics and the commodified body: An interview with Donna Dickenson', *Studies in Social Science* 10:2 (2016).

[58] Charles Taylor, 'Democratic degeneration: Three easy paths to regression', The American Academy in Berlin Fritz Stern Lecture (2017).

[59] P. Critchley, 'Aquinas, morality and modernity – The search for the natural moral law and the common good', *Academia* (2013).

[60] M. Thompson, 'Autonomy and common good: Interpreting Rousseau's general will', *International Journal of Philosophical Studies* 25:2 (2017).

[61] H. Varden, 'The General Will and Reform in Kant's Legal-Political Philosophy', European Consortium of Political Research (ECPR), Conference Paper (2017).

Locke and Mill but equally of Aquinas's anti-gnostic universalism, the general will of Rousseau, Kantian categorical imperatives and even Aristotle.[62]

AN ALTERNATIVE VALUE FRAME: RESPECTFUL RESPONSIBILITY TO AND FOR ONESELF

Although each of these standard principles of value has clearly attractive features, we have seen that they each carry noticeable shortcomings. It will now be argued that these shortcomings preclude them from being seen as pre-eminent guides in the management of new technologies, although this does not disbar them from the value field.

We have seen in Chapter 1 that the pre-eminent means for reconstituting and protecting privacy is the use of technology constructed on a conceptual foundation of respectful responsibility to and for oneself. It would be a surprise therefore if the value frame recommended as the basis of managing our relations with technology was not founded on the same principles.

Before proceeding to the advantages that this foundation has in relation to these other values, it is worth restating the principle elements of this alternative framework.

Existential Values

First, there is a notion of existential awareness upon which respectful self-responsibility rests. At the centre of this is that one is both allowed and encouraged to arrive at one's own frame of meaning. That is, one does not adopt, let alone embed, any frame of meaning such as those of the dominant ideologies of the trajectory. This does not indicate a necessary fragility of an existential frame of meaning, although it does point to the likelihood of a frame that evolves. It does not veil the absolutism of existence but embraces that condition. This is a gate not only to freedom but also to the sense of responsibility that is to and for oneself, but respectful of others. That includes a refusal to assume responsibility for another, although helping others in their search for that would be encouraged due to the advantages that would come from making these principles common. Taking responsibility for others who are incapable or handicapped in such a search – the very

---

[62] The author has presented elsewhere arguments that Hobbes, Smith, Locke, Mill and Rousseau have contributed to a trajectory of political mythology in which the citizen is induced, socialised or compelled to subject themself to the State in response to claims that the State will deal conclusively with their existential fears and desires; see *The Mythological State and Its Empire*. I have also argued that the notion of a mythological trajectory applies beyond politics to include Deity, the Market and now Technology. In that context, Aristotle and Aquinas are seen to contribute significantly to the formation of a broader myth; see chapters 2 and 3 of D. Grant and L. Bennett Moses, *Technology and the Trajectory of Myth*.

young, the aged, the infirm, others who are struggling or resistant to striving for such a condition or who intrude on the self-responsibility of others disrespectfully – is necessary, so long as that is itself undertaken with full respect. None of this precludes – in fact, it typically involves – that, in taking responsibility for oneself, one can and should enter mutually respectful arrangements with similar others on which one is obliged to deliver. This is not a matter of trust but is before trust, which may well follow. Consequently, among the principal elements is that the citizen is not merely allowed but is required to develop the skills, resources, decision-making and general capacity for self-reliance and ongoing self-development, including regarding the evolution of technology.[63]

This notion has wide implications: first, for the institutional framework as well as for civil society, which are explored in detail in following chapters; second, for the management of new technologies, the spread of which we have examined regarding the neuroscientific field, and the management of which we shall look at in Chapter 6 through a proposal for a new moral-technological frame. Finally, it has an implication for the other main 'value principles' that we have just examined. We shall now look at these.

Self-Responsibility and Other Values

We have just seen that *human dignity* is vacuous in absolute terms in that, in the world of serious ideological contest, a particular ideology can claim that acts to eliminate other ideologies – even violently – can be a display of both social and theological dignity. We have also seen that the claim that human dignity is the source of the capacity for moral reasoning has negative Kantian overtones which overshadow the more important value of agonistic response against the widely demonstrated human capacity to degrade and subject others. A much less dogmatic framework than human dignity is needed to deal with these unfortunately common sides of human nature. Human dignity is a valuable characteristic, but we are more likely to see a framework not locked in dogma where there is a promotion of respect between individuals who are urged to be self-reliant. Dignity is the result, not the foundation, of self-reliance and respect.

We have also just seen that the notion of *liberty* is locked within a highly contested field of meaning: Are the dominant interests of Church, State and Market those we should look to for protection of our liberties, or are they pre-eminent threats, and what role is technology playing in this? We saw in Chapter 3 that this theme of contradiction extends across a wide range of aspects of life in a liberal democracy – from health to education, to security and crime control, from the use of technology to finance and to religion – and within each there are strong

---

[63] See also D. Grant, *The Mythological State and Its Empire*, pp.9–12; D. Grant and L. Bennett Moses, *Technology and the Trajectory of Myth*, pp.209–210.

arguments on the side of individual rights and liberties but also on the side of State intervention, commercial viability and religious dogma. This has been complicated by the intrusion of technologies into personal practices, deeply informing and thereby subverting decisions by the citizen who willingly submits.

Against all this, there appears to be a need to develop a new paradigm in which the responsible citizen is moved to the centre of gravity in considering the nature of liberty. There are several immediate implications of such a shift. The first would be that technological solutions to questions that affect liberty would rarely, if ever, be the first step. That is, rather than extending the traditional framework to include – and progressively be replaced by – technological solutions, this is a move in the other direction away from the field in which dominant interests have in practice long decided questions of liberty. Both technology and the traditional institutional framework would move aside to make the respectful responsible citizen, rather than the demands of their dominant interests, the centre of attention. This is not the complete supplanting of technology, let alone of law, dogma or the market, only that the purpose of these forces would be to cooperatively enhance the development of respectful self-responsible behaviour by the citizen. We will see what that means in Chapters 7–10.

Neither is it to dismiss the wide range of conundrums we have just referred to from Chapter 3, only to state that these need to be looked at in a completely different light – in a new paradigm – and so with fully different outcomes. Again, the magnitudes of the trajectory need to be no longer forms to which we subject ourselves. On the contrary, their purpose should be to promote this sense of respectful, self-reliant liberty. Located within these conditions, this is a new sense of liberty.

We have also looked at *identity* as a key factor in technological management, making the point that such a notion of a sense of ourselves within our world view – as comprised of our fears, desires, goals, intentions, what we value and so on – includes not only how we want to relate to technology but more broadly what we see as an authentic life. We also saw that behind these – often contradictory – elements there are forces operating strategically which impact on each element and on how they relate to each other. Our religious views – if we have those – our political beliefs, our commercial and consumer attitudes not only undergo change over time but reflect what forces we are subject to as we form and try to sustain some kind of coherent world view. In turn, each of these affects our attitude towards technologies, whether these are seen as vital services embedded in our practices or whether they are a constraint to living in the world more freely or something of each of these.

In short, we cannot understand how to deal properly with these technologies, for example, how they should be regulated and used, without an appreciation of these formative influences. What is their nature and their purpose, and, importantly, do their ideas and practices contribute to an authentic sense of self, how we would choose to be in the world in the sense indicated by Heidegger?[64] Or do they lead us into beliefs and practices that primarily serve other interests, such as those of the trajectory? If the latter is the case, we would then ask what kind of reimagining will allow a more authentic, existential sense of self, through which we as individuals decide the beliefs and practices we are happy to have in common with others – or, respectfully, not – and impose on the world in place of the dominant world views, to which we are largely subject. This would be a new Kantianism, in which authenticity would mean taking responsibility for oneself both immediately and in a broader, strategic sense in which we accept existential reality and deal with that without subjection to ideologies and interests that claim to provide relief from it.

Such an undertaking would not mean forgoing the wide range of sensible arrangements that help us navigate the world in relative safety, but it is asking about the broader elements of what we think about, how we behave and where we place ourselves in the context of competing world views to develop each our own. This is especially relevant in considering the personal impact of new technologies, by which our sense of identity is to be increasingly exposed to progressive and radical transformation, as we have seen regarding neuroscience.

Our consideration of *equality* is also revealing, in that, sitting behind the obvious problem of understanding what equality actually is – Does it relate to rights, to distribution of resources, to life opportunities? – there is the more profound 'centre of gravity' issue. That is, irrespective of repeated reference to the rights, capabilities, experiences, conditions of existence, and aspirations of citizens, the centre of gravity in addressing these matters typically defaults to Deity and to the State and the Market, wherein the contents and limitations of equality are formed and overseen. Therefore, if equality is to be fully experienced by the citizen and not ultimately be an imposition from the magnitudes of such dominant ideologies, the right and aspirations of the citizen to be responsible for themself must be at the heart of – and not the consequence of – promotional sociopolitical arrangements.

These foundational, 'centre of gravity' issues regarding equality are what lie behind – and raise questions about – such issues as how the notion of rights plays out in the political field and beyond and, more broadly, the nature of government authority and legitimacy, the range of its policies and the relation of these to the nature and quality of individual capacity and opportunity; the meaning of both dignity and consent; and the justifications for distributing resources – that is, what equality is and how it works in a political community. These all look very different in a trajectory-centred arrangement than they would where the respectful, self-reliant individual is at the centre.

Importantly, this question is also at the heart of how we might relate to new technologies. Given that self-responsibility has at its core not only self-reliance but also the enhancement of the individual, then access to emerging technologies by all

---

[64] M. Heidegger, *Question Concerning Technology*, 10–11.

is centrally important. We have seen this regarding neuroscience. But the matter goes beyond that since, as the speed of technological innovation increases, the risk of, say, artificial intelligence overtaking and then taking over human capacity means that it is crucially important that citizens both are offered and embrace a technological capacity to cope with the impact of this, technologically and socially.

The consideration of *human rights* as a frame for the management of new technologies shows that, despite the high status of this value principle, there are significant problems to be addressed, both broadly and when the focus is on one's own body. Regarding the latter, we saw some advantages in an arrangement which features the notion of gifting combined with a donor's retention of an interest within a property rights frame. However, we also saw that this still needed to deal with the incursion of political and commercial interests, even into communal rights. We also saw that the notion of inherent value was problematic and that the desire for control should not be regarded as anathema.

What is required is a workable frame which includes these three elements but which does not rely on the pragmatism of property rights combined with communality. This is provided by the principles proposed here, in that I can gift my body parts and be allowed to retain an interest in their subsequent disposition, making that gifting conditional. This frame also allows changing my body, even dramatically, without being criticised for rejecting the status quo by wanting to be in control. In fact, even beyond corrective intervention, such changes are central to the enhancement of which such self-responsibility is partly comprised. What is of value is not some inherent status but what will promote self-responsibility. All this avoids the property rights frame so far as my body is concerned. The key here is the rejection of any crude account of Cartesian dualism, that is, of any notion that I am in some simple way separate from my body. It is the rejection put by Heidegger in defence of an authentic existence,[65] and it is this sense of existentialism that informs the principles herein as the basis of a new sense of privacy.

Given these connections between existential authenticity, respectful self-responsibility and the body, it is appropriate to make some broader remarks about the relationship between the body and new technologies since these connections also provide the rationale for the notion of privacy presented in this work. Respectful self-responsibility regarding the body is comprised of three areas. The first relates to external intrusion into the body, where – in the context of protecting the integrity of the body – the priorities include setting conditions, arrangements, opportunities and limits for enhancements, and denying any downloading of data of any kind without the express permission of the citizen and subject to any such download being consistent with an ability to show respect for others, that is not for malevolent purposes.

---

[65] M. Heidegger, *Being and Time*, s211, 254.

170 *Privacy, Its Values and Technology*

Second, regarding the forgoing of one's body, where the priorities include denying any upload of neurological or originating data or the provision of other body parts unless gifted to another and whether or not conditions are applied by the donor. Such conditions would not apply where the State has justifiable reasons for monitoring data due to threats from crime or terrorism, and where judicial approval is received; metadata may be gathered by the State without such express approval so long as that is justified by crime control and to prevent terrorism; corporations may gather personal data so long as there is pre-existing approval from the citizen but may not sell that data outside conditions set by that citizen. Further, no citizen may sell themself into slavery as that is a denial of self-responsibility. No one may sell their data or body parts except for express, respectful purposes, that is, not for 'any reason the buyer may determine', as that also is forgoing of self-responsibility.

Third, regarding the condition of the body, the citizen must be primarily responsible for one's health to ensure that minimal call is made on routine procedures funded by the community, to ensure that any body parts passed on are in an acceptable state and to ensure that intervention is, whenever possible, for enhancement rather than corrective purposes.

It can be added now that these provisions begin to give a fuller sense of the foundational place of respectful self-responsibility within the broader context of human rights examined above. That is, they point to how the individual needs to take control not just of their body – including their neural content – but also of their beliefs, acquisition of self-sustaining skills – including regarding advancing technologies – political participation, post-conviction rehabilitation and personal information. None of this denies the necessity for the reimagining of the social institutions necessary to promote this acceptance of responsibility, as we shall see.

What is required in developing a viable sense of the *common good* is not one which plays down or sees as risky a reliance on a strong individualism but one which reimagines individualism in a manner that incorporates a notion of the common good through respect. We should turn away from the political theorists mentioned above in this regard to the extent that they fail to do so. Self-responsibility – the notion that no citizen should assume responsibility for another through any singular determination of the conditions of existence of that other – forms the basis of such a strong individualism but it has implicit within it the notion of mutual respect.

Together, these two principles can well found a notion of the common good, while at the same time resisting the intrusion of external dominant interests, this by reimagining social, political, commercial and technological institutions. As an example, the protection of the human genome as developed by the Human Genome Project can stand beside the right of a citizen to manage and amend their personal genome both for therapeutic correction and for enhancement, so long as no risk was taken to either concurrent or generational genomic conditions. That is, I am responsible for my genome but must show respect for others in changing it. That is, regarding genomics, there are dual protections while allowing enhancements. A further example concerns education, where there are multiple responsibilities. On one hand, the citizen is responsible to engage in educational programmes which sustain a sense of human commonality, thereby showing respect. On the other, there should be no restrictions on personal enhancement, so long as there is no malevolent purpose in that. In this field of personal enhancement, beyond enhancement that a citizen might prefer for personal reasons, there is a responsibility to sustain an awareness and competence regarding technological advances, say, in self-generating artificial intelligence, so that developments there do not outstrip the human capacity for managing them. This is a different sense of the common good. Concerning climate change, it is incumbent on each citizen to voice strong views and take proper action regarding any interest which continues to threaten the state of the climate. Beyond that, each citizen must accept personal responsibility for any behaviour within their own sphere of influence which degrades the climate. Regarding nuclear arms, there is little to be said, as their very presence reveals the intention to – put politely – both assume responsibility for others and display a lack of respect for them.

In the context of the ever-increasing intervention of technologies into our conditions of existence, the notion of *personal responsibility* for moral and rational decision-making will be increasingly important. Will neurotechnological interventions change our awareness or our moral frame or our rational capacity? Technology is, of course, not the only qualifier for these capacities. It needs to take its place alongside such other qualifiers as our inherent or acquired biological, psychological and social factors, each of which is also increasingly affected by technologies. The result may well be an expanding evolution of each of these factors, but how determinative are they? They may still leave a zone of responsible – albeit constrained – autonomous decision-making, but the task remains of understanding the nature and effect of these qualifiers, both singly and in combination.

If one accepts that it is difficult to convincingly attribute this rational but qualified decision-making that makes up personal responsibility in some straightforward way to our 'mental states' or to a patchwork of learned social customs, norms or moral codes, might there be another approach to understanding personal responsibility? Also, could such an approach enclose the two senses of responsibility referred to above, that is, this sense of rational decision-making and the sense of me taking on a commonly agreed set of principles and practices? These two may not be unrelated, but they are not the same.

It is an argument put here that between neurological disposition and autonomous decision-making is a field populated not just by a patchwork of learned customs and practices but by an array of ideas and practices promoted by institutions – typically, theological, political, commercial and now technological – that are managed strategically by dominant interests which both cooperate and compete and the purpose of which is a dual 'claimed benefit and subjection' of citizens. This argument is also that these strategies impact on both neurology and behaviour and so on decision-making and responsibility, in both senses of the latter. It is these strategies to which we respond differentially – typically complying, even unthinkingly, but occasionally resisting – in making decisions and being responsible, also in both senses. From that, our behaviour is not neurologically determined but, significantly, impacted by social constructs that are strategically deployed but not hardwired into us. This is far from determinism.

The challenge then is how to become aware of and respond to this complex, influential field. The argument here is that this can be realised not by attributing too much to neurology or mental states or traditional notions of socialisation. It can be realised by awareness of the ideas and practices that are attributable to the mythological magnitudes of the trajectory as their champions claim to generate particular forms of the 'self' and then determining not to forgo one's responsibility for oneself. Such would be a form of life with echoes something akin to Heidegger's authentic, existential living. Doing so will allow a sense of self that is responsible in a different way, one that is to no one else and for no one else, except for those who require support. This also provides a context for responding to – along with the predecessor magnitudes – the new technologies in ways which are not determinative.

The issue of *liberal democratic regulation* properly involves the debate about whether the State should be constrained from surveilling personal data and personal lives more generally, on the one hand, and its responsibility to protect citizens by gathering data about crime, terrorism and economic indicators, on the other. This is usually resolved by referring to the notion of non-domination rather than non-interference. Domination would be arbitrary interference. However, non-domination allows the State to intervene in the interests of the citizen on the basis of presumed consent, while liberalism would regard that as controversial, although Pettit – who popularised this account – then developed a second iteration by adding that the power of the State over its citizens will not be arbitrary if the people have an equal share in controlling the State's exercise of power. The problem is that the flaws in the first iteration are not corrected with the second. That is, the first iteration suffers from the weakness that, because the State interferes in my life on the basis of what is commonly regarded as the interests of citizens, it does not mean that I necessarily regard such intervention as in my interest. I may wish to behave in a manner contrary to commonly regarded principles but would do so respectful of others' self-responsibility. So, such intervention is arbitrary. This is not resolved by giving people an equal share in controlling State power. That move still leaves me subject to the common view about what the State should be empowered to do. It is still arbitrary interference on the same grounds.

In that context, non-consensual surveillance of my data by the State would not be allowed, and any judicial approval to explore it non-consensually would need to first have a supply of evidence of potentially significant wrongdoing on my part. Corporations, with their restricted responsibility to protect individual liberty, should have no right to capture metadata or personal data except under conditions outlined above for human rights. Further, the issue of the subconscious level at which commercial corporations operate, especially regarding their marketing strategies, is more significant than is generally recognised. That is, marketing is a strategy which combines the claim of the satisfaction of desire on condition of subjection to the commercial regime, the purpose of which is downstream manipulation. Data collection is now a central part of this entire 'claimed satisfaction-subjection' strategy. Resisting this would not preclude the voluntary sharing of information by the citizen either to help in the provision of enhancement services or in the interests of community health standards.

The important point is that these elements – the constructed corporate magnitude, the dominant interests that manage them, the strategic claimed satisfaction of desire on condition of subjection and so on – are all key elements in the modern mythologies that are intended to distance and camouflage our attention from existential concerns. The State is another such magnitude and it operates in a similarly sublimated manner, claiming to have the same impact by distancing our existential fears on condition of our subjection to it.

This leads to the acknowledgement that liberal democratic regulation – the regulation of technology by the State in this case – needs to be seen in this context. The State is not – never has been – a straightforwardly functional representative entity but one that operates – through a governmentality – on the basis of subjection, the camouflaging of existential concerns and the claimed resolution of constructed fears and desires. Its regulation of technology is – like technology itself – saturated in these mythological layers of meaning, and we need to be sure that regulation is not used to subject citizens based on the claim of eliminating fear and satisfying desire. So, again, it is a personal strategy of moving the respectful self-responsible citizen to centre-stage and the reimagining of the State and the Market and the forcing of technology into a properly functional – not mythological – role.

A Further Note on the Bourgeoisie

It is appropriate at this point to again reflect on the comments in Chapter 4 regarding the bourgeois characteristics of which our current common notion of privacy is largely comprised, due to the impact of the mythological magnitudes on our psychological space and in which the bourgeoisie have played a key role. Respectful self-responsibility would not fall prey to such dispositions as 'heritage' sexuality, class-inspired political activism, exploitative capitalist entrepreneurship, protective domesticity, exaggerated consumerism, defensive self-discipline and self-determination and as beneficiaries of algorithmic technology. Nor – to the considerable extent to which the bourgeoisie contributed to it – would it allow the manipulation of the flow of information which thereby subjects individuals. There would be no absence of psychological fragility, but its source would be the absolutism of reality, not the forces of the magnitudes of State and Market. Respectful self-responsibility would be a substantial immunisation against these and so would allow a different sense of privacy.

We can now proceed to explore what a sense of privacy that honours this preferred ethical framework might look like.

6

A New Sense of Privacy

The new account of privacy presented here is founded on this revised ethical frame and is developed in response to the manifest shortcomings of present accounts. Neither of those two accounts addresses the implications for privacy that rests in the primary human condition and is of the most private significance. That is the absolutism of reality, the existential question. That is, they do not go to the heart of privacy. Neither do they see the strategic nature of the dynamic that has produced the large part of what have become our private concerns. In fact, they repeat it. Neither are they set up to deal with the algorithmic presumptions, intrusions and opportunities of emerging neuroscience.

Each in its own way not only conceives of privacy in the context of its own time, but does so by reflecting or allowing the intrusive power of the mythological magnitudes. The result is that, on one hand, the Constitutional account has emerged as the protection of a confidential space, in which each individual seeks to be left alone so that they may pursue a self-fashioning, protected in this by a range of constitutional and legal provisions. In short, an account for the bourgeois individual. On the other hand, each of the information flow arguments contributes elements to an account that would preserve a flow of preferred information within a social context but, although it has the door open to an explanation of the dynamics that 'select' the flow of information, does not do so in the context of the dominant dynamics at work and which determine that selective flow. They are more focused on the movement of information in the current social context than with the dynamic that constitutes both social context and information flow. Each is thereby a mythology-tolerant account.

So the first principle of a new privacy must be an acceptance of existential reality. This is thereby an awareness of the mythological dynamic and thereby, in turn, a refusal to subject oneself to – or to be induced into spending most of one's time attempting to constrain – any of the ideologies whose claims to deal with that reality are conditional on subjection to its regimes of idea and practice.

The implication of this first principle is that, consistent with the nature of existential living, one accepts existential fear and desire and goes about determining ways to deal with and to use these as motivation to live authentically and self-responsibly in respect for others. Further, one determines one's own frame of meaning. We have explored the dimension of this already, but it means that *privacy is the 'to and for oneself' of that ethical frame*. Privacy needs to be seen as inseparable from this frame. This, in turn, means that one needs to be allowed, encouraged and required to be self-reliant', not reliant on another and with none other reliant on oneself, subject to sensible caring principles for particular others, as already outlined. 'To and for oneself' is the second principle of privacy. This combination of factors is an optimistic, not a 'cynical' approach.[1]

Further, since self-responsibility cannot be achieved by the individual alone, there needs to be information sharing and cooperation with key public and private agencies to realise the goals of self-responsibility. This would include the substantial extent to which self-responsible citizens would demonstrate respect through the spectrum of personal and collaborative relationships. This information sharing and cooperation is the third principle of the new privacy.

Further again, part of self-reliance in a fast-changing technological world will require one not only to be presently self-reliant but also to plan for future change. Technology is a part of this, including neuroscientific self-enhancement. Neuroscience should be embraced, albeit conditioned and applied in a manner that promotes self-responsibility. This conditional embrace is the fourth principle of privacy.

Regarding information, it is a key for this new privacy that a citizen owns, manages but conditionally forgoes their data. Such ownership allows them to think through what is meaningful for them and to plan their existential life goals uninterrupted by others. Because existential living is the goal, this is not, as it is with Floridi et al., the central but a derivative element, and it is the fifth principle.

Finally, because this sense of privacy will need to rely on – and cannot be subject to – any of the magnitudes, then the agencies which are presently a part of the contemporary organisational infrastructure would need to be reimagined as purposed to promote respectful, existential living and not the exploitation of the individual. This is the sixth principle of privacy and is the subject of the following chapters.

We shall now explore these principles in more detail, but, in short, such an exploration will produce a new sense of privacy which withdraws completely from – and requires the reimagining of – the modern mythological dynamic that has to now constituted the ideas and practices of all the social, political and technological

---

[1] O. Stavrova et al., 'Victims, perpetrators or both? The vicious cycle of disrespect an cynical beliefs about human nature', *Journal of Experimental Psychology: General* (2020), doi:10.1037/xge0000738.

infrastructure normalised within us. Some may argue that there are echoes of both constitutional and information flow accounts of privacy in this. It is better to see that appropriate elements of those have been drawn into a fully new account, the foundations and practice of which are a complete reversal of current accounts of privacy. The individual, suitably made self-responsible, is at the centre of – not the product of – this account. Being distinct from current alternatives – Constitutional, information flow and informational ontology – there is no 'being left alone' to pursue one's confidential self-fashioning. It cannot be reduced to an idea about the contextual, selected flow of information, since information flow – even if at optimal levels – is merely one indicator of the new arrangements of existential privacy. Finally, neither can it resolve into information as an ontological state, as that is an algorithmic reconstruction of the ineffability of human reality, even if that is largely decoded and the reconstruction is protected by an ethical code.

THE WAY FORWARD

To further emphasise the range of counter-forces with which this new account will have to deal – that is, beyond the wide range of forces already presented and bringing these further up to date – we shall first note a variety of current developments which further demonstrate the techniques of subjection. Then, following the presentation of the essential elements of a new, preferred notion, we shall look at the leading current alternative proposal, which will thereby be revealed to feature various flaws, albeit among a range of attractive features. Finally, in this chapter we shall look at a selection of well-recognised privacy conundrums and how their resolution would be advanced by the application of the new privacy model.

Counter-forces

Beyond the standard range of online data and image-based methods available and the potential of the neuroscientific advances we have looked at, there are quite recent new opportunities being taken up by the State to increase the surveillance and subjection of citizens technologically. Faggella has identified at least seven new technological developments which are being adapted or designed for the purpose of surveilling citizens. These include smart glasses for widespread facial recognition, AI-enabled body cameras to enable racial profiling, EEG headbands for emotional surveillance, smart school uniforms to track students, 24/7 wristbands to be worn by criminals, robotic birds for covert civilian surveillance, and social credit scoring.[2] It is noticeable that many of these are more prominent in weakly or non-democratic countries. However, this should not be regarded as a salve to those in other

---

[2] D. Fagella, 'Artificial intelligence for government surveillance: 7 unique use cases', Emerj (24 November 2019).

jurisdictions who are concerned about such developments, especially given the demands upon democratic governments to optimise provisions of security. Such demands enable governments to utilise both their increasing technological armory and their rapidly expanding databases to both monitor and profile citizens at will.

Fagella also canvasses the dramatic, imminent evolution of AI – including advances in neuroscience, in artificial general intelligence (AGI) and the related emergence of non-human intelligences – and takes the fully credible view that these will be disruptions in both senses of that word. From this he joins an increasing band of prominent experts who urge cooperative planning regarding the kind of human intelligence that we might set as goals, thereby to try to avoid the kind of human crisis which will likely otherwise emerge if the resolution of these issues is left to the competitive instinct.[3] The latter point is emphasised by the manner in which large technology corporations – the Market – are influencing the rules that will govern AI. We saw in Chapter 2 that, regarding the release of the EU Ethics Guidelines for Trustworthy AI, Metzinger not only dismissed the argument that AI can be trustworthy but stated that his advice to the EU that certain AI uses should be prohibited – such as autonomous weapons and social credit scoring – was ignored following representations by well-known technology corporations through the trade group DigitalEurope.

A VERY DIFFERENT VIEW OF PRIVACY

As we now move forward into the presentation of a new account, it is appropriate to keep in mind the principles we have just looked at. They are informed by the argument that the approaching wave of neuroscientific technologies requires a gestalt shift in how we think about privacy. We will inevitably become increasingly embedded – neurologically – in the technological world of artificial intelligence. We therefore need to find a way to accommodate this embedding – in fact, to embrace it due to the advantages it will bring – while sustaining a sense of self that we as individuals determine. This will require a new, very different sense of privacy, not one that is tied to the bourgeois heritage of much privacy thought or which attempts to convert it fully into the currency of information (as either flow or ontology). It must not only embrace technology but also promote respect by ensuring the State and the Market do not gather or share our personal information – except through independently authorised methods for reasons of security – including about oneself as generated within forms of social cooperation. This new privacy must be tied to the personal enhancement of physical, psychological and cognitive capacities that will sustain self-responsibility. In that, its embrace of neuroscience must be engineered to allow this two-way flow of social and educational knowledge,

---

[3] D. Fagella, 'The international governance of AI – We unite or we fight', Emerj (9 September 2019).

embedded in practice, in a manner that still allows for the conservation of know-ledge about oneself – beyond all this necessary exchange – so that we may continue to enjoy our personal thoughts and plans alone or in company. Finally, because this is all against the grain of much State and Market practice, this notion of privacy must be embedded in – and cannot be understood as separate from – reimaginings of the ways in which the State, the Market and Technology operate. Privacy is thereby a field that operates across this range of the 'to and for oneself' of 'respectful responsibility to and for oneself'. By this it will be possible for humanity to deal – constructively rather than defensively – with the looming developments in neuro-science, of which we have so far seen only the first wave.

The New Privacy Will Be Progressive and Conservative

This account of privacy is founded on two combined notions, one 'progressive' and one 'conservative'. Together, these would comprise a *personal technology strategy* which produces this combination of respect, enhancement and the embrace of technology in a manner that is non-mythological. Due to that, existential fear and desire are not anathema but are embraced, its opportunities sought. It also embraces a particular kind of social integration but changes the nature of both State and Market. By all that, it also produces a new sense of Regulation and of the Rule of Law.

Progression and Conservation – Broad Themes

A dominant means for the establishment of this new socially progressive-conservative framework must itself be technology. That is, the respect, enhancement, rule of law, regulation and institutional practice envisaged here are all facilitated to a substantial degree by technical redesign. What this means is that, rather than adopt pre-designed technological solutions to these challenges, the citizen must – first and foremost – have primary 'technological skin in the game' by which they engage the world and which has embedded in it, as its primary purpose, the citizen's self-defined interest as a respectful subject. Such personalised technology would deter-mine all that is allowed to be uploaded, shared, maintained or downloaded, among other functions. This personal technology would not be neurally embedded, although – in time as its functioning and credentials were thoroughly tested – the possibility of occasional neural connection could be possible.[4]

---

[4] I am grateful to Professor David Grayden, Clifford Chair of Neural Engineering in the Department of Biomedical Engineering, Melbourne School of Engineering at the University of Melbourne, who has been cautiously optimistic about the ultimate feasibility of the model presented here should the science continue to develop in this field. Nonetheless, I take full responsibility for the arguments put here.

180   *A New Sense of Privacy*

This technology would operate through a software network of subject-designed algorithms[5] and ultimately within a quantum-based blockchain arrangement that could engage any external technology designed to upload or download data from and into a personal, discrete, external information pod. It would have embedded within it one's personal technology strategy which would evolve over time. Given the reservations expressed in Chapter 2 concerning the reality-constructing nature of data and algorithms, the data and algorithms here would be a reflection of the design requirements of the citizen, not provided off the shelf to them, designed by others. It would thereby interface all online elements of a citizen's engagement with the reimagined State and Market institutions outlined below in Chapters 7–10.

The key here is that, through this technologically realised personal technology strategy, we need to accept the inevitability of the individual as embedded in the technological world, but here as agent and not as subject. This arrangement dispenses with the idea of one of the key elements of traditional notions of privacy, the strict boundary, replacing this with an interactive but controlled interface through which the citizens exerts agency. The software is both a protective and an enabling device under the full control of the agent, except where the State exercises independently authorised intervention for security purposes. It would operate via an interactive data pod, external to the individual, which filters data uploaded to authorised agencies as well as within any potential implant or download. It thereby houses an abiding statement of the aspirations and responsibilities of the citizen. With the likely eventual cognitive downloading of data, such filtering would be uncontroversial regarding the downloading embodied in most sensory corrective or routine enhancement devices but would be seriously tested regarding ideational or behaviour modification. For example, one can imagine the attraction to law makers of imposing neurological changes to give effect to behavioural change. For the principle of respectful self-responsibility to be sustained, the status of the 'non-normalised' would be no different to that of 'citizens'. That is, no technological 'solution' could be imposed neurally.

A distinction between this arrangement and other models of personalised technology, such as is proposed by either Domingos or Goertzel, needs to be restated. For Domingos, the model would negotiate the world on behalf of the citizen: it would filter emails and reply on one's behalf; check credit card bills and dispute improper charges; complete tax returns; renew subscriptions; identify a solution for a medical ailment and run it by one's doctor; identify job opportunities and be interviewed by the company's model as to one's suitability; suggest candidates to vote for; or screen potential dates and work with the date's model to pick a restaurant

---

[5] A. Knutas et al., 'A process for designing algorithm-based personalised gamification', *Multimedia Tools and Applications* 78 (2019):1353; this is distinct from algorithms designed by others but tuned to what data-based predictions say about her interests – see M. Zanker et al., 'Measuring the impact of online personalisation: Past, present and future', *International Journal of Human-Computer Studies* 131 (November 2019): p.160.

or search for entertainment. One's model would be targeted by the models of the purveyors of every product and service and be screened by it for one, and it would learn from one's feedback and upgrade itself. Much of this is brought together through the placement of all of one's data with a single corporation which would protect it and dispense it on one's behalf for various purposes in line with one's instructions.[6] Goertzel envisions a far wider and deeper role for AI in a world run by artificial general intelligence (AGI). He sees the evolution of a global brain to which all are connected so that it develops adult human-level common sense intelligence which is integrated with the technical intelligence of AGI expert systems. The end of all this is an arrangement in which we would see the construction of 'genius boxes' to answer all questions and in which total surveillance would see the disappearance of politics, death and so on.[7] The point with both of these is, of course, that the systems they envisage do not preserve the respectful self-responsibility of the individual but transfer it to AI-based systems. They are both thereby mythological, a manifestation of the Absolute Self.

Beyond being conceived in the manner described, the preferred system can be further enhanced by a series of additional measures. These would include the use of AI systems that doubt themselves and so would make more credible enhancement proposals by embracing uncertainty[8] – because AI does not fully understand the results of its actions, the use of AI is designed with an 'undo', that is, reversibility[9] – and by regular auditing of others' algorithms to identify the full range of their inherent data and design biases.[10] This would be the place where a self-sovereign identity carried by a quantum-based blockchain would be both progressive and conservative by virtue of its nodal database structure.[11]

Progression – Some Specifics

The progressive element would be a plan that represented the required enhancement – 'requirement' being key in the context of the demythologisation of one's life – of individuals through the embrace of these technologies.[12] Rather than a carte

---

[6] P. Domingos, *The Master Algorithm*, pp.267–276.

[7] B. Goertzel and Ted Goertzel, *The End of the Beginning* (2015), pp. 710–716.

[8] Will Knight, 'Google and others are building AI systems that doubt themselves', *MIT Tech Review* (2018).

[9] 'Researchers are building AI with an undo', *The Download MIT Tech Review* (27 November 2017).

[10] Organisations like ORCAA (O'Neil Risk Consulting and Algorithmic Auditing) are emerging to undertake the task of external auditing to assess algorithms for fairness.

[11] P. Diamandis, 'Blockchain breakthroughs coming in the next 5 years', Singularity Hub (7 June 2019).

[12] One suggestion that has been made in this area, that is, the relationship of humans with machine intelligence, is to design robots that fear death so that their sense of vulnerability would ensure they care more about what they do and think. One might observe that this might also motivate their machine learning to protect themselves from humanity and so become

blanche for self-indulgence, this would be primarily for the acquisition of skills and knowledge that actualised the principle of self-responsibility but also would be the framework for information exchanges in one's online personal and collaborative relationships. It also would include details of any entertainment experience that was not subjecting.

Guided by the personal technology strategy – and operating through one's personally designed algorithms – this plan would involve engaging with reimagined State and Market agencies, the function of which would be to support the individual's chosen enhancements, so that they can develop all elements of that strategy. The agency is subsidiary in this, although its support would be subject to certain priorities, such as giving equal emphasis to the fulfilment of the citizen's responsibility to be familiar with the latest technological developments – to avoid 'falling behind' as that development progresses – and actively denying assistance in any sought enhancement that would constrain the individual's respect for self-responsible others. The responsibility of all agencies would extend to mentioning any rehabilitation or enhancement that might progress the individual's own strategy. Given the continual auditing of data downloaded to the personal, external nodal 'pod', well-tested innovative learning methods of the future may become acceptable as means of 'occasional', second-stage – that is, following the comprehensive stress test of the system – direct neural uploading and downloading, although the prospect of direct neural connection to the cloud – itself a repository of potentially mythological data – needs to be approached with extreme caution.

This current action plan for implementing the strategy, located nodally and separate from the citizen but under their control, would thereby contain a range of elements, some of which would be shared conditionally with State or Market institutions. These may include inter alia current aspirations and activities, for example, regarding sought medical interventions; skills development activities; priority communication initiatives; virtual entertainment initiatives; virtual therapeutic planning and experience, including augmented reality and virtual reality; and so on. It would be a port of call for auditing agencies. However, it would always be continually monitored by the citizen themself as the technology must be always presumed to be capable of error and bias. This would be in particular to ensure that, apart from registering an interaction with the citizen – for example, a purchase transaction, an online enquiry or a course registration and result – the plan would preclude any 'profiling' of the individual allowed unless specifically approved by them for the purpose of promoting further enhancement. That is, there would no accumulating external individualised data bank of the kind currently employed by State and Market.

---

more wary and thereby a threat. K. Man et al., 'Homeostasis and soft robotics in the design of feeling machines', *Nature Machine Intelligence* 1 (2019): p.446.

A Very Different View of Privacy 183

VR and AR would play an important role in this overall strategy. Given its capacity to demythologise individual lives, these technologies would be the means by which citizens would be refamiliarized – in a controlled environment of the kind currently used successfully for post-traumatic stress disorder (PTSD) therapy and with any digital recording subsequently available only to the citizen themself – with the existential realities and opportunities within the natural and social worlds. Such experiences would then remain as reminders of the mythologising potential of State and Market – and Deity – even when these are begun to be reimagined in the manner that we shall see in Chapters 9 and 10.

As an operational rule, all this is a reversal of present arrangements whereby the centre of gravity rests with the dominant interests of State and Market.

Conservation – Some Specifics

The purpose of the conservation element of the model would be various. It would act as a digital library to include the template of the strategy, amended as the plan evolves but retaining the history of initiatives taken, successes and failures regarding skill acquisition and planned virtual experiences. It would be a locale for the resource and service contracts with citizens that would emerge when the citizen decided on their content and it would include risk management and audit provisions regarding this overall system as it related to each citizen, regarding the effectiveness of all personally designed data and algorithms and regarding the personal data authorised by the citizen for sharing with State, Market and others.

There are two principal sets of relationships which, along with their design and use of technologies, will determine the outcome of the conservation element of the proposed privacy model. To set those relationships properly in place – and ensure they begin for the first time to operate non-mythologically – the model would first require immediate and extensive collaboration between researchers and regulators to establish necessary principles, legislation, collaborative monitoring and sanctions regarding technology redesign for the purposes of personalisation. Under that process, new technologies would from the design stage be blocked if they were intended to intervene unilaterally in the personal technology strategy. All this would be audited by the personal algorithms to identify any residual bias.

As with the plan, given the necessary ownership of data by the citizen, no institution would be able to gather or share personal data from this personal digitised library without approval, including between State and Market.[13] Related data must

---

[13] See F. Cate and J. Dempsey, *Bulk Collection – Systematic Government Access to Private-Sector Data* (Oxford University Press, 2017), where they state at p.5 that 'Transparency about systematic access remains weak' and at p.191, regarding the United States, 'DARPA's TIA programme foreshadowed the potential of how machine learning techniques, when trained on the right data sets, might assist in "predictive policing" and predictive intelligence efforts. Given this

184   *A New Sense of Privacy*

be protected by encrypted, unhackable, quantum technology[14] wherein the techni-
cian forgoes all rights of access to it. That would be a demonstration of respect for
the individual. It would not prevent the accessing of personal data for genuine
security purposes, as long as there is independent – say, judicial – examination and
authorisation of that and an explanation given to the citizen wherever appropriate.
Nor would it disallow the receipt of personal data for the purpose of the State
planning to deliver resources to satisfy the reasonable enhancement demands of
citizens. This is in marked contrast to current practice where not only are vast
amounts of personal data gathered, but they are shared widely for individual profiling and a range of other surveillance-related purposes, including for both security
and commercial purposes. It cannot be denied that mining data directly from the
brain would be an attractive strategy. Given the forces currently at play and the wide
sources of data, establishing ownership of personal data by the citizen is required as a
first step in the transition to non-mythological arrangements. This does not absolve
the need for each citizen to share personal data – fully protected – that may benefit
others, as a means of the individual showing respect. Sensitive personal health data
would be an example. All this should apply whether or not the data is depersonalised
or aggregated, with permission.

Beyond that, a range of personal information should be protected from mining.
This would be concerned with the confidential development by the individual of
their personal technology strategy. It would also include the personal expressions
and experiences that come with thinking through the fears and desires associated
with existential reality. Some of these, even, will be shared in confidence if a citizen
chooses to explore these through social relationships or through such means as
virtual reality or downloads of these neurally once the strategy is formed.

Alternative Accounts

Given that many of the issues regarding the widening presence of technology in the
lives of individuals, often ominously, are now increasingly appreciated, there has
been a range of attempts to address the reasonable expectations of individuals. The
present work is such an attempt but there are, of course, others. One of the most
significant efforts in this regard, particularly because it attempts – albeit unsuccessfully in the final analysis – to address many of the key issues, is the work of the
Institute of Electrical and Electronics Engineers (IEEE), especially in its attempts to
explore and refine the notion of Ethically Aligned Design.[15]

---

   potential, the government's desire and need for more private-sector data will only continue to
   increase.'
[14] Y. Sodeyoka, 'Unhackable Internet', *MIT Technology Review* (26 February 2020).
[15] IEEE, *Ethically Aligned Design (First Edition)*, pp.3ff.

A *Very Different View of Privacy* 185

In its *Ethically Aligned Design (First Edition)*, the IEEE presents a number of principles as imperatives:

- Respect for internationally recognised human rights
- Increased human well-being as a success criterion
- Empowerment of individuals to have access to and control of their data (the create/curate/control frame)
- Provision of evidence of the effectiveness and purpose of artificial and intelligence systems (A/IS)
- Transparency of every A/IS decision
- Provision of unambiguous rationale for all decisions made
- Prevention of potential misuse and awareness of risks of A/IS
- Adherence of creators and operators to knowledge and skill required for safe and effective operation.

This frame invites a number of comments. On the positive side, it correctly identifies the fundamental need to transfer control and ownership of personal data to the individual, right down to the individual transaction. This is, as we have seen, one of the centrepieces of any non-mythological account of privacy. It also emphasises the need for the design and operation of technologies to be relative to an ethical framework and unsurprisingly recommends the international human rights framework as preferred in filling that role. From this it follows, as they say, that A/IS must be transparent, demonstrably useful and focus on individual well-being. It also recommends that data management should also be subject to auditing to prevent misuse. Those processes would work well within a non-mythological frame.

The major shortcoming of this array of provisions is, of course, that it makes no attempt either to guide the individual to self-responsibility – let alone recognise the central importance of existential conditions and the personalisation of meaning in an account of privacy – nor therefore to reimagine the State and the Market to complement that. The result is that those institutions remain as mythological magnitudes, free to continue to seek the induced subjection of the individual to their respective and joint governmental aspirations. For example, making A/IS more transparent does nothing to counter the subjecting mythological claims by State or Market about distancing existential concerns and dealing conclusively with constructed concerns of the individual. It may make those claims more attractive. Similarly, 'creating, curating and controlling' one's data[16] does nothing to counter mythological claims by dominant interests, which can remain the basis of those processes. Thereby, the technologies – in particular, of neuroscience – will retain their ever-increasing potential for subjection. We have also seen in Chapter 5 that simply referring their new data control guidelines to international human rights[17]

---

[16] Ibid. p.110ff.
[17] Ibid. p.9.

and well-being[18] codes is problematic outside of a non-mythological institutional frame. Similarly, outside such a frame, the monitoring of algorithms[19] and related educational principles[20] is ultimately unhelpful. That frame is the subject of the final four chapters in this work.

Other recommendations by the IEEE are also problematic. Their admirable defensiveness regarding individual data control causes them to miss the importance of sharing data when it would – respectfully – promote the self-responsibility of others without degrading that of the author. Further, the proposal to embed values in AI/S is fraught.[21] As we have seen, commonly recognised values fall short of arrangements which would ensure an existential honesty, so the opportunity for citizens to be morally unconstrained apart from respect for others and the duty to be self-responsible is unavailable. Whatever other values were embedded in AI/S, the inevitable result would be that presumptions about available options would be pre-emptive. The notion of 'nudging' robots would be similarly pre-emptive and should be ruled out.[22] Finally, perhaps because of their erroneous attraction to classical ethics[23] – Adam Smith and Kant were, as we have seen, consummate mythologists whose thought was ultimately about promoting the dominance of the Market and Deity, respectively – the IEEE focus is heavily laden towards the individual which, although appropriate, is done at the cost of ignoring crucially necessary changes in the purpose and activities of the institutions of State and Market, that is, beyond merely seeking to apply standard ethical frameworks there.[24]

A final example of how IEEE thinking is skewed is its treatment of affective computing. As we have mentioned, the concern of the IEEE is to ensure that AI/S should not amplify or dampen human emotional experience.[25] This fails to see the significant benefits of certain technologies, especially VR but also AR, in refamiliar-ising citizens – in a safe environment – with the experience of existential fear and desire. Given the lifelong mythological embedding of citizens, the process of demythologising human experience so that the seductions of technology – espe-cially regarding claims about an Absolute Self – can be resisted in the neurological age becomes a challenge. Certainly, a frame of demythologised regulation, law, State and Market practice will be fundamental, but adding a personal experience of demythologised existential fear and desire regarding both the natural and social environments could be of real assistance, educationally.

---

[18] Ibid. p.70.
[19] Ibid. pp.36, 59, 135.
[20] Ibid. p.118.
[21] Ibid. p.169.
[22] Ibid. p.97.
[23] Ibid. p.37.
[24] Ibid. p.130ff.
[25] Ibid. pp.6, 90ff.

Some Applications of New Privacy   187

In the end, these shortcomings strongly constrain what is otherwise an admirable attempt to shift the individual to the centre in the production and management of personal data. Those constraints allow the mythologising that typifies the magnitudes – even within their post-absolutist, engaged phases – so that the value of the IEEE frame is devalued.

Somewhat in a similar vein, the MyData movement has a range of admirable principles which are aimed to place the individual at the centre of their personal data control. These include that individuals should be empowered actors in their management of their online and offline lives with the right to manage their own data and privacy; that such data needs to be easily accessible and usable, so that it is a personal resource; and that there be decentralised management of such data that eases both agency regulatory compliance and changes of service providers for individuals.[26] As of February 2020, the EU Data Strategy became quite closely aligned with these principles.[27]

This approach shares with the IEEE framework the important aim of a citizen-centric approach to personal data but, like that network, does not give sufficient acknowledgement either to the inevitability of the deep embedding of citizens in neural technology nor therefore to the importance of reimagining the purposes of the agencies of State and Market to promote individual enhancement with the protections and controls that it champions. It therefore does not have an ultimately realistic understanding of the necessary evolution of the notion of privacy. Like IEEE, it goes halfway.

SOME APPLICATIONS OF NEW PRIVACY

A selection of indicative, practical examples will now be presented to give a sense of how this new privacy model would work. These will be taken from operational practice as well as from case law. In all these examples, it is to be taken that any intense monitoring by authorities of the activities of individuals or organisations should be under the authority of independent judicial officers, unless stated otherwise. That would include the examination of metadata and, ultimately, personal data.

As a broad principle, the position here is that matters of privacy as proposed – whether regarding issues of respect, of progressive interactive engagement with State and Market or of the conservation of personal data–based skills and experiences – are best dealt with not by a legislated tort but by relying wherever possible on the courts under common law to set and adjust the parameters. Early precedents would be required, guided by the Constitutional provisions we will explore in Chapter 8.

---

[26] A. Poikola et al., 'MyData – A Nordic model for human-centred personal data management and processing' (White Paper), *Ministry of Transport and Communications* (2014).

[27] *MyData Global Newsletter* (21 February 2020).

A litmus case that has long been prominent in current privacy thinking is that regarding the relationship between media and celebrity, often presented as one between free speech[28] and the rights of the individual. In the new concept of privacy being proposed here, there is no right to collect personal information – including images – of any celebrity, so long as they are behaving respectfully and are responsible to and for themselves. No right lies with media to breach such privacy conditions simply because there might be some salacious interest or commercial value in aspects of such lives. This principle was tested in the case of Michael Douglas and Catherine Zeta-Jones.[29] Unfortunately, the appeal, which concerned the publication of illicit wedding photographs, was determined by the fact that their privacy had already been infringed by the publication when, on the criteria being presented in the present work, privacy was not an issue for other reasons. That is, that the appellants were not ultimately concerned with privacy but only with exclusive publication of photographs by media of their choice. Those matters to one side, the press had no right to publish given that the appellants were acting in a self-responsible manner, and matters of so-called public interest therefore lay in their own hands. That is, only they had the right to end their privacy in the matter or not.

A very different example, drawn from the potential of current neurological research, would be that of the extension of one's personal cognitive substrate, referred to in Chapter 2. It might appear at first that the privacy issue would be difficult to address, given that the 'extension' might be programmed to gather external data to assist in the resolution of challenges, problems or opportunities identified by the citizen. Access to this substrate by supportive agencies of State or Market might be argued to be a breach of the rights of that citizen to control all downloads of data. But this problem would be resolved by ensuring that the extension is, in its nodal form, separate from the citizen's natural brain, and the presence within the extension of software that embodies the personal technology strategy, which would thereby act as an early warning of unauthorised intrusion and as a filter against any suspicious 'data virus' of that kind. Should such new data be judged not to be in breach, it would be 'accepted' as a contributor to the potential solution to the identified problem or opportunity. A further protection would be the other range of conservation measures, including the authorised status of the delivering agency and the principle of reversibility before download into the biological brain of the citizen.

Regarding governance, it is not a breach of respect for citizens to explore anti-democratic sentiments or even to do so in company. Beyond that, any action planned by the citizen to pursue those sentiments would be a breach of respect

---

[28] A wider consideration of the important issue of free speech, especially by the media, and its proper constraints will be undertaken in Chapter 8.

[29] *Michael Douglas and Catherine Zeta-Jones* v. *Hello! Limited in the Supreme Court of Judicature Court of Appeal (Civil Division)* (21 December 2000).

for others and disallowed, unless that action comprised raising issues for debate. Therefore, security provisions would allow the State – not under delegation to sectors of the Market – to monitor for signs of such planned action, ultimately but not pre-emptively to access personal data under independent judicial authority. Further, the principle of respect would allow a citizen with those sentiments, on the one hand, to formally withdraw from exercising their franchise but, on the other, not generally to withdraw from jury duty, thereby denying respect to an accused. On the other hand, due to the demonstrated influence of dominant interests on the democratic process, the sources of all funding for the organisational aspects of political parties should be publicly available, and costs for the electoral process should come only from public funds. The monitoring of attendance at public political events and of online political communication would not be allowed unless separate evidence of significant anti-democratic action were available. This would include the use of facial recognition – an issue that is to be compounded with the universalisation of sensors and the Internet of Everything – which also should not be used either in the electoral context or as a general surveillance method unless there was justification to identify individuals who were demonstrated or likely security threats. On the other side of this issue, representatives of dominant interests of any kind – including of the magnitudes of Deity and the Market or of any special interest group – who are politically active should be publicly acknowledged. Fully open, agonistic and rational debate is the goal here, not dominant sectional interest. One would expect that the generational change required for this would commence with the reimagining of the purposes of State and Market, as outlined in Chapters 8 and 9.

In the debate between the State and the individual regarding security, the default position is that the individual – being supported by reimagined State and Market – is to be considered as pursuing self-responsibility with respect. The first priority is not the interests of State or Market. Those institutions should then, as a secondary function, maintain a properly constrained regime of monitoring for signs of threat, which would include the gathering of anonymised data to allow for proper planning in both its security and broader service provision functions. This security regime would convert to more intense surveillance when specific evidence of likely wrongdoing was available. Information concerning particular individuals would typically be shared with them once matters were concluded, but without divulging the mechanics of security procedures. The activities of security agencies should, like that of both the State and the Market more generally, be the subject of close parliamentary oversight. Given the proven strategy of media outlets in generating fear for commercial purposes – separate from its proper function of reporting valid threats to the community in a non-sensational manner – a press council should have and use powers to examine media activities and impose appropriate constraints or penalties regarding any incursion into the lives of self-responsible citizens.

Regarding the internet and social media, these should not be unconstrained fora, given their ever-increasing role as a source of information and thereby their vulnerability to influence of the widest range of individuals and organisations. They should not be the captive of State or Market, both of which should nonetheless promote respect and information regarding enhancement programmes. Regarding copyright or ownership of online content, ownership of the provided content would remain with the content providers – State, Market broadly or individual citizen – who could set conditions of use, unless contracts allowing other use were agreed, whether by sale or gift. Digital identifiers should be used for any uploading or downloading of content – and blocking provisions built in by design – but not for browsing. Deletion rights should attach to owners of content. The State should maintain an anonymised metadata monitoring regime of these fora for security and cyberbullying tracking purposes and respond in the manner outlined above. Cookies should continue to be used with subject approval, but the information gathered is not to be shared with any other agency. The collecting agency is not to profile the subject or then share such a profile unless specifically authorised. 'Do not track' options should be universalised. Beyond the risks already mentioned, the Internet of Things can provide a valuable medical and social monitoring service.

There is of course a burgeoning case law regarding the internet. Three cases of interest include the following:

- *The Author of a Blog* v. *Times Newspapers*,[30] wherein the anonymous blog author unsuccessfully sought an injunction to prevent him being identified, even though, as a police officer, he was publicly revealing matters pertaining to police practice. He failed in the application on various grounds, including that his status as a police officer was a matter of public interest. The new privacy would have protected his anonymity via robust whistleblower legislation given that what he was revealing was in the public interest.
- *Cynthia Moreno et al.* v. *Hanford Sentinel*,[31] where the case tested whether an author who posted an article on Myspace.com could claim invasion of privacy when that article was republished in a newspaper and in which, for the purposes here, 'no such reasonable expectation of privacy existed'. If the litigant had not authorised the information to be broadcast more widely, the new privacy would have delivered success in her case.
- *Angel Fraley* v. *Facebook*,[32] in which the litigants alleged that Facebook's Sponsored Stories violated the Right of Publicity Statute and the

---

[30] *The Author of a Blog* v. *Times Newspapers*, High Court of Justice Queen's Bench Division before Eady J (4 June 2009),

[31] *Cynthia Moreno et al.* v. *Hanford Sentinel Inc et al.* in the Court of Appeal in the State of California (Super. Ct. No. 06CECG04125AMC).

[32] *Angel Fraley et al.* v. *Facebook Inc., a corporation, and DOES 1-100*, United States District Court Northern District San Jose Division Case No. 11-CV-01726-LHK .

common law doctrine of unjust enrichment by appropriating their names, photographs, likenesses and identities for use in paid advertisements without their permission. In this case, certain claims were dismissed and others denied, except for that regarding unjust enrichment, which was granted. The new privacy would have endorsed that decision.

Each of these cases demonstrates the fragility of the current notion of privacy in the context of the forceful technologies of the internet. They are also a reminder that it is typically the claims of the dominant interests of State and Market, in particular, that induce the subjection of individuals, including the forgoing of personal data. That is, the internet is a principal player in the mythological landscape, and there needs to be express rights of data ownership and disposal, along with constant alerts, given to citizens regarding this.

Regarding financial and employment issues, the default position is that citizens are to be treated as potentially respectful and self-responsible. In the consequential process of affirming that, both State and Market agencies would have to post and promote 'respect' principles and to ensure that all employees are continually but not oppressively engaged to determine means by which they may improve their skills and knowledge in pursuit of a self-responsible way of life. This should proceed by incentive rather than by punishment. Neither the State nor sections of the Market other than the citizen's preferred agencies should have access to credit details and bank account information, except under such particular circumstances as reasonable suspicion by police of a crime. Given the extensive presence of biases, any judgments based on the application of algorithms should be challengeable in an independent tribunal. If grounds otherwise exist for such agencies as taxation, investigative agencies, courts and so on and the financial affairs of the subject are a matter of relevance, then access should be granted subject to the usual provisions herein. Tax returns should otherwise be confidential. Potential employers should not have access to an applicant's financial records, although a reasonable range of testimonials, selected by the potential employer, should continue to be allowed. This should not include access to postings on social media. Employers could then not have access to or use information directly from an employee's private life to make employment-related decisions. Generally, an employer has no legitimate direct interest in an employee's private life. Employers have no right of access to an employee's computer, emails or mobile telephones unless matters of concern have been raised formally. State legislation will be required to specify the dimensions of such matters, clarifying the fair expectations of employer and employee. Given the level of potential risk, employees of transport and security agencies – including police – should be made aware of their responsibilities and, if intelligence gathering reveals legitimate concerns, personal monitoring – such as drug testing and baggage checks – should be imposed subject to the standard conditions herein.

Relevant health and education information would be made securely and confidentially available to relevant State agencies, given their responsibility to understand, respond to and promote the general enhancement of each citizen. Such information would be the subject of regular, 'not to be further disseminated' consideration between the agencies, represented by single agents – including the general medical practitioner where appropriate – to prevent overkill, to encourage the pursuit of the citizen's self-responsible goals. These discussions should avoid any sense in which the State presents itself as making mythological claims or threats. They should always take place in the context of existential realities and incentivising the use of benign technological means (e.g., VR or AR but never direct neural download) to do so. Similarly, but not so extensively, due to the persistence of its profit motive and even despite its reimagined non-mythological status, the Market should promote opportunities to help realise both respect (a sign of which is the absence of exploitation) and the opportunities for increased self-responsibility. In this context, citizens should have access to their health records and explanations as to their significance. For their part the citizen has the responsibility to notify any health or educational condition that may impact services to them. Security and health agencies would have the responsibility to undertake monitoring programmes regarding common diseases, including online, without accessing personal information unless reliable evidence requires that and in which case the subject should be engaged. Students not only have the right of access to their educational records – held confidentially – but have the right and obligation to be fully engaged so that a plan for existential living is elaborated. Importantly, curricula would be presented in an existential context, utilising all available technological aids and in a safe environment. Parents but not potential employers should have direct access to such data, the latter having to rely on certified copies from educational institutions. School surveillance technology is appropriate in schools that demonstrate a need for it to establish a safe environment but not generally.

For those who adopt beliefs in a Deity, an expectation of privacy may seem reasonable. However, the position here is not only that Deity is a mythological magnitude but that the dominant interests of this magnitude presently exert significant influence on the democratic process. There is no separation of Church and State in real time. As a consequence, any significant financial contributions to Church administration – whether from individuals or Market organisations – would be publicly listed, as for political parties. A good example of the overlap between Church and State is the very substantial amounts of public funding allocation by State education agencies to Churches for education. This is anathema to principles of self-responsibility, as it favours one magnitude – Deity – by another – the State. Such allocations are thereby in strong pursuit of perpetuating mythological arrangements. Regarding the practices of the confessional, there would be no expectation that disclosures would be exempt from criminal or civil prosecution where that is a factor. State law has precedence. This is a key factor in assuming self-responsibility and respect for victims.

Some Applications of New Privacy

Regarding law enforcement, the investigative process should be understood differently from any post-conviction circumstance. Before conviction, the accused remains a citizen, albeit a suspect. Consequently, all standard rights of citizenship – and thereby the protection of personal information from the media – should accord, subject to an independent officer determining flight or other risk. The media has no right to report other than the bare facts of prosecution. They should not be invited to attend the arrest, as is now common, and should be precluded from pursuing a public 'trial by media' prior to the court trial by procedural and evidentiary constraints. This does not apply if the accused then pleads guilty. If a person is found not guilty, then court records should be expunged. Post-conviction, during the sentencing process, the court has the right to explore the private life of the convicted person. If the person is convicted, then an entirely different frame is to be established. The offender is to be engaged – not subjected – in a regime which sets out a programme intended to establish the skills and knowledge in them which will allow them not to reoffend – to show respect – and to become fully self-responsible. Custodial sentences are not for punishment – either by physical abuse or as a meaningless waste of time – but are to be focused solely on preparation for return to the community. Such persons are to be shown respect if they themselves engage in this process properly. This raises the question of sentencing and its structure, a matter we shall return to in Chapter 9.

More broadly, a range of behaviours should be allowed in private – especially by consent – that are precluded in public. Without descending into bourgeois notions of privacy, this refers to a range of victimless activities such as in regard to sexual practice, smoking marijuana – although this is a health matter – and so on. Regarding the disclosure of criminal records to potential employers, this should not be required if a person has been living self-responsibly. The caveat to this is that if a citizen seeks employment in an area related to an offence they have committed (former embezzlers seeking employment in a financial institution, child molesters seeking work in a school, or former addicts seeking employment in a hospital), then there should be a statutory obligation to disclose – since the person is still demonstrating the search for self-responsibility – and preclusions would apply. When such people are released from custody, and have demonstrated in pre-release programmes that they have acquired the skills and knowledge to live self-responsibly, then it is not required that local community members are advised of their record. However, as a precaution in this transition period, local police should be advised and technology-based monitoring of the location of such offenders would be appropriate for a period where preferred by the releasing authorities.

Finally, regarding the environment for the family and a range of groups in civil society, the argument may well properly be that they should not be subject to particular intrusions. Families should be allowed to raise children and such groups to go about their activities, especially those that are accepted as beneficial to others. The caveat, of course, is that, especially regarding the family, they have the

194 A New Sense of Privacy

particular function of fostering the respectful and self-responsible behaviour of children. Without thereby authorising any additional interest of the State, they are properly seen as having a function that precedes that of a reimagined, supportive State and Market. Appropriate pre-birth learning experiences should be available and participation vigorously encouraged.

On the other hand, various other groups can properly be seen as having carriage of the protection of specific cultural values, for the protection of which they can claim additional levels of privacy, especially when those values are under threat from more dominant values and those values are sought to be maintained within a respectful frame. As was demonstrated in *Foster and Others* v. *Mountford*,[33] there was an attempt to prevent publication of an academic work by Mountford which included revelations of Australian Aboriginal cultural and religious secret ceremonies. Muirhead J. issued a restraining order and damages in his judgment on the case. This is an interesting case in that, although the cultural aspects included religious elements and were thereby mythological, the practices involved demonstrated no disrespect for other citizens and were based on this group being culturally appropriate. This was a case of relative, not absolute, self-responsibility but which was respectful.

Given that we are about to begin an exploration of the reimagining of the law and regulation necessary to sustain this new notion of privacy, it is appropriate to consider now two legal opinions relevant to key current understandings of the nature of privacy. These give a sense of what we are attempting in the present work to forgo and replace, and as an aide-memoire in that exploration.

The first is the classic, still much revered opinion expressed by Warren and Brandeis.[34] We have already referred extensively to this in Chapter 3, but we might remember that the authors agreed with the view of Cooley J. that privacy was the right 'to be let alone',[35] as 'the intensity and complexity of life ... have rendered necessary some retreat from the world' but 'modern enterprise and invention have, through invasions upon his privacy, subjected [the citizen] to mental pain'.[36] They were especially concerned with the then-increasing intrusion of the press and included publication of items obtained by technology, for example, by photography. They did not deny that there were continuing circumstances where publication was appropriate, including inter alia matters of general or public interest,[37] where it was in accord with the law of slander and libel[38] and so on. They say, finally, that 'the common law has always recognised a man's house as his castle, impregnable, often,

---

[33] *Foster and Others* v. *Mountford and Rigby Limited Supreme Court of the Northern Territory* (Australia) before Muirhead J (3, 6 December 1976).
[34] S. Warren and L. Brandeis, 'The right to privacy', *Harvard Law Review* 4:5 (1890): pp.193–220.
[35] Ibid. pp.193–196.
[36] Ibid. p.196.
[37] Ibid. p.214.
[38] Ibid. p.216.

Summary of Part I 195

even to its own officers engaged in the execution of its commands. Shall the courts thus close the front entrance to constituted authority, and open wide the back door to idle or prurient curiosity?'[39]

The second points to the cultural relativity of the notion of privacy.[40] As Whitman states, 'Continental law is avidly protective of many kinds of privacy in many realms of life, whether the issue is consumer data, credit reporting, workplace privacy, discovery in civil litigation.'[41] Yet 'As for American law, it too is obsessed with privacy', exemplified by the attitudes of privacy attached to abortion, public nudity, telephone tapping and so on.[42] In short, 'Evidently, Americans and continental Europeans perceive privacy differently.... We possess American intuitions – or, as the case may be, Dutch, Italian, French or German intuitions. We must make some effort to explain this fact before we start proclaiming universal norms of privacy protection.'[43]

As we begin to consider regulation and law in relation to privacy, these two papers thereby cause key questions to be raised again in the context of the argument being put in the present work: whether, when one is considering privacy, the notion of 'being let alone' has any relevance in an environment where the individual brain is becoming – and will continue to be – increasingly connected to and embedded in intelligent technology, and whether the variability of the content of 'privacy' makes any specified notion of its content so broad as to be virtually inexhaustible. That is, beyond specified matters that the respectful self-responsible citizen is to share confidentially, the content of what is private should be up to the citizen themself, and that will vary widely between citizens. What is proposed here goes well beyond these two questions. It also goes beyond other notions of privacy founded on better control of information flow – since most information is produced in the context of mythological processes – and on any ontological reduction of individuals to information as that is mythological at two levels: the reduction is mythological and the content is mythological. These are matters that need to be accommodated in any non-mythological notion of regulation and law.

SUMMARY OF PART I

Part I has been concerned with the significance of emerging neuroscience for the idea and practice of privacy and with various contextual factors by which that significance needs to be understood.

---

[39] Ibid. p.220.
[40] J. Whitman, 'The two western cultures of privacy: Dignity versus liberty', *Yale Law Journal* 113 (2004): pp.1152–1160.
[41] Ibid. p.1156.
[42] Ibid. pp.1158–1159.
[43] Ibid. p.1160.

A New Sense of Privacy

Neuroscience is becoming a tool for clinical therapy and enhancement unlike anything seen before, its force due to its foundation on the fast-evolving capacity of algorithmic technology. The speed of this evolution, and that it is being championed by highly regarded practitioners, is delivering to neuroscience a pre-eminent, even dominant, status. However, this dominance is obscuring the facts that, not only does algorithmic technology have deep limitations, but it is also leading to a progressive subjection of humanity to its regimes that has not been properly acknowledged.

A key effect of this subjection is that the connecting of humans to algorithmic technology, increasingly through bi-directional data exchange, will demolish our current notions of privacy – a field already fraught with shortcomings – even as it repairs and enhances cognitive capacities. These notions are not only outdated – the product of former historical scenarios – but they are so riddled with contradictions that they barely provide value to individuals. This will worsen with the deep intrusions of neuroscience. We need an entirely new conception of privacy.

The challenge of developing a new conception can be seen in the revelation that subjection by algorithms echoes the historical instances of wide subjection that have preceded it. This is the recurrence of a dynamic that explains the human disposition to subject oneself to absolute magnitudes if claims are made that existential concerns will be eliminated. The dominant interests who have promoted this dynamic – serially through Deity, State and Market – have claimed that existential concerns can be banished, but do so by shifting the focus onto constructed fears and desires which they claim to conclusively deal with. This shift is allowed by the normalising that has characterised their respective ideas and practices over historical time and which has provided the content of how we have understood privacy: an assembly of historical ideas and practices. This recurring – mythological – dynamic is the foundation of the present elaboration of algorithmic technology, by which an Absolute Self is promised but which will deliver absolute subjection.

A concept of privacy is required that can resist deep algorithmic intrusion without losing the offer of clinical therapy or cognitive enhancement. Since *responsibility to and for oneself* is the preferred antidote to any application of this mythological dynamic, it is presented as the foundation of a new account of privacy. This is due not only to the manner in which it counters this dynamic but also to its credentials as a new ethic. This new conception therefore embraces algorithmic technology but is conceived such that it is the individual citizen who must control every aspect of the interface with this technology. This is the meaning of responsibility to and for oneself, the 'to and for oneself' comprising the new understanding of privacy. This is not to say that this reconception is sufficient, as it will require to be supported by the institutions of the social infrastructure, the focus of Part II.

PART II

Regulation

Part II has been concerned with the reimagining of the social infrastructure in a manner that will support and encourage the individual pursuit of the existential responsibility to and for oneself.

Such a reimagining would require a reconsideration of the notion of regulation, conceived here not as prescriptions and proscriptions that are derivatives of legislation but as the foundational framework of any systematic attempt to change human behaviour, in particular. In this, the focus has been on the nature of the presently dominant notion of regulation, responsive regulation.

A critique of this notion has been presented, based on its key elements and their consequences. These elements include that this system is not, as claimed, founded by the cooperative search for outcomes then adopted by the citizen but on the power of the administering agency. The source of this confusion can be traced back to the reliance of this sense of regulation on the political theory of republicanism proposed by Pettit, which equally claims to promote liberty but does so by relying on the unjustified intrusion of the republican state into the affairs of citizens.

A key consequence of this confusion is that the champions of responsive regulation promote what they perceive as the advantages of the spread of regulatory control away from the organs of State and thereby across the social fabric. They acknowledge the risks of this but are prepared to rely on a plethora of monitoring processes to complement what they argue are the strengths of self-regulation. The critique of this arrangement presented here is based on the argument that this is a modern extension of the long historical processes of normalisation – that is, in this case subjection – that was a feature of the emergence and demise of the respective mythological magnitudes of Deity, State and Market. This normalisation is further reinforced by the wide adoption of the methods available through information technology.

The argument was then presented that it is within the law that search for a framework which can avoid this sense of ongoing normalisation can be found.

That is, law as a framework which can promote responsibility to and for oneself rather than subjection. This, however, would require a significant reimagining in its Constitutional and legislative context but each of which is available by a reworking of current legal principles. More significantly, the notion of the rule of law would require a move away from the currently dominant anatomical approach and a refocusing and elaboration of the potential in the teleological approach. This new focus would lead to the reformation of State and Corporate agencies as purpose-based, fiduciary entities. In this, the role of trust would become secondary to the principle of responsibility to and for oneself, which such entities would promote.

Against this background, the argument was put that both State agencies and Market corporations need to be seen, in their present form and activity, as mythological entities. That is, as relics of their respective eras of dominance as magnitudes but still empowered due to their modern adoption of the capacities of regulatory dispersal and algorithmic Big Data capture and manipulation, all of which have undermined viable notions of accountability. It would be against such principles and practices that State and Market entities could – even within the existing legal framework – be reimagined as actively promoting each citizen as responsible to and for themselves. Existential reality rather than mythological subjection could then emerge into the lives of all.

7

Reimagining Regulation

The notion of privacy we have just looked may be coherent, but it cannot stand alone. It depends upon the gradually increasing take-up of the notion of respect by and for individuals and the willingness of citizens to accept that living and thinking mythologically can be forgone by shifting to an existential, self-responsible way of living. So that this notion does not stand alone, each citizen would benefit from the reimagining of a social and political environment that would support them in this re-gearing of their life. These would not be insignificant changes – for example, in the institutional policies and practices of the State and the corporations of the Market – and they not only would take time but would themselves require changes in the Constitutional, legal, legislative and regulatory framework by which they are informed. To further complicate this reimagining, such institutions and corpor-ations – should they not experience such transformation and forgo their current mythological strategies – would likely be active resistors to these changes, effectively making the individual transformations difficult if not unlikely. That is, without these environmental changes, the continuing vulnerability of individuals to the claims of dominant interests and to the developments in neural intrusion would remain. In fact, these claims would be increasingly difficult to resist, if not in fact be irresistible.

The next point that needs to be made is in respect to the decision to explore the regulatory framework here before examining what might be considered by some as the more significant Constitutional, legal and legislative features of the institutional landscape. The reason for this is straightforward. The broad argument in this work is that each of the mythological elements of the trajectory has been or is progressively being engaged to convert its absolutism into a sympathetic form – losing that absolute status and so entering a growing field of failed but persistent elements: we live in a field of the ideas and practices that are the residue of these failed absolutist magnitudes. This persistence takes two forms, that is, the residual interest in regaining its absolute status and the conversion of much of its power into

200 *Reimagining Regulation*

regulation, thereby compensating for the loss of its absolutism through a micro-scale control of the wide social fabric.

This is not therefore to deny the existence of forms of 'sovereign' power wielded by the institutions of these magnitudes or that their dominant interests ever forgo the desire to re-establish the power of the Deity, the State and the Market in absolutist form. It is only to say that, in this dynamic field, these magnitudes have been variously engaged to be 'sympathetic', but this engagement ironically manifests itself in the form of regulation. It is in the nature of this mythological regulation to both constrain the magnitude but also to cover the social field so that its purposes are achieved by also constraining the individual subject. It does this to a level of efficiency that sovereign power could not. Foucault discovered this in *Discipline and Punish*, where he saw the inefficiency of sovereign punishment replaced by the regulation of punishment in its disciplinary form.

A COMMON VIEW OF REGULATORY POWER

The view that the regulatory framework is, even with its weaknesses, a general good is a common one. For example, for Shleifer:

> The American and European societies are much richer today than they were 100 years ago, yet they are also vastly more regulated. Today we live in houses and apartment buildings whose construction – from zoning, to use of materials, to fire codes – is heavily regulated. We eat food grown with heavily regulated fertilizers and hormones, processed in heavily regulated factories with publicly monitored technologies, and sold in heavily regulated outlets with elaborate labels and warnings. Our means of transport, including cars, buses and airplanes, are made, sold, driven, and maintained under heavy government regulation. Our children attend schools that teach heavily regulated procedures and play on playgrounds using government-mandated safety standards.[1]

Shleifer proceeds to examine three ways in which economists think about economic regulation, asking, in particular, whether growth has been in spite of or due to it, given the positive correlation indicated between growth in regulation and growth in income. The theories he identifies and considers are Pigou's public interest theory, Coase's contracting theory and Stigler's capture theory. Public interest was the subject of severe criticism by the Chicago School of Law and Economics, for whom the Market can be trusted to sort out failures without intervention by government, which ignored the success that has accompanied significant increases in regulation. Coarse extended this by arguing that, where the Market failed, the necessary corrections can be made by the courts through their jurisdictions involving contract, common law and tort. Stigler questioned whether government was benevolent or

---

[1] A. Shleifer, 'Understanding regulation', *European Financial Management* 11:4 (2005): p.439.

competent, arguing that the Market captures the political process. In particular, for Shleifer, the arguments of the Chicago School failed because they placed too much theoretical faith in private ordering and in the courts and, empirically, failed to recognise that we live in a society which is richer, more benign and more regulated.[2]

The proposal that comes from his review suggests there are four options available to a society to enforce regulation – market discipline, private litigation, public enforcement through a regulatory agency, and State ownership through nationalisation[3] – these reflecting ascending levels of public control. They reflect, at the extremes, a choice between disorder and dictatorship. He sees each option on the continuum having strengths and weaknesses. Among a range of findings, Shleifer concludes that empirical examination of various jurisdictions indicates that deregulation works best in developed economies, by the establishment of specialised courts as an alternative to regulation, and, in those still developing, competition and market discipline are a viable alternative if they are working efficiently.[4]

RESPONSIVE REGULATION – THE PRINCIPLES

The value of the analysis by Shleifer is that it pegs out ground that is presently although variably occupied by a currently dominant regulatory theory, that of *responsive regulation*.[5] This is built around a pyramidal strategy[6] which, at the base, accepts that most individuals or agents will be compliant with the established regulatory regime and then progresses vertically through six categories of increasing non-compliance towards a recognition that some will be fully non-compliant. Each category is associated with a response from the authorities, from maintaining subject awareness and education for the compliant, through shaming, up through deterrence by sanctions then ultimately prosecution and/or loss of operating licences as appropriate for the fully non-compliant.

The nine principles of responsive regulation reveal how this strategy is claimed to be driven:

- Think in context by not imposing a preconceived theory
- Listen actively and structure dialogue that gives voice to stakeholders, seeks and monitors agreed outcomes; that builds commitment by helping actors find their own motivation to improve; and that shows resolve to stick to a problem until it is fixed

---

[2] Ibid. pp.440–442.
[3] Ibid. p.442.
[4] Ibid. p.449.
[5] J. Braithwaite, 'Fasken Lecture – The essence of responsive regulation', *University of British Columbia Law Review* 44:3 (2001): pp.475–520.
[6] Ibid. pp.482–483.

- Engage the resistors with fairness, showing them respect by using their feedback to improve regulatory design
- Praise those who comply, support any innovation, nurture innovation and help leaders pull laggards through new ceilings of excellence
- Signal that you prefer to achieve outcomes by support and education
- Signal but don't threaten a range of sanctions that can be escalated through to the formidable as a last resort
- Network pyramidal governance by engaging a wider network of partners as you move up the pyramid
- Elicit active responsibility (for making outcomes better in the future), resorting to passive responsibility (holding actors responsible for past actions) when active responsibility fails
- Learn; evaluate how well and at what cost outcomes have been achieved; then communicate lessons learned.

This model has been applied across a range of social, political and economic fields. These include risk management, theories of public accountability, global governance, human rights, labour migration, consumer protection, crime control, restorative justice, tax havens, regulation of competition, urban sustainability and the management of the environment.

We shall return to analyse this scheme shortly – and to an exploration of these applications in Chapters 9 and 10 – but it can be said here that Braithwaite has coincidentally utilised as many of the elements in the Shleifel analysis as can be fitted together in one system. Neither 'no government is necessary' nor 'full government control' could fit his rationale, but he has included willing compliance and criminal prosecution, respectively, and various combinations between those. This shading of the elements allows him to develop a dynamic whereby all subjects – irrespective of their level of compliance – are managed within a thoroughgoing regulatory environment. This points to the question of the extension of the regulatory framework right across the social field and thereby to the value of the Foucauldian accounts of the nature of governmentalisation and discipline.

REGULATION AS BIOPOWER, THE PLANNING OF SPACE AND ALGORITHMIC DETERMINISM

We have seen in Chapters 1 and 4 that the idea of the Absolute State slowly emerged as it became clear, through the intellectual and political conditions surrounding the Reformation, that the idea of a Deity with which there could be no negotiation was unsustainable. But even if it was able to be engaged in that way, it could then not be seen as absolute in the sense needed for it to 'realise' the absolutism of existential reality and then – the believers hoped – be sympathetic to them by virtue of their good deeds. We saw that the Absolute State was conceived to fill that emerging

Absolutist lacuna. Hobbes described the nature of such a State almost poetically. We saw that, as with all mythological magnitudes, the dominant interests of the State argued that only by individual subjection could their claims concerning their immediate fears and desires – which distanced and camouflaged their existential concerns – be satisfied. That was the inducement. This inducement did not stand alone, of course, as the absolute power of the State was also brought to bear to enforce subjection on those who demurred. The argument here is that this mythological 'inducement to be subject through an act of imagination' is the very significant hidden factor in a proper understanding of the history of institutional life in modernity.

However, this mythology also camouflaged other processes, those which acted to attain a micro-fine control or subjection of individual beliefs and practices. These have been the processes of governmentalisation and discipline which have subjected through the progressive creation or subjectification of the individual from the sixteenth century. We have seen that Foucault identified these two associated strategies and highlighted that the original notion of 'police' was a key to the transformation of the principles of the Christian pastorate for the purposes of promoting the orderly – with a certain sense of comforting – growth of the forces of the emerging State:

> Police has more need of regulation than laws. We are in a world of indefinite regulation, but always regulation.... We are in a world of the regulation, the world of discipline. That is to say, the great proliferation of local and regional disciplines we have observed in workshops, schools and the army from the end of the sixteenth to the eighteenth centuries, should be seen against the background of an attempt at a general disciplinarisation, a general regulation of individuals and the territory of the realm in the form of a police based on an essentially urban model.... Commerce, town, regulation and discipline are, I think, the most characteristic elements of police practice as this was understood in the seventeenth century and the first half of the eighteenth century.[7]

But the operation of these has persisted, even thrived, into the contemporary era. We can see at least three fields in which this persistence is in evidence.

The first relates to the nature of biopower, understood by Rabinow and Rose as comprising truth discourses about the 'vital' character of human beings, authorities competent to speak that truth, strategies for intervening in collective existence in the name of life and death, and modes of subjectification by which individuals work on themselves in the name of individual or collective life or health.[8] This has led to a politics of death – thanatopolitics – in the hands of absolutist States, but it more commonly takes the form of either letting die or making live, that is, strategies for

---

[7] M. Foucault, *Security, Territory, Population*, pp.340–341; see also A. Johnson, 'Foucault: Critical theory of the police in a neoliberal age', *Theoria* (December 2014): p.12.

[8] P. Rabinow and N. Rose, 'Biopower today', *Biosocieties* 1 (2006): pp.195–207.

managing life. Their focus is on the fields of race, population and reproduction, and genomic medicine. With these we have the entry of genomic mapping,[9] reproductive technologies[10] and genetic health interventions,[11] each of which lends itself to a regulatory framework that enables a biopolitical management of the health and life of both individuals and populations.

But there is a further significance here. There has been a range of observations about Foucault's shifts in terminology – not the least from biopower to governmentality,[12] that is, how they relate. It might be one view that biopower as management of bodies evolves in his thought into the broader notion of governmentality as management of populations. The view of the present work is different, that is, that biopower as the management of life and death is more fundamental due to its distancing of existential concerns by medical means, and the resolution of these is the key to the preparedness for individual and social subjection which comprise the wide forms of governmentality.

The second relates to the manner in which regulation is used in the urban planning context to construct governance arrangements and thereby to distribute individuals within space, to prescribe regimes of practice, to establish regimes of surveillance and to normatively control human behaviour. Such an analysis of urban planning reveals not only the suitability here of the Foucauldian frames of discipline and surveillance but also that it is typically taken up within a regulatory framework and that the outcome ultimately sought is self-regulating compliance rather than enforcement:

> Foucault utilised a panoply of spatial metaphors in his work. The most renowned of these is Jeremy Bentham's architectural figure of the Panopticon and its application.... Planning literature shares this emphasis on the Panopticon, which has been described as an axiom for contemporary socio-political conditions, illustrating how surveillance and control are reproduced in the fine grain of daily life.[13]
>
> Several points can be derived by applying these broad concepts to land-use regulation and enforcement. Land-use planning is itself a practice of distributing individuals in space, and may be understood as an important component of the art of distributions, forming part of a wider set of practices designed to create governable spaces.[14]

---

[9] Ibid. p.206; see also M. Johnnson, 'Integrating selection mapping with genetic mapping and functional genomics', *Frontiers in Genetics – Evolutionary and Population Genetics* (December 2018).

[10] P. Rabinow and N. Rose, 'Biopower today', p.208; see also S. Kim, 'Reproductive technologies as population control: How pronatalist policies harm reproductive health in South Korea', *Sexual and Reproductive Health Matters* 27:2 (2019).

[11] P. Rabinow and N. Rose, 'Biopower today', p.211; see also M. Almeida, 'Human enhancement: Genetic engineering and evolution', *Evolution, Medicine and Public Health* 2019:1 (2019).

[12] For example, see J. Oksala, 'From Biopower to Governmentality', in C. Falzon et al. (eds.), *A Companion to Foucault*, pp.320–336 (Wiley, 2013), p.324.

[13] N. Harris, 'Discipline, surveillance, control: A Foucauldian perspective on the enforcement of planning regulations', *Planning Theory and Practice* 12:1 (2011): p.65.

[14] Ibid. p.62.

Regulation as Biopower, the Planning of Space and Algorithmic Determinism 205

In addition, a Foucauldian perspective directs attention to the effects and impacts of enforcement on those who are the subject of regulatory practices. It also raises questions about the ethical implications of encouraging citizens to monitor and report on each other.[15]

[M]any traditional planning enforcement teams (are being) recast as compliance teams ... how they can facilitate efficient and effective systems and institutional frameworks that encourage individuals and organisations to self-regulate.[16]

The third field is that of algorithmic regulation, which can be reactive or preemptive. For Yeung, such regulation comprises three forms: standard setting to enforce behavioural norms, the gathering and monitoring of information to detect violation of those norms, and administering sanctions where the only human role is to input data.[17] From these, algorithmic regulation is properly seen as a form of social ordering[18] and thereby a means of risk control and actuarial justice.[19]

This raises a range of questions. These include that the incomprehensibility of Big Data makes reliance on algorithms essential (dataism), that this can be argued to hide the anti-democratic nature of such reliance,[20] and that the reliance for revenue on mass data collection constitutes 'surveillance capitalism' and this in turn generates general mass surveillance.[21] There are also legal questions relating to both informational privacy and the risk to individual rights posed by profiling individuals, and the absence of the opportunity to challenge algorithmic decisions, especially given the lack of transparency, the inaccuracy and the errors of such decisions, even if they are converted to 'recommender' systems. All this can erode the collective moral and cultural fabric.[22] For Yeung, much of this may be overturned by the introduction of redesigned, computer-mediated contracts that allow bilateral participation in the setting of terms.

Hildebrandt also asks interesting questions, including regarding algorithmic regulation and the rule of law.[23] Given the proliferation of artificial legal intelligence (ALI), she raises questions about the extent to which computational systems increasingly infuse not only government legislation but also administration and adjudication. This may lead to algorithmic-friendly drafting of legislation, to the automation of administration and administrative decisions and to courts employing ALI. Hildebrandt asks if this will lead to legislation becoming self-executing, whether legal judgment could be conflated with prediction, whether automated systems will run on

---

[15] Ibid. p.72.

[16] Ibid. p.58.

[17] K. Yeung, 'Algorithmic regulation: A critical interrogation', King's College London Dickson Poon School of Law Legal Studies Research Paper 2017-27, pp.6–8.

[18] Ibid. p.11.

[19] Ibid. p.15.

[20] Ibid. p.18.

[21] Ibid. p.20.

[22] Ibid. p.26.

[23] M. Hildebrandt, 'Algorithmic regulation and the rule of law', *Philosophical Transactions of the Royal Society* 376 (2019): 20170355.

206 *Reimagining Regulation*

propriety software and whether they will be too complex, if will they be testable and contestable, how all this would change the nature of interpretability and so on.[24]

Distinguishing between code-driven and data-driven regulation of behaviour, Hildebrandt also raises concerns about the extent to which these algorithmic languages will take resulting regulatory systems away from the core adversarial checks and balances of the rule of law.[25] She suggests that a key element in the solution to this problem is ensuring that there is an agonistic process engaging data scientists, expert lawyers and citizens to ensure that the design of such systems has such core principles embedded within them.[26]

Comment

It will be immediately clear that, in the context of the broad argument being put here, these various features of regulation are anathema. This broad argument is not averse to regulation. On the contrary, regulation is essential as a means to guide the reimagined Law, State and Market that will be explored in the three chapters to follow. But the form of regulation to fulfil that role must be based on the core principles presented here. That would avert the kind of subjection that is founded on a form of regulation that induces or forces citizens to forgo self-responsibility through subjection.

THE CURIOUS CASE OF RESPONSIVE REGULATION – THE FASKEN LECTURE

Given these common features of regulation, we shall now explore its currently dominant form to determine the extent to which it does satisfy its core principles.

First, some definitions are presented.

Regulation is taken to be 'the intentional activity of attempting to control, order or influence the behaviour of others'[27] or, more widely, 'all forms of pressure to change the course of events, even the unintentional effects of agency'.[28] The notion thereby is beyond legal rules – such as governmental imposition of public obligations on private parties – and comprises political, social, economic and psychological pressures.[29] This is, in effect, the same as the claim in the present work that regulation is the foundation of these magnitudes that generate such pressures – and of Technology – and not merely an elaboration of law. Clearly, this is a wider frame than that of Shleifer.

---

[24] Ibid. p.2.
[25] Ibid. p.4.
[26] Ibid. p.7.
[27] J. Black, 'Critical reflections on regulation', *Australian Journal of Legal Philosophy* 27:1 (2002).
[28] C. Parker et al., 'Introduction', in *Regulating Law* (Oxford University Press, 2004) p.2.
[29] J. Colgan, 'The regulatory turn in international law', *Harvard International Law Journal* 52:2 (July 2011): p.324.

Responsiveness is taken to be the preference for collaborative strategies before enforcement when dealing with a non-compliant agent or agency to effect compliance or, as Braithwaite puts it, '[R]egulators should not rush to law enforcement solutions to problems before considering a range of approaches that support capacity-building'.[30]

What Is Curious

In the Fasken Lecture, Braithwaite presents responsive regulation as a two-part, 'paradoxical'[31] strategy of collaboration and enforcement to effect compliance. However, seen more clearly, this is a single strategy of enforced compliance thinly masked by techniques of inducement. The engagement of the non-compliant agent cannot be straightforward collaboration – that is, it is not a decision freely taken to work together for the benefit of either or both or other parties, including between those of unequal status – if it always stands in the shadow of enforcement. That is, the application of fear is a transparent constant in responsive regulation and that is not the sense Braithwaite gives to collaboration.

We should therefore not be too easily distracted by such terms as 'capacity building',[32] 'listening', 'praise', 'fairness', 'nurture', 'communicate',[33] 'self-regulation',[34] 'supports',[35] 'respectful',[36] 'ethical appeals',[37] 'empathy', 'internalisation of the values of law' and 'worthy of trust'.[38] Braithwaite elaborates these qualities in a strategy which he says is theory-independent, which emphasises listening to and seeking commitment from the subject in a manner characterised by fairness and respect, that is, open to regulatory redesign, that promotes support and education of the subject to build capacity, that signals but refrains from engaging formidable sanctions, that prefers active rather than passive responsibility of the subject and that communicates lessons learned.[39] All this is placed in the context of a 'just law'[40] and a 'just legal order and a caring civil society',[41] with the chance to argue unjust laws.[42] If there is punishing to be done, this is preferably done by punishing oneself.[43] In

---

[30] J. Braithwaite, 'Fasken Lecture', *UBC Law Review* 44:3 (2011): p.480.
[31] Ibid. p.475.
[32] Ibid. p.475.
[33] Ibid. p.476.
[34] Ibid. p.478.
[35] Ibid. p.480.
[36] Ibid. p.484.
[37] Ibid. p.488.
[38] Ibid. p.489.
[39] Ibid. p.476.
[40] Ibid. p.489.
[41] Ibid. p.485.
[42] Ibid. p.488.
[43] Ibid. p.487.

208 *Reimagining Regulation*

fact, regarding the latter, there should be mere signalling – not threatening – sanctions that are formidable but are there only as a last resort.[44]

However, irrespective of the early timing of the introduction of these techniques into the interaction with non-compliant agents, what we should note first, as the foundation of this scheme, are terms such as 'shaming', 'law enforcement',[45] 'demanding interventions', 'punitive approaches', 'ultimately corporate capital punishment',[46] 'coercive control',[47] 'prosecutions unit',[48] the 'forces of law ... as somewhat invincible',[49] 'image of invincibility', 'belief of citizens in the inexorability of escalation' and 'spectre of punishment, threatening in the background'.[50]

THE ARGUMENT

The argument to be explored here, then, is that, if we are to give full consideration of the former tactics, this should be done only in the context of the latter, which are a primary condition for the engagement of the former. In doing so we shall consider why Braithwaite has argued for the broad strategy that he has. In that process we shall observe that, if there is collaboration actually going on – that is, a decision freely taken to work together for the benefit of either or both parties, even between those of unequal status – it is between potential enforcer and subject rather than negotiation about a range of possible outcomes between equally empowered parties. We shall offer a different answer than that provided by Braithwaite as to why this schema does not always work, that is, why some do not comply with any of these tactics,[51] and provide an observation regarding his rational choice argument.[52] The upshot is that Braithwaite is offering a theory – responsive regulation – that not only is not what it purports to be but also is yet another manifestation of a theoretical paradigm that needs to be replaced.

Pettit's Republicanism

Braithwaite is clear that the source of the values which inform his thinking in this area is the republican value of freedom as non-domination,[53] whose pre-eminent advocate is Pettit. I have argued[54] the problematic nature of that notion of freedom. Pettit – whose ostensibly principal aim is the elimination of fear – argues that non-

---

[44] Ibid. p.476.
[45] Ibid. p.480.
[46] Ibid. p.482.
[47] Ibid. p.486.
[48] Ibid. p.487.
[49] Ibid. p.488.
[50] Ibid. p.489.
[51] Ibid. pp.484–485.
[52] Ibid. p.487.
[53] Ibid. pp.485 and 486.
[54] D. Grant, *The Mythological State and Its Empire*, pp.166–186.

domination is not freedom from interference, which is the basis of the imposition of a suitable system of law, but freedom from intentional, arbitrary interference.[55] It is freedom even from the uncertainty that accompanies the prospect of arbitrary interference.[56]

Pettit hands to the republican State the full responsibility for creating and assuring this condition. Individuals cannot and should not pursue the creation of the condition of freedom. The State alone can and must do so,[57] and it does this through its coercive, widely dispersed, constitutional-legislative-institutional framework.[58] His notion of law plays a central role in this. Pettit rejects the Hobbesian claim that law is necessarily an invasion of freedom and endorses Harrington's claim that liberty in the proper sense is liberty by the laws,[59] which are general, intelligible, consistent, stable and promulgated in advance; otherwise, 'those who make, execute or apply the law may easily be given arbitrary power over others'.[60]

Founded on such republican law, specific areas of responsibility which Pettit urges on the State include external defence, internal protection, personal independence, economic prosperity and public life.[61] One profound effect of this fully empowered legitimacy is that the constitutional and institutional arrangements of the State are not merely responsible for allowing or causing individual freedom. They, and only they, are that freedom.[62] The upshot of this argument is that the State, which must track or further my interests and do so according to opinions of a kind I share, is enabled to interfere – his 'power of attorney'[63] argument – and it is not possible to see this interference as domination. The citizen is interfered with but not on an arbitrary basis.[64]

The problem is that Pettit shifts from an individual to a communal account[65] and then to a corporatised[66] and finally to a universal[67] account of such interests. This is a fatal shift, as it effectively disallows any interest that I may have in dealing with my fears or pursuing my sense of freedom with the support of redesigned institutions of State, even in a manner that is respectful of others. Pettit does state that 'an act of interference will be non-arbitrary to the extent that it is forced to track the interests and ideas of the person suffering the interference' but then says that 'my relevant interests and ideas will be those that are shared in common with others, not those

---

[55] P. Pettit, *Republicanism* (1997), pp.84–85.
[56] Ibid. p.85.
[57] Ibid. pp.6, 78, 92, 94, 104, 207.
[58] Ibid. pp.67, 78, 86, 93, 150, 177–180, 191–192, 230.
[59] Ibid. pp.38, 39.
[60] Ibid. p.174.
[61] Ibid. pp.150–170.
[62] Ibid. pp.81, 108, 260.
[63] Ibid. p.23.
[64] Ibid. p.35.
[65] Ibid. pp.36–37.
[66] Ibid. pp.138, 140, 141, 142, 145, 192.
[67] Ibid. pp.56, 68.

210 *Reimagining Regulation*

that treat me as exceptional, since the State is meant to serve others as well as me'.[68] For him, it is the coercive powers of the State which must be engaged to do so.[69] This is arbitrary interference as it is against my interests. More broadly, it undermines his argument that the State is an empire of laws not of men. Irrespective of his claim that the State is necessarily constrained by the laws, his denial that I may respectfully deal with my fears or pursue my sense of freedom in my own terms means that no republican argument about the rule of law per se will do as an argument for the effective constraint of the State. His State alone creates my freedom and does so, because it disallows my interests, in an arbitrary manner. Similar arguments then should apply to his arguments about the status of his constitutional arrangements,[70] separation of powers[71] and such counter-majoritarian arrangements as a bicameral legislature and a bill of rights.[72]

Pettit reinforces the corporatisation of acceptable interests with a sense of inclusiveness so selective that it is better seen as a pattern of exclusion. Included in this is his argument that, by his strategy of screening, 'the virtuous – "the choicest persons of the nation" – come to the top'.[73] This is elitist statism but it reaches bizarre levels when he characterises the necessity of trust by the citizen in the State as a relationship equivalent to that of a lover or a friend.[74] A further reinforcement of the elitist nature of Pettit's republican statism is his attitude towards the distribution of resources, wherein he denies equitable distribution on spurious grounds, that is, that adding resources to some will deprive others.[75] This is clearly of benefit to the wealthy, as his favour for the free market indicates.[76] Further, he argues that the intangible hands of (the negative of) shame and (the positive of) glory – that is, the importance of social approval – will best constrain agents of the State.[77] Pettit himself acknowledges the difficulties in applying this strategy,[78] but Rousseau, whom Pettit sees as a republican, had already seen the vacuousness and self-referentiality of opinion. For him, opinion was the problem, not the solution.[79] All this is compounded by Pettit's preference for concealment; that is, given the corporatisation of interest, then the unaligned individual will have little opportunity to challenge to the republican State, the effect of which is that 'the self-ruling demos or people may often run on automatic pilot',[80] only ineffectively challenged.

---

[68] Ibid. pp.55–56.
[69] Ibid. p.65.
[70] Ibid. p.86.
[71] Ibid. p.177.
[72] Ibid. p.181.
[73] Ibid. pp.63, 197, 214, 221, 223, 235.
[74] Ibid. p.268.
[75] Ibid. pp.161, 118–119.
[76] Ibid. p.205.
[77] Ibid. pp.255–256.
[78] Ibid. pp.236–237.
[79] J.-J. Rousseau, *Discourse on the Origin of Inequality*, p.166.
[80] Ibid. pp.186, 251.

The Argument   211

It is worth noting that, in his *On the People's Terms* – the text that followed *Republicanism* – Pettit's neo-republicanism moves the notion of non-domination in the direction of an individual freedom that is less vulnerable to the kind of State interventionism that he argues and that I have just criticised. Now free choice is to be able to select any of the options of choice regardless of what anyone else prefers one to do. This sounds fine, but he still leaves too much with the State – now 'subject to the equally shared control of the people' which 'must be democratic in a rich etymologically supported sense of the term'.[81] Regarding representation here, he says it should take two forms, responsive and indicative: the first required to respond to the demands of the represented, the second required to be so constituted or constrained as to further the ends that the represented may be expected to endorse.[82] Although he has made this move to more assured individual freedoms, his corporate notions of representation still ends a good distance from the notion of an individual being respectfully responsible to and for themselves, irrespective of his notions of representation.

Braithwaite Follows Pettit into the Trajectory

When one puts all of these features together – especially regarding the account of non-domination in *Republicanism* on which Braithwaite depends but which is not extinguished in *On the People's Terms* – we can say that the republican State intentionally assumes responsibility for its citizens. The breadth and depth of this assumption, because it requires the State to act in a manner that can be against what I see as my individual interests, is not only a profound form of domination effectively unchallengeable by the citizen but a domination that is arbitrary. The features of republican law, interest corporatism, exclusiveness as inclusiveness, screening, debate constriction, the institutionalisation of trust, the tolerance of wide inegalitarianism and promotion of the intangible hand all show that this State is not constrained to promote the respectful interests of individual citizens but is in effect fully empowered as an arbitrary, constitutive force. Rather than eliminate fear, it is a source of that. None of this is eliminated by his later reconsiderations, as we have just seen.

In fact, Pettit's republicanism sits well within the modern political mythology of the State.[83] That is, his republican State is the imagining – by its dominant interests – of a widely empowered but allegedly constrainable magnitude which distances our existential concerns and claims to deal with our immediate fears and desires on condition of subjection, by arbitrary intrusion if necessary. The republican State creates and maintains the conditions of my existence by this intrusion, thus denying my respectful interests.

---

[81] P. Pettit, 'Precis of the argument of on the people's terms', *Critical Review of International Social and Political Philosophy* 18:6 (2015).

[82] P. Pettit, 'On the people's terms: A reply to five critiques', *Critical Review of International Social and Political Philosophy* 18:6 (2015): reply to Miguel Vatter.

[83] See D. Grant, *The Mythological State and Its Empire*, pp.184–186.

Braithwaite's subscription to the republican value system, in particular, the notion of non-domination, therefore means that a proper understanding of his regulatory pyramid of supports and sanctions, especially as that rises to emphasise its most intrusive options that are ultimately administered in the interests of the non-compliant, would place it in the context of the arbitrary intrusiveness of Pettit's republicanism outlined here.

Comment

What should be drawn from all this regarding responsive regulation is that it would be expected that, aware of a range of formidable sanctions that rest on the table, non-compliant individuals and agencies would come to engage with those authorised to monitor and enforce in the development of capacity-building options. But this takes place in the shadow of fear. In that context, many citizens will make themselves subject to the Statist regime whether or not it is in pursuit of their own primary interests. Despite this expected outcome, Braithwaite acknowledges that a number refuse to comply. He puts that down to either incapacity or rational choice about the prospects of being prosecuted.[84] He does not see that there may be other reasons for non-compliance, based on a determination to protest what some non-compliant citizens see as evidence of a non-just legal order, non-just because it is against their interests. That is, republicanism may claim to present a 'just legal order', but, as we have seen, its disallowance of my private, respectful pursuit of my interests is arbitrary interference and so cannot claim to be a validly 'just legal order'.

Braithwaite may respond by saying that there are always both discursive and legal mechanisms that allow laws to be challenged and that this constitutes what is a 'just legal order'.[85] Against this, such individual appeals are powerless in the face of the heavy weight of opposition from the dominant interests of the trajectory. That is, dominant interests have the weight and power of history on their side as to how and by whom a 'just legal order' is determined.

IF NOT RESPONSIVE REGULATION, THEN WHAT?

State and Market need to be pursuing strategies by which they are converted to a frame which pre-eminently promotes the practice by citizens of the ethical principles put here. This applies as much to for-profit corporations as it does to agencies of the State. Then if a citizen or agency behaves in a manner that is contrary to those two principles, the response must be one that is focused on the better embedding of these principles in the thought and behaviour of the citizen or the agency through rational exchange or withdrawal of privilege, not punishment as it is presently

---

[84] *The Fasken Lecture*, pp.484–485.
[85] Ibid. p.485.

If Not Responsive Regulation, Then What? 213

understood. That loss can ultimately include programme-centred 'containment' for a citizen and close external and internal supervision or decommissioning for a corporation. Therefore, regulation needs to be reimagined not merely as an instrument operated by an authority to achieve a prescribed compliance but as a broader notion that requires standards that deliver these two non-mythological principles within and by that authority as much as it does of the citizen.

How these play out in detail will be the subject of Chapters 9 and 10, but here we can say certain things regarding what these responses are not:

- Regulation, properly understood, is not just – or even primarily – about the citizen but is as much about the nature of the institutional context. It is an opportunity first for fundamental institutional self-examination. It does not have a particular focus on the psychological character of the citizen, only on behaviour within that context. Any agency which does not have the non-mythological interests of the citizen as a purpose would need to be reimagined, as we shall see in Chapters 8–10.
- Regulation is therefore not to be about shaming, as 'disrespectful irresponsible behaviour' says as much about the shortcomings of the institutional framework.[86]
- Regulation is therefore not about the 'compliance' of the citizen with regulatory prescriptions until 'regulation' and 'compliance' are reimagined.[87]
- Regulation is not about punishment – even at the serious end of the spectrum of behaviour[88] – but about denial or loss of privileges (see the second bullet point above). It is about both identifying those institutional and individual shortcomings and developing means for both parties to change their approach to promoting respectful self-responsibility and working inexhaustibly on these with those resisting.
- Regulation should not be straightforwardly about eliminating risk, whether actuarial or sociopolitical.[89] Risk assessment is now widely used to protect dominant interests. Within the boundaries of the ethical principles put here, risk needs to be fully reassessed to enable a wider range of ideas and activities by citizens.
- Regulation is not about consumer protection per se as that focus is on constraining corporations within the context of their profit-seeking purpose. What is required is the transformation of agencies and entities so that the respectful existential conditions for citizens and the sustainability of the environment are

---

[86] Cf. N. Harris, 'Reintegrative shaming, shame and criminal justice', *Journal of Social Issues* (May 2006).

[87] Cf. C. Parker, "The compliance trap: The moral message in responsive regulation enforcement', *Law and Society Review* (2006).

[88] *The Fasken Lecture*, p.489.

[89] Cf. F. Haines, 'Addressing the Risk, Reading the Landscape: the Roe of Agency in Regulation' *Regulation and Governance* (December 2010)

purposes that are as prominent as profit seeking. Consumer protection is to be merely one element of this change of purpose. Employment conditions and patient rights within the health system would be others.

- Regulation of cyberspace should prioritise the interests of the user rather than the interests of the provider.[90] This is no threat to intellectual property once proper processes of design and certification are undertaken, as the operation of the respective technologies must be subject to reimagined purpose-based scrutiny and sanctions by way of loss of privilege or fines for the 'disrespectful'.
- Regulation should not identify the State as having a primary responsibility for nurturing capitalist accumulation[91] – whether by encouraging competition or any other strategy – unless the non-mythological interests of the citizens are among the most important of its purposes. It must not be responsible for promoting the process of commodification, as the transformation of all social relations into commodity relations reflects the colonisation of the State and its citizens by the Market.
- Against the grain of current Market-influenced arrangements, the regulatory system should not be implemented by non-State agencies[92] and entities or technologies, although public interest groups can play a secondary,[93] monitoring role. Even where the promotion of the self-responsible interests of citizens by agencies and entities is in place, scaled means of monitoring performance should always be in operation. The State would have to regain its primary function of executive administration on behalf of the elected government and thereby promote the re-establishment of proper levels of public accountability.

An Alternative Version of Responsive Regulation

Given the persistent, fearsome shadow of sanctions, including the most severe of corporate capital punishment and criminal imprisonment – and irrespective of the compliance with the 'collaboration' realised through that – Braithwaite's strategy must be seen ultimately as one of enforcement rather than collaboration. It is therefore internally contradictory at the deepest level. This is attributable to Pettit's republicanism, properly understood.

---

[90] Cf. Lennon Y. C. Chang and P. Grabosky, 'Cybercrime and establishing a secure cyberworld', *The Handbook of Security* (2014): 321–339.

[91] I. Alami and A. Dixon, 'State capitalism(s) redux? Theories, tensions, controversies', *Competition and Change* 24:1 (2020): pp.84, 86.

[92] Cf. C. Holley and C. Shearing, 'A Nodal Perspective on Governance: Advances in Nodal Governance Thinking', in *Regulation, Institutions and Networks*, P. Drahos (ed.) (ANU E Press, 2017).

[93] R. Rajabiun and C. Middleton, 'Public interest in the regulation of competition: Evidence from wholesale internet access consultations in Canada', *Journal of Information Policy* 5 (2015): p.63.

However, there is residual value in Braithwaite's strategy. If severed from the mythology of republicanism, his approach of seeking what would then be respectful collaboration remains of real value. This would need to be placed in a non-mythological context in which a 'just legal order' was not determined by dominant interests claiming to deal with 'constructed' concerns on condition of subjection. The mistake Braithwaite makes is to presume that an arrangement based on a republican legal system, that is, one which makes provision for legal challenges, is a just legal order. Although he appears to go some way to it, he needs to start far more firmly at the other end and consider the respectful existential interests of the individual citizen first and over the republican arrangements, displacing the dominant interests that promote those. All this leaves a place for sanctions, but they would be formed according to the manner in which the individual citizen or agency failed to pursue their interests in accordance with the ethical principles preferred here.

More broadly, it would be for the institutions of the non-mythological State to provide the support needed for citizens to develop. It would be their interests, and not those of the dominant interests of the trajectory, which would be provided for. This is not a merely servile function that such institutions would perform. There are long-unattended elements under the current arrangements which would be need to be addressed. Among these would be the failure to properly address the emotions – especially, existential fear and desire – a failure which has contributed so much to social and individual unease. Further, beyond institutional reform, the quantum change being wrought by a world dominated by emerging technologies may not find favour among many citizens. It may well be necessary to ensure that all citizens enhance their capacity to keep pace with the rapidly changing technological environment so that, for example, with the growing influence of artificial intelligence and virtual reality, it does not develop beyond our capacity to manage it. Wide awareness would be required for that. In such conditions, citizens may need to be brought to an understanding as deep as that which would reflect a behavioural code that promotes respect for all others.

In such a circumstance, the capacity building which could come from any wide revision of Braithwaite's schema would be fully tested. This would require a sense and practice of regulation vastly different from that currently promoted by current arrangements. In short, shorn of his mythological republicanism[94] and placed in the context of non-mythological arrangements of State, Braithwaite's search for collaboration would work far better than his present search does, irrespective of the current success that is claimed for it by interested parties. This would make available a sense of regulation vastly different from that which Foucault identified.

---

[94] It might be noted that Braithwaite retains his commitment to Pettit's republicanism. The Fasken lecture was published in 2011. In his paper with Y. Zhang, 'Persia to China: The Silk Road of restorative justice', *Asian Journal of Criminology* (2017), at p.3 he states that his views remain guided in part by that version of republicanism.

8

Regulation and the Law

Given the inadequacy of current regulation theory as means to pursue responsibility to and for oneself, we need to turn directly to law. As it happens, there is a sense of a reimagined rule of law that allows that.

The central theme of this reimagining is that law – to the substantial extent that it is a manifestation of the interests that dominate the engaged magnitudes of the trajectory – is a means of mythological subjection wherever it precludes respectful, existential autonomy. This is not the proper function of law, which should be concerned – like the proper functioning of the agencies that constitute those magnitudes – with promoting the awareness of the existential conditions for each citizen. That is the purpose of law but also the limit of it.

Because the mythological State and Market have been 'engaged' – allowing claims of its sympathy for each citizen – this consideration of law needs also to be seen in the context of the regulatory practice we have just considered, a practice which has spread across the social field. Regulation is the means by which subjection to the practices sponsored by the dominant interests of these magnitudes has progressed, but law sustains the validity of those mythological magnitudes. Therefore, law needs to be reconsidered. This is approached through four avenues.

As background to the exploration we are about to undertake, it will be useful to keep in mind elements of the enigmatic approach to law to be found disparately in Foucault. Specifically, one can say that he saw law as indicative, in the sense that it points to changing regimes of truth and power. Whereas sovereign truth and power was repressive, inefficient and extroverted, the disciplinary and governmental power that emerged in its shadow was productive, efficient and introverted, the world of 'police' regulation which strengthened the State. This in turn was replaced by a liberal and then a neoliberal form of governmentality which was based on the truth of specifics of knowledge, on what would be most productive and on the field of natural dispositions accompanied by individual freedoms by which individuals

Regulation and the Law

could take advantage of the rise of the market. Law changed to reflect these shifting regimes of truth and power.[1]

The move to neoliberal governmentality has been accompanied by a shift in the application of the law that reflects the shift to the neoliberal form of power. Examples of this are that corporations are increasingly being given the opportunity to have breaches dealt with by cooperative resolution, to settle and remain outside the law, while criminal matters are increasingly being settled by plea bargain, wherein the offender may be induced to plead guilty before the full force of the law is applied. Further, employers and employees may technically agree to settle upon a termination of employment triggered by either side, but whereby employers typically adopt this as a downsizing mechanism. These are examples of subjectification, wherein the subject is conceived of as a power and not a holder of rights: a neoliberalism which prefers the individual to exercise the capacity to act and make settlements rather than exercise rights. This is a new, neoliberal conception of the subject, and law is at the centre of this arrangement, facilitating this cooperation with power and intimately connected to the economy. It is not the departure from law but the ending of a juridical discourse.[2]

But in this, we might remember that Foucault does see an opportunity for what may be called 'resistant rights'. This is not any straightforward recognition of spectrums of juridical rights as commonly understood but a political capacity to choose, a critical affirmation. The sense of this is given by Golder, who inter alia sees Foucault's sense of rights as, first, ungrounded and illimitable: they cannot be based on some timeless and immutable essence of humanity but are a function of particular power–knowledge formations which themselves configure what is human. Second, they are the strategic effect of political struggle, that is, historical and political artefacts which reflect the contours of what is human within discourses and regimes of power: they can be made and unmade but not in a manner that finally affirms any form of power. Third, they can be seen as performative mechanisms which may even bring new communities into being.[3]

That is, both the law and the opportunity for resistant rights are best seen no longer as implacable, juridical formations but as reflections of the shifting field of contestatory power and knowledge. In mythological terms this shifting field is conditioned by the persistent remains of the impact of the magnitudes of the trajectory. We began to explore this in Chapter 4. What we will now begin to

---

[1] L. Brannstrom, 'Law, objectives of government and regimes of truth: Foucault's understanding of law and the transformation of law of the EU internal market', *Foucault Studies* 18 (2014): pp.175–182.

[2] A. Garapon, 'Michel Foucault: Visionary insight into contemporary law', *Raison Politiques* 52 (2013–2014): at 9, 16 and 24.

[3] B. Golder, 'Foucault's critical (yet ambivalent) affirmation: Three figures of rights', *Social and Legal Studies* 20:3 (2011): pp.286, 287, 290, 297.

consider is the manner in which this conditioning has been set and how we might find a way out of it.

THE NEED FOR A CONSTITUTIONAL FRAME
FOR A NON-MYTHOLOGICAL LAW

It is unsurprising that there is almost nothing in the field of jurisprudence which addresses this particular account of the mythological nature of either law or its increasingly powerful adjunct and successor, specified regulation. That is, there is no sense of the mythological dynamic either within or about current legal philosophy, legislative drafting or legal practice. So, a fundamental, Constitutional reference point is required. Perhaps the nearest that current provisions come to the protection of any sense of self-responsibility in the United States are various elements of the First, Fourth and Fifth Amendments to the US Constitution, as contained in the Bill of Rights. The First Amendment protects freedom of speech; the Fourth Amendment protects the right of people to be secure in their persons, houses, papers and effects against unreasonable searches and seizures – the 'privacy' right – and the Fifth Amendment provides that no person shall be deprived of life, liberty or property without due process of law. Some of these themes are echoed in Article 7 of the European Charter of Fundamental Rights, to wit, that everyone has the right to respect for their private and family life, their home and their correspondence, and that there shall be no interference by a public authority with the exercise of this right 'except such as is in accordance with the law and is necessary in a democratic society in the interests of national security, public security, public safety or the economic well-being of the country, for the prevention of disorder or crime, for the protection of health or morals, or for the protection of the rights and freedoms of others'.

These are all 'protections against' rather than 'provisions for', reflecting the prospect of unreasonable intrusions – or dominance – mainly by the State, whereas the provisions for self-responsibility that are presented in the present work are as 'provisions for'. Addressing that and the notion that the State – and the Market – should have the purpose of promoting self-responsibility seems a stretch. But we shall see that providing for such a purpose is well conceivable within current law, given suitable finessing. Taking the lead from that, we might say that various elements of the above amendments and provisions – the security of individuals in their freedoms – could be the basis of the kind of 'positive' Constitutional framework that would move self-responsibility to centre-stage.

This will always be confronted by the argument that a Constitution should be preeminently about constraining the State rather than empowering it. This chapter and those that follow are intended to provide for that constraining but in a manner that places the self-responsible citizen and their qualified, voluntary interests at the centre of the frame rather than as a secondary participant, as current circumstances allow.

The challenge in this is emphasised by the fact, apart from a handful of civil duties (such as to obey the law, to be loyal to the United States, to serve as an impartial juror, to serve in the armed forces when called and to vote), there is no elaborated account of the responsibility of citizens.[4] Further, the notion of personal responsibility – albeit more narrowly legal than the wider and deeper notion proposed herein – is regarded as only implicit in the US Constitution. As Judge Michael B. Brennan observed:

> The American Constitution is primarily a charter of government. The Framers recognized that the constitutional order that they created presupposed the concept of responsibility.... Without a general cultural insistence on a sense of personal responsibility, and its correlative – a sense of shame – any form of social organization faces trouble. This does not mean that in all instances the government is to define the content of individual obligations. But the government through the legal system should not actively undermine the fundamental sense of individual responsibility that is necessary for a civilised legal order.[5]

A sign of how challenging it will be to establish the adoption of the principles and practices of self-responsibility – unless supported by legal, political and commercial agencies – is the present move in the other direction. One example is the application of artificial intelligence algorithms to the judicial process, exemplified by the consideration of the replacement of judicial decisions by algorithmic determinations. This has real significance for the principle and practice of the separation of powers, thereby making this a serious Constitutional threat.

Michaels has responded to this development, pointing out that only judges can balance precedent with adapting the law to future circumstances, thus shaping the law; that many cases do not have a clear right answer; that the removal of judges would reduce the legal community and thereby the profile of the law and leaving law more susceptible to co-option; and that the removal of judges would dehumanise the law and its contribution to the sense of the human governance of society.[6] Further, complementing this at the framework level by redesigning laws and regulations into information and communication technologies (ICTs) not only creates new assemblages of law but also thereby moulds both the form and the content of laws and regulations. The outcome can be very different from the intention of the originating institutional settings and procedural frameworks:

---

[4] 'Constitutional Topic: Rights and Responsibilities', *US Constitution* www.usconstitution.net /constop_resp.

[5] Michael B. Brennan, 'The lodestar of personal responsibility', *Marquette Law Review* 88:2 (2004): p.375.

[6] A. Michaels, 'Artificial intelligence, legal change and separation of powers', *University of Cincinnati Law Review* 88 (2020 forthcoming).

220   *Regulation and the Law*

technology and law engage normativity in different ways.[7] It might well be observed that this is a paradigm case of the removal of responsibility not only from judicial officers but also from the prospect of increased personal engagement of the accused party in the judicial process. Consistent with what we have seen Chapter 2, this would be the imposition of algorithmic reasoning on the human realisation of justice.

But technology brings even wider and deeper implications for the US Constitution. That is, as Snead observes, emerging technologies are raising profound interpretive problems. That the Constitution is a product of the times in which it was originally conceived and then amended has, of course, been very widely explored. Those who undertook that work could not have conceived the questions now being posed by such fields as biotechnology. Should originalist textualism be sustained to preserve what was originally conceived, or does that limit and devalue the opportunities of emerging technologies?[8]

The general points here are that not only would Constitutional recognition of the principles of respectful self-responsibility be a challenge but the march of technologies that are subsuming self-responsibility – and the institutions that might protect those principles – is in the other direction. Two responses should be made to this. First, it is the very force of this march that makes the recognition of this principle all the more important. Second, as we have seen regarding certain elements of current US and European constitutional frameworks – for example, the views of Brennan J. – and as we shall see regarding the potential for purpose-based fiduciary principles, the field does exist to establish such a recognition by interpretation and legislative change. This field can also take comfort from the senses of rights that Golder sees in Foucault, senses that are uncoupled from forms of power, that are unconstrained by ideology and that are essentially performative in nature. Respectful self-responsibility would be so uncoupled, unconstrained and performative.

THE RULE OF LAW

We shall now begin to look at the notion of rule of law through the lens of these preferred principles. This will direct our consideration somewhat away from standard presentations and have it focus more on recent reconsiderations of that which are more relevant to the issue in the present work.

The rule of law forms one central element of the broader argument being put here. Many current accounts of it focus on its delivery, both institutional and procedural, arguing that there are essential features that any credible rule of law will display. A somewhat different approach, one preferred here, is adopted by those

---

[7] F. Contini and A. Cordella, 'Assembling law and technology in the public sector: The case of e-justice reforms', in *Proceedings of the 16th Annual International Conference on Digital Government Research* (May 2015), doi.org/10.1145/2757401.2757418.

[8] O. Carter Snead, 'Technology and the Constitution', *The New Atlantis: A Journal of Technology and Society* 61:5 (2004): p.62.

The Rule of Law

which explore the territory beyond these features and venture into the social contexts within which the rule of law sits – comfortably or not – to understand what informs it, what confronts it, what is shaped by it and thereby what it says about such a society. That is, looking at theories of the rule of law can say much about social beliefs and practices. A key factor in the latter is the nature of the social values that appear in such an exploration, as that will be taken here to be an indicator of the value of that respective rule of law: there are both positive and negative social values and they provide different foundations for the enterprise, some repressive and some liberating.

Prominent Views of the Rule of Law

Commentary and analysis of the current state of rule of law thinking abounds, so the challenge is to pick out from its many themes those that are relevant to the argument in the present work. There are few – if any – better places to start than with Krygier.[9] As Waldron has said of him: 'In 30 years of writing about the rule of law ... his writings have contributed a generous and interdisciplinary breadth of vision that is all too rare in this business ... Krygier's willingness to explore ... new directions and integrate them with one another is something that is sorely needed in the study of the rule of law.'[10] To which Phillip Pettit adds:

> Martin Krygier has made the rule of law his own.... Like a number of recent authors, he has made us keenly aware of its importance. Like a few of those writers, he has enhanced our understanding of what it requires. And unmatched by any of them, he has brought the style of a master to illuminating its connections with other ideas and its applications in day-to-day politics.[11]

For Krygier, despite the murkiness and exaggeration of the source and present use of the term 'rule of law', this is a valuable term which focuses attention on two matters of pre-eminent significance: the dangers of arbitrary power and the value of institutionalising its tempering. His critique of much current thinking leads him to suggest that the way forward is two-fold: be clear that arbitrariness in the use of power is the problem, then begin to imagine a social science that does not yet exist. This would require considering that it may be time to move beyond the rule of law to pursue the ideals that led us to it. Within the long tradition of rule of law thinking,[12] he sees an

---

[9] M. Krygier, 'The rule of law: Pasts, presents and two possible futures', *Annual Review of Law and Social Science* 12 (2016): 199-229.

[10] Jeremy Waldron, 'Martin Krygier's passion for the rule of law – Preface', *Hague Journal of the Rule of Law* 11:2–3 (2019): pp.251 and 253.

[11] P. Pettit, 'Athens and the rule of law: An essay in Honour of Martin Krygier', *Hague Journal of the Rule of Law* 11:2–3 (2019): p.289.

[12] M. Krygier, 'The rule of law: Pasts, presents and two possible futures', *University of New South Wales Law Review* 31 (2016): p.202.

ongoing concern about the pathologies of power, especially in its arbitrary form,[13] and how tempering it – not just narrowly through the courts – has been the repeating response.[14] He reaches back to Aristotle, Marsilius, the authors of the Magna Carta and Montesquieu, among others, and through to Selznick, Raz and Waldron in considering the range of the idea of the rule of law, including thin and thick accounts of it, but both of which he moves beyond.[15]

Krygier's way forward – a prospective social science – would ask key questions: What are the reasons for which people have clamoured and we might still clamour for the rule of law? Are they good reasons? What are the dangers to the values unearthed by such questions? What are the appropriate responses? His indicative response is that the answers to these questions will be found outside the law and within the broader society, especially in politics and the causality, variety and contexts therein.[16] Regarding this final point, the law may not be the ultimate reference in this, for example, regarding the separation of powers, which themselves may need to be more balanced – even blended – in the spirit of Montesquieu. We shall return to Krygier's approach shortly.

Anatomy and Teleology

First, we may usefully look somewhat more broadly to see where Krygier's view sits. At the risk of saying too little – or too much – this preface is not a detailed examination of the respective accounts of the rule of law by these other authors but is provided merely as a counterpoint to the work of Krygier. The key point is that each of these accounts, in one way or another, is what Krygier labels as anatomist: one way or another they present what they each see as the anatomical features of a good rule of law. This differs from those that are teleological, including his own, that examine the purpose of the rule of law. The argument of the present work is that any that fall into the latter category are more likely to allow an assessment of whether their rationale may contribute to a rule of law the purpose of which is to promote the principles put forward here, whereas anatomical models are more closely tied to the State as a magnitude.

Examples of an anatomical approach are those presented by Hayek, Bentham, Dicey, Rawls, Raz, Fuller and Waldron,[17] although we shall also consider the latter

---

[13] Ibid. p.203.
[14] Ibid. p.205.
[15] Ibid. p.215.
[16] Ibid. p.223.
[17] J. Waldron, 'The Rule of Law and the Importance of Procedure', in *Getting to the Rule of Law*, J. Fleming (ed.) (New York University Press, 2011), pp. 5 and 6, where we see his list of essential ingredients for proper legal procedure (including impartiality, trained judges, representation, right to presence, right to confront witnesses, properly attained prosecution evidence, right to present one's own evidence and argue the bearing of prosecution evidence, right to hear the tribunal's reasons for decision and right of appeal) along with the eight produced by Fuller.

The Rule of Law 223

in the following analysis of the teleological accounts. Krygier gives six reasons why this approach is wrong. First, the legal and institutional forms which are often the means invoked to deal with the social and political problems which are the focus of the rule of law often change more quickly than those forms; second, many new problems – such as those presented by the appearance of social media – arise about which these institutions have little to offer; third, when transplanted to new jurisdictions, such institutions can be widely out of place and even legitimise the power of incumbent dictatorship; fourth, conventional accounts pay little attention to the social causality – that is, from beyond the State – of the problems with which the rule of law is intended to address; fifth, the legal forms chosen to generate the rule of law can be complicit in its abuse, in gaming them; and sixth, non-lawyers are unlikely to ask about institutional forms in trying to see the point of the enterprise.[18]

For example, for Hayek, law should – anatomically – feature generality, impersonality, clarity, prospectivity, predictability and minimising discretion. He sees these generally as placed within the social norms that grew from traditions.[19] For Tamanaha, laws must be set forth in advance and stated in general terms; they must be generally understood, realisable by all and applied equally to all; there must be mechanisms of enforcement when they are breached; and so forth.

In the vein of constraining power, Fuller focuses on the eight internal principles of legal craftmanship that he believes have moral significance – the internal morality of law – and allow law to work with people on a moral basis of reciprocity: generality, publicity, prospectivity, intelligibility, consistency, practicability, stability and congruence.[20] Fuller sees law as the purposive enterprise of subjecting human conduct to the governance of rules and has such an inner morality, meaning that the practice of making and maintaining a legal system, ordered by social control, has practically necessary moral principles that impart practically necessary moral characteristics to the laws of that legal system and limit the powers of governors by ensuring a minimum of justice and fairness between governors and governed.[21]

In his anatomical approach, Raz identifies what he saw first as the five principles of the rule of law, that is, clarity, stability, public availability, generality and (only) prospective application. He then takes up the theme of the restraint of arbitrary power. For him, this amounts to seeing, in the context of the umbrella of custodianship, the rule of law as having a doctrinal status. This has the advantage not only of contributing to the restraint of arbitrary power but also of its universal application

---

[18] M. Krygier, 'Re-imagining the Rule of Law', Denis Leslie Mahoney Prize Public Lecture, Julius Stone Institute, Sydney University Law School, 7 September 2017, pp.9–13.
[19] For a critique of the mythological implications of drawing on such traditions as Hayek does, see D. Grant, *The Mythological State and Its Empire*, pp.146–165.
[20] K. Rundle, 'Fuller's internal morality of law', *Philosophy Compass* 11:9 (2016): p.499.
[21] L. L. Fuller, 'A reply to Professors Cohen and Dworkin', *Villanova Law Review* 10 (1965): p.655.

Regulation and the Law

across the law, whereby it aids examining and reforming law, thereby maintaining its broader relevance. So, it protects and advances the interests of the governed.[22]

Horwitz takes a somewhat different view, lamenting what he sees as the unpalatable consequences of rule of law thinking:

> It undoubtedly restrains power, but it also prevents power's benevolent exercise. It creates formal equality – a not inconsiderable virtue – but it *promotes* substantive inequality by creating a consciousness that radically separates law from politics, means from ends, processes from outcomes. By promoting procedural justice, it enables the shrewd, the calculating, and the wealthy to manipulate its forms to their own advantage. And it ratifies and legitimates an adversarial, competitive, and atomistic conception of human relations.... It may be true that restraint on power (and simultaneously on its benevolent exercise) is about all we can hope to accomplish in this world. But we should never forget that a 'legalist' consciousness that excludes 'result-oriented' jurisprudence as contrary to the rule of law also inevitably discourages the pursuit of substantive justice.[23]

Waldron, Krygier and Teleology

Against all this, there are two teleological approaches that seem relevant to the argument in the present work. The first is put by Waldron, the other by Krygier. The position here will be that the account presented by the former is unhelpful and that the latter's account is a much more significant attempt to deal with purpose, although ultimately it needs to be seen as having features that are the subject of the mythological analysis presented here.

The context of the argument put by Waldron is important. The reference points are democracy, human rights, free markets and private property, social justice and the rule of law. The latter is the field by which we are to deal with misbehaviour by crime, in commerce, in administration, by terrorism, for the marginalised and outsiders. It would not be an exaggeration to see his rule of law as foundational for all these elements of Western capitalist societies and a range of those in other jurisdictions.[24] From within this context, he sees that law protects dignity,[25] arguably one of the purposes of the law, given that the protection of dignity is inherent in the normativity of law and given that there is 'a wholesale connection between dignity and the branch of the law devoted to human rights'.[26] Although consistent with his procedural 'laundry list' approach,[27] Waldron argues that legal principles and

---

[22] J. Raz, 'The law's own virtue', *Oxford Journal of Legal Studies* 39:1 (2019): pp.1–15.

[23] Morton Horwitz, 'The rule of law – An unqualified human good?', *Yale Law Journal* 86 (1977): p.566.

[24] J. Waldron, 'The Rule of Law and the Importance of Procedure', p.3.

[25] J. Waldron, 'How law protects dignity', *The Cambridge Law Journal* 71:1 (2012): 200–222..

[26] Ibid. p.201.

[27] J. Waldron, 'The Rule of Law and the Importance of Procedure', p.6.

The Rule of Law   225

procedures either recognise, promote or protect individual human dignity. Specifically, the latter occurs through the demonstration of self-application of laws, the necessity of legal argument in courts, the change in individual status due to the upward equalisation of rank that has occurred over time, representation of the accused and the dignification of coercion by the State.[28]

Leaving aside the debates about the reality of equalisation and dignified coercion, there are several immediate grounds to question the argument Waldron makes. Semphill identifies some of these, primarily that Waldron ignores the reality that some laws, for example, those that related to the Nazi treatment of Jews, are dehumanising, and so, by that, procedure compounds the wrong.[29] He also points to the fact that the self-application of immoral laws – especially if motivated by fear – contradicts the principle of dignity.[30] In short, sidelining the contents of law comes at a high price and can subvert any claims to the protection of individual dignity by law and its procedures.

But there is a more fundamental problem with the arguments put by Waldron and that concerns the nature of dignity itself and thereby whether the protection – inherent or otherwise – of it can be a purpose of law, that is, whether it can be normative for law. For Waldron, dignity is a status concept.[31] With it, a person is recognised as having the ability to control and regulate their actions in accord with their own apprehension of norms and reasons that apply to them; that they are capable of giving and entitled to give an account of themself, an account that others are to pay attention to; and that they have the wherewithal to demand that their agency and presence among us as a human being be taken seriously and accommodated in the lives of others, in others' attitudes and actions towards them and in social life generally.[32]

The problem is that an active supporter of Al Qaeda or ISIS can claim all these dimensions of status. That is, dignity is culturally relative and the majority of people would not be guided by what such supporters regard as dignified. Waldron might respond by saying that these organisations are unlawful, and so marginal, rather than mainstream, and so cannot claim dignity based on these qualities, which are pointers to mainstream status and so are disqualified from having such status granted to them. A response in reply might be that in the earliest days of Christianity, the Christ and his followers were said to have not been mainstream, in fact, were a decidedly marginalised and radical group, even *lestes* or bandits or Zealots.[33] The point is that both groups can claim the status concept for dignity provided by

---

[28] J. Waldron, 'How law protects dignity', pp.205–219.
[29] J. Sempill, 'Law, dignity and the elusive promise of a third way', *Oxford Journal of Legal Studies* 38:2 (2018): pp.223, 225.
[30] Ibid. p.229.
[31] J. Waldron, 'How law protects dignity', p.201.
[32] Ibid. p.202.
[33] R. Aslan, *Zealot – The Life and Times of Jesus of Nazareth* (Allen & Unwin, 2013), p.78.

Waldron. It is a notion that sits within a wide range of social frames, all of which may exist within a single jurisdiction but not all of which would have their dignity recognised or whose dignity would be seen to be inherent within the law. Its relativity ranges too wide for Waldron's definition. As we saw in Chapter 5, other principles provide a better foundation or reference point for law, although their qualities go well beyond the features of dignity listed by Waldron.

The other teleological approach of interest – that argued for by Krygier – shifts the focus in a manner that not only identifies what he sees as the problem that the rule of law serves best to address – which the anatomical approaches do not do – but also moves on to talk about how the rule of law can provide a way of dealing with that problem. Whereas Waldron is concerned to say what value the rule of law serves, that is, dignity, Krygier's focus is on what he sees as the deep social problem presented variably by societies across the board. That problem is the arbitrary use of power, how we should respond to it and how we should think about these things before we start to argue for the implementation of a rule of law with particular features.

One need not look far to see why the arbitrary exercise of power is both a political and a moral problem. It is repeatedly in our face. We look to law to help deliver justice, fairness and equality, but none of this can happen if power is administered arbitrarily, that is, if power-wielders are not subject to regular control or limit, or if power is exercised in unreckonable ways or in ways that deny its targets the opportunity to be heard.[34] Krygier goes on to endorse the value of Shklar's liberalism of fear in saying that power needs 'above all' to be reliably and securely limited[35] but then goes on, like Stephen Holmes and Waldron following Montesquieu, to emphasise the need for strong governance so that necessary – but non-coercive – functions can be fulfilled. Government should not be emasculated but should be balanced by tempering. These non-coercive functions can channel, direct, facilitate and inform infrastructural strength.[36] Tempering is not a weakening but a toughening of power so that it is thoughtful and can do good. This is a key to his preferred rule of law.

Further, with Braithwaite, Krygier sees all this as insufficient. Contemporary capitalism needs a range of further institutions to temper power, including commissions, ombudsmen, auditors-general, ratings agencies, stock exchange regulation, competition authorities, prudential regulators and a vigilant civil society.[37] Finally, because power is exercised arbitrarily outside the State, this rule of law needs to be capable in this wider field and by drawing all the support it can from that field. There are many agendas that oppose the rule of law, but they have their own justifications.

---

[34] M. Krygier, 'What's the point of the rule of law?', *Buffalo Law Review* 67:3 (2019): pp.12–13.
[35] Ibid. p.18.
[36] Ibid. p.22.
[37] Ibid. p.26.

In short, this rule of law sees its wide political, social and economic significance.[38] It progresses the debate well beyond the anatomical approach in its teleology, not only constraining the State but doing so in a manner that enhances its resilience such that it will direct its capacity to do good, and sees its wider function across the social, political and economic fields.

There is no doubt that the power of the State needs to be managed. There is more than enough evidence of the need for that. However, as even Krygier's own account can be argued to show, the State is a powerful magnitude that has been engaged through myriad devices that claim to make it more sympathetic, so long as an individual subjects themself to its regimes. These suggest a mythological element. Further, we need to add to this that this engaged State is the source – through its post-absolutist regulatory form – of the exercise of an additional, different but widespread form of power which is also subjecting in nature: the regulating normalisation born of governmental strategies to reinforce that subjection that we examined in Chapter 4. Further again, it is a State that – as a Market State – encourages the Market to add its own economic subjection to that political subjection. No one could complain about tempering the State to claim it is not tyrannical but socially beneficial, yet that comes at the price of a normalising, regulating governmentalisation of the individual, the beneficiaries of which are dominant interests of State, Market and now Technology.

There are various moments at which these comments about Krygier's account of the rule of law are on display and allow a mythological interpretation of his broad arguments for constraint of power. First, his borrowing from Montesquieu, whose argument for the separation of powers – which admittedly Krygier is not excessively strict about as he varies the approach of Braithwaite[39] – arguably places him in the mythological field, concerned to constrain the absolutism of Hobbes's Leviathan.[40] Second, his acknowledgement, at least partial, of Shklar's liberalism of fear has strong parallels in the mythological argument that existential fear is at the foundation of the imagination of the magnitude of the State.[41] More important than these, his reliance on Braithwaite's adoption of Pettit's republicanism is a reliance on a mythological account of the State.[42] Krygier's rule of law not only deals with only one – the sovereign – of these two kinds of excessive power, and can be read to do so with mythological outcomes, but in doing so provides no focus on the other – normalising, regulatory – form and thereby allows not tyranny but systematic subjection. That is, if the 'tempering' of the State stops at preventing tyranny, then it misses much of the mythological subjecting that the engaged, regulatory Market

---

[38] Ibid. pp.28–29.
[39] Ibid. p.26.
[40] D. Grant, *The Mythological State and Its Empire*, pp.72–76.
[41] Ibid. pp.22–24, and M. Krygier, 'What's the point of the rule of law?', p.18.
[42] D. Grant, *The Mythological State and Its Empire*, pp.166–186, and M. Krygier, 'What's the point of the rule of law?', pp.15 and 16.

State has perpetrated in the name of 'civilisation'. It also allows this further subjection to go under his radar.

Constraining excessive and arbitrary power and the subjection that flows from it is necessary. But we should not do so, as we have, in a manner that allows its replacement by a different kind of subjecting power. We should remember that it has been through the constrained Market State that our political participation has been limited to a 'once in four years' visit to the ballot box while special interests occupy the parliamentary benches; that it promotes the mega-profit-seeking of large corporations while reducing worker wages and 'casualised' conditions to near-subsistence levels; that it both participates in and encourages the purloining of massive volumes of personal data under the guise of the demands of security and the health of the private sector through marketing the creation of desires; that it has allowed the spread of corporate AI strategies unchecked across an increasing range of activities and services, many of which subsume individual decision-making; that it takes part in and promotes the widespread regulation of individual practice across the socio-politico-economic field; and that it has largely stood by in the face of significant climate degradation to protect the interests of large oil and coal mining interests. Simply because all these have proceeded with little effective public resistance is more a sign of normalised subjection than endorsement. We need a different rule of law.

This other rule of law – which would deal with both types of excessive power, one arbitrary and the other systematically normalising and regulatory – would be one based on agencies being 'purposed' in law to give priority to citizens' respectful self-responsible interests, on the embedding of fiduciary trust law in agency practice to reinforce that priority and on a reconsideration of the notion of risk.

Before proceeding to fiduciary matters, we should return to Krygier. His way out of the problems of rule of law thinking centre on 'a social science that does not yet exist', including by looking beyond the law. Although the outcome of his deliberations is different from the non-mythological framework proposed here, his notion of exploring the sociological questions he suggests are a comfort to that framework.

We will remember that Krygier wished to proceed by asking a series of questions: What are the reasons for which people have clamoured and we might still clamour for the rule of law? Are they good reasons? What are the dangers to the values unearthed by such questions? What are the appropriate responses? His indicative answer is that the answers to these questions will be found outside the law and within the broader society, especially in politics and the causality, variety and contexts therein.[43] He even suggests empirical research to help provide answers to these questions. For Krygier, this science is civics or eunomics. The latter is a term coined by Lon Fuller and has the sense of the theory of good order and workable

---

[43] D. Grant, *The Mythological State and Its Empire*, p.223.

The Rule of Law

arrangements and that infuses the internal morality of law,[44] recognising constancies and regularities that persist through changes in social forms.[45] It focuses on legitimated power, adjudication and contract which seek to implement the common need, manifest in the collaborative articulation of shared purposes.[46] Here there are perhaps some echoes of Hayek's just society embedded in tradition.

But this does not address the issues with which the present work is primarily concerned. Certainly, the search for traditional senses of good order, of legitimated power and collaborative articulation of shared purpose as foundational notions of a rule of law is conceptual and perhaps even an empirical means of finding a way to resist tyranny, thereby tempering power in the civilised manner that Krygier intends. But falling back on traditions – even civilised ones – to explain the clamour for a rule of law does not fully explain why it is a clamour. This is not to say that he is uncritical of traditions,[47] only that his approach is different in character from that presented here, which is outside easily recognisable frameworks of criticism.

A point of clarification before proceeding further. The argument of this work is not that there is a single 'tradition' of which the West is comprised. Clearly, there are many – large and small – traditions resting there. Here we argue that the mythological trajectory is a frame, the dominant elements of which, singularly and together, have continued to heavily inform those traditions. Neither is it to say that many elements of our traditions are not agreeable. Clearly, there are many that are, but here the point is that, even when they are – with a law that is accountable, with a 'liberal' education, with the benefits of much scientific research, with aspects of improved conditions of living, with the wonder of the arts and so on – these exist within a frame that camouflages existential concerns ultimately through subjection.

So rather than looking around within the identifiable traditions of the West – for example, those with eunomic features – it is better to start at the bottom but beyond Shklar's liberalism of fear. Then we could understand that the rule of law is properly the answer to deeper – existential – conditions and that, given the opportunity, we can deal with and take advantage of that condition without being subject to the threats, claims and promises of mythological regimes. Further, we could see that, as their respective sovereign absolutisms have been 'called out' and they have been engaged to be more 'sympathetic', they have each – and often in partnership – sought re-ascendance through such other means as regimes of regulation and normalising subjectivation. So the search for unearthing traditions in the eunomic

---

[44] K. E. Dawkins, 'The legal philosophy of Lon Fuller: A natural law perspective', www.austlii .edu.au.journals.OtaLawRw5.pdf, p.76.

[45] Ibid. p.77.

[46] Ibid. p.78.

[47] M. Krygier, 'Too Much Information', in *Cosmopolitan Jurisprudence – Essays in Memory of H. Patrick Glenn*, Helge Dedek (ed.) (Cambridge University Press, forthcoming 2020), and M. Krygier, 'Conservative-liberal-socialism', *Symposium* 11:1 (2002).

230 *Regulation and the Law*

sense is circular, drawing on the very traditions that have given us the magnitudes in the first place. There is too much of Hayek's kind of mythologising here.[48]

In short, these questions can be better answered through the frame of the mythological analysis. In fact, there has even been – as Krygier calls for – some empirical, forensic analysis by the author of the manner in which mythological interests have generated legislation regarding recent technologies.[49]

So, we need to confront existential reality in a different way by a questioning of traditions, including the 'civilised' ones. This is not an abandonment of the lessons of the past but the need to examine those moments when those traditions allowed the emergence of tyranny. The occurrences of tyranny which have repeated devastatingly over the ages, and are so subjecting, are easy to spot. They must be resisted. But the traditions of 'civilisation' carry less easily detected regimes of subjection, and a valid rule of law needs to address this normalising subjection as well. This is the sense in which Krygier is correct, that is, that we need to look beyond the law. But looking into the traditions of Fuller or Hayek is only looking into the traditions fed by the ideas and practices generated by the long traditions of Deity and encapsulated in the democratic State (and more recently by such champions of the free market as Hayek). It is merely looking at mythological ideals. A deeper forensic is required, a dig into the very conditions of our existence. It has been proposed herein that unless the integrity and the 'thick' autonomy of the individual citizen is what is at the heart of a reimagined rule of law – and not the 'civilising' traditions – then subjection in its more normalising, regulatory form will persist, even if we temper arbitrariness and avoid tyranny. A reimagined law can play a key role in this.

A NEW RULE OF LAW: RISK, PURPOSE-BASED ORGANISATIONS AND FIDUCIARY TRUST

If we are to embrace a sense of responsibility strong enough to resist the force and spread of mythological idea and practice – in particular, one that is expressed in the claims on behalf of neuroscience – then we need a new attitude towards the law. Law and its regulatory colonisation of the social field needs – to the extent that it forecloses on existential reality – to be contested, reimagined and redesigned wherever it constrains the thick form of autonomy proposed in the argument here. This will mean opposing tradition in some circumstances, for example, the nature of the 'liberal' tradition analysed by Foucault, the Hayekian tradition of just conduct that delivered the free play of the neoliberal Market, the intrusive republican tradition described by Pettit or the technological traditions being developed as we speak, for example, that algorithms will inevitably transform our both us and our

[48] D. Grant, *The Mythological State and Its Empire*, pp.146–165.
[49] D. Grant and L. Bennett Moses, *Technology and the Trajectory of Myth*, ch.4 (by David Grant and Kenneth Yates) and ch.5.

world for the better. But it will mean affirming traditions wherever they promote self-responsible existence. This will be best delivered by reimagining the principles – legal and programmatic – on which agencies of State and Market operate.

This is the level of risk that needs to be taken, one that can follow through the long task of reform, including as that relates to constitutional and legal principles and to the functioning of the agencies of State and Market.

The reason for taking this risk, ultimately, is that accounts of the rule of law that seek various ways to constrain power, whether by demanding various anatomical characteristics or by teleologically identifying the values that will ensure power is not used arbitrarily, are in the end a range of means to constrain the State so that there will be equitable arrangements for citizens. That is, the frame of all these is mythological, the engagement of the magnitude. A different rule of law is needed, one which displaces and de-mythologises the State and locates the non-mythological interests of the citizen – suitably qualified – at the centre of our concerns. It is this particular combination of non-mythological citizen-law-State that can provide a setting in which the looming, far-reaching intrusions and opportunities of neuroscience can be properly managed.

Purpose-Based Agencies

A possible new frame for the rule of law, one with a new foundation for a new tradition, might begin with an assembly of ideas that includes the reconstituting of agencies, State and corporate, as purpose-based and which were guided by fiduciary principles. Such principles are typically understood in the context of fiduciary trust, as understood in law. We will see that this assembly is not quite enough but that it does provide a frame within which a fresh notion of law and a reimagined understanding of the nature of those agencies can be developed. To strengthen that frame we need to understand that fiduciary principles need to be reconceived on an even stronger foundation, since trust as such does not satisfy what a strong reconception demands. An argument for a different foundation, which makes the most of both purpose and fiduciary principles, will be put. In this trust would play a secondary role.

We begin by looking at the work of Rosemary Teele Langford, who has developed the notion of purpose-based governance within the Australian jurisdiction. Attempting to address the failing trust in societal institutions generally, an acknowledgement shared with the British Academy,[50] Langford sees purpose-based governance as a new way to deal with intractable governance issues, that it may provide an over-arching governance model and may serve to increase trust in institutions,

---

[50] C. Mayer, 'Reinventing the corporation', *Journal of the British Academy* 4:53 (2016); British Academy, *Reforming Business for the 21st Century: A Framework for the Future of the Corporation* (2018).

public and private.[51] In particular, it clarifies – is even essential to – assessing the best long-term interests of an entity. It can facilitate decisions regarding stakeholder demands, averting problems from a distributive justice model.[52] Importantly, purpose-based governance makes clear what responsible persons in an agency can and cannot do. An organisation's purpose could provide a constraining context for the range of what would then be secondary rules, such as conflicts and profits. It helps make better sense of compliance requirements and it helps create an entity's culture and values, which in turn can be the proper context for 'legitimating ethical and ideological decision-making'.[53] Most importantly – including for the broad argument of the present work – this model of governance helps an understanding of what law and regulation could look like in empowering responsible persons to focus on purpose.[54]

This model relies on obligations connected through loyalty to the purpose of the organisation. It is based on the realignment of the rules, relationships, systems and processes of an organisation with a clearly defined organisational purpose.[55] Langford explains that the model is better suited in the charitable context since those organisations are required to specify purpose due to financial incentives and the maintenance of charitable status, but, for her, these principles are also applicable to for-profit organisations. The model draws on fiduciary principles in that the interests of an agency cannot be determined without reference to the purposes of the respective arrangements and in that fiduciaries must subordinate their self-interest to the interests of the beneficiaries and thereby potentially to purpose.[56]

Under the current Australian regulations regarding charitable entities – to which Langford refers – the duties of responsible persons include, inter alia, the following:

- To act in good faith in the registered entity's best interests and to further the purposes of the registered entity
- Not to misuse information obtained in the performance of the responsible entity's duties
- To disclose perceived or actual conflicts of interest of the responsible entity.

Regarding for-profit entities, decisions and recommendations from a range of authoritative bodies such as courts, commissions and committees have made it clear that directors of companies must regard the interests of stakeholders when acting in the interests of their respective corporations.[57] What is also clear, however, is that

---

[51] R. Teele Langford, 'Purpose-based governance: A new paradigm', *University of New South Wales Law Journal* 42 (2020): at p.20.
[52] Ibid. p.4.
[53] Ibid. p.5.
[54] Ibid. p.6.
[55] Ibid. p.2.
[56] Ibid. p.3.
[57] Ibid. p.11.

under Australian law, company purpose does not currently play any clear role in corporate governance and regulation. Further again, very few large for-profit corporations articulate their purposes in their constitutions.[58]

Langford observes that, theoretically, the current corporate governance model could now be reconceptualised as purpose-based for non-profits and that this would provide a range of advantages for such entities, especially given the recent need for directors to protect stakeholder interest due to those pronouncements of courts, commissions and committees. There is also evidence that purpose-based corporations perform better on key metrics over time than others.[59] This highlighting of the responsibility of directors to protect stakeholder interest has the potential to generally promote the focus on stakeholder interests. This promotion thereby requires a nexus with corporate benefit, but this would 'provide scope for companies to pursue non-financial impact-driven outcomes and social returns. For example, directors of a company whose constitution included a purpose of benefit to all stakeholders, including shareholders, customers and clients, business partners and advisers, employees and the community.'[60] These would, of course, be high-level statements but could help create a culture of broad and attentive concern and would also allow shareholders the means to examine directors' performance or even launch legal action.

The British Academy reforms referred to by Langford involve changes to ownership, stewardship and regulation. In articulating their purpose, corporations would be required not to produce profits but to produce profitable solutions for the problems of people and the planet. Others have proposed replacing shareholder primacy with a legal norm of value creation.[61] That would require significant legal reform, but this should not displace current regulatory reform to address occupational health and safety, bribery, corruption, human rights, modern slavery and environmental obligations.[62]

Langford gives due consideration to the nature of the legal reform necessary to give substantial priority to social benefit purposes in comparison to stakeholder or shareholder interests. An example is how s.181 of the Australian Corporations Act arguably allows corporations to have purposes in addition to shareholder returns.[63] That is, directors are required to act in good faith in the interests of the company,

---

[58] Ibid. p.12.

[59] Ibid. p.13.

[60] Ibid. p.14, where Langford refers to the Rio Tinto Ltd. Governance Statement (2013).

[61] Ibid. p.16.

[62] Ibid. p.17.

[63] Despite his claim for shareholder primacy, Milton Friedman was one who also stated that companies can be incorporated for purposes other than profit: 'The Social Responsibility of Business Is to Increase Profits', *New York Times Magazine* (13 September 1970); Langford states that the introduction of a provision like s.172(2) of the Companies Act 2006 (UK) may serve to signal the permissibility of incorporation for purposes other than profit, a move that would also reassure directors.

and there is no explicit requirement that a company be formed solely to generate profit for members. She adds, regarding the provisions for directors to have regard for creditors' interests, to avoid conflicts of interests and profits, that:

> There is no reason why these requirements should not apply to directors of companies that adopt purposes other than shareholder profit. The same is true in relation to the duty of care in s.180, the duties to avoid improper use of position and information from position in ss.182 and 183 and duties to disclose material personal interests in ss.191 and 195. There is therefore no legal impediment arising from Australian law on directors' duties to the adoption of purposes.[64]

Any concern that directors are open to litigation for breach of duty if a company's purposes are not achieved in practice is unjustified. The same is true regarding the duty of care. That is, the duty of care does not require achievement of the company's purposes. Directors need only ensure that they have considered the company's purposes and have applied care and diligence in addressing these purposes.

All this raises the historical background of the interests of the corporation. Although the interests of the company are typically equated with those of shareholders,[65] this does not mean that shareholders' interests are equated with shareholders' returns. This may be related to the fact that companies were not originally formed as vehicles for shareholder profit. The original use of the corporate form identified by Langford and others was by municipal and religious bodies. They were used in relation to property left to the Church to distinguish between the natural person occupying a position as an official and the same person in their private capacity. This allowed property to pass to successive holders of the position, although it was also used to obtain a trading monopoly, generally in another jurisdiction. But the point is that what the for-profit corporation has generally become – a vehicle for shareholder returns – is a very different purpose than that for which it was conceived and, guided by Langford's principles, to which it can return.

Comment

What is clear, first, from the analysis by Langford is that there is considerable potential for agencies, both non-profit and for-profit, to adopt a 'purpose-based' model of governance. That potential rests within the current or within easily conceived law. Second, she identifies the potential for such a model to clarify a wide range of intractable corporate issues, especially the questions surrounding the way to deal with stakeholder interests. Third, the values pertaining to corporate culture, and thereby appropriate focus on customers, partners and employees, can be better considered. Fourth, this has the capacity to respond to the wide

---

[64] R. T. Langford, 'Purpose-based governance', p.18.
[65] *Greenhalgh v. Arderne Cinemas Ltd*, UK 1952 CL286.

disenchantment with corporate performance and standards. However, the fifth benefit of the analysis is the suggestion, which she also shares with those of similar mind in the United Kingdom, of the need for corporations to focus not on profits but on value creation and the associated issue of responding to the concerns and opportunities within the wider community. These all go to the point of what 'purpose' actually means.

For all this, Langford's work is a breath of fresh air. However, she still has not gone far enough. The revolution she is recommending remains prey to mythological thinking, that is: Which values are we talking about, and who will determine them? Which community concerns and opportunities should be promoted, and who will prioritise those? She shares with Krygier the challengeable position that bringing social values into the equation is enough to tap what people are concerned about. In the argument in the present work – as we saw in Chapter 4 – the development of social values has largely been the product of centuries of influence from the magnitudes and their dominant interests, who are primarily absorbed with making claims about distancing existential concerns, replacing these with constructed fears and desires and thereby benefitting from the subjection – both willing and imposed – of individuals keen to have these fears and desires addressed.

As a result, it would be appropriate to grasp the advances recommended by Langford and add the promotion of the respectful self-responsibility to the nature of the 'purpose' she recommends. One way to do so in a practical sense is through the application of a – redesigned – notion of fiduciary principles.

FIDUCIARY PRINCIPLES CAN DELIVER RESPECTFUL SELF-RESPONSIBILITY

Harding sets the consideration of fiduciary principles within the context of trust. In examining the relationship between these two notions, he makes the key elements of the operation of fiduciary law clear:

> In contrast to contract law, key rules of fiduciary law seem designed to ensure performance. For example. The 'no conflict' rule aims to prevent a fiduciary from being in a position in which her personal interests (or other duties) can improperly influence the discretionary decision-making in her principal's interests that is at the heart of her fiduciary responsibility. It is a rule designed to maximise the likelihood of due performance. Equally, the 'no profit' rule operates to deliver to the principal unauthorised profits made within the scope of the fiduciary responsibility, thus guaranteeing performance of the fiduciary's commitment to serve the principal's interest in relation to profits derived within that scope.[66]

---

[66] M. Harding, 'Contracts, Fiduciary Relationships and Trust', in *Fiduciaries and Trust – Ethics, Politics, Economics and Law*, P. Miller and M. Harding (eds.) (Cambridge University Press, 2020), p.59.

These two fiduciary principles are to ensure that the focus of the fiduciary is on the interests of the principal and not on herself. The sense of these would need, of course, to be realigned in the context of the proposal being put here, which is not concerned with profit for the principal as such. But seen within the frame of a purpose-based agency – and that is focused on the development of the respect, knowledge and capacities of which self-responsibility would be comprised – the theme of 'no conflict' and 'no profit' would ensure the focus of the State or Market agency on the 'interests' of the 'principal as citizen'. Here, the State or Market fiduciary would have as her function to work in genuine consultation with the 'principal as citizen' to deliver – within the context of available programme resources – what can realise respectful existential living. In short, a purpose-based fiduciary model for State and Market agencies could fulfil the principles of respectful self-responsibility.

However, we need to take this down to a deeper level to fill out the relationship between fiduciary and principal. We start by revisiting the characteristics of self-responsibility. We consider that, then place it in the context of respect. Self-responsibility is a 'thick' notion of self-reliance and autonomy, regarding both ideas and practices. It is a moral and material status. Such a notion would be strongly resistant to, especially, the claims by dominant interests of each of the magnitudes.

It comprises that self-responsible citizens, as subjects of the fiduciary relationship:

- are not responsible to another (this does not prevent such individuals entering into a wide range of formal and informal relationships, on grounds that honour this principle)
- are not responsible for another (save, for example, for various dependents), thereby allowing others to seek self-responsibility
- have no other that is responsible to or for her
- would not be subject to the ideas or practices of the regimes of the magnitudes generally but particularly, in the context here, any unexamined presumptions of the data and algorithmic designs embedded within neuroscience.

To allow that the search for such a status is available to every citizen, this status could exist only within a context of respect, its essential condition. Respect here is constituted by the following:

- leaving others be if they are acting in accord with the first principle
- responding to their requests for assistance as they (are required to) seek this status
- supporting those citizens incapable of doing so (the disabled, those with clinical psychological conditions or mental impairment, etc.)
- creating circumstances to encourage those struggling with or resisting this status while ensuring they are not harmed or shamed or harm or shame others

- recognising that someone who has not reached this status can respect those who have done so but those who have would 'conditionally' respect those who have not yet done so.

One key characteristic that brings this status and this condition closer together is that, to be due full respect, a person adopting these principles would be required to do what they undertake to do, including regarding their fiduciary undertakings. Thereby, they are not answerable to another person as such for not having done so but would be subject to loss of privileges in this regard.

TRUST

But there is more to the position presented by Harding regarding the nature of fiduciary principles and law, in particular, the notion of trust. For him, trust can be distinguished from confidence,[67] the former closely relatable to fiduciary relationships and the latter to social and technological systems. Confidence abstracts from human agency while trust focuses on people and their unpredictability. Without claiming these are fully separable, for him confidence typifies a contractual situation and is more about remedial consequences for non-performance, whereas trust is more about ensuring performance.[68] Further, for trust to form, the would-be truster must be able to adopt a perspective about the trusted as a person with agency, what sort of person they are dealing with.[69] Where there are systems interposed between them, trust is unlikely to take root.

To this point, there is nothing which is contrary to the nature of the fiduciary relationship within the context of promoting respectful self-responsibility. In fact, the notions that confidence is indicative of a contractual or systematic situation and that trust is more tuned to the personalised fiduciary relationship are something of an affirmation of these preferred principles. This is especially so if one takes the view that the arrangements which relate to the magnitudes are systematic in nature, and that points to its difference from the kind of personalised relationship being recommended here in the fiduciary relationship between those seeking and those assisting in the attainment of respectful self-responsibility.

However, if we press further into Harding's analysis, differences do begin to appear. First, for him trust can be – although not necessarily – directly relatable to the performance of the fiduciary, and this performance is relevant to the experience of trust in both directions:

[F]iduciary law's assurances of performance take on the character of clear statements about what that performance consists in.... The effect of this is to give to the

---

[67] Ibid. p.56.
[68] Ibid. p.59.
[69] Ibid. p.62.

fiduciary who seeks to be worthy of her principal's trust a roadmap indicating how to do so. The trustworthy performance of such a fiduciary might then trigger trust on the part of the principal who started out only with confidence in fiduciary law's assurances of performance.... In fiduciary relationships, inter-party trust and confidence in fiduciary law may thus develop in a virtuous interaction.[70]

As he states, 'A person is able to prove trustworthy by manifesting [such] appropriate or fitting attitudes, thereby showing the person who trusts her that she is disposed to, and does, respond appropriately to trust.'[71]

In the context of respectful self-responsibility, that is too tenuous a connection. There, trust would be based not on performance, which is bound to be variable, but on a recognition of the respectful self-responsibility of the fiduciary, the honouring of these principles ensuring the pursuit of the agreed goals whether or not the principal had full or only some lesser trust in them as fiduciary. Trust is thereby not irrelevant but is secondary to the display of self-responsibility by the fiduciary. There may even be circumstances where the principal is incapable of real awareness of the trust issues – due perhaps to mental impairment – in which case there should be no diminution of the fiduciary's optimal, self-responsible pursuit of set goals. Further, being self-responsible may mean doing other than what was agreed but still in the interests of the principal: tough love is an example. Proving oneself trustworthy is not the aim. Being self-responsible is the aim, and trust may or may not follow. If it does, it is valid only if it is inspired by self-responsibility.

Second, the issue of respect is, for Harding, directly relatable to trust. A particular instance of this is betrayal of trust, which can be seen as a display of lack of respect for the other person. He gives examples of this, from keeping one's promises – which can amount to respect for the truster – to being unfaithful to one's partner. Further, even if it is argued that trust makes no specific demands on my respect, as it is only mildly demanding, there are more determinative circumstances. I may not act selfishly against your interests if I know you trust me, especially if doing so would bring harm to you. I must respect your trust.[72]

Within the context of self-responsibility, trust is important in cementing social relationships and to indicate the reliability of systems and technologies, but it is not as foundationally important as respect. To respect is to acknowledge self-responsibility, and one earns respect through the search to attain that. Trust is a more ephemeral, though not unimportant, experience which may or may not be overlain on self-responsibility.

If these two amendments to Harding's accounts of trust and respect are accepted, then we can say that a purpose-based fiduciary model of governance – and thereby respectful self-responsibility – can be placed at the foundation of a governing

[70] Ibid. pp.59–60.
[71] M. Harding, 'Responding to trust', *Ratio Juris* 24:1 (2011): p.82.
[72] Ibid. pp.78, 79.

strategy. Thereby, agents of State or Market entities would be constrained in all their actions to promote these principles above all else. Through that, we would have an effective response to technologies, especially to the widening promises and potential of neuroscience, that seems destined to bring increasing subjection to the neuroscientific regime and its decision-making potential by virtue of its present inherent mythology. We would not form perspectives of trust regarding such promises unless those technologies progress these principles.

TRUST CLAIMED AS THE KEY TO INSTITUTIONAL AUTHORITY AND LAW

We can get a further sense of Harding's take on trust through Fox-Decent. For him, trust – especially as mutual trust – is a fundamental feature not only of institutional authority but also of law itself. To reach this conclusion, Fox-Decent returns to Hobbes, whom he sees as a champion of equity.[73] He understands Hobbes to be saying that the monarch is 'entrusted with power enough for [their people's] protection'.[74] The origin of this is the original covenant which took the individuals from the state of nature to a lawful existence. The origin of this covenant is that each agrees to 'give up my right of Governing my selfe, to this Man, or to this Assembly of men, on this condition, that thou give up thy Right to him, and authorise all his Actions in like manner'.[75] This is done as a means to limit the fear in the state of nature – or, in parallel, the social turbulence of mid-seventeenth-century England.

In focusing on the trust that Hobbes then talks about, Fox-Decent passes lightly over – in fact tends to downplay[76] – the absolutism of the Leviathan, which should be understood as the following:

> This is the generation of that great LEVIATHAN, or rather (to speak more reverently) of that *Mortall God*, to which we owe under the *Immortal God*, our peace and defence. For by this Authorite, given him by every particular man in the Common-wealth, he hath the use of so much Power and Strength conferred on him, that by terror thereof, he is inabled to conforme the wills of them all, to peace at home, and mutuall ayd against their enemies abroad.[77]

This terror and enforced conformity is an absolutism, and one which requires the total subjection of each individual to the authority of the sovereign. So, any sense of 'mutual trust' must be seen to be founded on this original covenant by which each individual forgoes all their powers of self-government to the Leviathan, who in turn

---

[73] E. Fox-Decent, 'Trust and Authority', in *Fiduciaries and Trust – Ethics, Politics, Economics and Law*, p.181.
[74] Ibid. p.181.
[75] T. Hobbes, *Leviathan* (Cambridge University Press, 1991), p.120.
[76] E. Fox-Decent, 'Trust and Authority', p.179
[77] T. Hobbes, *Leviathan*, pp.120–121.

240   *Regulation and the Law*

thereby can claim responsibility for their safety, which is the distancing of their existential fear. That subjection and that acceptance of the power and responsibility of the Leviathan is what Hobbes means by mutual trust, an exchange or mutual understanding which results in a gift of sovereign power from the people.[78]

The Leviathan is 'trusted' to exercise his total power to eliminate any unrest, the source of fear from within or without, and each citizen is 'trusted', having forgone all self-governing, to be fully submissive – to be 'subject' – to the authority of the Leviathan. The individual has liberty but only to the extent that they comply with the agreement to be ultimately subject.[79] This is not the mutual trust of 'political equals coming to agreement' in the normal sense. It is only by reconfiguring Hobbesian trust as trust in this normal sense that notions of equity and fairness – in the normal sense – can be attributed to Hobbes's notion of trust.

As a result of this move – by construing mutual trust as in that normal sense rather than as founded on Hobbes's basic tenet of absolute authority and individual subjection – Fox-Decent can proceed to see mutual trust as the linchpin of modern institutional authority, especially as represented by law. So, we have:

> I then explain how mutual trust informs law's authority such that law can be understood to pervade the spaces it creates or the liberty of its subjects and officials.[80]
>
> And yet, there is arguably a moral precept that connects the judiciary to litigants and the wider public, a precept that we now look to Hobbes to help unearth: mutual trust.[81]
>
> Running through Hobbes' conception of sovereignty, then, is an idea of mutual trust.[82]
>
> These questions matter because the answer, I suggest, lets us explain how the legitimacy and stability of sovereignty is necessarily a joint endeavour of sovereign and subject premised on mutual trust.[83]
>
> I now turn to elaborating a conception of mutual trust apposite to authority relations. I will then explain how a relational structure of mutual trust can supply a conceptual scheme for law's authority so as to fill with legal norms and principles the spaces within legal limits and across legal frameworks that law's positive norms create.[84]

Fox-Decent, following Baier, then manages to extend this notion into one in which the subject's trust is automatic, unconscious and unchosen: 'Whereas it strains the concept of agreement to speak of unconscious agreements and unchosen

---

[78] E. Fox-Decent, 'Trust and Authority', p.183.
[79] Ibid. p.186.
[80] Ibid. p.176.
[81] Ibid. p.179.
[82] Ibid. p.184.
[83] Ibid. p.184.
[84] Ibid. p.186.

Trust Claimed as the Key to Institutional Authority and Law 241

agreements ... there is no strain whatever in the concept of automatic and unconscious trust, and of unchosen but mutual trust.'[85] He states:

> I will now turn to sketching the role trust can play in the justification of legitimate authority, and will distinguish that role from the condition under which acts of mutual trusting productive of mutual trust can lend stability to well-ordered public institutions.[86]
>
> While subjects need not trust the State at the factual level or primary level, they nonetheless have a moral duty to relate to others on equal terms that they themselves are not entitled to set unilaterally. They can satisfy this duty while factually distrusting the state by possessing, at the secondary and moral level, Baier's 'unchosen but mutual' trust, a form of trust understood as a moral preparedness to be the subject of a legal order.[87]

In fact, these notions are built on the subjection of the mass of the community to authority, even though this absolutism has been tempered or 'engaged' by the evolution of democratic measures grafted onto it over three centuries by 'this assembly of men' and inspired by the thinkers of the political tradition.[88] These notions are built on a lopsided mutual trust between people with unequal influence and capacity, irrespective of this tempering. To have a sense of trust in the normal sense, we need to abandon Hobbes's (and the political tradition's) sense of it and promote a notion of it that reflects a non-subjecting relationship between parliamentarian and judge, on one hand, and the citizen, on the other. In fact, the respectful interests of the citizen should be recognised as having a pre-eminent status.

That would be founded not on trust or loyalty,[89] as with Fox-Decent, but on a self-responsibility promoted by a non-subjecting, genuinely fiduciary State. That is, a State in which the fiduciary relationship is based on all parties maintaining the standards of respect for others and responsibility to and for the fiduciary themself, thereby – to be unanswerable in this context – abiding by all undertakings given. Trust of a different kind than Fox-Decent's would then no doubt play a part as a secondary factor, indicating – though not invariably – how well the State 'promotes' in this way. There certainly would be no 'automatic, unconscious or unchosen' trust – except for the naïve – let alone at the foundational level. It would be self-responsibility, not Hobbesian mutual trust, that would produce a respectful, existential sense of 'law's authority', the 'connection of judiciary to litigants', 'legitimacy and stability of sovereignty' and 'authority relations', to use the phrases of Fox-Decent.

---

[85] Ibid. p.186 .
[86] Ibid. p.194.
[87] Ibid. p.195.
[88] See D. Grant, *The Mythological State and Its Empire*, pp.43–186.
[89] E. Fox-Decent, 'Trust and Authority', p.193.

242 *Regulation and the Law*

Trust and the Rule of Law

Against this 'Hobbesian' background, one can make similar comments about the notions of trust, the rule of law and accountability proposed by Postema. That is, if one gives due weight to the fact of the power transferred from each citizen to the State – a power that is normalised but still monumental – then the architecture of trust and accountability that Postema constructs on the rule of law is only the form of the attempt to temper that power in the civil and political realms. Certainly, that form in Postema is elaborate and well considered, but, as with Harding and Fox-Decent, the shifting of the focus to the form of the tempering unwisely camouflages the stalking threat within the Hobbesian covenant. It is far better to seek to eliminate that than to exhaust one's energies constructing more elaborate architectures of trust, accountability and rules of law to temper that threat.

As presented here, to be 'existential' in the sense intended here is the result of such a search. There, the citizen is not accountable to another but is respectful of every other as either actually existing or striving to exist in that manner. Due to those characteristics, each citizen would be expected to honour all undertakings, irrespective of external factors. That citizen, in turn, would be respected. This is not trust, which – as a psychological condition – may well be overlain on respect but is secondary to it. There is still a rule of law, but it is not founded on Hobbesian fear of the magnitude of State – especially when that is camouflaged by rationalities of trust – and which is a constructed mythology that claims to distance the absolute nature of reality.

The vigilance that Postema devotes to trust and accountability[90] would then be shifted to this social and political field of self-responsibility under this other rule of law, which would be progressively less concerned with the arbitrary exercise of power,[91] which itself would thereby be transferred back to each citizen and promoted by a purpose-based, fiduciary State (and Market, as we shall see). There is a sense of fidelity[92] in this new paradigm, but that would be better understood under the rubric of respect. We would not be concerned about the various shadings of trust[93] – including those recommended by Pettit – or non-trust, civic or political.[94] Therein, distrust[95] is a further refinement of the trust network generated by a need to cope with the Hobbesian covenant.

Postema is, like Harding and Fox-Decent, aware of the 'Hobbesian' covenant. He refers to the fact that 'human beings are at their motivationally weakest in

---

[90] G. Postema, 'Trust, Distrust, and the Rule of Law', in *Fiduciaries and Trust – Ethics, Politics, Economics and Law*, p.244.

[91] Ibid. p.244.

[92] Ibid. p.244.

[93] Ibid. pp.248–259.

[94] Ibid. pp.259–263.

[95] Ibid. pp.263ff.

circumstances where they wield power over the lives and fortunes of other human beings'[96] and that 'There is nothing essentially punitive about holding to account a person to whom great power is entrusted.'[97] However, like them, he focuses on means to contain the beast rather than looking for a way to change its very purpose.

Comment

To return to the very start, to the motivation of this work: we need to deal effectively with the extensive, reconstructive impact of neuroscience without forgoing the substantial benefits that will come from it. We need to be in control of it, not just socially but individually. We have seen that neuroscience is to be understood not only as an early twenty-first-century technological development for repair and enhancement but, since those who promote its benefits do so without acknowledging the wide and deep subjection to the regime that accompanies it, as having features displayed repeatedly throughout the history of the West by subjecting mythologies that have made the same claim on the same condition and claim.

To achieve these two, inseparable outcomes – promoting our well-being but retaining control of the process – we need to understand that history and to move to a new paradigm. That will require a new foundation to the moral code, a new notion of privacy built on that which embraces as well as controls this technology, and the support of reimagined law, as well as of the agencies of State and Market. In the final two chapters, we shall begin to explore this reimagining in relation to each of the latter two.

---

[96] Ibid. pp.269–270.
[97] Ibid. p.271.

9

Regulation and the State

THE STATE AS A REGULATING MAGNITUDE

A number of references have been made in this work to the mythological nature of the State. This idea depends on the argument that there is a demonstrable human disposition to deal with the fear of the absolutism of reality by imagining absolutist mythological magnitudes which materialise this reality so that it can be engaged to be made sympathetic to humanity. Existential concerns can thereby be distanced and replacement, constructed fears and desires can be conclusively dealt with. This requires the consequential subjection of individuals to the regime of idea and practice of the magnitude to empower its dominant interests to undertake this function. This schema was originally conceived by German philosopher Hans Blumenberg in *Work on Myth* and has been widely amended, developed and then applied to a consideration of various aspects of modernity by the author in this and previous works.

By this schema, we have the means to avoid confronting existential reality – or so the dominant interests of the magnitudes claim. The problem is that, once this engagement has taken place, the magnitude is no longer absolute and so no longer a materialisation of the absolutism of reality. A replacement magnitude is required.[1] This dynamic, which has repeated across the history of the West, has given us a trajectory of myth, as we have sought spiritual (through Deity), political (through the State), economic (through the Market) and now technological (through Technology in pursuit of the Absolute Self) means to avoid existential reality.[2] In other words, these are a series of misguided attempts to realise existential peace. However, these shifts from one to another of the magnitudes have not removed the accumulating subjections which individuals in the West have been required to digest over time, despite the levels of 'sympathy' that have been wrung from the magnitudes.

---

[1] D. Grant, *The Mythological State and Its Empire*, pp.19–40.
[2] D. Grant and L. Bennett Moses, *Technology and the Trajectory of Myth* pp.16–25.

The State as a Regulating Magnitude

This is the context in which we should see the State in the West. Its pretext was the demise of the absolute myth of Deity with Ockham, Pomponazzi and Luther, who together showed the unbridgeable distance between Deity and humanity, so there could be no engagement of the Deity to produce sympathy. To make matters worse, the popular sale of indulgences was thereby inherently corrupt. The ultimate result was that the search for a replacement form of absolutism that could be made sympathetic settled on the Hobbesian Leviathan. Locke instigated the process of engagement to realise this sympathy by arguing for the elaboration of representation and protection of certain individual rights, these being in turn developed further by the institutional separation of powers outlined by Montesquieu. Rousseau then progressed this sympathy through the notion of the general will, with its emphasis on equality and the common good, a general will which was to be taken up by Kant as he emphasised principles of right, law, justice, freedom and equality, individual independence, social contract and a constitutional State. Much of this has come down to us variably in the early Kantianism of Rawls and the republicanism of Pettit. This political tradition has thereby replaced the moral and material subjection of the individual to the Church with a political subjection to the 'sympathetic' democratic State, to its political mythology.[3]

The further argument here has been that this claimed conversion of the absolutist State to a sympathetic condition – what Krygier might call its tempering – has been transformed into an elaborate regulative phase which has reinforced democratic subjection with a second form of subjection that has spread out from the institutions of State and lays more intimately across the social field. It has been argued in Chapter 7 that the pre-eminent form of this regulative spread is now 'responsive regulation' as proposed by Braithwaite and others, a form that seeks to mirror the sympathetic institutions of the mythological State with a form of sympathy constituted by its 'responsiveness'. This is mythology, nonetheless, as the form of its exercise of power is ultimately absolutist in nature. We shall now look at some of the mythological credentials of Braithwaite's responsive regulation. Before doing so it needs to be stated that regulation is not inherently subjecting. It can be enhancing or enabling but for both good and bad. We shall look at an example of what a 'positive' sense of regulation might look like in the final section of this chapter. However, regulation is about social control, so the theme here is that, like the institutional arrangements of the State, the derivative regulatory arrangements are mythological whenever they claim to resolve our fears and desires on condition that we become subject to their regimes of idea and practice.

Regulatory Dispersal of Sovereignty, but What of Accountability?

There is clearly an increasing appreciation of the extent to which 'governance' exists outside the State, including in areas which are central responsibilities of the State.

---

[3] D. Grant, *The Mythological State and Its Empire*, pp.43–145.

246

This includes especially security, policing and prisons, but also now environmental monitoring; legal, health and educational services; and intellectual property.[4] This is an appreciation of the polycentric, nodal nature of governance wherein nodes are connected by networks. In one sense, there is nothing new here. Holley and Shearing acknowledge Foucault's observation – affirmed in this work but for mythological purposes – that power always was everywhere, its arrangements emerging, competing, shifting, disappearing and so on. They also acknowledge that the Hobbesian model of centralised power was always a mythology. So we have two key elements of the argument in the present work that the State is mythological and its form of power is reinforced by an arrangement dispersed idiosyncratically across the social field. To say that this dispersal is nodal is an extension of the basic two-part arrangement.

What Holley and Shearing, like Braithwaite,[5] do not consider is that the nature of this dispersed nodal power – typically located in the corporate world but also in civil society – can also be mythological. That is, that a node can subject people – more locally now – still based on the claim that being subject to local regimes is the preferred means of resolving fears and desires. The constitution of each node is a 'world', a 'human invention and reinvention' that is accomplished through governing processes[6] and the intention of which is to assemble capacities, knowledge and resources for 'shaping the flow of events'.[7] Researching them requires an investigation of four elements: their mentalities ('relating to how nodes think about a governance outcome – for example security or a safe environment'), technologies, resources and their institutions.[8] There is no mention here of the interests of individuals as individuals .

Neither is there any discussion of the accountability of nodes. Holley and Shearing do refer to various criticisms of nodal governance, in particular, to the tendency to exaggerated localism and the ignoring of other players in the vertical frame. This tendency is seen as an implied denigration of the State and its 'civilising' processes, this localism weakening State institutions to 'cede legitimacy to nodes of uncertain virtue', so encouraging vigilantism and the vilifying of certain groups.

However, the proper response to all this would be that, the further away from the State such nodes are, the lesser their capacity for both legitimacy and accountability. For better or worse, the Parliament and the Executive are the elected representatives

---

[4] C. Holley and C. Shearing, 'A Nodal Perspective of Governance: Advances in Nodal Governance Thinking', in *Regulatory Theory – Foundations and Applications*, P. Drahos (ed.) (ANU Press, 2017), p.172; see also C. Shearing and L. Johnston, 'Nodal wars and network facilities: A genealogical analysis of global insecurities', *Theoretical Criminology* 14:4 (2010): p.501.

[5] See the critique of Braithwaite's adoption of Pettit's mythological republicanism in Chapter 7 of the present work.

[6] C. Holley and C. Shearing, 'A Nodal Perspective of Governance', p.169.

[7] Ibid. p.165.

[8] Ibid. p.168.

of the people and should exercise authority on their behalf. Active delegation or allowing nodes to emerge spontaneously is thereby an increasingly significant risk, even with current standard institutional arrangements. It has been one of the strongest criticisms of privatisation that it allows politicians to avoid their responsibility and accountability. A stronger criticism of nodal governance is that, whether nodes are empowered or whether authority is more closely drawn back to the State, neither arrangement will avoid mythological implications unless specific strategies are developed to promote non-mythological arrangements of the kind we have just begun to look at. Given that Holley and Shearing acknowledge that one of the early – and still – primary foci of nodal power is criminology, especially policing and security, this will allow us to propose below a non-mythological model for that field.

Separately, we have already seen in Chapter 7 that Braithwaite, regarding his Fasken Lecture, has been behind much of the thinking around regulation, including as that might best apply both within and beyond the State to the Market and civil society, as players that can strengthen the effectiveness of the regulatory environment. We have seen that Krygier seeks to vary Braithwaite's account of this interplay as a separation of powers.

The key for Braithwaite is how to enforce regulation in the context of the move from the Welfare State to the Regulatory State and when players beyond the State – the market and civil society, thereby forming a tripartite arrangement – become key players in the process of enforcement.[9] We have seen in Chapter 7 that his response, 'responsive regulation', has become a dominant model for regulatory enforcement. It is a framework that seeks to combine encouragement in the early phases of engaging the potentially non-compliant, followed by increasingly stiffer sanctions if non-compliance becomes clear.

We can restate comments about Braithwaite's model. It is mythological, not merely in its borrowing of Pettit's republicanism but in its very operation. That is, the process by which the State first engages and is engaged cooperatively by those whose compliance is sought mirrors the manner in which the mythological magnitudes are engaged by public processes to convert their absolutism into a more sympathetic mode of operation. The 'sympathetic' mythological State has become the 'sympathetic' regulatory State. Within both, however, the sovereign power of the State remains. Braithwaite's regulatory model is merely an extension of the mythology of the State deeper and wider across the social field.

We get a strong sense of this also with *'smart' regulation* – that is, a pluralism that embraces flexible, imaginative and innovative forms of social control – intended as a means of harnessing 'governments as well as business and third parties' by broadening the regulatory framework and techniques.[10] Gunningham recommends that, in this pursuit of social control, it is preferable to include – along with

---

[9] C. Scott, 'The Regulatory State and Beyond', in *Regulatory Theory – Foundations and Applications*, p.269.

[10] N. Gunningham and D. Sinclair, 'Smart Regulation', in *Regulation Theory – Foundations and Applications*, p.133; P. Van Gossum et al., 'From "Smart Regulation" to Regulatory Arrangements', *Policy Sciences* 43 (2010).

traditional government regulatory strategies – international standards organisations; trading partners and those in the supply chain; commercial institutions and financial markets; peer pressure and self-regulation through industry associations, internal environment management systems and culture; and civil society in myriad forms.[11] But this is little more than regulation stretched wide across the social field. The non-government players are surrogates for the mythological State power.[12]

As to the modus operandi, Gunningham adopts Braithwaite's responsive regulation frame and the technique of escalating up the pyramid from persuasion through civil penalty to licence revocation as a last resort. To this it adds other instruments – for example, government-mandated information with third-party pressure – which facilitate the graduated, responsive and interactive strategy. In short, the role for government under smart regulation is to create the conditions for second and third parties to assume more of the regulatory framework, allowing the State to act more – but not exclusively – as a facilitator. The mix-and-match of instruments requires design for specific situations, but the categories include command and control, economic instruments, self-regulation through industry associations, voluntarism through individual firms, and educational, information strategies. One outcome sought thereby is for firms to go beyond compliance and is more likely when voluntarism is the driver. However, it is easily undermined by a lack of political will in applying the top end of sanctions for fear of offending business[13] and by government deregulatory strategies. This is a failure of accountability.

Smart regulation should be seen as an elaboration and sophistication of the spread of regulation from the State and out across the furthest reaches of the social field. It has the potential to significantly increase levels of social control. However, it is little more than a 'nuanced' development of Braithwaite's basic mythological model of social control. Even though regulatory activity is transferred from the State, these other manifestations have clearly adopted the authority once held by the State, and it thereby makes the basic model more 'artful'. Gunningham has recognised the value of voluntarism and he may well have explored that avenue more fully before settling on the dominant model of responsive regulation, with the mythological flaws he no doubt did not see. We shall do so at the end of this chapter.

We get a similar sense of this spread of social control from the notion of *meta-regulation*, primarily self-regulation. Again influenced by the thinking of Braithwaite, this notion came with the institutional embedding of 'regulatory review mechanisms into everyday routines of governmental policy-making' but has been extended out across regulatory space to agencies of State, Market and public interest groups.[14] So this includes the monitoring of regulation delegated by the State.

[11] N. Gunningham and D. Sinclair, 'Smart Regulation', p.134.
[12] Ibid. p.135.
[13] Ibid. p.144.
[14] P. Grabosky, 'Meta-regulation', in *Regulation Theory – Foundations and Applications*, p.149. In 'Regulatory Abdication in Practice' (University of Penn Institute for Law and Economic

The State as a Regulating Magnitude

Drawn from legal pluralism – that the law exists alongside other normative orderings – this regulatory pluralism allows for the relegation of the State to a lesser function, so leaving markets, communities and associations to dominate the field, even if typically under State purview. Here, governments have begun to steer rather than row, structuring the marketplace and monitoring activity. This leaves open not only the possibility of more effective applications of industry standards by market players but also the possibility of advantage being taken by them due to regulatory monitoring at a distance. To promote this situation, whole industries have grown up to assist businesses in compliance.[15]

But the trends are clear: governments withdrawing from regulation, so we have the rise of non-government regulators and the emergence of technology to enable these two trends. The latter has the extra advantage of personalising the monitoring of agencies right down to the individual citizens, although that can lead to unfounded witch-hunts as much as the identification of actual compliance failures.

Finally here, a further word on *public accountability*. Again drawing from Braithwaite, Dowdle presents a response to the crisis in public accountability, especially as that is perceived to be the result of Market privatisation and globalisation.[16] His argument is that the different notions of public accountability that abound are the product of different histories and different experiences but that they have tended to be harmonised by the bureaucratic mode of public accountability. That is, public accountability has come to be based on the outcomes of certain aggregated experiences that follow from elections, rationalising bureaucracies, judicial review, transparency and markets. He acknowledges that these produce a competing rather than a naturally evolving, coherent experience and that they each have had periods of ascendency in the quest for public accountability.[17] Yet despite this variegated heritage, they have been brought somewhat together through bureaucratisation and professionalisation of the institutional framework. This frame has not been effectively challenged by the emergence of deregulation, privatisation and so on. Even the more recent Market initiatives like devolution and contracting out have replaced one bureaucracy with another.

But recent changes have been disrupted by the need for flexibility – one might fairly argue due the rise of the Market – and by the localisation that has challenged, for example, American international dominance. So in fact there has been a

---

Research Paper 20-11 2020), Coglianese widely criticises the critical analysis by Simon in *Meta-regulation in Practice – Beyond Normative Views of Morality and Rationality* (Routledge, 2017). He argues that meta-regulation can work, although what she had done was present a case study in which it did not.

[15] P. Grabosky, 'Meta-regulation', p.154.

[16] M. Dowdle, 'Public Accountability: Conceptual, Historical and Epistemic Mappings', in *Regulation Theory – Foundations and Applications*, p.197; G. Turkelli, 'The best of both worlds or the worst of both worlds: Multilateral development banks, immunities and accountability to rights-holders', *Hague Journal on the Rule of Law* (2020).

[17] M. Dowdle, 'Public Accountability', p.201

250 *Regulation and the State*

fragmentation in the notion of public accountability,[18] different groups now looking to electoral, economic or judicial models while globalisation is looking, on the other hand, for more consistent expansion in the notion.

Dowdle responds to this fragmentation in a highly problematic manner. Due to this institutional fragmentation and because we each have our own unique epistemic background, we experience the notion of accountability differently. The result is that any search for a single, unified model is futile. Dowdle sees this as an advantage due to the interconnections of these individual backgrounds and the 'consilience' that can be drawn from such connections in the context of this fragmentation.[19] That is, the fragmentation, which prevents any final, coherent notion of accountability, can be the means to reach for a collaborative understanding of it. Further, he sees this as connecting to Braithwaite's notion of responsive regulation[20] and its search, at the lower levels of the pyramid, for communication that appreciates the perspective of the non-compliant.

The problem is that this leaves accountability prey to the power of the Market, which is at increasing distance from citizens' elected representatives. One could say that the account that he presents has the advantage of realism, in that it recognises the differentials that guide how we each see its nature and its operation. However, this bottom-up approach to accountability quickly runs into problems. First, individuals don't determine how State or Market agencies operate. This is immediately clear from his endorsement of responsive regulation, which he apparently sees as a field in which the perspective of the non-compliant can be better understood. However, this 'understanding' of the non-compliant, which allows some flexibility at the lower levels of response, ultimately comes up against the determination – including by the use of punitive sanctions – to ensure compliance. Dowdle does not see the subjecting mythology at the heart of responsive regulation, which ultimately is not about individual variation but about compliance.

This is not to say that a top-down approach, wherein the State or the Market should unilaterally determine the nature of their accountability to citizens, would be effective. That is even more blatantly mythological. There is another way, which we will explore shortly, and ironically it has within it one point made by Dowdle early in his analysis of the history of public accountability. That is that, from private law, an agent should conform to the demands of the principal.

The Regulatory State Impacts on Individuals

As it extends across social space, the responsive regulatory framework makes a significant impact on individuals. Within criminology, which is one of the first

---

[18] Ibid. p.204.
[19] Ibid. p.208.
[20] Ibid. p.210.

The State as a Regulating Magnitude

applications of this form of governance, we can see this regarding crime control. Here, networking that extends beyond the State has become prominent. Brewer points out that the source of this movement to networks came with the privatisations that accompanied the emergence of neoliberal economic and political theory, dislocating the State as the central guarantor of security.[21] The consequent fragmentation of social control even transcended the public/private sector divide by engaging multinational corporations and small businesses but also communities, associations and individuals.

Accompanying this shift – a manifestation of it – has been the move from reactive policing to a risk-management model made possible by increased data availability and surveillance. This is not simple devolution but a 'blurring of responsibilities in a technologically facilitated risk-based exercise to control and respond to crime'.[22] This fragmentation of responsibility has caused actors to seek variable coordination in networks with others to develop a patchwork of shared models.

This networking makes tracing the boundaries of nodal activity – and therefore the monitoring of it – difficult, as they can be both local and international or even virtual. There are no necessarily shared values or objectives. This has required the development of an account of the social structures of these nodes and networks.[23] One clear outcome is that they are not part of egalitarian horizontal structures, so only a few are well positioned to do effective work. The principal lessons from such accounts include that there is great diversity in private and public nodes, but with varying levels of connectedness, and so impact on individual citizens is often parochial. This does not exclude the central positioning and brokerage roles of some nodes, especially those of a public, governmental nature that engage private enterprises. Nor does it deny the emergence of private actors who now exercise control over segments of the security network, especially those with commercial significance and even to the exclusion of involvement of the State.[24]

This refocuses concerns about democratic accountability, given the potential for serious dilemmas of governance through the abuse of corporate power in administering crime and punishment. Such concerns are not to deny, for Brewer, the potential for increased functionality and greater efficiency in crime control through wider structures and better access to resources as crime control is 'pushed out of the bureaucracy'. This should make use of a meta-regulatory approach as a means to monitor performance.[25] But it is now unclear what decisions are being made concerning who is or is not prosecuted; what sanctions are applied; who is

---

[21] R. Brewer, 'Controlling Crime through Networks', in *Regulation Theory – Foundations and Applications*, p.448; K. Albertson, 'The marketisation of rehabilitation: Some economic considerations', *Probation Journal* 66:1 (2019).

[22] R. Brewer, 'Controlling Crime', p.450.

[23] Ibid. p.452.

[24] Ibid. p.456.

[25] Ibid. p.457.

252 Regulation and the State

imprisoned and for how long; what programmes are available to the convicted; what regimes of surveillance are applied, to whom and for how long; and so on. It is the individual who feels the formative impact of this proliferating accountability.

Accountability, Criminal Responsibility and Neuroscience

The other side of accountability is the issue of personal responsibility. This is particularly relevant regarding the administration of criminal justice, where neuroscience is raising important questions concerning the status of personal responsibility under State law.

Morse sees law as a folk psychological enterprise. That is, both doctrine and practice implicitly assume that human beings are agents who act intentionally and for reasons, who can be guided by reasoning and, in adulthood, are capable of enough rationality to ground full responsibility unless an excusing condition exists. As a result, he resists any deterministic challenges drawn from emerging – especially, cognitive, affective or social – neuroscience.[26] The folk psychological theory causally explains behaviour in part by such mental states as desires, beliefs, intentions, willings and plans. Biological, sociological and other psychological variables play a role, but folk psychology sees mental states as fundamental to a full explanation of human action.[27] Morse does not claim that the law cannot and should not learn from neuroscience, only that this science should continue to enrich and refine the sense of rationality in folk psychology and vice versa.[28]

Two responses need to be made to this notion of law. First, any move away from this can be seen as a move that erodes notions of personal responsibility. Examples of this are canvassed by Claydon when she refers to the neurological research which has indicated that 'attributing responsibility required flexibility ... [in] ... determinations of individual criminal responsibility, based on the age of the perpetrator ... on a case by case basis',[29] and that prosecutors and expert witnesses should be more sceptical in relying on the veracity of memory in contributing to evidence.[30] The point here is that, even as science begins to refine its research results, we need to be careful not to abandon the model of the responsible, rational individual. Second, on

---

[26] S. Morse, 'Law, Responsibility, and the Sciences of the Brain/Mind', in *Oxford Handbook of Law, Regulation and Technology*, R. Brownsword, E. Scotford and K. Yeung (eds.) (Oxford University Press, 2017), p.155; A. Bigenwald et al., 'Criminal responsibility and neuroscience: No revolution yet', *Frontiers in Psychology*, doi.org.10.3389/fpsyg.2019.01406.

[27] S. Morse, 'Law, Responsibility', p.156.

[28] Ibid. p.170.

[29] L. Claydon, 'Criminal Law and the Evolving Technological Understanding of Behaviour', in *Oxford Handbook of Law, Regulation and Technology*, p.348; N. Llamas et al., 'Neuroscience in youth criminal law: Reconsidering the measure of punishment in Latin America', *Frontiers in Psychology*, doi.org/10.3389/fpsyg.2020.00302 .

[30] L. Claydon, 'Criminal Law', p.351.

the other hand, folk psychology is itself a repository of constructed desires and beliefs and is thereby an inconsistent and variegated history of the mythological experience. We should not be drawn into either position. So, while the administration of criminal law – especially as it has devolved to agencies other than the State – needs to protect notions of rationality, it should do so in a manner that is not biased in favour of the beliefs and practices of any of the magnitudes.

In other words, these are complex issues which are not necessarily well-considered within the frame of traditional criminal justice administration. Their status is therefore likely to become even more tenuous as areas of the administration become devolved to private and community sectors with often quite different agendas. What we need is a criminal justice model which begins to take these issues on board in a way that, in acknowledging the impact of mythological subjection on beliefs and practices, promotes a non-mythological framework. This would place substantial pressure on regulatory governance with primarily economic or other sectional interests.

Comment

The State is properly seen as a mythological magnitude in its institutional arrangements. This sovereign power remains potent, even as engaged or 'tempered', and this generates a further strategy of social control as regulation ranges across the social fabric and into the embodied practices of individuals. This is so whether or not the networked nodal arrangement is monitored by smart or meta-regulatory frames. In fact, such monitoring can be argued to strengthen these nodes as means of social control by this disciplining of them. However, the complexities of administering justice, difficult enough within current criminological ideas and practices, will become far more complex as judicial and corrective power is increasingly separated into other, more widespread arrangements with other competing agendas, even more so as neuroscience makes itself felt in both prosecution and punishment.

THE STATE AND TECHNOLOGY

The State Becomes Digital

In addition to the spread of authority beyond the State comes a further level of complexity. That is the extent to which the State is transforming itself – at its very core – into a field of technology. Is the State becoming virtual? Various aspects of this question take the discussion not deeper but far wider than neuroscience.

The first point to recognise is the substantial extent to which the State is now a technological field. As they reach levels of sophistication well beyond their present state, developments in artificial intelligence, the internet of things, the exploitation of Big Data, the growth in predictive analytics and the use of blockchain is transforming the functioning of the State. The interfaces between State agencies and citizens will increasingly occur through chatbots (software able to converse and provide information and services) and robo-advisers (to provide financial and other advice based on the provision of a range of offered data).[31]

Add to that the prospect of the real-time digital management of such national infrastructure as roads, rail lines, ports, airports, water management, power generation, educational resources and information and communication networks that will be possible as every item becomes part of the internet of things; the 'localisation of these elements in 'smart' or digitally managed cities; the automation of regulatory compliance for a wide range of business and private activities; and the secure public storage of government documentation including the encoding of laws, statutes and 'smart' contracts generated without legal advice. Yet further, we see the online management of judicial and dispute resolution arrangements, some fully automated by using game theory. Government policies may be trialled virtually and public opinion about these monitored. Confidentiality standards – combined with transparency for involved parties – will likely rely on blockchain technology regarding much of this.[32]

It is immediately clear that these and other innovations will transform the nature of the State, thereby the very essence of the agencies that presently provide a very wide range of functions and services to the community. The design, generation, manipulation, interpretation and application of data is at the heart of these changes. This raises again the issues canvassed in Chapter 2, that is, the design and nature of the data and the algorithms through which all these changes will be managed and how these will increasingly re-create social and personal reality. It also points again to what these will require or demand of citizens, who must inevitably be brought into the regimes of practice of these digitised technologies. The viability of digitised identities and the impact on the status of personal data will be key factors here.

In this context, Sartor looks at the impact of communication technologies on human rights. He does so in acknowledging both the potential range of benefits – including economic development, culture, education, public dialogue and even moral progress – and the potential risks – including alienation, inequality, surveillance, profiling, automated assessment, virtual constraint and loss of normativity.[33] Against that background, he sees the challenges for human rights, many of which – such as freedom, dignity, equality, identity, privacy – we have looked at in Chapter 5, both through and outside the international human rights frame. In short,

---

[31] Z. Engin et al., 'Algorithmic government: Automating public services and supporting civil servants in using data science technologies', *The Computer Journal* 62:3 (2019): p.448.

[32] Ibid. p.449ff.

[33] G. Sartor, 'Human Rights and Information Technologies', in *Oxford Handbook of Law, Regulation and Technology*, pp.425–433; 'Human Rights and Technology – Discussion Paper' (December 2019), Australian Human Rights Commission, chapter 12: Proposals and Questions, pp.289ff.

The State and Technology | 255

the development of information and communication technologies poses both opportunities and significant challenges for every formal human right. Government should, in Sartor's view, adopt a proactive role in discerning where these technologies differentially impact.[34]

The position in the present work is that we cannot look straightforwardly to the State to address these important issues. The State itself, in its various functions, is as much a player in this field. Its role as potential adjudicator and promoter of rights needs to be seen in the wider context of the interests that have colonised and which utilise it. In fact, it is the argument here that the very nature of the State needs to be reimagined.

State as Digitally Avaricious

We saw in Chapter 1 that one of the fields of knowledge that affirmed the tide of mythological normalisation was that, even for the normalised, monitoring never stops. It is in this context that we should see that the transition of the State to a near to total digital arrangement is being complemented by its agencies drawing together not only vast amounts of data on both functional performance and individual behaviour. They are clearly also drawing equally vast data resources from the private sector. In that, the State is clearly threatening, if not breaching, at least present notions of privacy. A study of systematic access by governments to private sector data across leading jurisdictions to this information found the following:[35]

- In most, if not all, countries studied, existing legal structures provide an inadequate foundation for the conduct of systematic access, both from a human rights perspective and at a practical level. Laws are vague and ambiguous and government interpretations of them hidden or even classified; practices are opaque and oversight mechanisms absent or limited in scope.
- In every country studied, even those with otherwise comprehensive data protection laws, access for regulatory, law enforcement and national security purposes is often excluded from those laws; or it is treated as an accepted purpose for which access is authorised.
- Overall, there had been, until recently, relatively little discussion of the complex legal and political issues associated with asserting jurisdiction over data stored in other countries or relating to citizens of other countries.
- Although standards for real-time interception of communications for law enforcement purposes are high in most surveyed countries (but not

[34] G. Sartor, 'Human Rights and Information Technologies', pp.447–448.
[35] F. Cate and J. Dempsey, *Bulk Collection – Systematic Government Access to Private-Sector Data* (Oxford University Press, 2017), pp.6–7.

256 *Regulation and the State*

China or India), standards for access to stored communications held on third parties was less consistent.

- Regarding standards of government access to communications in national security investigations, almost half of the countries do not have provisions requiring court orders for surveillance undertaken in the name of national or foreign intelligence gathering.
- Most countries handle travel and financial data under laws requiring routine bulk reporting for specified classes of data.

Cate and Dempsey draw conclusions in key areas: new digital technologies make it increasingly easy for governments to collect, store and process information on a massive scale, and governments are exploiting this; as internet-based services have globalised, trans-border surveillance has flourished; national security legal authorities have become increasingly powerful since 9/11; and the expansion in powers has been supported by extreme secrecy.[36]

Clearly, 9/11 and the Snowden data releases have triggered and publicised a substantial expansion in data collection and interpretation for the purposes of national security. Predictive analytics and personal profiling, along with wider surveillance techniques, are intended to fill the knowledge gap to help prevent further events of those kinds. But if one looks at the mythological implications here, then the State and Market magnitudes are working in harmony for purposes that protect dominant political and economic interests, through this exponential increase in data collection and its manipulation, making easier the subjection of individuals. It is perhaps a sign of the depth of this subjection that little constraint is placed on these activities through public protests.

Sociologist Chris Parenti has traced the history of surveillance in the United States back to its early use in monitoring of slaves, through World War II when the Nazis used IBM computers to institute the 'final solution'. As he stated in an interview:[37]

> The State has to set limits on the private sector and on itself, on other parts of the State. That's no foolproof method but I think it's all we have. The main issue here also is a society organised around a profit motive. That has to be put into check by democratic State power. There's a contradiction around the nature of the State ... [it] ... developed in increasingly despotic directions throughout modernity; but at the same time I think that there's another side to State power, that is as the government, which is embodied not in the police and the military but in other aspects of government – the more democratic parts of representative government – that have to be nurtured and used as a counterbalance against the police and surveillance core of the State. So it's a seemingly contradictory argument, but really there's no individual escape from this.

---

[36] Ibid. pp.43–45.
[37] C. Parenti, 'Surveillance in America', radio interview regarding his book *Soft Cage: Surveillance in America from Slavery to the War on Terror* (2003), station KPFA, Berkeley, CA, transcript published by *American Behavioral Scientist* on 1 June 2005, p.7.

Other Key Features of the Digital State: Data, Surveillance, Democratic Values and Regulation

Against this background of the State as a tempered magnitude – as a consequential generator of wide regulatory power and as a principal player in the world of technology – it is proper to consider a range of unresolved issues in related fields. Thereby we can consider what the proper function of the State would be across these other fields of activity, especially regarding a non-mythological mode of operation, a consideration of which will then follow.

Given the pre-eminent role of the State regarding data acquisition, the function of *data brokering* has particular relevance for the legislative and regulatory capacity of the State and its connected networks. Data brokers commonly collect, sell or otherwise make available personal data for the development of individual profiles for marketing and risk mitigation purposes. The data can come from credit and debit card transactions, public records, online tracking cookies, smartphones and so on. It is usually collected without the permission of the person to whom the data applies. Even in terms of one of the currently dominant notion of privacy – to be left alone – this collection constitutes a deep intrusion. Calls for the reform of this industry have longevity.[38]

But data brokerage also needs to be seen in the context of the massive data capture, sale, storage, algorithmic interpretation and application between State and Market, as well as 'State to State', 'Market to Market' and 'State to Market'.[39] We have just seen a summary of the former in Cate and Dempsey at note 35, but the State also needs to be understood to be both a buyer and a seller of data,[40] not just a gatherer. It cannot thereby be asserted about the State in some simple way that its concerns are strictly about promoting the interests of the citizen by accepting responsibility for issues of security, the economy or infrastructure planning. The reason is that State gathering and use of personal data is done without advice to or permission of the citizen. That is, this is done by presumption that the subjection of the citizen, based on mythological claims, does not require permission. That its dominant interests have that view is attested by their failure to establish any external – for example, judicial – affirmation of the necessity for such personal data capture. This is especially so where the data has been captured and provided by an external node or network.

This should not prevent data capture by the State. There are legitimate management and planning requirements, and many of these can be addressed through

---

[38] A. Ashley Kuempel, 'The invisible middleman: A critique and call for reform of the data broker industry', *Northwestern Journal of International Law and Business* 36:1 (2016).

[39] See, for example, the Data Sharing and Release Act proposed by the Australian Productivity Commission in 2017.

[40] M. Hicken, 'What information is the government buying about you?', *CNN Money* (13 October 2013); N. Lindsey, 'State DMVs selling personal data for millions of dollars in profit', *CPO Magazine* (18 September 2019).

258 Regulation and the State

aggregation and anonymising data, but the capture of personal information should always have the citizen's approval, unless judicial review allows confidential collection. The latter applies in particular to capture for security reasons. Further, there are two other, complementary reasons why the State should be seen as a legitimate data collector. First, as we have seen, the model of self-responsibility proposed here as the basis of the new model of privacy requires the citizen to provide a range of data to State agencies so that necessary resources can be made available for that and so relevant health conditions can be relayed. Second, given the new model of the State as a purpose-based fiduciary agency – which we are about to explore – then the State would have no reason except to have the interests of the fully engaged citizen as its rationale.

This is thereby the reason for *Big Data* to become an increasing resource for a range of State activities. That is, managed under the auspices of a purpose-based fiduciary set of agencies with the promotion of the existential interests of the individual as its rationale, Big Data would no longer be a means for exploitation of the citizen but a means to promote the citizen's interests. The conditions already outlined in Chapter 6 would apply; that is, all personal data beyond what was required to be shared to promote the citizen's – and others' – respectful self-responsibility would be protected. This would include all the data downloaded by agencies into the personal data node outlined in that chapter. Such an arrangement would provide a widely elaborate framework for both the balancing of group and individual fairness proposed by Mark MacCarthy[41] and the principles of the EU Data Protection Directive (Directive 95/46/EC).

There are matters of concern associated with Big Data, of course. Where data-driven education is adopted by the State and develops into a model centred on virtual learning (with all its continual data collection, the application of algorithmic assessment and long-term data retention), on private sector decision-making (replacing pedagogical decision-making) and on data-driven content and metrics, then we have a major shift in educational principles.[42] This can be addressed by the new purpose-based fiduciary model.

A matter requiring particular attention is the role of the State in the adoption of widespread *facial recognition*. Its proponents claim its value in security, crime control and medical and psychological diagnoses[43] and in satisfying the lifestyle demands of consumers, thereby with real value for the State and its Market allies. However, if one looks at the wider picture, there are significant issues. First, it seems inevitable that meanings can be algorithmically built into such images, that such captured images will be 'augmented' by the personal profiles garnered from the fast-

---

[41] M. MacCarthy, 'Standards of fairness for disparate impact assessment for Big Data algorithms', *Cumberland Law Review* 48:102 (2017).

[42] E. Zeide, 'The structural consequences of Big Data–driven education', *Big Data* 5:2 (2017): pp.164–172.

[43] N. Martinez-Martin, 'What are important ethical implications of using facial recognition technology in health care?', *AMA Journal of Ethics Policy Forum* (February 2019).

increasing collection and analysis of personal data. Thereby, it is an extension of GPS systems, adding images of the individuals and associates and locations to such profiles. This immediately raises not only the incidence of error and cultural bias – as well as the prospect of identity theft through hacking – but also the broader problem associated with the algorithmic creation of reality explored in Chapter 2. Second is the reverse issue of the potential for such 'located' images to be added to other scenarios, for example, regarding security or law and order but also regarding education, welfare and the commercial opportunities they offer, serving those agendas. In these circumstances, the only valid first condition seems to be that such 'recognition' take place only with the consent of the citizen, unless authorisation is obtained from an independent judicial source.[44] This could then be augmented, as West suggests, by limiting data storage time, restricting data sharing, providing clear signage in public areas, mandating accuracy standards, mandating third-party assessments, reducing collateral data collection, requiring opt-in for marketing purposes, certifying users and valid field testing.[45] But this would best be set in the context of such a broader State policy agenda as that proposed in Chapter 6, where the responsibilities of citizens to provide a range of data – this may include some data by way of facial recognition – are conditioned by the confidential preservation of a full range of other data.

An especially thorny issue for the State, one not near resolution, is how to set conditions for a citizen to have the right to *delete personal records*.[46] This is not a reference to 'going off the grid', to be forgotten, which seems too much of a challenge in many jurisdictions. This refers to having records or the searches for one's name deleted if one chooses. A citizen should have a proper level of control over what is said about them online and in other media. What 'proper' means is, of course, the issue. The Court of Justice of the European Union has grappled with this and produced a position of principle:

> where the right to freedom of expression is being balanced against the right to respect for private life, the right criteria in the balancing exercise include the following elements: contribution to a debate of general interest, how well known the person concerned is, the subject of the report, the prior conduct of the person concerned, the method of obtaining the information and its veracity, the content form and consequences of the publication, and the severity of the sanction imposed (on the party invoking freedom of expression).[47]

[44] Y. Welinder, 'Face recognition privacy in social networks under German law', *Communications Law Bulletin* 31:1 (2012).

[45] D. West, '10 actions that will protect people from facial recognition software', *Brooking Institute Online Series: AI Governance* (31 October 2019).

[46] S. Kulk and F. Zuiderveen Borgesius, 'Privacy, Freedom of Expression and the Right to Be Forgotten in Europe', in *Cambridge Handbook of Consumer Privacy*, J. Polonetsky, Omer Tene and Evan Selinger (eds.) (2018).

[47] *Satakunnan Markkinaporssi Oy And Satamedia Oy v Finland* App no. 931/13 ECtHR (21 July 2015) para 83.

The argument in the present work is that these principles favour freedom of expression somewhat too much, although they are in sympathy with much in this argument. The fundamental principle is that, if someone is acting in a respectful, self-responsible manner, there can be no claim on their personal circumstances except for any enhancement that they choose in search of self-responsibility. Certainly, a citizen is to respect other citizens, and that means that there should be a sharing of information that contributes to that as 'common interest', but one's public profile or one's priors should play no part in that. These points are emphasised if the information was improperly obtained. However, if there were evidence of 'non-responsible' behaviour, then these protections would lose an amount of their force consistent with the 'gravity' of the incident and taking into account the consequences of the publication.

A further issue – one that brings us back to the field of regulation and in a manner that concentrates attention again on the often seamless networking between State and Market – is the extent to which *privacy self-regulation* has been successful, whether the State and interest groups should have a more prominent role in this and how that could be effective. This is the field which for Rubenstein contains State regulation at one end (e.g., as prescribed by the EU in its General Data Protection Regulation), voluntary self-regulation by the Market at the other and a range of other options between these, sometimes including the participation of consumer advocacy groups as a means of co-regulation.[48] The tenor of Rubenstein's approach is that the middle ground, where the sets of interests can be brought into the contest, is a better place to deal with these problems than the restrictions or laxity of either end of the spectrum.

This raises the broader issue of the regulation of cyberspace, a particularly troubled arena. Henriksen has made clear, in describing the relatively recent failure of the UN Group of Governmental Experts to develop an international legal framework, that this is a field riven by sovereign differences even about such fundamental principles as a preferred normative framework. The result is that strategy, politics and ideological differences are the dominant factors in the functioning of information and communication technologies.[49] Among the confounding factors are the protection of sovereign foreign policy agendas drawn from ideological world views, differences over internet openness, the growth of regionalisation, the increasing role of such non-State players as think tanks and research institutes, the exercise of influence by the tech industry and continuing disagreement over the norms that should guide regulation.[50]

---

[48] I. Rubenstein, 'The Future of Self-Regulation is Co-Regulation', in *Cambridge Handbook of Consumer Privacy*.

[49] A. Henriksen, 'The end of the road for the UN GGE process: The future regulation of cyberspace', *Journal of Cybersecurity* 5:1 (2019): 1–9.

[50] Ibid. pp.4, 5, 6, 7.

The State and Technology   261

Further to this issue of the *governance of cyberspace* is that of the *governance within cyberspace*. Here the focus is that regulation is taking place but in the forms of both code – as Lessig and Katyal argue – and self- or private regulation. There are different views about whether the State should attempt to control code, with all its inherent vulnerabilities to criminal activity, or whether it should be left as open source. Following Braithwaite, Chang and Gunningham add to this question the view that self-regulation in its various forms is preferable to intervention by State or industry bodies, as self-regulation encourages the 'responsiveness' that regulation does well regarding the interests of any particular entity.[51] This thinking is extended by Brenner regarding cybercrime, where she argues for the involvement of the private sector, including individuals as civilians.

Put together, this is a complex set of issues. It seems that, frankly, governance at the international level is at best a long way off. In the absence of that, perhaps the only way forward is to seek a series of bilateral or multilateral partnerships involving sovereign State and industry participants to develop smaller-scale structures and arrangements to promote the full range of activities, but with the interests of the non-mythological individual citizen at its centre. This goal would be somewhat easier to fulfil within the frame of a reimagined State and Market and of the purpose-based fiduciary kind we are about to look at. The present mythological, data-driven State or Market will likely do little to promote such interests. In fact, in all these examples, the State is a contributor more to the problem than to its solution due to its inherent mythological features and its consequential close alliance with the Market.

A further, particular set of challenges for the State is that of the *friendliness of artificial intelligence*. We shall look at two: the *enhancement/privacy question* and the *morality question*. We have touched on both in different contexts but revisit them here as they are key issues for the State's relationship to technology. Regarding them, we can say that the field of cognitive tools will continue to develop but is already at the point where, with 'extended mind' developments, these will function in a manner that is as significant as the product of much of our cognitive capacity.

Regarding the *enhancement/privacy question*, these 'AI extenders' may be best seen as a version of brain–machine interfacing and thereby inseparable from the function proposed in the argument for the development of artificial general intelligence. They can be physically or virtually external to us but loosely connected to us or fully embedded with our brains, which thereby take over and make the artefact redundant. This is the not-uncontested view – given the argument that such extensions cannot be agents so cannot cognise – that the vehicles of our cognitive representations need not be instantiated by sets of neurons in the brain. There are variations within these two ends of the spectrum. The argument in the present work

---

[51] L. Chang and N. Gunningham, 'The Governance of Cyberspace', in *Regulation Theory – Foundations and Applications*, p.538.

262 *Regulation and the State*

is that it will become increasingly clear that the user will change their reasoning process in response to the design of the task to be undertaken through the 'extender' and that the skills of the individual user will co-evolve with the technology.[52] These tools, coupled with our biological systems, will increasingly offer enhanced cognitive abilities, for example, memory, sensorimotor capacities, perception, planning, comprehension, expression, decision-making, emotional self-control, navigation, comprehension, reasoning and so on.[53]

There are clear lessons from all this. They include the prospect of the comprehensive embedding of the citizen in the technology; that with the continuing development of AI, the extension will outstrip the cognitive capacity of the citizen; that the citizen will thereby forgo cognitive skills – and a feeling of confident capacity – to the extension; the prospect of third-party ownership of the extension; the embedding of moral principles within the extension to guide its performance; issues of responsibility when the extension makes a mistake; intimacy that becomes surveillance; and so on.[54]

Regarding the *morality question* more generally, some like Floridi argue that a series of participants undertaking various functions can produce a result that has moral implications: morality is already distributed.[55] The problem with that argument is that the moral outcome from the activity of the neural extension lacks intention. No one sought that outcome, right or wrong. The further question is that of algorithmic design for ethical principles. The Brookings Institute has raised this,[56] and we have seen in Chapter 5 that the IEEE has the issue at the centre of its focus in the *Ethically Aligned Design* report. However, we already saw there that finding the appropriate principles is not straightforward. How to address this has been a central concern of the present work. This is a field of research properly directed by the State, although that would likely be too great a challenge at present given what has been just been said regarding the inherent disposition of the current State form.

The problems facing the allied field of *privacy by design* is well accounted for by Bygrave.[57] He sets out the history of the challenge of even achieving semantic clarity, and that this ultimately saw Privacy by Design as the common terminology, with principles such as:

- Proactive not reactive; preventive not remedial
- Privacy as the default

---

[52] J. Hernandez-Orallo and K. Vold, 'AI Extenders: The Ethical and Societal Implications of Humans Cognitively Extended by AI', *AIES'19 Conference* (2019) p.507.

[53] Ibid. p.511.

[54] Ibid. p.512; see also R. Heersmink, 'Distributed cognition and distributed morality: Agency, artefacts and systems', *Science and Engineering Ethics* 23 (2017): pp.436–437.

[55] L. Floridi, 'Distributed morality in an information society', *Science and Engineering Ethics* 19:3 (2013): p.729.

[56] M. Kearns and A. Roth, 'Ethical Algorithm Design Should Guide Technology Regulation', Brookings Institute (online 13 January 2020).

[57] L. Bygrave, 'Hardwiring Privacy', in *The Oxford Handbook of Law, Regulation and Technology*, p.756.

A Way Forward 263

- Privacy embedded into the design
- Full functionality: positive sum not zero sum
- End-to-end lifecycle protection
- Visibility and transparency
- Respect for user privacy.

There are two sets of challenges facing the implementation of these principles by the State. The first is acknowledged by Bygrave himself.[58] That is, there has been serious difficulty getting traction with them, including with the Market (thereby with consumers), with governments, with designing engineers, within the legislative process and thereby with realising legitimacy and with their operationalisation. Dominant interests, solely and together, have been more concerned with the advantage to be gained by accessing, not defending, personal data. The other challenge is, as we have seen, to reach a notion of privacy which goes beyond the straightforward 'being left alone' or 'better managing information flow' concepts which have been the mainstay of normalisation into mainly bourgeois culture.

A WAY FORWARD

To recap the route to this point, we see that the State has changed from a sovereign entity to a distributed regulatory network that is enmeshed in the Market. It is not disempowered by this but merely operates through different means. However, the persistence of its formal institutions and agencies means that it is still for now 'identifiable' and, through its dominant interests, may seek mythological re-emergence as an absolutist magnitude. At the same time, the State – while it has become the regulatory State – is utilising its privileged access to Big Data and new interpretive techniques to transform the social field from an analogue to a digital arrangement, including regarding such key functions as security, justice, education, welfare and infrastructure management. The central concern raised in the present work is that the imminent availability of increasing amounts of neural data – and the capacity to alter that both structurally and regarding its content – will provide for unforeseen levels of control. So new models of both State and Market are now needed.

The next challenge is to begin to conceive of a notion of the State which addresses all these pressing issues. This will need to recognise the mythology of its current, tempered form, then see that the search by its dominant interests for its re-ascendance has come in the form of its wide coverage of social space through regulation and, more recently, through the opportunities of technology – a number of which remain problematic – the latter especially in partnership with the Market.

---

[58] Ibid. p.762.

264   *Regulation and the State*

What might such a notion look like? Since the present mythological form of the State is founded on the forgoing of existential self-responsibility by every citizen, then a viable notion of the State should seek the practical establishment in governance of the ethical principles presented here. This would be a gestalt shift in the perception of the nature of the State. However, we have seen that, without such a shift, the widely pervasive intrusions and algorithmic reconstructions of personal identity and cognitive autonomy that are approaching with the applications of neuroscience are likely to be overwhelming.

We have also seen in Chapter 8 that fiduciary principles, especially when combined with the notion of purpose-based entities as described by Langford, offer promise in this regard. However, we also saw there – in the work of Harding, Fox-Decent and Postema – that fiduciary principles need a stronger foundation than trust. So, we need an account of the State as a purpose-based set of institutions and agencies that operate on fiduciary principles and which thereby do not promote mythological subjection. Miller presents a fiduciary account of the State, albeit one closely aligned with principles of political trust. However, although his account goes a long way towards the kind of fiduciary State that is sought in the present work, underlying mythological themes still come through. Once these are dealt with, we can see what a non-mythological reimagining of the State could look like.

THE FIDUCIARY STATE

The account of government presented by Miller focuses on its relationship with political trust, specifically how that reveals the nature of fiduciary government. This account can move us towards a notion of a non-mythological State, but the mythology within his account needs to be removed. I shall attempt to do that before returning to the value of Miller's account.

First, fiduciary government needs to be uncoupled from political trust as a foundational alliance. Trust can have a place in a fiduciary State but at a secondary level. To explain, trust is a valuable human ethical principle and is an important element in the way we navigate the world. However, we have seen from the comments on Harding, Postema and especially Fox-Decent that political trust is inherently mythological in that it typically reflects the political subjection of the citizen. We see this in Hobbes's originating covenant, which was a response to the social turmoil in England in the mid-seventeenth century – the English Civil Wars of 1642–1651, at which latter date *Leviathan* was written – and which justified an absolutism in the form of King or Parliament through a claim that the safety of the subjects would be assured so long as they forwent any skerrick of legitimate self-governance. This was a covenant clearly weighted in favour of the sovereign, who was ceded widespread powers while subjects received the promise of peace and fair treatment: the sovereign 'trusts' the population to avoid unrest and the populace 'trusts' the sovereign – empowered by their very subjection – to quell any unrest that

The Fiduciary State

may originate from among them and external others but also then to rule fairly. Democratic reforms in the meantime have of course tempered this absolutism, but the fact remains that the self-responsibility of subjects remains traded for incremental improvements in their conditions of life.

The argument by Fox-Decent – in favour of legitimate political authority and the rule of law that results from this mutual trust – almost completely washes out of the debate this absolute power of the State and this subjection of individuals, the two elements which remain at the heart of the political landscape. Given that this combination of empowerment, on one side, and subjection offset by the promised distancing and camouflage of existential fear, on the other, is at the heart of the mythological analysis, then Fox-Decent is presenting a veiled mythological account of political trust. Trust may come back into the debate, although not at the foundational level given it by Fox-Decent and only in a non-mythological form.

It may properly be said that Miller adopts a similar position. For him, although he acknowledges that 'our subjection to government is inescapable', he believes with Pettit that – as a consequence – 'the reality is that we have no choice but to manifest political trust'.[59] This takes us into Miller's enthusiasm for the republicanism of Pettit more generally, and it is there that we can see the mythological themes.

The background to this analysis is that the account of the republican State provided by Pettit is thoroughgoingly mythological. We have seen in Chapter 7 that this form of the State is entitled – even required – to intrude into the affairs of the citizen if it is regarded by authorities as being in the citizen's interests, even if they are behaving respectfully of others but not pursuing an interest that is shared with others. This is thereby arbitrary interference by the republican State.[60] This is a key point among a range of evidence of Pettit's mythological credentials.[61] Among that range are comments regarding Pettit's view of trust, including that the pursuit of civility would properly have citizens 'put themselves in the hands of public officials, be they police or politicians or bureaucrats, even when that reliance is not supported by the existence of effective constraints on those officials'.[62] He also states, 'I am never so safe as when I am in the hands of a lover or friend.'[63] This call for trust as of a lover or friend is a veil over the arbitrary but systematic interference in one's life that republican officials are entitled – even required – to pursue. That is, it is a veil over the mythological status of the republican State.

Against this background, we can make various observations about Miller's further reliance on Pettit. First, 'democratic government entails political trust in an objective sense. And indeed, Pettit has said as much.... Our political agency is a matter of

---

[59] P. Miller, 'Political (Dis)trust and Fiduciary Government', in *Fiduciaries and Trust – Ethics, Politics, Economics and Law* (Cambridge University Press, 2020), pp.233, 241.
[60] P. Pettit, *Republicanism*, p.65.
[61] See D. Grant, *The Mythological State and Its Empire*, pp.166–186.
[62] P. Pettit, *Republicanism*, p.262.
[63] Ibid. p.268.

266   *Regulation and the State*

our capacity to decide *whom* to trust, recognising that we must trust *someone* to govern.'[64] Second, 'I take it that, insofar as the republican conception of political trust advances descriptive claims, it is engaged in a process of characterising elements of an underlying political reality ... how we ought to understand the democratic franchise, party politics, deliberative political processes and political institutions.... Put simply, the suggestion is that much *political activity*, within and beyond political institutions, is underlain by political trust or involves ongoing negotiation over the terms of a trust reposed and undertaken.'[65] Third, 'Another attraction of Pettit's republican framing of political trust is, of course, that it dovetails nicely with the idea of fiduciary government and suggests a broader conceptual continuity between objective trust and fiduciary relationships',[66] especially through representation.

What is being presented here is an argument that Pettit's republican theory, especially with its emphasis on political trust, is the context not only for understanding the key elements of political activity and institutions but also for the nature of fiduciary relations. However, given the mythological nature of Pettit's republicanism, one might observe that it takes these elements, including fiduciary relations and government, in the wrong – mythological – direction. This is a direction that could have been avoided if Miller had reordered various of the elements of his argument. That is, if he had given greater emphasis to one element that he does recognise, that is, the 'inescapable' subjection to the 'faceless monolith' of government power, and to one he underplays, that is, that 'Some citizens likely do, if rarely, trust in government and in public officials.'[67] The latter should be seen as a varied manifestation of generalised rather than particularised trust.[68] That is, the power of government – and the claims made on its behalf – is the means by which individuals are induced, normalised or forced into subjecting and trusting relations. If he had withdrawn these elements from the – republican – background to the nature of fiduciary relations, then that element could be progressed differently and non-mythologically.

Next, Miller might have then conceived fiduciary relations – as the basis of fiduciary government – in the manner that Fox-Decent does, that is, 'thickly', though without promoting it to a 'theory of everything'.[69] That would work only if emphasis was given to a purpose-based or mandated nature of the State that prioritised the – non-mythological – promotion of existential conditions for the citizen. Then the fiduciary State could focus not only more widely on human rights generally and on environmental rehabilitation but on specifically providing the

---

[64] P. Miller, 'Political (Dis)trust and Fiduciary Government', p.233.
[65] Ibid. p.234.
[66] Ibid. p.234.
[67] Ibid. p.232.
[68] Ibid. p.229.
[69] Ibid. p.226.

negotiated resources citizens require to become self-responsible. The priorities of dominant interests could then be made secondary to that, if not eliminated. That status would then guide, as Fox-Decent recommends in a different context, 'constitutional structure, substantive law, and institutional practice that bear on the roles and responsibilities of legislators, judges, administrative agencies and members of the executive branch',[70] that is, the kind of rule of law that was proposed in Chapter 8.

In short, shorn of its mythology, Miller's fiduciary State – when combined with Langford's principle of purposed-based agencies that honour the interests of citizens as fiduciary 'principals' – could undertake the creation of non-mythological existential conditions founded on respect. It could do so in a manner that promotes citizens' self-responsibility in an environment not initially of mutual trust but of mutual respect. In this context, the array of State functions, especially including the gathering and use of data and other technologies, would be guided by the non-mythological dynamic, especially under the approval of the citizen unless judicial review authorised otherwise.

PRINCIPLES OF A NON-MYTHOLOGICAL JUSTICE SYSTEM

Non-mythological social arrangements, promoted by State and Market, can be outlined in a straightforward manner, but we will first present, by way of contrast, an example of what mythological principles – increasingly common – look like in operation.

Mythological Justice

Given that the administration of justice is at the heart of the responsibilities of the State, we can properly look closely at this in considering the application of mythological principles and the possibility of a non-mythological alternative.

First, as we have just seen, certain State jurisdictions have deployed facial recognition technology, developed by the Market, despite evidence that it applies a range of biases, especially regarding gender and race.[71] Beyond this, generalised public surveillance is also commonly being carried out with AI through the use of cameras and drones; cell phone and social media data is being monitored through 'geofencing'; police can gain access to homeowners' cameras regarding commission of crimes; and justice administrations have trialled the use of algorithms to make risk assessments on recidivism, that is, for predictive purposes. We have already seen in Chapter 1 that these techniques form an important part of the constant monitoring of marginalised groups that is central to mythological normalisation. The Brookings

---

[70] Ibid. p.227.
[71] R. Ray, '5 Questions Policy Makers Should Ask about Racial Recognition, Law Enforcement and Algorithmic Bias', Brookings Institution (online 20 February 2020).

268 *Regulation and the State*

Report asks whether jurisdictions have consulted their communities regarding the deployment of these technologies, what the safeguards are regarding proper and effective use, how biases will be identified, what 'beyond consent' provisions can be introduced to deal with the proliferation of data networking beyond first collection, and how AI can be used for more effective police training and offender skills development, including through virtual reality.

The use of virtual reality need not be mythological. In fact, it can provide a positive use for AI, including more generally beyond its use in justice administration. The first four questions, however, point to mythological issues. That is, they not only are founded on compromised data sets but, more significantly, point to the imposition of a priori judgments and are therefore replete with the arguments about the implications of post-Kantian algorithmic Idealism examined in Chapter 2. One explanation for their growing popularity is that they exhibit the mythological dynamic: dominant interests of the magnitudes of State and Market claiming that existential and then constructed fears will be distanced, camouflaged and conclusively dealt with so long as all accept submission to the anti-crime technological regime. In this, the suspect and the judicial officer are abstracted in a process of dehumanising technology.

Certain of these themes are picked up by Marks, Bowling and Keenan in their consideration of 'automatic justice':[72]

> New scientific techniques, data collection devices and mathematical analytical procedures are having a profound effect on the administration of criminal justice. They are blurring the boundary between the innocent person who should be able to expect freedom from State intrusion and coercion and the 'reasonably suspected' person for whom some rights may justifiably be curtailed. These same technologies are also blurring the boundary between the accused and the convicted. The established process that distinguishes the collection of evidence, the testing of its veracity and probative value and the adjudication of guilt are being automated and temporally and procedurally compressed.[73]

These authors go on to say,

> It may be that … the traditional criminal justice model … is no longer fit for the purpose of explaining criminal justice practice or constraining State power. Our deepest concern is the emergence of a potentially unfettered move towards a technologically driven process of automatic criminal justice. It may be that a stronger right to privacy and enhanced data protection rights could prove a more solid foundation for building a model that will protect fundamental human rights and civil liberties in the long term.[74]

---

[72] A. B. Bowling and C. Keenan, 'Automatic Justice? Technology, Crime and Social Control', in *Oxford Handbook of Law, Regulation and Technology*; A. Zavrsnik, 'Criminal justice, artificial intelligence systems, and human rights', *ERA Forum* 20 (2020): p.567.

[73] A. B. Bowling and C. Keenan, 'Automatic Justice?', pp.724–725.

[74] Ibid. p.725.

Principles of a Non-mythological Justice System 269

In the argument in the present work, the authors are right to identify the threat posed by technological crime control and that changes to the current criminal justice model are needed. However, seeking to address these important issues by bolstering the dominant notion of privacy and the current suite of human rights will not achieve what is required, especially as neuroscientific technologies proliferate, for example, in predictive methods, crime detection and punishment. The current model is founded on claims about the effectiveness of widespread submission to the regimes of law and governance in eliminating the fear of crime. Clearly, those claims have been a failure, given ever-rising prison populations. The current model is failed mythology, and the full emergence of algorithmic neuroscientific technology will constitute further submission, not the long-claimed elimination of fear. What could address these issues would be a gestalt switch to an existential model founded on non-mythological conditions and promoted by purpose-based fiduciary principles.

Non-mythological Justice

Non-mythological justice would be founded not on algorithmic prediction, prosecution and sentencing but on the denial of the mythological arrangement which algorithmic justice promotes. The value of such a reimagined approach is, at least, that it may help address the continuing problem of the growth in prison numbers in jurisdictions across the Western world.[75]

First, the notion of an offence needs to be reconfigured so that it references the degree to which behaviour is disrespectful of others and indicative of a failure to take responsibility for no other. It is not hard to envision this in the criminal field, where misdemeanours reflect low levels of disrespect and the most serious acts of violence commonly reflect optimal disrespect. In response, the processes of criminal investigation and prosecution – which would challenge the application of AI at its foundations – would place significant reliance on identifying the motivation for criminal behaviour alongside the evidentiary process. Here, a system wherein police undertake their investigative work in tandem with the prosecutorial agency has particular advantages to promote a wider focus. The forensic identification of such motivation, which need only in a minority of offences become deeply psychological or psychiatric – given the most crimes are conditioned merely by social

---

[75] The author claims some expertise in this area, having been engaged for twenty years across the justice system in Australia: early as a court-based Probation Officer, through to operational Director of Prisons in three separate Australian States over ten years, having repeatedly provided policy advice to governments in this area over this period, and having been Director General of a wide Ministry of Justice which held responsibility for the Crown Law Office, courts administration and across adult and juvenile correctional administration. He is the author of *Prisons – The Continuing Crisis in New South Wales* (Federation Press, 1992). That publication argued that prisoners should retain the status of citizenship when incarcerated, and it thereby can properly be seen as a forerunner to key arguments put in the present work.

circumstance – would identify those characteristics that would recommend enhancing dispositions to be prescribed by the courts. Further, so-called victimless offences would also be calibrated to reflect the secondary impact on others of such behaviour, for example, one's family or other dependents. Even where there was no such dependency, the issue of the respect of the individual for themselves – and the associated relevance of being responsible for oneself – would keep these as relevant offences.

In the corporate sphere, there would be a similar recalibration. The current policy of regarding business as largely, even primarily in a different, 'corporate' jurisdiction would be replaced by the notion that illegal practices which had an ill-effect on citizens were examples of a failure to act both respectfully and self-responsibly and would attract criminal significance. Wherever there was such a foreseeable effect, corporate wrongdoing would be dealt with under the criminal jurisdiction. In fact, given the widespread social devastation cause by corporate offences, these offences should be regarded as equivalent to the most serious criminal activity by individuals.

When it came to the sentencing phase, this too would be framed by the principles of respect and self-responsibility. Traditional notions of personal punishment, with their residual Christian themes of retribution, would be expunged. All that would matter would be to deal with the offender's disrespect and their realising of a self-responsible way of life. This would also downplay the pervasive notion of the display of State power. Instead, a sentence would be imposed – for both previously 'criminal' and 'corporate' matters – which reflected the level of disrespect and the absence of self-responsibility. Typically, for both community-based and custodial dispositions, this would include a minimum and a maximum period whereby the offender would be given an opportunity to demonstrate an appreciation of the level of disrespect they had displayed and the shortfall of their self-responsibility revealed during the pre-conviction process. The offender themself would in effect determine the actual length of the imposed disposition. This would be done by engagement with active programmes of skill enhancement and by overt indicators of awareness of the importance of respect, not only towards victims. There would be no negative, intimidatory 'shaming', as recommended within the mythological model proposed by Braithwaite's responsive regulation.

In the corporate sphere, there would be the need for 'corporate' individuals to personally and actively demonstrate an appreciation of respect, as well as contributing – proportionate to the assets of the corporation and themself – a diversion of resources to programmes that enhanced the self-responsibility of citizens, especially those who experienced the disrespect shown by the directors of the corporation. This entire enterprise would be guided by the purpose-based fiduciary principles.

In all this, there would need to be a return of responsibility to the State – and away from the Market – for the delivery of the elements of this proposed system. Irrespective of the adoption by both State and the Market of purpose-based fiduciary principles, this forgoing of responsibility that the State has arranged by the regulatory transfer of responsibilities to the Market needs to be seen as a degradation of democratic principles of accountability. Justice is not to be considered as a means of deriving profit. A non-mythological justice arrangement would reverse this well-established trend.

Such a non-mythological dynamic is readily applicable beyond the administration of justice. In health and education, in particular, the reversal of the functioning of the State to operate on the basis of purpose guided by fiduciary responsibility to the citizen and based on the proposed principles is readily conceivable.

10

Regulation and the Market

THE MARKET IS MYTHOLOGICAL

It is easy to see the mythology in the Market. Not only is it now practically impossible to conceive it as separate from and secondary to the State across the social infrastructure, but, in its own right, it is the field wherein existential desire – as the empowering force to deal with existential anxiety – is camouflaged by the widest range of its constructed desires.

The modern Market emerged from the failure of the absolute State – through the differential excesses of its authoritarian and welfare forms in the mid-twentieth century – whereby a new mythology was required. The neoliberal Market, a direct product of those excesses, emerged to fill that vacuum. The rise of this form of the Market came with the emergence of German ordo-liberalism and American anarcho-liberalism, both of which can be seen with Foucault as instances of the repeating liberal response to crises in governmentality. It was no longer about the Market existing in a space created by the State but about the economy serving as the principle, form and model for a State which, because of its defects, is mistrusted by everyone on both left and right.[1] One economic theorist who bridged ordo-liberalism and anarcho-liberalism was Hayek, whose views became especially influential.[2]

Heavily impacted by the cultural destructiveness of Nazism, Hayek argued strongly against any dominance by the State and strongly for what he saw as the values of traditional cultural heritage.[3] For him, the *rules of just conduct*, of which the market order is a pre-eminent product, are the slowly evolving and well-tested

---

[1] M. Foucault, *The Birth of Biopolitics* (Palgrave Macmillan, 2008), p.117.

[2] Ibid. p.161.

[3] For a more extensive account of the mythological significance of Hayek's social economics, see D. Grant, *The Mythological State and Its Empire*, pp.146–166, and D. Grant and L. Bennett Moses, *Technology and the Trajectory of Myth*, pp.53–58.

The Market Is Mythological

social traditions that generate spontaneous orders so long as they are not subject to external constraint. These rules are not prescriptive but are the limits of acceptable behaviour. Typical of these constraints are such constructed orders as government – with its inherent potential for totalitarianism – which is better left to manage a narrow range of activities such as the coercive powers[4] of a law which must be only abstract and negative; the national security; and dispensing an ultra-thin notion of welfare.

These rules should be seen not as creating spaces of individual freedom but as means of subjection to the requirements of the Market order, which will create a new and better life for all through their often-uncomfortable creation of civilisation. They are not a mechanism for the production of social justice[5] and they are not embarrassed by the emergence of monopolies. These rules do thereby create the opportunity but not the certainty for all participants to satisfy their needs.[6] Freedom is to be understood within the market context, which also not improperly produces great wealth. It will mitigate against arbitrary power.[7]

The problem for Hayek is that this kind of neoliberalism has entrenched an inequality by which large numbers of citizens are excluded from satisfying their needs due to their subjection to these rules of just conduct and thereby to emergent dominant interests which are often protected from market competition by direct and indirect State sponsorship and due to their market dominance.

This combination of claims regarding the satisfaction of – constructed – desires made by dominant interests on condition of subjection to the Market regime is classically mythological. These rules of just conduct should be seen within the processes of normalisation outlined in Chapter 4. That is, Hayek's slowly evolved, well-tested social traditions not only are the direct product of the failed absolutisms of Deity and State but are the form of the residual field produced by those engaged magnitudes and used to justify the subjection of individuals to the normalising regimes of his neoliberal Market, the new Absolutism of the mid-twentieth century. This is especially relevant to Hayek's comments regarding the corporation, as 'an aggregate of resources', including that it should never 'even be obliged to consider in its decisions whatever is regarded as the public or social interest, or to support good causes or generally to act for the public benefit'[8] and that 'it is not monopoly as such but only the prevention of competition that is harmful'.[9] Such prevention of competition is, of course, not uncommon in the real world of neoliberalism.

---

[4] F. A. Hayek, *Law, Legislation and Liberty*, 3 vols (Routledge, 1998), 1:131; 3:46.
[5] Ibid. 3:93.
[6] Ibid. 2:115.
[7] Ibid. 2:99.
[8] Ibid. 3:82.
[9] Ibid. 3:83.

274   *Regulation and the Market*

The Mythology of Salomon *v.* Salomon

Against this background, and given the long prominence of the corporation as an emblematic force of the Market, it is appropriate to make some comments about the legal and Constitutional context in which the corporation has emerged and thrived. We will begin with the implications of *Salomon* v. *Salomon*.[10] The *Salomon* decision is widely regarded as having established the fundamental principle that a registered company is a separate legal entity, distinct from its shareholders, and is to be treated as any other independent person with its own rights and liabilities. It has its own personality. This notion was further refined during the twentieth century by gradually differentiating and disconnecting the legal nature of shareholdings from the ownership of the company's assets.[11]

Salomon thereby also confirmed the legitimacy of the 'one person' or 'private' company. There was a proliferation of such companies after 1870, and for interesting reasons. These included that their limited liability provisions were valuable in the volatile environment and that it was a corporate form that favoured the family-controlled enterprises in Britain at the time: for the wealthy of England, it was preferable to seek investment from family members or close associates.[12] Thereby family-run private businesses became politically powerful and their interests were promoted over those of their creditors.

The *Salomon* decision also has implications for the establishment and functioning of corporate groups, the main purpose of which in Britain in the 1890s was to reduce competition and raise prices.[13] It was applied to groups of companies where a subsidiary was held to be a separate legal entity from its parent company and others in the group. The effect has been that courts were reluctant to 'pierce the corporate veil', even where tort claimants sought to recover damages from a holding company in a group other than tortfeasor company. This favours the shareholders of the parent company at the expense of creditors of companies in a corporate group where risky or negligent behaviour occurs or there has been externalisation of costs,[14] thereby creating a moral hazard. In response to this circumstance there have been an increasing number of cases allowing tort victims to bypass *Salomon*[15] under the duty of care principle.

The point is that such use of *Salomon* has clear mythological elements. We have dominant interests (the owners of the parent company) making claims about – and

---

[10] *Salomon* v. *Salomon & Co. Ltd* (1897) AC 22 ('Salomon').
[11] P. Lipton, 'The mythology of Salomon's case and the law dealing with the tory liabilities of corporate groups: An historical perspective', *Monash Law Review* 452 (SSRN 2015): p.458.
[12] Ibid. p.465.
[13] Ibid. p.475.
[14] Ibid. pp.479, 481.
[15] See *CSR Ltd* v. *Young* (1998) Aust Tort Reports 81-468; see also J. Payne, 'Lifting the corporate veil: A reassessment of the fraud exception', *Cambridge Law Journal* 56:2 (1997): pp.284–290.

The Market Is Mythological 275

thereby inducing investors regarding – the pursuit of the satisfaction of their constructed fears and desires on condition of subjection to a corporate regime which, in the end, exploits them. The owners have, on the other hand, created a personated magnitude which does deal with their own fears and desires. *Salomon* thereby allows the corporation to be considered as an entity with the mythological Market.

The Fourteenth Amendment and the 'Personal' Powers of Corporations

The Fourteenth Amendment of the US Constitution, which had been passed in 1868, draws out various matters, at the centre of which is the now-questioned status of the American corporation as an empowered person:

> The [Supreme] Court's decisions in this area seem to assume that a corporation is a 'person' under the Constitution and is thus entitled to many of the same rights as a natural person. However, the Court has never established a test to determine what a constitutional person is or whether a corporation meets such a test. Instead, the Court has continually borrowed metaphors from corporate theory to analogise the corporate entity to the 'person' protected by the Constitution. These metaphors of corporate theory are frequently deployed in an 'ad hoc', arbitrary manner; different corporate metaphors have been used within the same case, even in interpreting different portions of the same Constitutional Amendment. The result is a foundational problem in corporate law, for the Court has granted corporations constitutional rights without engaging in the preliminary inquiry of whether a corporation is entitled to them under the Constitution.[16]

The significance of this is that the Court has created a legal fiction – one might say legal myth – of personification. Beyond that, because the Court has used three vastly different theories of corporate personality doctrine,[17] there is a 'schizophrenic' nature inherent in corporate identity. To this unlikely mix was added, in the 1970s, the argument that the corporation lacked a sense of social responsibility and accountability, both economically and socially. In response, defenders of corporate autonomy – in what must be said is an artificial debate – utilised the 'law and economics' arguments, which amounted to a resistance to any government intervention. That debate continues.

---

[16] J. Krannich, 'The corporate 'person': A new analytical approach to a flawed method of constitutional interpretation', *Loy. U. Chi. J.* 37 (2005): p.62.

[17] These are: corporations as artificial entities, intangible in nature and existing by virtue of the State's authority; corporations as aggregate entities, with the State replaced by the autonomy of the American citizen as the fountainhead of corporate existence and the start of the advocacy for recognition of individual rights in collective form; and corporations as real entities, as natural creatures to be recognised apart from its owners and existing autonomously from the State. Ibid. pp.67–86 passim.

276 Regulation and the Market

Against this historical background we have the indeterminacy of the notion of personhood within the Constitution, which identifies no particular characteristics of the person nor therefore a test for what it is.[18] Nor has the Court attempted to set forth definitive characteristics of the notion, except for using that suite of metaphors to justify different rights, the result of which is the emergence of a Constitutional 'person' distinguishable from the natural person to whom the 'Constitutional' term refers.[19]

The Court's consideration of Constitutional corporate rights has proceeded along with this mixed series of notions and metaphors. Its early pronouncements that a corporation was Constitutional under the Fourteenth Amendment set the stage for increasing corporate rights, but which today nearly equate to the rights of an individual. Yet that has left a particular Constitutional interpretation, given the lack of a test for Constitutional personhood: there is no sign in the original Amendment that it was intended to create Constitutional persons as opposed to natural persons. It was conceived to protect newly freed slaves.[20] Yet the counter-intuitive expansion of corporate constitutional rights proceeded on that basis. In fact, beyond the Fourteenth Amendment pronouncement, these rights include double-indemnity protection and that commercial speech is protected under the First Amendment.

There could be little doubt that, in the context of 'the pervasiveness of modern business corporations',[21] Constitutional recognition and the consequential attribution of a range of powers equivalent to that of natural persons raises the status of the corporation to almost inestimable heights when compared with the citizen. In the context of such a strident Market economy as that in the United States, corporations should be seen as constituent or subsidiary magnitudes. That is, the Fourteenth Amendment, and other Constitutional applications, has been used to affirm the mythology of the corporation.

Regulatory Capitalism

In the context of this legal and Constitutional background, it is appropriate to restate that regulation has – through the symbiosis of State and Market – gradually and thoroughly engaged, transformed and spread this adaptation of sovereign power wide across the social field, to the extent that State power has increasingly become corporate power. One of the consequences is the notion of regulatory capitalism: to properly understand the regulatory State, we need to place that phenomenon in the context of regulatory capitalism, whereby we can see

[18] Ibid. p.90.
[19] Ibid. p.91.
[20] Ibid. p.95.
[21] Ibid. p.100.

The Market Is Mythological

a constitutive interpretation of the role of regulation – a perspective that focuses on the role of regulation in the continuing expansion, adaptation and transformation of capitalism. In this interpretation, states constitute markets and markets constitute the state. Not only are the state and its regulation necessary conditions, they are also the causal factors behind the creation and institutionalisation of markets.[22]

This perspective is argued to offer a broader and more rewarding understanding of what is going on, 'certainly more than the idea that the current order is about the "free market" or that liberalisation, privatisation and deregulation are about the retreat of the state or depoliticization'.[23] That is, the state has to protect the functioning of the capitalist system 'and even nurture it. In this sense, it is not fully autonomous.'[24] This concept points to a world 'where statist regulation coevolves with civil regulation, national regulation expands with international and global regulation, private regulation coevolves and expands with public regulation, business regulation coevolves with social regulation, voluntary regulations expand with coercive ones and the market itself is used or mobilised as a regulatory mechanism'.[25] We are thereby in a quite thoroughgoing regulatory frame, where regulatory practices – beyond being embedded in political, economic, political, private and social fields – actually constitute those fields. Central to all this is the notion of commodification, which – for Levi-Faur, following Marx,[26] Polanyi and Offe – has evolved from an account of the transformation of non-wage labourers into wage labourers but now refers more generally to the transformation of social relations into commodity relations: 'It specifies the conditions under which *every* citizen becomes a participant in commodity relations.'[27] This is complemented by decommodification – the withdrawal and uncoupling of an increasing number of social areas and

---

[22] D. Levi-Faur, 'Regulatory Capitalism', in *Regulation Theory – Foundations and Applications*, p.290; D. Levi-Faur, 'The rise of regulatory capitalism: The global diffusion of a new order', *The Annals of the American Academy of Political and Social Science* (2007), doi.10.1177/0002716204272371; D. Levi-Faur, 'Regulatory capitalism and the reassertion of the public interest', *Policy and Society* 27:3 (published online 2017).

[23] D. Levi-Faur, 'Regulatory Capitalism', p.291

[24] Ibid. p.292.

[25] Ibid. p.293.

[26] Marx analyses labour relations as being not what they seem, that is, direct social relations between individuals at work. Instead, they comprise material relations between persons and social relations between things. For him, value does not 'stalk about with a label describing what it is. Instead, it converts every product into a social hieroglyphic. Later on we try to decipher the hieroglyphic, to get behind the secret of our own social products'; in K. Marx, *The Marx-Engels Reader*, 2nd ed., R. Tucker (ed.) (Norton, 1978), pp.319–322; see also Cahill, who states, '[In] the current context, even just halting neoliberalisation would be a welcome development. It would stymie the practice whereby capital and political elites force the costs of the crisis onto labour. It would also halt the forcing of people into greater levels of market dependence for their basic needs by maintaining current levels of decommodification'; D. Cahill, 'Beyond neoliberalism? Crisis and the prospects for progressive alternatives' *New Political Science* 33:4 (2011): p.489.

[27] D. Levi-Faur, 'Regulatory Capitalism', p.294.

278   *Regulation and the Market*

social groups (surplus labour power) from market relations – and recommodification – the administrative and political reform of human commodification processes where they become obsolete.

In parallel to this dynamic, Levi-Faur proposes that regulation should be seen not just as constraining or even as also empowering but also as constitutive, the latter typified by any field of activity which could not exist but for the rules by which it is constituted. For him, a prime example of the latter is capitalism, whereby regulation is *for* – not *of* – capitalism. That is, it is constitutive of capitalism.[28]

There are a number of points of response to this account of regulation. First, it is a good argument for the proliferation of regulation from the State across the social field, although this work emphasises that the mythological engagement of the State has significantly diminished the wide range of its sovereign power. Levi-Faur allows for this by stating that 'the claim of a monopoly (by the State of the means of violence) does not suggest *actual* monopoly either now or in the past. A claim is just a claim, no more no less, and there are gaps with regard to the *actual* monopoly over the regulatory distributional authority just as there are gaps with regard to the actual monopoly of the means of violence.'[29]

Second, the argument in the present work is that, regarding the operation of the regulatory dynamic, this mythological engagement of the State is thereby both a constraint on its sovereign power and a constitution of its redesigned function as a facilitator of the Market, while the Market is widely empowered and constituted by regulation. Regulation is the post-Sovereign but still mythological form of power, but the Market is no more constituted by regulation than the State, as that forgoes much effective power to the Market.

Third, the suite of commodification, decommodification and recommodification – and that *every* citizen becomes a participant in commodity relations – affirms the argument here that the material nature of the Market has significantly subsumed the social and the political. That is, in parallel to Floridi's transformation of every individual into information, we live not in a world that is desocialised or depoliticised but in one where, largely, those aspects of living have become embedded in the Market, which thereby establishes citizens and the elements of their lives as commodities, that is, unless and until they lack value as commodities or resist that categorisation – when they are actively decommodified – or can be reimagined as commodities – when they can be recommodified. One can also see these categories as active in the disposition of data, whereby the Market itself operates by perceiving the citizen increasingly – and largely – technologically. This 'commodification' is the mythological subjection of the individual through the replacement of the 'existential' claims of an ascendant Market that has been widely enabled by the transfer of sovereign State power, but which operates across both these magnitudes

[28] Ibid. pp.295–296.
[29] Ibid. p.293.

The Market Is Mythological 279

in the form of regulation. In short, the elements of regulatory capitalism display an order which goes to affirm the principal argument here regarding the underlying dynamic. They are anathema to a respectful existential manner of living.

Corporate Motivation

It has already been put that corporations, as constituent magnitudes empowered by regulation, seek the subjection of citizens to their commercial regimes by claiming that such subjection will lead to the distancing and camouflage of their existential concerns and that their constructed fears and (especially) desires will be dealt with conclusively. However, how such claims are made adds to that. Commercial offerings are not merely the result of invitations to participate and enjoy but are more strategic. That is, desires are not simply realised and responded to but are typically created.

Trentmann is clear about such created desires and the easy credit which fuels them. We saw some of this in Chapter 4 regarding the impact of this on Market subjectivation, but it is also revealing to explore how commercial corporations have developed methods for that. From early in the late modern era in the United States, 'Production no longer satisfied real wants. Wants were now created and manipulated by advertising and a value system that equated the good life with personal possessions. This cycle relied on 'an inherently unstable process of consumer debt creation', as Vance Packard had identified.[30] For Trentmann, the manipulative account of post-war advertising was too simple and should be seen as part of a broader movement, its success depending on a cross-fertilisation with State and society. Market research became credible 'because it intersected with a more general advance of a whole variety of related forms of social research: mass observation, opinion polling, expenditure surveys, audience research and, also, direct attempts by the State to understand their citizens in order to promote healthy or national products ... It was a commercial-State-social science research complex',[31] reflecting the inextricable post-war elements of the 'consumer, democracy and capitalism' package that was to be retold by the neoliberals in the 1990s.[32]

Interestingly, Packard took aim at market researcher Ernest Dichter, who argued that, for consumers, products possessed a personality, even a 'soul'. 'Wanting stuff was not frivolous. It was about self-fulfilment. This idea had affinities with the Enlightenment as with recent psychological theories of self-realization. Where Dichter went further was to see the profusion of possessions as a passage in human

---

[30] F. Trentmann, *Empire of Things*, p.302, herein referring to Vance Packard's *The Hidden Persuaders*. This view of the manipulative tactics by the Market through advertising and other means remains. See also pp.362, 677.

[31] Ibid. p.319.

[32] Ibid. p.273.

280   *Regulation and the Market*

liberation. Market researchers were akin to therapists, teaching people to forget about original sin.'[33] One might better say, to forget about existential reality.

As have just seen, the Market did not act by itself in promoting consumption. From the New Deal in the 1930s[34] through to the acknowledgement in 2008[35] that public expenditure – through infrastructure, social transfers, services – had been crucial in both lifting standards of living and facilitating consumer spending, the State has been a key facilitator in the Market's drive to create and satisfy consumption.

Further, the promotion of credit – of debt – in all this may be seen quite differently from the view of Packard that it was destabilising. That is, it is not destabilising of the economy but can properly be understood as strategic and induced a subjection of the consumer-citizen which becomes structural. Its growth has been stellar: by the inter-war years, paying in instalments financed 2-6 per cent of consumer expenditure in the United States and Western Europe, but by 2006, unsecured consumer credit made up 25 per cent of disposable income in the United States. Once mortgages are added in, we see that by, 2007, total household debt as a share of gross disposable income stood at 140 per cent in the United States.[36] The Market, with the support of the State, had over these decades lured the consumer-citizen into a position where the creation and satisfaction of a vast array of desires has tied them into a position of thoroughgoing subjection. Beyond being a series of choices, consumerism has become a well-embedded way of life:

> We have stressed the contributions of States, ideologies and social movements. That does not mean that consumers have been passive bystanders, merely that these institutions shaped the context in which they lived their lives.... To have any chance of success, proposals that hope to create more sustainable lifestyles need to appreciate the personal meaning people take from their things.[37]

It may be said then that corporate motivation regarding consumerism takes the constructed desires of the individual, begins to satisfy them – with strong support from the State – and extends them to wants beyond needs. This provides a created sense of liberation on the part of the consumer but comes at the price of an ever-increasing credit-debt that is widely subjecting. This has become so prevalent that it is now regarded as normal. Behind this elaborate scene the elements of the mythological dynamic are clear: dominant interests of the corporate magnitude, claims about and the satisfaction of constructed desire which distance and camou-flage existential concerns, and subjection.

---

[33] Ibid. p.316.

[34] Ibid. p.286.

[35] J. Stiglitz, A. Sen and J.-P. Fitoussi, *Commission on the Measurement of Economic Performance and Social Progress* (2008), p.16.

[36] F. Trentmann, *Empire of Things*, p.409.

[37] Ibid. pp.681–682.

Comment

The argument so far has been historical, placing the corporation – as an emblematic form of the Market – against a mythological, legal and Constitutional background. It has also explored its emergent modus operandi as inextricably integrated in the regulatory frame extended from the State, and looked at its motivational drive. We now need to consider it in the context of the digital age, and how these historical circumstances are being brought together and transformed through the power of algorithmic technology.

CORPORATE BEHAVIOUR IN THE DIGITAL AGE

It is without question that the corporate world is not only a primary user but also a primary generator of digital capacity and so of information. We shall now look at several aspects of these two fields germane to the broad argument here. This will not be to deny that corporations can and do interact with consumers on a navigable playing field but is to say that this field is already significantly biased and, as we have just seen regarding the corporate regulatory nature of capitalism and the prevalence of credit, is now almost always coloured by this mythological context.

Before we look at the most obvious issue in this particular digital world, that is, the corporate use of data, we need to bring back into focus the argument in Chapter 2, that is, that algorithms are not mere interpreters of data but have data created for them and then interpret that in a manner conceived by their designers. This has become a vast field in which algorithms do not represent a largely common reality but actively create and re-create that. This constructivism is the context for understanding their use by corporations.

A key outcome of the corporate use of algorithms is that, as part of these re-creations, they not only shape individual lives – for example, as is shown by the surveillance, search, filtering, forecasting and production of data on social media[38] – but take this to a high level of personalisation: the effect of algorithmic application is increasing individualisation, commercialisation, inequality and deterritorialization while at the same time decreasing transparency, controllability and predictability.[39] By that, this is a reconstruction of individual consciousnesses and thereby culture, knowledge and norms, that is, the social order and the meaning and value of democracy.[40]

There is, of course, no single order being here replaced by a single algorithmic order, but the argument is that democracy should allow the co-existence of a range

---

[38] N. Just and M. Latzer, 'Governance by algorithms: Reality construction by algorithmic selection on the internet', *Media Culture and Society* 39:2 (2016): p.240.

[39] Ibid. p.238.

[40] Ibid. p.246.

of relatively compatible social orders, which are therefore being constrained – if not repressed – by algorithmic interpretation and construction. Due to the capacity of algorithms to particularise knowledge and interpret data, this is felt most deeply at the individual and micro-social level, whereby meaning can be not only personalised but also – as 'universal' meanings are promoted by augmented reality – generalised, leaving individuals more impacted. This effect has then grown further as machine learning allows algorithms to constantly refine and develop such interpretations. The result is an increase in the opacity and unpredictability of what is presented as reliable information, that is, information the reliability of which has not been agonistically tested.

In the face of these rapid changes, government policy development is difficult.[41] But inadequate levels of scrutiny mean that algorithms are thereby becoming both actors and institutions, as well as norms and rules, in governance. This is not to say that algorithms themselves exert power.[42] That would be a wrong assumption – a mistake in attribution – which absolves the designers, their sponsors and policy makers from responsibility.[43] This is also the issue of algorithmic agency and responsibility. That is, even when it comes to be claimed by agents of artificial intelligence that their products have passed the Turing test, wisdom would call for strong demonstrations of this over a long period before such attribution is made, and even then there should be a 'human driver behind the wheel'. Once we forgo that responsibility, we have effectively made a quantum change to all human fields that could not be recovered. We have explored this issue in Chapters 2 and 6 in regard to developments in brain–computer interfacing.

Again, the mythological dynamic is here in full view: corporate magnitude, their dominant interests, claims about satisfying constructed concerns that distance and camouflage existential concerns, and individual subjection.

The Dimension of the Problem of Corporate Algorithms

We can get a sense of the vastness of this data mining and monetisation from two other pieces of research, produced by Christl[44] and Zuboff.[45] To say that the size and growth of this is monumental is a clear understatement, given that the number of individuals, the transactions mapped and the monetary value of each of these categories runs in the billions. Referring to the biases in algorithmic data manage-

---

[41] Ibid. p.251.
[42] Ibid. p.245.
[43] Ibid. p.254.
[44] W. Christl, 'Corporate Surveillance in Everyday Life – How Companies Collect, Combine, Analyse, Trade and Use Personal Data on Billions', *Report by Cracked Labs* (Institute for Critical Digital Culture), Vienna, June 2017.
[45] S. Zuboff, *The Age of Surveillance Capitalism* (Hachette Book Group, 2019).

ment,[46] Christl identifies various categories of corporate entity that undertake this exploitation of data on a mass scale. These include those involved in media, telecommunications, internet service provision, financial services and the public sector. Among the principal agents of these intrusions into personal data are the risk data industry (for credit scoring, identity verification and fraud scoring in real time, investigating consumers), the marketing data industry (ranking and prioritising consumers, programming advertising,[47] connecting offline and online data, managing behaviour in real time, identity resolution, much of this done through such consumer software systems as consumer identity and access management and master data management) and the consumer data broking industry.

Recent developments include the growth of a range of strategies. *Digital tracking and profiling* operate beyond loyalty programmes and consumer credit reporting and now identify postcodes and residential building types, as well as tracking web browsing, social media activity and smart device use. The data from all these sources can be triggered by a single interaction by the consumer. There is *large scale aggregating and linking of identifiers*, the consequence of which is the drawing together of large amounts of data on each of billions of individuals to allow inference about behaviour.[48] '*Anonymous' recognition* is the effect of dubious claims by data brokers, for example, that personal details have been anonymised when all that is often done is replacing a name with a hashtag that remains linked to the name and can be easily mined again. The ranking of individuals in terms of their past activity and potential commercial value is common, this produced by mining the wide range of characteristics about a person available through one's offline and online activity. This allows predictive assessments of future behaviour through the use of statistical correlations that generate levels of probability. As Christl notes, except for the companies, no one really knows the accuracy of these profiles, due to the lack of transparency in the process.[49]

Real time monitoring of behavioural data streams allows data companies to track every purchase that is linkable to a particular advertisement, thereby obtaining data on what triggers individual behaviour.[50] This can include tracking a person's activity across an entire day. None of this known to the citizen. *Mass personalisation* is the provision of personalised service on the large scale. For example, Facebook utilises the data it collects to make 200 trillion decisions a day to decide on content relevant to each of its users.[51] Facebook has also *experimented on people* by selecting

---

[46] W. Christl, 'Corporate Surveillance', p.5.
[47] It might be noted in fact that social media advertising is expected to become increasingly personal and then vanish due to the augmented overlaying of messaging on items in the internet of things and other fields and through sensored monitoring and prediction of wants. P. Diamandis, 'How Advertising Will Get Way More Personal – And Then Vanish Completely', Singularity Hub (12 February 2020).
[48] W. Christl, 'Corporate Surveillance', p.69.
[49] Ibid. p.72.
[50] Ibid. p.73.
[51] Ibid. p.75.

284   *Regulation and the Market*

particular suites of data, thereby nudging a noticeable increase in voter turnout, and did so without alerting the subjects of the experiment. In fact, online advertisers routinely show different advertisements to different groups to test responses for commercial purposes.[52] One of the outcomes of all this is *mission creep*. That is, how information about everyday life behaviour is being 'promoted' for the making of automated decisions about individuals in such important areas of their lives as insurance, finance, employment and law enforcement.[53]

The point here is that the data management and exploitation practices of corporations has reached into the very heart of the lives of individuals for the purposes of commercial advantage. It is a matter not only of seeking to monetarise personal data but of pre-emptive attempts to access standard resources within traditional forms of life so the data can be 'read' by algorithms. One might describe this as the algorisation of life, much of which is occurring in a non-transparent manner.

This has extended the mythological dynamic. Individual citizens are now so bound into such subjection to the corporate-technological matrix that the sense that the dominant interests of the corporations are making a *claim* to deal conclusively with constructed fears and desires is disappearing into an increasing subjection. The reality of the mythological dynamic is thereby being revealed. Perhaps there are echoes here of the repressions drawn out of various religious creeds and certain State absolutisms. That is, with current and emerging technologies as tools, the corporations of the Market are attempting to re-ascend to a near-absolute status. This is the context for the emerging, but far wider, capacities of neuroscience.

One attempt at a valid theoretical base for accounts such as is provided by Christl comes from Zuboff. The theme of her argument is that surveillance, different from capitalism, feeds on the thwarting of self-determination that emerged with neoliberalism.[54] This is characterised by the wilful disregard for the boundaries of private human experience and for the 'moral integrity of the autonomous individual', producing an extraordinary asymmetry in the division of learning.[55] Here, 'personalisation' is a camouflage for aggressive extraction from the depths of human experience and an entrée into the new world of behaviour modification where individuals are deprived of a right to the future.

Much of this is not new, although she is surely right in what she says. Where she does appear to venture onto new ground is through the notion of the rise of instrumentarian power and its materialisation as a Big Other. Here she sees the transformation of the Market into a project of total certainty but which produces claims that are unimaginable outside the digital milieu. It ultimately produces a society which is a confluent hive mind, as might be conceived by machine learning,

[52] Ibid. p.78.
[53] Ibid. p.79.
[54] S. Zuboff, *The Age of Surveillance Capitalism* (Profile Books, 2019), p.18.
[55] Ibid. p.19.

Corporate Behaviour in the Digital Age

and in which the 'freedom' of each individual machine is subordinated to the knowledge of the system as a whole. There is no sense of an individual's right to sanctuary. This is a coup from above, for her.[56]

In fact, she has unknowingly assembled – but without connecting the dots and with the deeper implications unfulfilled – various elements of what is presented in the present work as the mythological dynamic. First, she sees the significance of the post-war emergence of the neoliberalism of Hayek and his choosing the Market over democracy due to his dread of totalitarianism.[57] Second, she sees the manner in which Facebook manipulates the emotional states of online subscribers, monitoring mood shifts over a period, so that its predictive products not only can detect sentiment but can also predict how emotions are communicated at different points during any week, matching each emotional phase with appropriate messaging for the maximum probability of guaranteed outcomes.[58] Third, Zuboff conceives what she calls the Big Other, a

> ubiquitous networked institutional regime that records, modifies and commodifies everyday experience from toasters to bodies, communication to thought, all with a view to establishing new pathways to monetisation and profit. Big Other is the sovereign power of a near future that annihilates the freedom achieved by the rule of law. It is a new regime of independent and independently controlled facts that supplants the need for contracts, governance and the dynamism of a market economy. Big Other is the 21st-century incarnation of the electronic text that aspires to encompass and reveal the comprehensive immanent facts of market, social physical and biological behaviours. The institutional processes that constitute the architecture of Big Other can be imagined as the material instantiation of Hayek's 'extended order' come to life in the explicated transparency of computer-mediation.
>
> These processes reconfigure the structure of power, conformity and resistance inherited from mass society and symbolised for over half a century as Big Brother. Power can no longer be summarised by that totalitarian symbol of centralised command and control. Even the Panopticon of Bentham's design ... is prosaic compared to this new architecture.[59]

This Big Other is the mechanism through which surveillance capitalism works. One key impact of this, beyond the continuous exploitation of personal data and behaviour modification, is the reduction of the individual to the lowest common denominator – under the guise of personalisation – and so the end of sanctuary for the individual.[60]

---

[56] Ibid. pp.20–21.
[57] Ibid. pp.37, 108, 497.
[58] Ibid. pp.304–305.
[59] S. Zuboff, 'Big Other: Surveillance capitalism and the prospect of an information civilisation', *Journal of Information Technology* 30 (2015): pp.81–82.
[60] S. Zuboff, *The Age of Surveillance Capitalism*, pp.376, 477.

If Zuboff had mined the notion of emotional exploitation deeper and identified the existential concerns as an abiding condition of the constructed day-to-day fears and desires, then she would have seen not only why the mass of individuals willingly subject themselves to the technological regime – there is still a disposition beneath the apparently imposed subjection – that makes claims that optimise that subjection. She also would have seen that the Panopticon was a symptom of an emerging absolutism of the mythological State which ultimately collapsed in the totalitarianism of the mid-twentieth century, an event that brought Hayek to the fore as a champion of the absolute Market. Then she would have seen that her Big Other is nothing but the latest manifestation of the trajectory of mythologies, dating back to the Absolute Deity. In short, she saw key elements of the latest version of the Market mythological magnitude – as it fully exploits current information technologies – but did not mine them deeply enough or see the bigger picture that comes from aligning these more closely.

This approach to the application of algorithmic technology by the Market, whether by Zuboff or the full mythological account presented more broadly in the present work, could be considered by some as somewhat pessimistic. In her assessment of algorithmic regulation, Yeung does not come down on either side of this question but does provide an account which emphasises the very considerable and increasing power that such regulation has – in a world of the application of machine learning to Big Data – across the social, economic and political fields. This is especially so when decision-making is devolved to such algorithmic processes, either reactively or pre-emptively, to manage risk or deliver justice.[61] When the achievement of policy goals is the focus of such techniques, we can see both the opportunity for genuine progress and the availability of opportunistic justification. Either way, we are looking at a new form of social ordering, driven by the presumptions built into the algorithms.

Yeung raises various other problems that come with this dataism, including that it focuses on symptoms rather than problems, that it encourages the growth of State and Market activity (since there is never enough data) and that citizens become data entrepreneurs. She adds a fourth, although it would be an advantage in a non-mythological arrangement, that is, that individuals use data to take more responsibility for themselves, for example, regarding their health and personal security.[62] Regarding all these issues, however, she is right in pointing to their political implications. This point is extended by her consideration of Zuboff's surveillance capitalism. In that context she raises such legal problems with this new surveillance as its undermining of due process and the threat to fundamental rights due to the 'fragmentation' of the individual, of substantive

---

[61] K. Yeung, 'Algorithmic regulation: A critical interrogation', *Regulation & Governance* 12 (2018): pp.509, 511.
[62] Ibid. p.513.

equality,[63] problematic developments as we have seen. Just as challenging is the threat to human agency, particularly in the context of the distribution of decision-making that we looked at with the devolution of regulatory responsibility. Democratic principles are thereby at risk from the associated lack of transparency.[64]

These observations by Yeung are all affirmations of the broad point here that corporations have the capacity to take – and typically are taking – the opportunity of algorithmic technology and Big Data to explore the intimate details of individual citizen's lives with the intent of modifying behaviour for profit. This is an exploitation of the predictable disposition of individuals to accept – or even seek – subjection to, in this case, the corporate-technological regime due to claims made by the dominant interests. However, this circumstance is not an inevitability, and there is a way for corporations, as there was for the State, to reverse this increasing trend. This will include an argument that algorithms can be a contributor to individual well-being, so long as they – and the data they manipulate – are co-designed by and remain under the control of the individual citizen.

THE WAY FORWARD

One might respond to the risks and excesses of the corporation – especially those in the neoliberal frame – in two ways: first, through resistance, and there is a range of approaches within this strategy. Prominent among these in recent times has been the response to neoliberal restructuring that was imposed on the economies of Egypt, Greece and the United Kingdom and which saw large public protests around 2010. An analysis of this movement revealed, however, that understanding this response as a straightforward resistance to neoliberalism is not justified.[65] That research concluded that these protests were as much about the lack of democracy, social justice and dignity as they were about neoliberalism. The responses were more complex than the revelation of a straightforwardly anti-neoliberal sentiment directed against austerity.[66] A clearer pointer to individual resistance has been identified in Japan, where neoliberal values were rejected by corporate employees who adopted a 'silent' approach of adopting competitive subterfuge, turning inward and stronger desires for stability and security: a different kind of alienation that neoliberal typically generates.[67]

Second, given the sparse response of the State to the excesses of neoliberalism – in fact, in the argument here, the State is a promoter and captive of neoliberal

[63] Ibid. p.515.
[64] Ibid. p.516.
[65] A. Ishkanian and M. Glasius, 'Resisting neoliberalism? Movements against austerity and for democracy in Cairo, Athens and London', *Critical Social Policy* 38:3 (2018).
[66] Ibid. pp.20, 21.
[67] N. Gagne, 'Neoliberalism at work: Corporate reforms, subjectivity and post-Toyotist effect in Japan', *Anthropological Theory* (February 2019), Online First, pp.1, 22.

corporatism – consideration is being given to the prospects of a fresh reinterpretation of the human rights framework to give assurance of a multidimensional equality that extends to civil, political, economic, social and cultural rights 'beyond the neoliberal paradigm'.[68]

However, whatever the success of such strategies, for all the reasons just set out and especially including its inseparability from the mythological State, the weight of gravity rests currently with the corporate neoliberals and their practices. Therefore, nothing short of a direct approach is likely to de-mythologise such corporations. It will be useful in doing so to briefly revisit the genesis and history of the corporation. This will help to explain the preferred strategy to be outlined.

Key Factors in the History of the Corporation

Corporations were not always in the form or had the practices that they have now:

> The early modern corporation was an instinctively and inherently social entity. The global chartered trading companies of the 17th to 19th centuries, backed by the imperial ambitions of their governments, were mandated to increase trade and economic prosperity, but were simultaneously expected to provide employment, housing and medical and educational services in their trading localities.... The history of the corporation puts in clearer perspective the current criticisms against publicly traded, multinational behemoths, seen to be exploiting regulatory arbitrage and driven by short-term profit targets to the detriment of social, fiscal and environmental concerns. The long history of the corporate form demonstrates that social purpose was not incidental to the privilege of incorporation; instead, it was inseparable from the right to incorporate. It is within the power of the State to devise forms that meet this ambition.[69]

Beyond the deep social problems visited by such trading companies in the colonial phase, we can see that the connection between commercial and social purpose began to unravel in the nineteenth century, as incorporation laws were liberalised along with changes to the common law. One consequence was the barring of donations to charities as *ultra vires* or beyond their legal powers. In effect, 'the corporate legal form that had originally been designed for public benefit was thus then legally prohibited from funding charitable institutions, as it was considered against the interests of its shareholders'.[70] Although corporate endowments to private foundations continued and attempts were made to mitigate their power and promote

---

[68] G. MacNaughton, 'Equality Rights beyond Neoliberal Constraints', in *Economic and Social Rights in a Neoliberal World*, G. McNaughton and D. Frey (eds.) (Cambridge University Press, 2018), p.17.

[69] L. Davoudi et al., 'The historical role of the corporation in society', *Journal of the British Academy* 6:s1 (October 2018): p.18.

[70] Ibid. p.34.

industrial democracy,[71] as corporations grew in size they became effectively unchallenged.[72]

It has been a reawakening to the earlier history that has recently stimulated moves for corporate reform in various jurisdictions, for example, in France and the United Kingdom. The French National Assembly passed Article 61 of the government's Action Plan for Business Companies' Growth and Transformation. The purpose is to make businesses more sustainable and in line with collective social and environmental interests, thus redefining the very definition of corporate purpose.[73] Three things flow from such legislative change: corporations must consider the social and environmental stakes of their activities; corporations can define a purpose beyond profit; and corporations can adopt a new corporate form in line with these changes, including a second board to assess the success of these new purposes. In the United Kingdom, parallel reforms are on the agenda:

> [The corporation] should be reconceived as a means of commitment to the promotion of the interests of its customers and communities as well as enhancing the wealth of its investors. This requires a careful reconsideration of the purpose of the corporation and its associated forms of ownership and governance. The humanities have a vital role to play in all this.[74]

Mayer adds:

> Re-establishing trust in corporations requires a re-invention of the corporation that involves redefining the fiduciary responsibilities of its directors to uphold its stated purpose and to entrust its controlling ownership to those who are responsible for ensuring that the directors satisfy their fiduciary responsibilities.... The corporation today is inhumane. It is inhumane because we have taken humans and humanity out of it and replaced them with anonymous markets and shareholders over whom we have no control.[75]

These observations lead us back to the views about purpose-based organisations advocated by Langford and her emphasis on the value of the application of fiduciary principles to corporations outlined in Chapter 8. In that context, Langford also refers to the work of Sjafjell and Taylor,[76] who advocate the replacement of the social norm of shareholder primacy with a legal norm of value creation, by creating

---

[71] Ibid. p.38.
[72] Ibid. p.36.
[73] B. Segrestin et al., 'When the law distinguishes between the enterprise and the corporation: The case of the new French law on corporate purpose', *Journal of Business Ethics* (2020), https://doi.org/10.1007/s10551-020-04439-y.
[74] C. Mayer, 'Reinventing the corporation', *Journal of the British Academy* 4 (2016): p.53.
[75] Ibid. p.70.
[76] B. Sjafjell and M. Taylor, 'Clash of Norms: Shareholder Primacy vs Sustainable Corporate Purpose', University of Oslo Faculty of Law, Legal Studies Research Paper Series No. 2019-56.

290 *Regulation and the Market*

sustainable value within the planetary boundaries while respecting the interests of investors and other involved parties.

The question to be asked is how, as with agencies of the State, for-profit corporations can be brought to a condition where they not only recognise but actively promote the respectful self-responsibility of each citizen within a community. As have seen from the above analysis and the observations by Mayer, the present state of the corporation is far from that condition. Although it is an important step forward, it does not go far enough to say:

> Giving purpose more of a role in the corporate sphere would solve some of the issues surrounding the extent to which companies can consider and promote stakeholder interests and provide scope for companies to pursue non-financial impact-driven outcomes and social returns. For example, directors of a company whose constitution included a purpose of 'benefit to all stakeholders, including shareholders, customers and clients, business partners and advisers, employees and the community' or 'to foster the growth of (the company) for the benefit of all stakeholders' would have more leeway and mandate to consider and promote stakeholder interests than directors of a company whose purposes were 'to maximise long term shareholder value through responsibly and sustainable investing in mining and related assets' or 'to deliver long-term total shareholder returns, taking proper account of employees, customers and others with whom we do business as well as with the communities and environments in which the company operates'.[77]

There is no mention of the interests of individual citizens who lie outside the immediate sphere of interest of any such company, let alone any reference to promoting any individual's respectful self-responsibility.

NEW CORPORATE STRATEGIES TO PROMOTE RESPECTFUL SELF-RESPONSIBILITY

There are two guiding principles that need to be kept in mind as we explore ways forward. These are to be seen within the context of fiduciary principles and are the following:

- Corporate strategies are to promote value for the community generally and, specifically, the respectful self-responsibility – that is, to themself and for themself – of any citizen whose interests can reasonably be seen to intersect with those of the corporation.
- Corporations must not introduce strategies that degrade or preclude a high quality of life across the community generally nor the realisation of the respectful self-responsibility – that is, to and for oneself – of any citizens whose interests can reasonably be seen to intersect with those of the corporation.

---

[77] R. T. Langford, 'Purpose-based governance', pp.14–15.

These would be significant challenges for any corporation. However, it will be remembered that these provisions would operate within the context of Constitutional, legislative changes to give effect to the same principles and that all this would take place within a reconceived rule of law and regulation. Progressively, case law would build to provide precedents in the application of such principles. These contextual factors would mitigate the obvious challenges that the application of these principles will present for the accountability of corporate directors.

There would appear to be two avenues worthy of consideration by which corporations might be brought to this preferred condition, so long as one first accepted that corporations could adopt a 'purpose' whereby they would promote the respectful self-responsibility of the individual. The first is through the duty of care principles as they could apply to corporations. The second is the potential to exploit the fiduciary responsibilities of directors towards stakeholders, beyond shareholders.

Regarding the duty of care provisions of corporations, there is a range of provisions that characterise the director as having a duty of care to the company,[78] but these do not go to the point being recommended in the present work. We can see that a corporation can be held accountable for producing products that cause damage. In *James Hardie Industries (JHI) PLC v. White*,[79] the New Zealand Court held that, through its holding companies, JHI had a duty of care to take all reasonable steps to ensure the products did not cause damage but were fit for purpose. This avenue thereby does not progress the issue of respectful self-responsibility very far, even though it does go some way towards the second guiding principle above.

Regarding the responsibilities of directors towards stakeholders, we can start – with Jean du Plessis – by acknowledging that most Western corporate law models are still based on the shareholder primacy model where shareholders and senior corporate executives can be enriched while other stakeholder interests can be legally ignored.[80] From this, du Plessis identifies seven principles of current corporate law, to each of which he attributes mythological status. These include the following:

- Directors need to direct their duties only to profit maximisation for shareholders.
- Shareholders own the corporation.
- Directors need only consider shareholders' interests 'as one can only serve one master'.
- To be responsible to all means that one is responsible to no one.
- Directors are the agents of the shareholders as their principal.

---

[78] I. Ramsay and R. Austin, *Ford, Austin and Ramsay's Principles of Corporate Law*, 17th ed. (2017), at 8.010.3.

[79] *James Hardie Industries PLC v. White* (2018) NZCA 580.

[80] J. du Plessis, 'Myths about underlying theories and principles of corporate law and other ways of recognising the interests of all stakeholders', Annual CLTA Conference, Auckland University (4–5 February 2019); see also J. du Plessis, 'Shareholder primacy and other stakeholder interests', *Corporate Governance, Corporate Responsibility and Law* 3 (2016) C&SLJ238.

292　　　*Regulation and the Market*

- Agency cost will be too high if it is not left to the shareholders to hold directors to task.
- Directors' duty to act in the best interests of the corporation means they must act in the best interests of the shareholders as a whole ('corporators as a general body').

In a series of references to case law – or the absence or misinterpretation of it – du Plessis urges the forgoing of each of these myths. Such commentary can be seen as an ideological clearing of the decks, but the question remains regarding the next step on the way forward. We might see a further move in the direction preferred here by reading the value of s.181 of the Australian Corporations Act (2001) to mean that a director must act in good faith in the best interests of the corporation as a whole – as a separate legal entity – and for a proper purpose.

Such a reading would include that the corporation had interests including but also other than those of shareholders. Thus, as du Plessis puts it, and as should be seen as consistent with fiduciary principles:

> Directors, in exercising their powers and discharging their duties under Section 181 (1) (a), can have regard to the interests of any group, groups, person, or persons as long as the consequences of the actions taken, are taken in good faith, judged in context of the particular actions taken, and are in the best interests of the corporation as a separate legal entity.[81]

THE NEED TO GO FURTHER

Yet none of this brings us to the point where the corporation is not only not preventing but is actively promoting these capacities of the individual, in the sense that has been described in the present work. That is, citizens would have responsibilities to be respectful of others and to develop their self-responsibility. The State and the Market – reimagined in the manner outlined here – would need to take the initiative with each citizen in this regard and the citizen would need to accept that initiative in partnership across a range of fields (e.g., security, health, education, skills development and so on), including technologically, but beyond that have no purchase on the life of the respectful, self-responsible citizen.

What this means is that the corporation must be managed in line with these same principles, which is to say that fiduciary principles need to be redefined. Directors would no longer operate merely in the interests of the corporation, employees,

---

[81] J. du Plessis, 'The Purpose of the Corporation Redefined: Recent Developments in Australia and the US', Ross Parsons Corporate Lecture, Sydney Law School, University of Sydney (2 March 2020), www.youtube.com/watch?v=if91SzqT71I&feature=youtu.be; see also I. Esser and J. du Plessis, 'The stakeholder debate and director's fiduciary duties', *SA Mercantile Law Journal* 19:3 (2007).

investors, shareholders and the community. The notion of community needs to be broken down to mean the interests of all citizens taken individually. Wherever someone's interests can reasonably be said to intersect with the corporate interests – especially given the 'promotional' responsibilities of the reimagined corporation – then the focus needs to be on the person's respectful self-responsible interests.

This would require the extension and reimagining of not only the notion of purpose as described by Langford but also the notion of fiduciary principles, which for her encloses the notion of purpose-based governance.[82]

Roadblocks to Further Progress

There are, of course, roadblocks to making further progress in this regard. For example, regarding fiduciary duties, in Australia – unlike Canada – there has been a particularly restrictive interpretation given to the scope of such duties, which in essence are tied to the preclusion of conflict of interest and profit taking by fiduciaries. The source of this restrictiveness is the difficulties created by an expansive interpretation of such duties as it relates to the laws of contract, agency and trusts.[83] Further, the notion of stakeholderism – according to which corporate leaders should give weight not only to the interests of shareholders but also to those of all other corporate constituencies (including employees, customers, suppliers and the environment) has come under criticism as it would not actually benefit stakeholders share.[84] Bebchuk and Tallarita, commenting on the US jurisdiction, canvas reasons why stakeholderism is an 'illusion': director and CEO remuneration aligns their interests with those of shareholders rather than with those of stakeholders,[85] and there is little evidence that, in the past, directors have used their discretion to protect stakeholders – for example, in the acquisition of companies – where they have done so for shareholders. They go further to claim that stakeholderism would actually be detrimental to economic performance and society, primarily because history shows that it would insulate corporate leaders through the absence of such means to ensure accountability as voting rights, and because it would impede, limit and delay policy reforms due to diverted resources and increased reliance on corporate self-regulation.[86]

Others see difficulties in such issues as accountability and tension between multiple purposes. For example, in Australia, the authors of the federal

---

[82] R. T. Langford, 'Purpose-based governance', p.1.

[83] R. T. Langford, 'High Court of Australia on Fiduciary Theory', in *Fiduciary Duty and the Atmospheric Trust* C. Sampford, K. Coghil and T. Smith (eds.) (Taylor and Francis, 2016), p.203.

[84] L. Bebchuk and R. Tallarita, 'The Illusory Promise of Stakeholder Governance', Harvard Law School Forum on Corporate Governance (posted 2 March 2020).

[85] Ibid. p.30.

[86] Ibid. p.53.

government's Corporations and Market Advisory Committee (CAMAC) Report noted that the Company Directors' Report on the Social and Fiduciary Duties and Obligations of Company Directors, by the Senate Standing Committee on Legal and Constitutional Affairs, opposed any move to introduce legislation obliging directors to have regard to the interests of groups other than shareholders in making decisions. It considered that a mandatory provision could place directors beyond the control of shareholders without enhancing the rights of other parties. It stated:

> To impose a duty to act fairly between entities as diverse as creditors, employees, consumers, the environment, is to impose a broad and potentially complex range of obligations on directors. Such a duty could be vague... Without a legally-ordered set of priorities between the various groups, it would be difficult for any claim by one group to be upheld, as the directors' action could probably be characterised as being in the interest of some other group or groups. The question of who could enforce the various duties in the courts would also be difficult.[87]

In response, various arguments have been put to the effect that there are ways forward, even within the current constitutional-legislative frame, whereby directors can be seen properly to take up responsibilities to others rather than shareholders alone. Blair and Stout argue for director autonomy:

> Careful analysis consequently highlights the danger associated with a simplistic rhetoric of shareholder primacy that treats the interests of 'the shareholders' as synonymous with the interests of 'the firm'. Nine times out of ten, corporate policies that serve the shareholders' interest may serve the interests of other corporate constituents as well. It is important, however, for corporate directors to recognise and respond to situations where this is not the case. Of course, this subtlety comes with a cost. The mediating board model replaces an easily measurable goal (raise the price of the firm's shares) with one that is far more complex and difficult for outsiders to observe (maximise the value of the firm as a whole). In the process it emphasises the importance of ensuring that mediating directors operate in an environment where both the economic and social variables encourage them to behave trustworthily.[88]

This argument promotes the idea that the corporations, through the directors, should have regard for social factors as a means to maximise the value of the firm. In the argument here, the respectful self-responsibility of individual citizens is such a social factor, and it adds value to the firm to promote this, since individuals with such characteristics strengthen the community due to their refusal either to submit to exploitation by others or to exploit others in the manner that, as we have seen, many corporations currently do.

---

[87] 'The Social Responsibility of Corporations', Report of the Corporations and Markets Advisory Committee of the Australian Government (December 2006), p.98.

[88] M. Blair and L. Stout, 'Director Accountability and the Mediating Role of the Corporate Board', Cornell Law Faculty Publications Paper 759 (2001), p.446.

The Need to Go Further

In this regard, Langford refers to developments which embed community interest in corporate purpose, for example, the UK Companies (Audit, Investigation and Community Enterprises) Act which in 2004 introduced community interest companies which are subject to a community interest test.[89] Further, s.172 (2) of the Australian Companies Act 2006 allows companies to adopt a purpose other than the benefit of its members, thereby effectively enabling a public benefit purpose. As she states, this raises the issue of multiple purposes and the consequential problems for directors' duties but points to case law which, in such circumstances, requires directors to pursue a balancing of such purposes.

This in turn requires a revitalisation of directors' duties, which is allowable under current Australian corporation law. For Langford, the core duties traditionally imposed on directors of for-profit companies are the duty of care, skill and diligence; the duty to act in good faith in the interests of the company (including dealing with the dual masters of purpose and profit); the duty to act for proper purpose; and duties to avoid unauthorised conflicts and profits.[90] Langford sees no inherent conflict between these and the notion of purpose-based for-profit corporations. In fact, the introduction of purpose would for her provide the opportunity for the revitalisation of both corporations and the duties of their directors.

This line of thinking, as we have seen, is affirmed by du Plessis, but he extends the implications of the above arguments to assert that principles of corporate social responsibility should be aligned with contemporary community expectations and, further, that those principles be enforceable as a right that would be included in directors' social duties.[91] This would be aided by an extension of non-financial reporting requirements.[92]

The point of all this is that the roadblocks may properly be seen as the products of established corporation theory and practice, emphasising a range of threats to corporate success should the various changes outlined here be introduced. In response we may say that the protective function that the narrow application of fiduciary duties plays for corporations does not preclude fiduciary principles being used as a guide to a reimagining of the corporation. We may also say that the threats and alleged illusory nature of stakeholderism as presented are a very narrow corporate defensive strategy to deal with issues that can be the basis of sensible, 'good faith' corporate management. Further, regarding multiple purposes, there is no reason why shareholders, investors and employees cannot be invited to align with a corporate purpose designed to focus on the respectful self-responsible interests of individuals with whom corporate activity intersects. There need be no irresolvable issue of accountability as a result.

---

[89] R. T. Langford, 'Use of the corporate form for public benefit – Revitalisation of Australian corporate law', *University of New South Wales Law Journal* 43:3 (2020): p.7.
[90] Ibid. p.10.
[91] J. du Plessis, 'Corporate social responsibility and contemporary community expectations', *Company and Securities Law Journal* 35:30 (2017): pp.45–46.
[92] J. du Plessis, 'Corporate governance, corporate responsibility and law', *Company and Securities Law Journal* 69 (2016): p.74.

296 Regulation and the Market

OUTLINE OF A NON-MYTHOLOGICAL CORPORATION

We can progress the idea of such a corporation by looking at certain key features of which it would be comprised. Prominent among these would be the optimal conditions for consumer relations, broadly defined. After looking back briefly to the contextual issues, we shall look briefly at several fields, that of competition theory, consumer protection, data management and employee relations.

Broad Context

In the context of the two principles listed above, the first point is that such a corporation would exist within the reimagined frame of a non-mythological regulation, Constitutional and legislative provision and the reimagined rule of law. This would be supplemented by the adoption of the strategies just outlined, that is, by the application of fiduciary principles, purpose-based governance, stakeholder primacy and community responsibility principles and reporting.

That is, corporations would have a frame within which the forgoing of the mythological strategies could be pursued, those strategies that cause them to make mythological claims to promote conditions of subjection. Such conditions include where the decisions by individuals are increasingly forgone to corporations that have applied such tactics as data theft, data mining, profiling, predictive analytics and individualised nudge-marketing.

Second, the broad, well-established trend of regulatory transfer from State to the Market would need to be – preferably – reversed or at least initially subject to far more extensive reporting requirements regarding their promotion of existential conditions for respectful individual development. This would not allow a means of surveillance of citizens except regarding serious security matters.

Competition

The guiding issue here regarding competition law is the relationship between an economic approach and a social market approach, that is, how to ensure that market interests retain a close focus on societal concerns. In a world dominated by neoliberal economic theory, there has been increasing tension between the two, with the former now well established as ascendant. This has been a matter of increasing significance, for example, within the European Union, where there are calls for a recalibration of competition law so that the market itself would provide a well-designed balancing of market interests and societal interests.[93]

---

[93] A. Gerbrandy, 'Rethinking competition law within the European Economic Constitution', *Journal of Common Market Studies* 57:1 (2019): p.138; J. Mulder, '(Re)conceptualising a social market economy for the EU internal market', *Utrecht Law Review* 15:2 (2019): p.27.

Such interests include sustainable corporate operations, improved worker conditions, the reduction of social exclusion, the pursuit of a 'living wage', environmental protection and the wide proliferation of 'minimum standards'.[94] All these would lie in the context of a 'circular' economy, that is, one that is based more on cooperation between economic agents, that holds a long-term view on economic relations and that acts on a notion of corporate responsibility that is wider than economic profit.[95] Such a notion is very much in tension with a European economic model still too heavily influenced by the ordo-liberal economic theory from which it emerged.[96] This recalibration is a strategy that would enable – but not fulfil – the pursuit of non-mythological practices by corporate directors.

Consumer Protection

Consumer protection has been a highly active field. A range of statutes has been introduced over time to protect the consumer against shoddy or exploitative or dangerous practices and goods. These were in response – especially between 1965 and 1975 – to a new consumer environment which included, for example, the increasing distance and increasingly impersonal relationship between buyer and seller, more 'sophistication' of marketing techniques, pre-packaging of goods making them difficult to assess, the widespread marketing of consumer credit, conflicts of interest between business practices and consumer needs, poor access to litigation and redress, and, importantly, the growth of multinational corporations and monopolies which placed the consumer at a disadvantage.[97] All this took place in the context of a growing international consumer movement, for example, with the formation in 1960 of the International Organisation of Consumers' Unions that in 1995 became the Consumers International as it spread across the globe. Along the way, despite opposition from the United States, the Guidelines for Consumer Protection were adopted by the United Nations in 1985.

However, in the late 1980s, government priorities moved away from such regulation of economic development as neoliberal economic rationalism came to dominate. Government consumer affairs agencies were integrated into industry portfolios where they became of secondary importance. It was only when the poor consumer-related practice of many corporations emerged through deregulation, self-regulation and other measures that governments were forced to take up again the interests of consumers. There had been the emergence of incomprehensible contract terms, the prohibitively expensive cost of court action and the emergence of extra-regulatory practices, for example, in the financial services sector.[98]

---

[94] J. Mulder, '(Re)conceptualising a social market economy', p.23.
[95] A. Gerbrandy, 'Rethinking competition law', p.132.
[96] Ibid. p.129.
[97] John T. Wood, 'Consumer Protection: A Case of Successful Regulation', in *Regulation Theory – Foundations and Applications*, pp.641–642.
[98] Ibid. pp. 646, 648.

298   *Regulation and the Market*

The lesson here is that it is an unreliable method of ensuring fairness to rely on the goodwill of corporations the purpose of which is to satisfy shareholders' search for profit. The adoption of purpose-based corporate governance operating on fiduciary principles would begin to reverse this. But that, as has been argued, is only the first step towards the reimagining of corporations that would have as their purpose the protection and promotion of the interests of any respectfully self-responsible citizen with whom their corporate practices intersect.

Corporate Use of Personal Data

There is an ever-increasing range of applications and uses of personal data, some personally and socially beneficial but many that are certainly are not so. In canvassing how corporations should deal with personal data, it might be remembered that the proposal outlined in Chapter 6 is based on a combination of rules: first, that respect for other self-responsible individuals and the obligation to pursue one's own self-responsibility requires individuals to share certain data with authorised State or other agencies, albeit on a confidential basis. This will include the right of security agencies to intercept data when, having satisfied an independent judicial officer, there is reason to believe that a security or serious criminal offence is planned or is being committed. It will also include the need to share certain health data, should one have acquired or be at risk of acquiring a communicable disease, and data concerning programme participation which is relevant to an awareness of existential issues and for the acquisition of skills that enhance self-responsibility.

Second, beyond that, personal data is to be under the systematic control – both in the first instance and regarding 'downstream' use – of the individual and may be protected through any methods that the individual determines, short of denying access to those bodies just identified. This data includes, for example, geographic location, online search activities, financial transactions and social media activity. Within that category of protection, although subject to both sets of rules, will lie any external device through which the subject may be engaging other data sources, including those that would be the means of ultimate direct neural upload or download. The co-development by each citizen of their own personal data and algorithms to undertake these roles and functions would be a key part of this broad strategy. In the context of these principles we can consider various issues that remain controversial in the use of data by corporations.

Preferred Manner of Data Use by Corporations

Pre-eminent among such issues are those brought to light by the application of corporate algorithms to Big Data. This is important due to concerns that such algorithms are – in the argument here – predisposed not only to preferred outcomes but to reconstructions of reality that give priority to corporate interests. Various

Outline of a Non-mythological Corporation

proposals are being considered to rectify the first of these by an algorithmic redesign that delivers considerably more fairness in this process.[99] There is no sign of any recognition of the latter.

Regarding issues of privacy, we have seen in Chapter 3 that current approaches include either a Constitutional/rights or a social context approach. Both of these were considered as mythological. Therefore, we should not look to them to reverse the decontextualization that occurs through the application of algorithms to individual or Big Data.[100] Instead, we should see decontextualization as a means of mythologically subjectifying the individual, so any application of algorithms to these data fields – not at all invaluable in itself[101] – must be based on the ownership of personal data by the individual and that no outcome of such algorithmic analysis – in policy development or in application – can be seen as valid or applied to individuals without exposition and consent of the citizen at the points of both collection and reuse. This particular provisionality will always apply. These provisions are only to be left to Market agencies if they have demonstrated the embedding of fiduciary purpose–based principles that are 'existential'. More generally, Big Data mining needs to be reversed to serve the interests of the respectful self-responsible individual, who should be provided with the tools to explore the data sets authorised by individuals and agencies to develop strategies each for their own self-enhancement and enjoyment.

The issue of surveillance has already been referred to, but a particular application of that is the growing trend to establishing *smart cities*, with continuous monitoring of functions, public spaces and the citizens. These are promoted as the optimal means to manage an ever-increasing urbanisation and the provision of wider ranges of choice for individual behaviour.[102] Clearly, one has to see this development as a derivative of Bentham's Panopticon, with its purpose of constant surveillance of inmates within a prison from a single central point, such that the inmates control themselves due to the belief that they are under such constant surveillance, whether or not they are. The argument against this is that dystopic concerns will be overcome by progressive trust through access to de-identified (or anonymised) data. Irrespective of the shaky claim that re-identification of data can be prevented in an age which emphasises security and data mining, the basic principle must be that the centre of gravity will still lie with the data collectors, especially in a time of Big Data – and the biases and transferability of ownership of that – which must be

---

[99] M. MacCarthy, 'Standards of fairness or disparate impact assessment of Big Data algorithms', *Cumberland Law Review* 48:102 (2018): p.143.

[100] M. MacCarthy, 'Privacy policy and contextual harm', *I/S: A Journal of Law and Policy for the Information Society* 13:400 (2017).

[101] S. Dash, 'Big data in healthcare: Management, analysis and future prospects', *Journal of Big Data* 6:54 (2019): pp.23–25.

[102] K. Finch and O. Tene, 'Welcome to the Metropticon: Protecting privacy in a hyperconnected town', *Fordham Urban Law Journal* 41:5 (2016): article 4, pp.1605–1617.

consistently resisted. There is a balance issue here, of course, that in protecting the individual we do not deny the rights imperative. This balance could be explored through the use of anonymised individuality, say, in vehicular or pedestrian traffic flow where an anonymised 'unit' could take the place of any identified citizen.

A non-mythological approach would emphasise data control by the individual at the point of collection, which would allow the use of an effective 'off switch' or 'do not track' applications, and by access to explicability and challengeability of data. In this context, profiling of individuals without express consent would be anathema. This should not extend to a 'right to be forgotten', as respectful self-responsibility would require the confidential sharing of selected data, as described in Chapter 6. On a positive note, genuinely anonymous data and data assembled from authorising individuals would be explorable by existentially conditioned individuals for the means to enhance their existence in their own terms, from the triviality of traffic flow to the crucially important aspects of skills development.

Given the argument here that *personal data ownership by the citizen* – along with data sharing and data production – has a key role in the resistance to corporate data predation and thereby in the promotion of respectful existential living, it is appropriate to look at the European Union's General Data Protection Regulation (GDPR) which operates under the umbrella of fair information practices (FIPs). Key elements of this regulation, which was introduced in 2018, include provisions for consumers to withdraw consent (Article 7) and the right to be forgotten (Article 17). It includes provision for data protection by design and by default (Article 25) and the recording of all processing activities (Article 30). In principle, therefore, it regulates and enables enforcement of the right of each citizen to high-quality access, rectification, deletion and objection within data collection and processing and so appears to be a significant step forward in the management of their personal data by citizens and by data service providers and processors.[103] The shortcoming of all this, valuable though it is regarding the broad argument herein in that it 'levels the playing field' considerably, is that it does not place responsibility on corporations to actively promote the self-responsibility of the citizen by searching for data – at the behest of the citizen – that can promote that status. The GDPR constrains but does not sufficiently promote.

By way of addendum to this issue, it might be noted that such processes as data collection, credit scoring, personal profiling and algorithmic design are not inherently the source of subjection. They are so only when left in the hands of corporations – or States – the purposes of which are mythological. Placed fully under the control of the respectful self-responsible individual, they can be a series of means by which the success of the pursuit of such non-mythological outcomes can be assessed.

---

[103] C. Hoofnagle et al., 'The European Data Protection regulation: What it is and what it means', *Information and Communications Technology Law* 28:1 (2019): pp.67–69.

Employee Relations

One final but eminently important element in the reimagining of the corporation as purposive and 'existential' is that of employee relations. Historically, in what has been called the industrial era – stretching from the mid-eighteenth century up to the late 1970s – economic production was generated through vertically organised corporations supported by a stable workforce. During this time, workers unionised to pursue better wages and conditions at a time when jobs were long-term. However, from the late 1970s – as neoliberal economics and globalisation began to take hold – the workplace saw the applications of information technology, with the consequence that corporations began to be organised horizontally, work began to be outsourced to subcontractors[104] spread far and wide, and production was coordinated by means of such technology. The result was that workers' share of GDP reduced into a 'wage gap' which also saw the share paid to investors, shareholders and management rise, often significantly.[105]

Further, this restructuring has blurred the lines between employer and employee, thereby leading to disputes as to the status of subcontractors, and so making the notion of collective bargaining far more difficult, to the advantage of investors and shareholders:

> The definition of an appropriate bargaining unit has lost meaning not only because it is based on outdated definitions of who is an employer and who is an employee, but also because it assumes a relationship among employees in one or more physical locations that may not be true in the 'workplace of the new information technology', although initiatives are being pursued under the National Labour Relations Act to attempt to address these issues.[106]

There are roadblocks to this, of course, comprising the constant pursuit of management to seek flexibility in both production and employment, so resisting job security and a range of so-called employment benefits. Much of this is complemented by arguments that the impact of technology on job losses will be moderate, as new jobs will emerge. Others make a very different point, citing driverless vehicles, robotised construction and further widening of the wage gap, making many products unaffordable to a larger group. Even skilled technology and other professional workers will

---

[104] K. Dau-Schmidt, 'Trade, Commerce and Employment – The Evolution of the Form and Regulation of the Employment Relationship in Response to the New Information Technology', in *Oxford Handbook of Law, Regulation and Technology*, p.1056; also K. Dau-Schmidt, 'The impact of emerging information technologies on the employment relationship: New gigs for labor and employment law', *University of Chicago Legal Forum* 2017 (2018): article 4; for a perspective of the emergence and applications of AI in the corporate sector, none of which has a first focus on the individual citizen, see D. Faggella, 'The Changing Landscape of AI Priorities for Business Leaders', *Emerj AI Research* home page.

[105] T. Picketty, *Capital in the Twenty-First Century* (Belknap, 2014), p.356.

[106] K. Dau-Schmidt, 'Trade, Commerce and Employment', pp.1062–1063.

302 *Regulation and the Market*

be increasingly replaced by advances in the self-learning characteristic of machine learning algorithms.

At one level, all this points to a need for subsidised re-education, health insurance and income insurance for support during retraining and after retirement. But these will not come from collective bargaining. A different paradigm is needed. Undoubtedly, the confluence of neoliberal economics, globalisation and information technology (especially now in the form of machine learning AI) has allowed capital to undertake a restructuring of the economy without any serious consideration of the needs of labour, in fact, to seek to replace it. But at another level, a call for an initiative to address these three elements – education, health and retirement[107] – should not just be seen in the context of the impact of the use of technology by corporations. It can be placed in the much wider context of the need to re-purpose corporations under both fiduciary principles to promote personal, non-mythological existence which could see citizens repeatedly reskilled for independent living.

Undertaking the reforms we have been considering would also place the Market and the State within a new frame of regulatory law and practice so that each citizen is prepared for the arrival and spread of the new neuroscience, a spread the advantages of which we should not resist. This will mean the abandonment of current notions of privacy and the development of a notion of that which will – within a new ethics that drives this new sense of regulation – embrace neuroscience so each citizen, rather than be subject to the deep intrusion allowed by the unchecked emergence of that algorithmic neuroscience, can develop an authentic, enhanced sense of themselves on their own terms.

SUMMARY OF PART II

Searching for a means to support self-responsibility, we examined Responsive Regulation and argued that, as a way to change human behaviour, its co-operative approach obscured its reliance on the intrusiveness of the methods of the Republican State, so denying self-responsibility. This has been exaggerated by the dispersal of the normalising regulatory regime across the social fabric, whereby it reflects the claims of the dominant interests of the mythological magnitudes of Deity, State and Market. The search for infrastructural means to promote self-responsibility is better sought in a rule of law and in State and Market forms which eschew the spread of digital exploitation and instead convert those magnitudes to a purpose which prioritises the fiduciary interests of each citizen.

---

[107] T. Piketty, *Capital in the Twenty-First Century*, p. 481.

Bibliography

Barney, W. L. (ed.). *A Companion to 19th-Century America*. Blackwell, 2006.

Blumenberg, H. *The Legitimacy of the Modern Age*. MIT Press, 1995.

Blumenberg, H. *Work on Myth*. MIT Press, 1985.

Braithwaite, J. 'Fasken Lecture – The essence of responsive regulation'. *University of British Columbia Law Review* 44:3 (2001).

Braithwaite, J. 'Types of Responsiveness', in *Regulation Theory – Foundations and Applications*, P. Drahos (ed.). Australian National University Press, 2017.

Braithwaite, J. and Y. Zhang. 'Persia to China: the Silk Road of restorative justice', *Asian Journal of Criminology* 12:1 (2017): 23–38.

The British Academy. *Reforming Business for the 21st Century: A Framework for the Future of the Corporation* (2018) (published online)

Brownsword, R., Scotford, E., and Yeung, K. *Oxford Handbook of Law, Regulation and Technology*. Oxford University Press, 2017.

Christl, W. 'Corporate Surveillance in Everyday Life – How Companies Collect, Combine, Analyse, Trade and Use Personal Data on Billions'. Report by Cracked Labs (Institute for Critical Digital Culture), Vienna, June 2017.

Christian, B. and Griffiths, T. *Algorithms to Live By*. Henry Holt, 2016.

Dau-Schmidt, K. 'The impact of emerging information technologies on the employment relationship: New gigs for labor and employment law'. *University of Chicago Legal Forum* 2017: Article 4 (2018).

Descartes, R. *Discourse on Method and Related Writings*. Penguin, 2003.

Descartes, R. *Meditations on First Philosophy*. Oxford University Press, 2008.

Domingos, P. *The Master Algorithm*. Allen Lane, 2015.

Drahos, P. (ed.). *Regulation Theory – Foundations and Applications*. Australian National University Press, 2017.

Dunn, J. *The Political Thought of John Locke*. Cambridge University Press, 1995.

du Plessis, J. 'Corporate social responsibility and contemporary community expectations'. *C&SLJ* 35:30 (2017).

du Plessis, J. 'Myths about Underlying Theories and Principles of Corporate Law and Other Ways of Recognising the Interests of All Stakeholders', Annual CLTA Conference, Auckland University (4–5 February 2019).

du Plessis, J. 'The Purpose of the Corporation Redefined: Recent Developments in Australia and the US', Ross Parsons Corporate Lecture, Sydney Law School, University of Sydney (2 March 2020).

du Plessis, J. 'Shareholder primacy and other stakeholder interests'. *Corporate Governance, Corporate Responsibility and Law C&SLJ* 3:238 (2016).

Elias, N. *The Civilising Process*. Blackwell, 2003.

Floridi, L. 'The Ethics of Algorithms: Mapping the Debate'. *Big Data and Society* (July–December 2016).

Floridi, L. *The Ethics of Information*. Oxford University Press, 2015.

Floridi, L. 'Four for a theory of informational privacy'. *Ethics and Information Technology* 8:3 (2006).

Floridi, L. 'The logic of design as a conceptual logic of information'. *Minds and Machines* 27:3 (2017).

Floridi, L. 'What the near future of artificial intelligence could be'. *Philosophy and Technology* 32 (2019).

Floridi, L. and Cowls, J. 'A unified framework of five principles for AI in society'. *Harvard Data Science Review*, no. 1 (2019).

Floridi, L., Cowls, J., Beltrametti, M., and Chatila, R. 'An Ethical Framework for a Good AI Society: Opportunities, Risks, Principles and Recommendations'. *ResearchGate* (November 2018).

Foucault, M. *The Birth of Biopolitics*. Palgrave Macmillan, 2008.

Foucault, M. *Discipline and Punish*. Vintage, 1979.

Foucault, M. *Governmentality*. In *The Foucault Effect*, G. Burchell, C. Gordon and P. Miller (eds.). Harvester, 1991.

Foucault, M. *Security, Territory, Population*. Palgrave Macmillan, 2007.

Fox-Decent, E. 'Trust and Authority', in *Fiduciaries and Trust – Ethics, Politics, Economics and Law*, P. Miller and M. Harding (eds.). Cambridge University Press, 2020.

Francis, L. and Francis, J. *Privacy – What Everyone Needs to Know*. Oxford University Press, 2017.

Gaukroger, S. *The Emergence of a Scientific Culture*. Oxford University Press, 2006.

Goertzel, B. and T. Goertzel (eds.). *The End of the Beginning – Life, Society and Economy on the Brink of the Singularity*. Humanity+ Press, 2015.

Grant, D. *The Mythological State and Its Empire*. Routledge, 2009.

Grant, D. *Prisons – The Continuing Crisis*. Federation Press, 1992.

Grant, D. and Bennett Moses, L. *Technology and the Trajectory of Myth*. Edward Elgar, 2017.

Hahn, S. *Lord Have Mercy – The Healing Power of Confession*. Darton, Longman and Todd, 2017.

Harding, M. 'Contracts, Fiduciary Relationships and Trust', in *Fiduciaries and Trust – Ethics, Politics, Economics and Law*, P. Miller and M. Harding (eds.). Cambridge University Press, 2020.

Harding, M. 'Responding to trust', *Ratio Juris* 24:1 (2011).

Hayek, F. A. *Law, Legislation and Liberty*. Routledge, 1982.

Heidegger, M. *Being and Time*. Blackwell, 1997.

Heidegger, M. *The Question Concerning Technology and Other Essays*. Harper, 1977.

Hobbes, T. *Leviathan*. Cambridge University Press, 1991.

Hunter, I. *Rival Enlightenments*. Cambridge University Press, 2006.

Institute of Electronic and Electrical Engineers. *Ethically Aligned Design*, first edition (published online).

Kant, I. *Critique of Pure Reason*. Palgrave Macmillan, 2007.

Kant, I. *Practical Philosophy*. Cambridge University Press, 1996.

Kenyon, A. and Richardson, M. *New Dimensions in Privacy Law*. Cambridge University Press, 2010.

Bibliography

Kierkegaard, S. *Fear and Trembling*. Cambridge University Press, 2006.

Krygier, M. 'Conservative-liberal-socialism'. *Symposium* 11:1 (2002).

Krygier, M. 'The rule of law: Pasts, presents and two possible futures'. *Annual Review of Law and Social Science* 12 (2016): 199–229.

Krygier, M. 'Too Much Information', in *Cosmopolitan Jurisprudence: Essays in Memory of H. Patrick Glenn*, Helge Dedek (ed.). Cambridge University Press, American Society of Comparative Law Series, forthcoming 2020.'

Krygier, M. 'What's the point of the rule of law?' *Buffalo Law Review* 67:3 (2019).

Langford, R. Teele 'Purpose-based governance: A new paradigm'. *University of New South Wales Law Journal* 42 (2020).

Lilti, A. *The Invention of Celebrity*. Polity, 2017.

Locke, J. *Two Treatises of Government*. Cambridge University Press, 2003.

Luther, M. *Here I Stand*. Hendricksen, 2011.

Madary, M. and Metzinger, T. 'Real virtuality: A code of ethical conduct. Recommendations for the good scientific practice and the consumers of VR-technology'. *Frontiers in Robotics and AI* (2016). doi: 10.3389/frobt.2016.00003.

Matthew, C. *The Nineteenth Century – The British Isles 1815–1901*. Oxford University Press, 2000.

Metzinger, T. *Being No One – The Self-Model of Subjectivity*. MIT Press, 2004.

Mill, J. S. *On Liberty*. Pelican, 1974.

Miller, P. 'Political (Dis)trust and Fiduciary Government', in *Fiduciaries and Trust – Ethics, Politics, Economics and Law*, P. Miller and M. Harding (eds.). Cambridge University Press, 2020.

Minsky, M. *The Emotion Machine*. Simon and Schuster, 2006.

Montesquieu, Charles-Louis de Secondat, Baron de la Brede et de. *The Spirit of the Laws*. Cambridge University Press, 2002.

Moore, Adam D. 'Privacy, Neuroscience and Neuro-surveillance'. January 2020, ResearchGate.

Moore, Adam D. *New Oxford Annotated Bible*. New Standard Version with The Apocrypha. Oxford University Press, 1950.

Nilsson, N. *The Quest for Artificial Intelligence*. Cambridge University Press, 2010.

Nissenbaum, H. *Privacy in Context: Technology, Policy and the Integrity of Social Life*. Stanford University Press, 2010.

Ockham, W. *Quodlibetal Questions*, trans. A. J. Freddoso and E. Kelley, 2 vols. Yale University Press, 1991.

Pettit, P. *Republicanism*. Oxford University Press, 1997.

Postema, G. 'Trust, Distrust, and the Rule of Law', in *Fiduciaries and Trust – Ethics, Politics, Economics and Law*, P. Miller and M. Harding (eds.). Cambridge University Press, 2020.

Richardson, M. *The Right to Privacy*. Cambridge University Press, 2017.

Rousseau, J.-J. *The Social Contract and Other Later Political Writings*. Cambridge University Press, 2003.

Simmel, G. *Georg Simmel: On Individuality and Social Forms: Selected Writings*, D. Levine (ed.). University of Chicago Press, 1971.

Simmel, G. 'The Secret and the Secret Society', in *The Sociology of George Simmel*, K. Wolff (ed.). Free Press, 1950.

Theunissen, M. *Kierkegaard's Concept of Despair*. Princeton University Press, 2005.

Trentmann, F. *Empire of Things*. Penguin, 2017.

van Krieken, R. *Norbert Elias*. Routledge, 1998.

306   *Bibliography*

Yeung, K. 'Algorithmic regulation: A critical interrogation'. *Regulation & Governance* 12 (2018).

Waldman, A. 'Privacy as trust: Sharing personal information in a networked world'. *University of Miami Law Review* 69:559 (2015).

Waldron, J. 'How law protects dignity'. *The Cambridge Law Journal* 71:1 (2012).

Waldron, J. 'The Rule of Law and the Importance of Procedure', in *Getting to the Rule of Law*, J. Fleming (ed.). New York University Press, 2011.

Zuboff, S. *The Age of Surveillance Capitalism*. Profile Books, 2019.

Index

Absolute Deity, 9, 96–104, 286
Absolute Market, 9, 105–128
Absolute Self, 2, 5, 13, 19, 50, 56, 70, 124, 128, 181, 186, 244
  in neoliberalism, 124
  in pursuit of technology, 4
  technology and, 8–9, 91
Absolute State, 9, 104–117, 202
Absolute Technology, 128–137
absolutism of existential reality, 7, 71–72
accountability, in modern State, 245–250
Action Plan for Business Companies' Growth and Transformation (France), 18
agencies of the State, 12, 18
agency, Foucault on, 116
algocracy, risk of, 47
algorithmic determinism, 202–206
algorithmic regulation, 205–206
algorithmic technology, 25
  application of, 42–45
  in brain research, 38–40
  constructivism, 46–51
  corporate use of, 298–301
  ethical issues, 139–140
  in neuroscience, 41–42
  normalisation and, 129–134
  use by corporations, 281–282
algorithms, seeing ourselves as, 5
alienation, 122
alternative frame for normalisation, 92–95
American Medical Association, 131
anatomy, teleology and, 222–224
Angel Fraley v. *Facebook*, 190
anonymous recognition, 283
applications of new privacy, 187–195
arbitrary power, 221, 223, 228, 273

artificial general intelligence, 12, 30, 181, 261
artificial intelligence, 25–28
  embedding in, 178–179
  friendliness of, 261–262
  future of, 138–139, 178
augmented reality, 67–68
Australian Corporations Act, s. 00181, 233
authentic existence, Heidegger on, 128–129
Author of a Blog v. *Times Newspapers*, 190
automatic justice, 268

barrier between oneself and the world, 6
Bayesian decision theory, 39
BCI. *See* brain–computer interface
Becker, Gary, 120
behavioural data, 283
Bender, A., 49
Bentham, Jeremy, Panopticon, 93, 134–135, 204
Berry, Jasmine, 60
bidirectional interfaces, brain function, 34–36
Big Data, 172, 258, 298–301
  large-scale aggregating and linking of identifiers, 283
  personal information and, 75
Big Other, 284
Bill of Rights (US), 218
biopower, regulation as, 202–206
black box problem. *See* interpretability
Blumenberg, Hans, 244
body, technologies of, 161–163
body swapping, 63
Bonnet c. Societe Olibet (1882), 77
bourgeoisie
  consumption by, 131
  and culture, 263
  and the emergence of the State, 109

308 Index

bourgeoisie (cont.)
  habitus, 8
  individualism, 83
  normality, 9
  privacy theory and, 74
  psychological space, 109
  sense of privacy, 80, 173–174
  on sex, 104
  significance of, 135–136
  use of credit by, 125–127
brain–body connection, 30
brain-to-brain communication, 34, 36
brain–cloud interface, 36
brain–computer interface (BCI), 4, 34–36, 261, 282
brain function, 32–33
  bidirectional interfaces, 34–36
  expanding, 36–41
  modifying through algorithms, 60
  technological developments in studying,
    29–30
  technology and, 33–34
brain imaging, algorithmic interpretation, 39–40
brain organoids, 30
brain-scale networks, simulation of, 37
brain–substrate extension, 37
Braithwaite, J.
  Fasken Lecture, 206–208
  problems for, 214–215
  on regulation, 212, 247
  on republicanism, 211–212
Brandeis, L., 77, 79, 81
  view of privacy, 194
Brennan, Michael B., 219
Brewer, R., 251–252
British Academy reforms, 233
Brookings Report, 267–268
Business Companies' Growth and Transformation
  (France), 289
Bygrave, L., 262–263

CAMAC Report, 294
capitalism
  regulatory, 276–279
  restraint of, 226
capture theory, 200
Capurro, R.
  critique of Floridi, 10
  on digital enlightenment, 141–143
care, exhibiting, 129
case law, privacy and, 75–83
catallaxy, 118
categorical imperatives. *See* Kantian Idealism
Catholic sacraments, 96
Centre for the Study of Existential Risk, 71

charitable entities
  corporations barred from donating to, 288
  regulations regarding, 232
Chicago School of Law and Economics, 200
Christian deity. *See* Deity
Christianity
  Lyon on, 92
  normalisation of the Deity, 96
  as proto-State, 105
Christl, W., 18, 284
citizens
  as consumers, 123
  digital embedding of, 4
  personal data owned by, 300
  responsibility of, 219
civil society, privacy and, 193–195
civilising process, 116
Civilitas, 110–113
Claydon, L., 252
cognitive embeddednes, 80
collaborative brain–computer interface, 34–35
Commandments, Ten, 98–101
commodification, 17, 278
common good
  as ethical principle, 163–165
  respectful self-responsibility and, 170–171
communications technologies. *See* technology
Companies (Audit, Investigation and Community
  Enterprises) Act (2004) (UK), 295
Companies Act 2006 (Cth), 295
competition law, 296–297
confession
  Foucault on, 102–104
  as mythological subjection, 96–98
confidence, trust vs, 237
connectome scanning, 37
consciousness, streams of, 32
conservative privacy, 12, 179–181, 183–184
Constitutional privacy theory, 74–83, 175
constructivism, 46–51, 54, 57, 67, 70, 135, 155, 281
consumer protection, 297–298
consumerism
  as debt to the Market, 125–128
  under neoliberalism, 121–122
consumers, 120–121, 123–128
consumption
  linked with deforestation, 62
  market promotes, 279–281
  trends in, 112
contracting theory, 200
Convention on the Elimination of All Forms of
  Discrimination against Women, 149
Convention on the Rights of Persons with
  Disabilities, 149

Index

corporate behaviour. *See also* corporations
  data collection, 172
  in the digital age, 281–287
  motivation for, 279–281
  powers of corporations, 275–276
  Salomon v. Salomon, 274–275
  use of algorithms, 298–301
  use of personal data, 298
  wrongdoing, 270
corporations. *See also* corporate behaviour
  history of, 18, 288–290
  non-mythological, 296–302
  reimagining, 18–19
  rights of under democracy, 158–159
Corporations Act (2001) (Cth), 292
Court of Justice of the European Union, 259
credit
  availability of, 125
  as debt, 125–127
crime control, 251, 269–271
criminal justice
  regulation of, 252–253
  reimagining of, 21, 268
Csikszentmihalyi, M., 121
culture, 49, 60, 113
  and consumer, 126
  corporate, 232–242, 248
  neurally embedded, 48
cyberspace, governance of, 17, 260–261
Cynic *parrhesia*, 143
Cynthia Moreno v. Hanford Sentinel, 190

data, as culturally designed, 5, 17, 46–47, 49, 51
data brokering by the State, 257–258
data collection by corporations, 173
data mining, 282
debt. *See* credit
decision-making
  modes of, 45
  respectful self-responsibility and, 171–172
deep convolutional neural networks (DCNNs), 66
deep generative multiview model (DGMM) algorithm, 40
deep learning, 26–40, 42–43
Deity
  belief in and privacy, 192–193
  normalisation of, 96–104
  normalising, 96–104
  notion of, 31
  quashes existential fear, 73
democracy,
  as ethical principle, 158–159

depression,
  treatment with VR, 63
deregulation, 13, 126
determinism, 32, 156–157, 172, 202–206
Dichter, Ernest, 279
digital age
  corporate behaviour in, 281–282
  ethical challenge for, 142
digital embedding of citizens, 4
digital enlightenment, 142
digital ethics, 144–146
Digital Geneva Convention, 149
digital metaphysics, 51
digital tracking and profiling, 283
dignity, 11, 79–80, 141
  as ethical principle, 149–151
  dignitarian arguments, 77
  respectful self-responsibility and, 166
  as status concept, 225
directors
  motivations of, 293
  obligations of, 233, 292–295
dissociative experiences with VR, 65
dominant interests, 2–3, 7, 16, 50, 65, 67, 101, 123, 146, 183, 211, 263, 284
Domingos, Pedro, 12, 43–45, 54, 60, 180–181
Dowdle, M., 249–250
downloading, 12, 89, 169, 180, 182, 190
du Plessis, Jean, 18, 291–292, 295
Dumas v. Liebert (01867), 77
Dworkin, R., 161

economistes, 107
educational information, 192
Elias, N.
  arguments of, 8
  on etiquette, 137
  Foucault and, 113–115
  on habitus, 109
  view of State, 109–110
empathy, improving, 62
employment issues
  employee relations, 301–302
  privacy and, 191–192
enforcement of regulation, 207–208
enframing technology, 128
enhancement, 5, 7, 12, 20, 34, 57, 59, 92, 112, 123, 130, 133, 135–136, 159–170, 173, 176–184, 187, 190–192, 260–261, 299
enhancement therapies, 133
enhancement/privacy question in AI, 261
Entick v. Carrington (01765), 75, 82
environment of privacy, 1–2
epistemic agency, 65

310 *Index*

equality
  as ethical principle, 159–161
  respectful self-responsibility and, 168–169
Ethically Aligned Design project, 59, 140, 146,
  184–187
ethics
  common ethical principles, 149–165
  concerns raised by algorithms, 139–140
  Floridi on, 139–140
  privacy and, 10–11
  reference points for activity, 146–149
  respectful self-responsibility and, 144–146
  technology and, 143–146
Ethics Guidelines for Trustworthy AI (EU), 42
eunomics, 228
European Union
  Court of Justice, 259
  European Charter of Fundamental Rights, 15,
  218
  European Convention of Human Rights, 78
existential concerns, 7–10, 96, 127, 204, 279, 286
  camouflaging of, 136
  evidence of, 72–73
existential living. *See* respectful self-responsibility
existential reality
  absolutism of, 7, 71–72
  acceptance of, 175–176
existential values,
  self-responsibility rests on, 165–166
expansion microscopy, 37
experiential learning through VR, 63
experiments on people, 283
explainable machine learning (XAI), 39, 41
explicability. *See* interpretability
extension of privacy, 75
Eye of God, 93

facial recognition technology, 258–259
failures, trajectory of, 3
false memories in children, 66
family, privacy and, 193–195
Fasken Lecture, 206–208
fear, neoliberalism and, 122
Felix c. O'Connell (o1858), 77
fiduciary principles, 271
  Australian law, 293
  Market based on, 289–292
  respectful self-responsibility and, 235–237
  State based on, 264–267
  trust and, 237–242
financial issues, privacy and, 191–192
Floridi, L.
  Capurro's critique of, 10
  on ethics, 138–141

Kant's influence on, 52–55
  ontology, 10, 52–54, 88
fMRI techniques, 35
folk psychology, 252
Foster and Others v. *Mountford*, 194
Foucault, M.
  on agency, 116
  on confession, 102–104
  on consumers, 120–121
  Discipline and Punish, 108–109, 200
  Elias and, 113–115
  on governmentality, 21, 105–107, 109, 114–116,
  124, 133, 173, 204, 216, 272
  on justice, 119–120
  law in, 216–217
  on the Market, 119
  on *parrhesia*, 10, 143–144
  on pastorate, 8, 14, 96, 102, 104–105, 203
  on policing, 15
  on regulation, 203
  on resistant rights, 217
  spatial metaphors, 204–205
  work of, 8
foundational dynamic, 2–4
Fox-Decent, E.
  on the rule of law, 265
  on trust, 239–242
France. *See also* French National Assembly
  case law in, 77
  corporate regulation in, 289
freedom. *See also* liberty
  protection of, 151
  under neoliberalism, 121
French National Assembly, 18
Fuller, Lon, 223, 228
Future of Life Institute, 71

Gallant, Jack, 35
Gee v. *Pritchard*, 76, 82
General Data Protection Regulation (EU), 300
genetic intervention to improve cognitive
  performance, 34
Germany, case law in, 77
Gintis, H., 48
God. *See* Deity
Goertzel, Ben, 181
governance. *See also* State
  of cyberspace, 260
  outside the State, 245
  while maintaining privacy,
  188
governmentality, 21, 105–107, 109, 114–116, 124, 133,
  173, 204, 216, 272
  neoliberal, 217

Index

origins of, 105
Griffiths, Tom, 42–43
Griswold v. *Connecticut*, 81
Guidelines for Consumer Protection (UN), 297
Gunningham, N., 247–248

habitus, 8, 109, 137
Haferkamp, H., 115
haptic skills, improving, 63
Harding, M.
    on fiduciary principles, 235
    on trust, 237–239
Harvard Business Review, 131
Hayek, F. A.
    on law, 223
    on the Market, 117–120, 272–274
health issues, privacy and, 192
Heidegger, M.,
    on authentic existence, 128–129, 144
Hildebrandt, M., 205–206
Hobbes, T., 116
    Leviathan, 239–240, 264
Hohwy, J., 47
Holley, C., 246
homo digitalis, 142
homo oeconomicus, 120
Horikawa, Tomoyasu, 35
Horowitz, Morton, 224
household debt levels, 280
human cognition, 49
human dignity. *See* dignity
human rights
    as ethical principle, 161–163
    respectful self-responsibility and, 169–170
    values and, 145
Human Rights Act (1998) (UK), 78

IBM Smart Cities project, 49
Idealism, 25, 45, 50–53, 55, 57, 60, 77, 102
identity
    as ethical principle, 154–156
    respectful self-responsibility and, 167–168
IEEE. *See* Institute of Electrical and Electronics
    Engineers, 12, 59, 140–146, 184, 186–187, 262
iHuman report, 25–26
immersed multimodal environments, 64
immersive virtuality, 62
individuals, impact of regulation on, 250–252
information flows
    privacy and, 6, 175
    status of, 74–75
information sharing and cooperation, 176
informational idealism, 55–57
informational ontology, 10

informational privacy theory, 74, 83–89
Institute of Electrical and Electronics Engineers
    (IEEE), 59, 140–146, 184–187
institutional authority, 239–242
institutional self-examination, 213
insurance, purchasing, 131
interests of the user, prioritising, 214
internal morality of law, 223
International Covenant on Civil and Political
    Rights, 148
International Organisation of Consumers' Unions,
    297
internet, privacy on, 190–191
interpretability, 26
interventionist technologies, 20
intrusion, notion of, 29
invisible hand, 119

James Hardie Industries v. *White*, 291
Japan, response to neoliberalism, 287
Johns Hopkins Institute, 72
just, meaning of, 119
justice system
    mythological, 267–269
    non-mythological, 267–271

Kantian Idealism, 5, 46, 78–79
    on algorithms, 47–48
    categorical imperatives, 150
    deeper themes, 51–52
    on Deity, 139
    in Floridi, 52–55
    as mythological, 55–57
Kierkegaard, S., 71
Kitayama, S., 48
Krygier, Martin
    on civics, 228–229
    on rule of law, 15–16, 221–222
    on teleology, 226–228

L'Homme-machine, 109
land use planning. *See* urban planning
Langford, Rosemary Teele, 16–18, 231–235, 264,
    267, 293
    on corporate purpose, 295
    on fiduciary principles, 289
    work of, 18
law
    enforcement of, 193
    regulation and, 216–243
    reimagining, 15–16
    rule of, 220–234
    trust key to, 239–242
Lawrence v. *Texas*, 81

Legg, S., 143
Levi-Faur, D., 276–278
liberal forms of governmentality, 15, 108, 172–173
liberalism, 108, 158, 172, 226–227, 229
liberal-utilitarian ways of thinking, 76
liberty
  as ethical principle, 151–154
  Mill on, 151–154
  respectful self-responsibility and, 166–167
living existentially. *See* respectful self-responsibility
Locke, John, 75, 245
Lyon, David, 92–95

Machiavellianism, 67
machine learning, 38–39, 57, 130, 140, 282, 286, 302
magicalising, 117
magnetic receptors in the brain, 30
magnitudes of the trajectory, 216–217, 235–237
Manokha, I., 134–135
Manola v. *Stephens*, 77, 82
marginal groups, predictive algorithms and, 132
Market
  accountability and, 250
  captures the political process, 201
  consumers and, 123–128
  equality under, 160–161
  exercise of power, 13
  as mythological, 272–281
  myth of, 3
  normalising, 105–128
  regulation and, 272–302
  reimagining, 17–19, 21
market research, 124
marketing, 120–121
Maslow's hierarchy of human needs, 121
mass personalisation, 283
master algorithm project, 43–45
media
  protection of information from, 193
  relationship with celebrity, 188
mercantilism, 109
meta-regulation, 248
Metzinger, T., 42, 69
Mill, John Stuart, 76, 151–154
Miller, P., 264–267
mission creep, 284
morality question in AI, 262
Morse, S., 252
mortality awareness, 73
multivariant pattern analysis (MVPA), 68–69
MyData movement, 187
mythological justice, 267–269
mythological magnitudes, 2, 72, 136, 172–173, 185, 216, 244, 247

mythological trajectory
  history of, 57
  Kantian Idealism, 55–57
  of the Market, 272–281
  neuroscience in, 57–59
  in sociopolitical practices, 81–83
  traditions informed by, 229
myths of secularisation, 93–94

nanotechnology, 33–34
narcissism,
  exploring through VR, 67
neoliberalism, 127, 217
  consumers in, 120
  emergence of, 272, 285
  freedom in, 121–123
  governmentality, 15, 217
  origins of, 108
  resistance to, 287
neural overlays, 59
neural plasticity, 35
neurohybrids, development of, 38
neuronal activity, false positive readings, 45
neuroscience
  breadth and depth of, 28–29
  conditional embrace of, 176
  and criminal justice, 252–253
  impact of, 243
  interpretation of, 16
  mythological trajectory, 57–59
  as powerful dynamic, 1
  technology and, 4–6
Neurotechnologies for Human Cognitive Augmentation, 26
Nissenbaum, 83, 86, 88–89
nodal governance, 246–247
non-mythological existence. *See* respectful self-responsibility
non-mythological justice, 269–271
non-mythological privacy, 12
normalisation
  algorithmic, 129–134
  compliance and, 19
  by Deity, 96–104
  Foucault on, 102–104
  by the individual, 20, 72
  by the Market, 105–128
  principles of, 95–96
  privacy as history of, 91–92
  results of, 9–10
  seeking new values, 7–10
  by the State, 104–115
  strategies of, 7
  by technology, 128–136

object consciousness, 55
objective nature of privacy, 75
offence, notion of, 269
Olmstead v. *United States*, 78
On Liberty, 76
On the People's Terms, 211
ontology, 10, 52–54, 88, 138–139, 144, 177–178
optogenetic techniques, 33
O'Shaughnessy, John, 121

Packard, Vance, 279
pain control, 63
Panopticon, 93, 134–135, 204
Parenti, Chris, 256
Pariseau-Legault, P., 133
parrhesia, 143–144
pastorate, 8, 14, 96, 102, 104–116, 203
Pavesich v. *New England Life Insurance Co.* (1905), 78
personal algorithm, 179–180, 183, 298
personal cognitive substrate, 188
personal data. *See also* information flows
    corporate use of, 298
    deletion of, 259
    ownership by the citizen, 300
personal responsibility,
    respectful self-responsibility and, 171–172
personal technology strategy, 12, 179–183, 188
personality disorders, 31
personality, exploring through VR, 67
Pettit, Phillip, 14, 158–159, 172, 214, 227, 230, 242, 245, 247, 265–266
    on Krygier, 221
    on republican State, 265
    Republicanism, 208–211
Piaget's theory, 46
plasticity of the self, 68–70
policing strategy, 14, 106
    Foucault on, 15, 203
political activity, trust required for, 266
political obligation, 161
politiques, 107
Pollard v. *Photographic Company*, 82
Postema, G., 242–243
post-Kantian Idealism, 50–51, 60, 70
power
    arbitrary exercise of, 226
    regulatory, 200–201
power-of-two-based permutation logic, 40
precautionary principle, 142
predictive algorithms, risks in, 129–134, *See also* algorithmic technology
predictive processing (PP), 47–48

prices and wages, 118
primal cognitive experience, 30–32
Prince Albert v. *Strange*, 76, 82
privacy
    Constitutional, 75–83
    by design, 262–263
    environment of, 1–2
    functioning of, 11–12
    new account of, 175–195
    new values for, 10–11
    present understandings of, 73–75
    as respectful self-responsiblity, 144
    selective flow, 83–90
    self-regulation of, 260
    theory of, 6–7
    to and for oneself, 20
private sector data, State access to, 255–257
progressive privacy, 12, 179–183
property rights over body parts, 162
Prosser, W., 78
prostheses, 33
Proteus effect, 65
psilocybin, clinical use of, 72
psychoanalytic insights, confession and, 97
psychological space, 9, 132
psychopathy, exploring through VR, 67
psychotherapy for the middle-aged, 73
public accountability. *See* accountability, in modern State
public interest theory, 200
purpose-based organisations, 16–17, 21, 230–235, 238, 242, 258, 261, 264, 266–271, 289, 293, 295–296, 299

raison d'état, 106–108
Raz, J., 223
real-time monitoring of behavioural data, 283
reality, 44–45, 50, 53, 67, 155, *See also* senses of reality
    constructing, 58
regulating magnitude, State as, 244–245
regulation
    defined, 206
    impact on individuals, 250–252
    law and, 216–243
    Market and, 272–302
    for the new privacy, 13–15
    reimagining, 21, 199–215
    and the State, 244–271
regulatory capitalism, 17–18, 276–279
regulatory dispersal of sovereignty, 245–250
rehabilitative vs enhancement therapies, 133
remote neural devices, 58

314 Index

Report on the Social and Fiduciary Duties and Obligations of Company Directors, 294
reproductive technologies, 162–163
republicanism. *See* Pettit, Phillip
resistance to subjection, 143
resistant rights, 217
respect, for others, *See also* respectful self-responsibility
respectful self-responsibility, 5
  corporate strategies for, 290–292
  digital ethics and, 144–146
  as ethical principle, 165–174
  ethics and, 10
  fiduciary principles and, 235–237
  relation to other values, 166–173
responsibility, as ethical principle, 156–158
responsibility to and for oneself, 10–11, 129, 144–145, 165–174, 179
responsive regulation, 206–208, 250, 270
responsiveness, defined, 207
Richardson. M., 76, 79–80
right to be let alone, 78
Roe v. *Wade*, 81
Romantic view of human nature, 76
Rousseau, Jean-Jacques, 245
Royal Society *iHuman* report, 25
rule of law, 220–234, *See also* law
  current notions of, 15
  new approach to, 230–231
  trust and, 242–243
rules of just conduct, 119, 272
Russell, Stuart, 27, 41

Sahakian, Barbara, 35
Salomon v. *Salomon*, 274–275
Sartor, G., 254
secularisation, myths of, 93–94
security, while maintaining privacy, 189–190
selected flow of information, 83–87, 177
self
  plasticity of, 68–70
  technologies of, 134–135
self-determination, 284–286
self-regulation of privacy, 260–261
self-representation, 68
self-responsibility. *See also* respectful self-responsibility
  in ethical framework, 146
  technology and, 11
  transfer of, 19
Semphill, J., 225
sentencing, 270

sex, confession and, 103–104
shareholder primacy model, 291
Shearing, C., 246
Shleifer, A., 200–201
Simmel, Georg, 79
smart regulation, 247
smart cities, 299
Smith, Adam, 119
social class, predicts consumption, 130
social cognitive neuroscience, 68
social conditions, variations in, 2–4
social dynamic, as mythological, 1–4, 7, 10, 16, 50, 60, 72, 88, 91–92, 95, 112, 116, 125, 127, 164, 175–176, 268, 279, 282–285
social infrastructure, 1, 272
social media
  privacy on, 190–191
  VR and, 66
social traditions, 273
sociopolitical practices, 81
socio-technological frame, 12
Southey v. *Sherwood* (o1817), 76, 82
sovereign power, 15, 74, 95, 107–109, 113, 124, 200, 229, 239–240, 263, 278
  care for subjects of, 107
  exercise of, 13
  regulatory dispersal of, 245–250
Spies v. *Illinois* (o1887), 82
spinal cord–spinal cord connection, 34
stakeholders
  benefit to, 18, 290
  directors' responsibilities towards, 291, 293
State
  absolutism in, 202
  as digitally avaricious, 255–257
  data brokering by, 257–258
  equality under, 160–161
  liberal democratic regulation, 172–173
  must be non-mythological, 15
  need for management, 227
  normalisation of, 104–115
  regulation and, 244–271
  reimagining, 16–17
  rights of under democracy, 158
  surveillance technologies, 177–178
  technology and, 253–263
Stotts, J., 97
streams of consciousness, 31–32
stress treatment, with VR, 63
subjection, 3, 5, 8, 89
  countering, 177–178
  as normalisation, 91–96
  resistance to, 143
  technology used for, 145–146

Index

subjectification
  bourgeois, 109
  as identification and subjection, 108
  neoliberal, 217
substrate, 35, 37–38, 58, 188
sum-product networks (SNPs), 43–45
surveillance. *See also* Panopticon
  Eye of God theories, 130
  of normalised individuals, 21
  Parenti on, 256
  by the State, 177
surveillance capitalism, 205, 285–286
Swanson, L., 47
sympathetic engagement, 200
synaesthesic experience, 34
synthesised data, 138
system justification theory, 122

Tamanaha, B., 223
technology
  Absolute Self and, 4, 8–9
  brain science and, 29–30
  Constitutional implications, 220
  impact on the State, 16
  liberty and, 152–153
  neuroscience and, 4–6
  normalising, 128–136
  privacy and, 138–143
  progression and conservation,
    179–181
  of the self, 134–135
  the State and, 253–263
  technologies of the body,
    161–163
  used for subjection, 145–146
teleology
  anatomy and, 222–224
  Waldron on, 224–226
Ten Commandments, 98–101
tradition of mythologists, 56
trajectory, 19, 50, 56–57, 69, 144, 172, 215, 286, *See also* mythological trajectory
  of failures, 3
transplant technologies, 162–163
Trentmann, F., 18, 125–126, 279
trust, 86, 88
  fiduciary principles and, 237–242
  institutional authority and, 239–242
  rule of law and, 242–243
trustworthy AI, 42

unit of identification (UI), 65
United Kingdom
  availability of credit in, 126
  corporate regulation in, 289
United Nations
  Conventions, 148–149
  Universal Declaration of Human Rights (1948),
    147–148
United States, privacy theory in, 77
  United States Constitution. *See also* Constitutional
  privacy theory 77–78
  Fourteenth Amendment, 275–276
  as frame for law, 218–220
Universal Declaration of Human Rights (1948),
  79
uploading, 12, 37, 58, 89, 182, 190
urban planning, 204–205

value systems, 138–146
  human rights and, 145
  normalisation of, 7–10
  for privacy, 10–11
  privacy and, 21
van Krieken, R., 115
victimless activities, 193
virtual reality (VR), 61–62
  benefits of, 62–64
  exposure therapy, 63
  in justice system, 268
  problems with, 64–67
  visual hallucinations induced by,
    66
von Jhering, R., 77

wages and prices, 118
Waldman, A., 88
Waldron, J., 224–226
Warren, S., 77, 79, 81, 194
Whitman, J., 195
whole brain simulation, 38
Wilde, Oscar, 82
Williamson, B., 49
Wrenn, Mary, 122
Wyatt v. Wilson, 76, 82

Yeung, K., 286–287

Zamora, D., 114
Zuboff, S., 284–286

CPSIA information can be obtained
at www.ICGtesting.com
Printed in the USA
LVHW011357030821
694404LV00012B/867